THE EMPIRE OF APOSTLES

THE EMPIRE OF APOSTLES

Religion, *Accommodatio*, and the Imagination of Empire in Early Modern Brazil and India

ANANYA CHAKRAVARTI

UNIVERSITY PRESS

OXFORD
UNIVERSITY PRESS

Oxford University Press is a department of the University of Oxford. It furthers the University's objective of excellence in research, scholarship, and education by publishing worldwide. Oxford is a registered trademark of Oxford University Press in the UK and in certain other countries.

Published in India by
Oxford University Press
2/11 Ground Floor, Ansari Road, Daryaganj, New Delhi 110 002, India

First Edition published in 2018

ISBN-13 (print edition): 978-0-19-948508-6
ISBN-10 (print edition): 0-19-948508-9

ISBN-13 (eBook): 978-0-19-909360-1
ISBN-10 (eBook): 0-19-909360-1

Typeset in ScalaPro 10/13
by Tranistics Data Technologies, Kolkata 700 091
Printed in India by Replika Press Pvt. Ltd

To
Professor Dain Borges
and
Professor Muzaffar Alam

CONTENTS

List of Figures ix
Acknowledgements xi

Introduction 1

1. From Contact to 'Conquest' 26

PART I IN SEARCH OF THE INDIES

2. Other Indies 55
3. The Living Books 95

PART II *ACCOMMODATIO* AND THE POETICS OF LOCATION

4. José de Anchieta and the Poetics of Warfare 135
5. Christ in the *Brahmapuri*: Thomas Stephens in Salcete 178

PART III RELIGION, *ACCOMMODATIO*, AND THE IMAGINATION OF EMPIRE

6. Theatres of Empire: António Vieira and Baltasar da Costa in Brazil and India 231
7. The Empire of Apostles 280

Epilogue 315
Glossary of Key Terms 322
Bibliography 326
Index 349
About the Author 356

FIGURES

1.1 The Malabar Coast in 1498 27
1.2 Coastal Brazil, Mid-Sixteenth Century 40
1.3 South and Central India, Mid-Sixteenth Century 46

2.1 Xavier's Travels in the Indian Ocean 61

4.1 Manuscript of Poem Describing Six Savages Dancing, *Os Machatins* 161

5.1 Page from the Earliest Known Manuscript of *Discurso sobre a vinda de Jesu Christo* 202
5.2 Marsden Manuscript of Stephens's *Kriṣṭapurāṇa* 223

6.1 Dutch Assaults on the Portuguese Empire, Seventeenth Century 232
6.2 António Vieira (1608–1697) 235
6.3 Baltasar da Costa's Sketch of Roberto Nobili as a *Sannyāsi* 254

ACKNOWLEDGEMENTS

> Gratitude—is not the mention
> Of a Tenderness,
> But its still appreciation
> Out of Plumb of Speech.
>
> —Emily Dickinson

This book was researched and written across five continents and seven years. Along the way, I incurred deep debts for which profound gratitude is meagre payment indeed. I was fortunate to receive generous financial support for my archival research from various institutions, including the University of Chicago, USA, the Social Science Research Council's International Dissertation Research Fellowship Program, USA, and the American University in Cairo, Egypt. I am also grateful to the Max Weber Programme for Postdoctoral Studies, European University Institute, Italy, and Antonella Romano in particular, for allowing me the luxury to write in an office nestled in a Tuscan garden. My stay in Lisbon was facilitated by the institutional hospitality of the Fundação Oriente, the Centro de História de Além-Mar, Universidade Nova de Lisboa, Portugal, and the Instituto de Ciências Sociais da Universidade de Lisboa, Portugal. Eduardo Kol Carvalho, Pedro Cardim, and Ricardo Roque deserve special mention for their help in facilitating my stay.

The materials for this book were drawn from a large number of archives including the Arquivo Nacional and Biblioteca Nacional in

Rio de Janeiro, Brazil; the Archives and Special Collections, SOAS Library, SOAS, University of London, and the Stonyhurst College Archives in the UK; the Goa State Historical Archives, the Thomas Stephens Konknni Kendr, and the Krishnadas Shama Goa State Central Library in Goa, India; the Jesuit Archives of Madurai Province in Shembaganur, India; St Aloysius College, Mangalore, India; the Archivum Romanum Societatis Iesu, the Archivio Storico di Propaganda Fide, and the Biblioteca Nazionale in Rome, Italy; and the Arquivo Nacional Torre do Tombo, the Biblioteca Nacional, the Biblioteca da Ajuda, the Academia das Ciências, and the Arquivo Histórico Ultramarino in Lisbon, Portugal. At these institutions, Fr Edward Jeganathan and Fr Irudiyaraj, Blossom Xavier Souza, George Rodrigues, Jan Graffius, and Winifred Assan were especially helpful. Among the many friends I made during my research, I wish to thank in particular Paolo Aranha, Joanna Elrick, Manuel João Magalhães, and Ricardo Ventura, not just for their friendship but for their intellectual companionship.

This book was conceived and nurtured at the University of Chicago, where my teachers, interlocutors, and friends were invaluable critics and ardent supporters of this wildly ambitious project. Mauricio Tenorio was an early champion of my ambition to bring together the two 'Indies', and his historical vision and love of poetry were constantly inspiring. I am also profoundly grateful for the rigorous and careful feedback I received from Jorge Flores and his generous support over the years. At the University of Chicago, I benefited from two intellectual homes. I thank the members of the Latin American History workshop and the community of scholars of South Asia, as well as the staff of the Department of History, the Center for Latin American Studies, and Committee for Southern Asian Studies during my time there. I thank especially Alicia Czaplewski, who is sorely missed. Romina Robles Ruvalcaba exists in a category by herself—soul sister. If, as Rulfo tells us, time is heavier than the heaviest burden man can bear, she has lightened my load, as a historian and as a person, every day. I also thank Sonam Kachru, not just for sharing his brilliant mind, formidable erudition, and many, many cigarettes over the years, but for his patience, his kindness, and his unflagging loyalty and support.

I have benefited enormously over the years from the feedback and help of various colleagues. Thanks are due to members of the Early Modern History Workshop at the University of Chicago and Elisa Joy Jones, as well as my colleagues at the European University Institute, particularly Jennifer Hillman. Ines G. Županov provided me with a platform to share my work at its earliest stages, and I am most grateful to her and the participants of various workshops hosted at the Centre d'Études de l'Inde et de l'Asie du Sud, Paris, France, especially Joan-Pau Rubiés, for their feedback. Thanks are due to Ricardo Roque and the members of the collective working on colonial mimesis at Instituto de Ciências Sociais, and to Tom Cohen and the attendees of my workshop at Catholic University of America, Washington D.C., USA, especially Sanjay Subrahmanyam and Fr John O'Malley. Perhaps the single most important forum for shaping this final manuscript was the book workshop held by my colleagues at Georgetown University, Washington D.C., USA. Many thanks to John McNeill, Bryan McCann, Dagomar Degroot, Toshihiro Higuchi, Kate de Luna, Mubbashir Rizvi, and Suze Zijlstra for their generosity, time, and advice. I am particularly grateful to John Tutino, without whose careful editorial eye this book would not be what it is. Thank you for helping me see the forest past the trees.

I thank the anonymous reviewers; Trishula Patel and Jakob Burnham; William Nelson; and the editorial team at Oxford University Press, New Delhi, for their help in preparing and improving the manuscript. Many thanks to Fr Leon Hooper and the Woodstock Theological Library, Georgetown University Library, and the Jesuit Maryland Province, USA, for permission for the gorgeous cover image of this book. I also thank the directors of the Archivum Romanum Societatis Iesu, Rome, Italy; Archives and Special Collections, SOAS Library; Academia das Ciências, Lisbon, Portugal; the British Library's Endangered Archives Programme, UK; and the John Carter Brown Library, Brown University, USA, for permission to reproduce the images in this book.

I thank my ever-patient, supportive, and loving family. The love of peregrination that my parents, Rupa and Sarvajit Chakravarti, inculcated in me is reflected in this work. I am grateful for the curiosity and open-mindedness I learned from them. Thanks to my sister Aparupa for making sure I ate, slept, and stayed human through gruelling months of writing. Thanks, too, to my aunt Choi Chatterjee, in whose footsteps I follow and whose endless founts of creativity inspire me. Though they are not here to see this work, the imprint of my grandparents, Deb Kumar and Nonda Chatterjee, is apparent in every page.

Last but by no means least, I wish to thank the two people who have most deeply shaped my scholarship over the years. Professor Borges's erudition and generosity continue to sustain me, many years after I had the pleasure of whiling away an afternoon in his office, learning how to read and think with both breadth and depth. Professor Alam provided me with the finest apprenticeship I could have hoped for in the art of historical scholarship. I thank my two mentors for providing a model for the kind of scholar I aspire to be: curious, humble, generous, rigorous. I dedicate this book to them.

INTRODUCTION

> We must now consider the process by which this [Christian] history of past centuries was transmitted to new worlds ... It was only a question of time before Europe would expand toward America and in part toward Asia, continents that were lacking in great cultural protagonists. Still later, Europe would begin to make further incursions into these two continents, Africa and Asia ... which it would seek to transform into European franchises, into colonies.[1]

This is how Pope Benedict XVI explained the 'universalization of European culture' to the Italian Senate on 12 May 2004. His address on the state of Europe focused on the need to return to its roots to address the challenges of the present.[2] For him, the 'cultural and historical concept' embedded in 'Europe' received concrete form with the advent of Islam. The new faith disrupted the unity of the Mediterranean world, creating the tripartite division between Europe, Africa, and Asia familiar today.[3] (It is unlikely that a citizen of al-Andalus, who could travel seamlessly from the depths of Iberia to the Maghreb and the Mediterranean shores of the Levant, would have experienced such a disruption—but his ilk are not the subjects of this history.) 'Amid this process of shifting borders,' Benedict XVI argued, 'a theology of history was constructed ... rooted in the Book of Daniel', in which the formation of the *Sacrum Imperium*

[1] Ratzinger, 'The Spiritual Roots of Europe', 64.

[2] Ratzinger, 'The Spiritual Roots of Europe, 64.

[3] Ratzinger, 'The Spiritual Roots of Europe, 51–2.

Romanum laid the foundations of Europe.[4] Then, inevitably, invincibly, Europe marched outwards: America and parts of Asia and Africa, lacking a 'protagonist' of the stature of Christianity or Islam, lay fallow until Europe, fulfilling its destiny, expanded to sow its seed in these cultural wastelands.

Although Benedict XVI's disquisition is better read in the spirit of theology rather than history, the mythology of the 'age of discoveries' is remarkably resilient—and not merely in the popular imagination.[5] The same sense of momentousness and inevitability that infuses Benedict XVI's essay informs many accounts of the early modern European expansion—even those that are highly critical of Europe's history of imperialism. Like Benedict XVI, these accounts are based on a teleology that culminates in the re-making of the globe into a series of 'European franchises, into colonies'.

Nevertheless, while the mythological aura surrounding Europe's expansion has not faded away, most writers today would balk at the explicitly Christian interpretation of the history Benedict XVI offered. Scholarly analyses of Europe's expansion are often studiously secular, with religion often reduced to a footnote. For Benedict XVI, this historiographical lacuna is another symptom of the graver illness that has beset Europe. The march of divine history was slowed, in his eyes, not through the agency of Asians, Africans, and Amerindians, but through developments in Europe's own intellectual history. The Enlightenment ushered in 'the victory of the post-European techno-secular world'. Europe increasingly abandoned the spiritual foundations of its identity, replacing its Christian roots with a multicultural secularism. Benedict XVI lamented that 'the time has apparently arrived to affirm the value systems of other worlds, such as pre-Colombian America, Islam or Asian mysticism'.[6] The alarm he rang resounds today. As Europe confronts the bodies piling up on its shores, drifting on the deadly waves of conflicts in its erstwhile

[4] Ratzinger, 'The Spiritual Roots of Europe, 5–4.

[5] In the case of the Portuguese empire, Gilberto Freyre's thesis of *lusotropicalismo* held sway till the late 1990s, when, beginning with Cláudia Castelo's seminal work (1998), Portuguese scholars began to dismantle the mythology of the benign nature of Portuguese imperialism.

[6] Ratzinger, 'The Spiritual Roots of Europe', 66.

colonies; as it contemplates Turkey's entry into its union; as it looks askance at the non-white residents of Molenbeek or the *cités* of La Courneuve, Benedict XVI is hardly alone in his anxiety regarding Europe's 'crisis of identity' in a multicultural, secular world.

In another address given in Aparecida, Brazil, Benedict XVI countered the orthodoxies of multicultural relativism with a reading of Latin America history. He portrayed the pre-contact populations of Latin America and the Caribbean as 'knowing and welcoming Christ, the unknown God whom their ancestors were seeking, without realizing it, in their rich religious traditions'. Their cultures were made 'fruitful' by Christ, so that 'the proclamation of Jesus and of his Gospel did not at any point involve an alienation of the pre-Columbian cultures, nor was it the imposition of a foreign culture'.[7] The encounter of Christian Europeans and indigenous peoples of Latin America, therefore, was not one of colonial violence. It was the beginning of a process of cultural synthesis, since 'authentic cultures are not closed in upon themselves ... but they are open, or better still, they are seeking an encounter with other cultures, hoping to reach universality through encounter and dialogue with other ways of life'.[8]

Benedict XVI's views on the spread of Christianity have a venerable genealogy, both theologically and in the development of the missionary church.[9] The mechanism by which the Church has remained and continues to remain open is that of conversion. Conversion, in this view, allows the possibility of surmounting the incommensurability inherent in cross-cultural encounter, so that converts may one day achieve a 'new synthesis'.[10] Yet, in light of his earlier pronouncements, it is hard to escape the conclusion that for Benedict XVI, 'authentic

[7] Benedict XVI, 'Address of His Holiness Benedict XVI', Aparecida, Brazil, 13 May 2007.

[8] Benedict XVI, 'Address of His Holiness Benedict XVI', Aparecida, Brazil, 13 May 2007.

[9] The theological *locus classicus* is Paul (particularly, Galatians 3:28), which has nourished a long tradition of thought on universalism, and whose echoes are apparent in Pope Benedict XVI's speech.

[10] On incommensurability in cross-cultural encounter, see Pagden, *European Encounters*, 238.

cultures' are really only those that are willing to capitulate to a specifically *European* tradition of Catholicism.[11]

Naturally, the speech provoked scathing criticism in Latin America for its blatant evasion of the violence and destruction—cosmological, material, demographic, and cultural—that attended the continent's evangelization. Humberto Cholango, president of the confederation of the Kichwa peoples of Ecuador, even while affirming the vitality of Catholicism in contemporary indigenous culture, took exception to the Pope's claim that 'the utopia of going back to breathe life into the pre-Columbian religions ... would be a step back.'[12] Cholango reminded Benedict XVI that the sword of empire had been one of the most effective weapons in the Church's arsenal in Latin America. There are good historical reasons why the contours of the global Church today are still largely indistinguishable from the erstwhile boundaries of Europe's empires.

This book places the relationship between Church and empire at its centre, in the hopes of decolonizing our understanding of both. The intention is not to reduce the Church to a handmaiden of European imperial expansion, a functionalist view of the role of religion that does disservice not least to the complex history of the indigenous adoption of Christianity.[13] Indigenous peoples were not yoked to Christianity through European imperial coercion alone and often embraced the faith for their own reasons.[14] Moreover, the universal ambitions of the Church were distinct from, though related to, the expansionist drive of Europe's kingdoms. While the

11 On Benedict XVI's 'nearly absolute' rejection of 'every possible interpretation of inter-religious dialogue in a syncretic sense', see Aranha, 'Roberto Nobili e il dialogo interreligioso?' 146–7.

12 Cholango, 'Respuesta indígena al Papa Benedicto XVI', available at http://www.voltairenet.org/article148222.html.

13 Vilaça argues that Wari adoption of Christianity solved an aporia central to their cosmology (Vilaça, 'Cristãos sem fé'; Vilaça, 'Conversão, predação e perspectiva'). Wilde, in *Religión y poder en las misiones de Guaraníes,* contends that active support of educated indigenous elites was crucial to the Jesuit Guaraní missions.

14 Examples include the case of King Alfonso I of Congo and the case of the Parava in India in their struggle against rival Muslim groups, discussed later.

synergy between Europe's empires and the Church expanded the boundaries of both, the Church's drive towards universal conversion could and often did run counter to the demands of temporal dominion. Furthermore, with the rise of an increasingly independent papacy, Rome could function almost as a rival metropolitan node in the imperial networks of the Catholic empires. As this book demonstrates, when the Dutch and other imperial rivals threatened Portuguese dominion, the Church was content to seek other political partners in its evangelical pursuits.

Still, imperialism itself in the early modern era was not innocent of religion. European expansion occurred during a period in which religious culture still pervaded every aspect of life.[15] Thus, insistently secular histories of empire of this period are vulnerable to a (wishful) presentism, if not outright anachronism. Standing at the opening to the waters that carried the Portuguese around the world, Benedict XVI, ever mindful of the 'theology of history,' referred precisely to this amnesia. He reminded his listeners of 'the powerful cultural tradition of the Portuguese people, deeply marked by the millenary influence of Christianity and by a sense of global responsibility'. It was the 'Christian ideal of universality and fraternity', he claimed, which had inspired 'the adventure of the Discoveries and ... the missionary zeal which shared the gift of faith with other peoples ... an "ideal" to be realized by Portugal, which has always sought to establish relations with the rest of the world'.[16]

Just as in Aparecida, Benedict XVI's deliberately anodyne words softened the crucial role of imperial domination in the history of missionary work—a history of which he is painfully aware in today's decolonized world. Yet, his Eurocentric vision of the 'universal' Church; his insistence on the place of the Church at the heart of a European identity; and his uncompromising, almost millenarian belief in the divine destiny of both are living remnants of a particular *imaginaire*, which this book hopes to historicize and, ultimately, dismantle.

[15] See Somerville, *The Secularization of Early Modern England*; Taylor, *A Secular Age*.

[16] Benedict XVI, 'Address of His Holiness Benedict XVI', Cultural Center of Belém, Lisbon, Portugal, 12 May 2010.

This book explores how missionaries of the Society of Jesus working in the non-European world—specifically, Francis Xavier (1506–1552), Thomas Stephens (c. 1549–1619), and Baltasar da Costa (1610–1673) in India and Manuel da Nóbrega (1517–1570), José de Anchieta (1534–1597), and António Vieira (1608–1697) in Brazil—sought to fashion an apostolic empire that both coincided with and exceeded the temporal boundaries of early modern Portuguese dominion. Their mandates were neither straightforward, nor singular. Rather, they struggled to balance the exigencies of three primary commitments: the first, to a notion of the meaningfulness and specificity of their particular local missionary space; the second, to the universal enterprise of Catholic evangelism; and the third, to the global ambitions of Portuguese temporal domain.

The careers of these Jesuits, spanning the mid sixteenth to the late seventeenth centuries, frame two key moments of crisis in the Catholic notion of universal Christian empire: the dissolution of the unity of the Church and the end of Iberian domination of the enterprise of European empire. Their lives thus run parallel to and reflect the arc of the first phase of European imperialism.[17] Over the course of this arc, these missionaries weighed and prioritized these three commitments differently. Moreover, the relative importance of these competing mandates was contingent upon their particular location. Through their attempts to inscribe and understand their actions within these three scales of meaning—local, global, and universal—a religious imaginaire of empire emerged.

In retaining the French usage here I draw attention to the cosmological nature of the term: as Steven Collins puts it, the word 'imaginaire' refers to 'objects of the imagination, the ensemble of what is imagined, without implying falsity; it can also refer to specific imagined worlds, and so can be used in this sense in the plural'.[18] This book traces not only the discursive contours of this imaginaire of empire, but also its relationship with the world that it represented. It investigates the ways in which this imaginaire developed and spread, in reaction to and sometimes in resistance to a changing world and how it facilitated action within the world for these missionaries.

[17] The periodization is from Pagden, *Lords of All the World.*

[18] Collins, *Nirvana and Other Buddhist Felicities*, 73.

In doing so, I keep in view a chasm that is often blurred in histories of empire: the difference between the messy realities of power in colonial spaces and the grandiose discursive productions of empire that attended these activities. The subjects of this book were thwarted at every turn by indigenous interlocutors, by their masters in Rome, and by the inadequate power and dubious political will of the Portuguese imperial apparatus. Yet, in their writings, they bequeathed a blueprint of imperial thinking, whose traces are still with us today: modes of classifying the peoples of the world in hierarchical schemas, in which the European sits at the apex; conceptual cartographies, in which the far-flung corners of the world serve as colonial outposts to a European centre; and a sacralizing vision of empire, in which the realities and naked violence of imperial power are eventually erased. In part due to Jesuit epistolary conventions, this triumphalist vision found widespread circulation, while the ambiguities and disappointments of colonial experience were relegated to private conversations and internal archives. The sense of inevitability that attends even contemporary understandings of Europe's dominion is an echo of their millenarian assertion of the divine destiny of the Church travelling on the back of empire.

In imbuing their local missions with meaning, missionaries saw in them manifestations of the universal Church, just as the universal claims of the Church found concrete expression in their particular mission. The dependence, however uneven and contingent, of the evangelical project upon the temporal dominion of the Portuguese meant that local missions also became theatres within which global geopolitics played out. By the same token, in their eyes, the abstract universalism of the Church could be given form in the globe-encompassing ambitions of Portuguese rule. The religious imaginaire that they elaborated, therefore, provided a means to suture the local, the global, and the universal into a holistic vision of empire.

Local, Global, Universal: *Accommodatio* and the Evolution of an Imperial *Imaginaire*

In tracing the entangled history of early modern Portuguese imperialism and the evangelical Church, the Society of Jesus is a particularly attractive focus of study. The order gained influence early on with both the papacy and the Catholic nobility of Europe and took the lead in missionary activity abroad. The Jesuits were thus highly influential in both the imperial and the missionary enterprise.[19] Furthermore, their institutional structure allowed them to develop a global vision. The tightly knit, diasporic order placed heavy emphasis on written communication between its members and headquarters. The knowledge generated in specific mission-fields, including practical strategies for engaging indigenous peoples, was circulated amongst its members throughout the world.[20] The sophistication of Jesuit governance and administration allowed the society to maintain a globally dispersed membership, without sacrificing the coherence accorded by a centralized structure.[21] As such, the Jesuits were ideally placed to imagine and situate their activity within a broader context. Even as they struggled to find appropriate means of conversion within their local contexts, Jesuit missionaries were always aware of the wider implications of their activity from the point of view of the Portuguese Crown, the Catholic Church, and their own order. In their understanding of the dialogic process of the creation of Christian subjects of the universal Church in local missions, the Jesuits provide an ideal group to investigate how local conditions shaped the development of a trans-local imperial imaginaire.

What then was the mechanism by which a series of particular mission spaces was transformed in the imagination of these missionaries into an imperial landscape? When the future saint Francis Xavier set sail for the Indies, he envisioned only the rich harvest of pagan souls that he would reap in those faraway lands. Yet, very quickly he had to contend not only with the variety and specificity of the various

[19] On Ignatius's correspondence with the leading Catholics, see deNicólas, *Powers of Imagining*, 301.

[20] Juan Polanco presented a list of twenty reasons for the importance of epistolary exchange for the Society, including: (*a*) to keep the Company united and strong in the face of distance; (*b*) to keep members motivated and to provide them with practical and spiritual guidance; (*c*) to grow the order and its reputation; and (*d*) to aid centralized decision-making. See Juan Alfonso de Polanco to the Society, 27 July 1547, *Sancti Ignatii*, I: 536–41.

[21] Friedrich, 'Government and Information-Management'. On epistolary production in the missions, see Županov, *Disputed Mission*.

cultures of these 'pagans', but also with the significant challenge their cosmologies could present to the Christian message. It was a lesson future missionaries to the Indies would learn well and for which the missionaries fashioned a solution based on a principle enshrined in Jesuit praxis from the very beginning: *accommodatio.*

Accommodatio enjoined the spiritual preceptor to adapt the Christian lesson to the capacity and dispositions of his audience.[22] Its theological roots lay in the Judaeo-Christian exegetical principle that 'the Scriptures speak a human language'. This opened the metaphorical and allegorical language of scripture to hermeneutic interpretation that was sensitive to the time and place of its elaboration.[23] The concept intertwined rhetoric and theology: Augustine, in explicating why Jewish customs were now condemned by the Christian God, had drawn upon Cicero's notion of appropriateness in *De Oratore.* Thus, 'the rhetorical notion of the appropriate, the fitting, allowed Augustine to sustain simultaneously the ideas of divine immutability and of historical change'.[24] Augustine's crucial temporalization of Cicero's rhetorical concept eventually paved the way for Jesuit missionaries to add to it a spatial dimension: the principle of accommodatio allowed missionaries to transcend the contingencies not only of time but also of space, in spreading the Christian message. Accommodatio thus involved negotiating the tension between the universal and eternal law of the Christian God and the necessarily contingent, limited nature of the humans who received that law. In concrete terms, it involved the willingness of the missionary to adapt to or even adopt those cultural practices of his flock that he deemed free of the taint of idolatry.

By its very nature, the practice of accommodatio demanded from the missionary a disciplined sensitivity to the local realities of the mission space and its peoples. No wonder then that its practitioners have left us some of the richest proto-ethnographic accounts of the peoples among whom they laboured: testaments to the lifetimes that were devoted to the study and evangelism of their alien flock. Yet,

[22] The eighteenth annotation of Ignatius of Loyola's *Spiritual Exercises* enjoins the giver of the exercises to adapt them to the dispositions of the persons who wish to receive them.

[23] Funkenstein, *Theology and the Scientific Imagination,* 202–89.

[24] Ginzburg, *Wooden Eyes,* 110–12.

the years spent in these missions and the understanding and even respect for indigenous cultures that it engendered did not blind Jesuit missionaries to the broader structures within which they laboured. In other words, the deep devotion to a particular mission space did not preclude the missionaries from attending to the universal aspirations of the Church or the global ambitions of their imperial patrons. Moreover, the practice of accommodatio was not innocent of the exercise of power: it was adapted as a weapon of the relatively weak precisely in those territories where the simple confluence of imperial arms and missionary authority was not enough to compel conversion.

One of the central arguments of this book is that it was precisely through the practice of accommodatio that Jesuits came to place the myriad locales of their acquaintance into the much broader conceptual geographies of the Portuguese empire and the universal church. The knowledge that they gleaned from these local mission spaces would eventually be shaped into the logic of empire. Knowledge of other peoples was ordered into hierarchical ethnological schema, in which European civilization was not only placed at the apex but was divinely ordained to rule all other peoples. Moreover, their knowledge of local spaces, which were initially imbued with meaning in relation to a universal Church, led eventually to a Eurocentric conceptual cartography of empire.

Writing from the Margins

The dialectic between the local and the global inscribed in accommodatio (and which is also characteristic of the dynamic of empires) necessitates a methodology that allows analysis at a variety of spatial scales.[25] This is a challenge that this book addresses through the use of historical biography. The process by which the disparate corners of the world (Brazil, India, 'Europe') went from being just that to becoming hierarchically organized nodes of an empire requires the writing of the coterminous histories of these three regions.[26]

[25] On varying scales of analysis, see Revel, *Jeux d'échelles*.

[26] My approach here is indebted to Subrahmanyam's notion of connected history: Subrahmanyam, *Explorations in Connected History*; Subrahmanyam, 'On World Historians in the Sixteenth Century'.

Biography provides a manageable way to trace vast historical trends while resisting the schematic macro-historical tendencies of much of 'world history'. As David Nasaw puts it, biography 'offers a way of transcending the theoretical divide between empiricist social history and linguistic-turn cultural history without sacrificing the methodological or epistemological gains of either'.[27]

There is, however, another more profound reason for choosing this methodology above others. Biography favours the exploration of the ways in which an individual moulds himself, and is himself moulded in terms of external presentation and internal self-cultivation. This methodology is, therefore, particularly appropriate to this study, centrally concerned as it is with the practice of Jesuit accommodatio.[28] Missionaries self-consciously, though heteronomously, shaped their encounter with their non-European others through the practice of accommodatio. Moreover, it was through the unintended effects of this process of self-development, effects that were determined by their specific non-European context, that these missionaries came to view themselves as imperial actors and to develop a peculiarly imperial imaginaire.

Of all the missionary groups labouring outside Europe, the Jesuits most consciously theorized and performed the cultivation of the self. The towering figure of Ignatius at the centre of the order provided a model of the Jesuit self. The *exemplum* offered implicitly by Ignatius's life and the guidance given explicitly through his writings amounted to a comprehensive programme through which to fashion oneself as a Jesuit, both at the spiritual and interior level, and its more worldly and exterior manifestation.[29] Thus, Jesuits who set off for India and Brazil

[27] Nasaw, 'Introduction', 576. See also the introduction to Eaton, *A Social History*.

[28] Since the postmodern critique of subjectivity, scholarship has tended to ignore the former aspect in favour of a performative understanding of the self. See, for example, Margadent, 'Introduction', 7. My approach is closer to Barbara Taylor's view that '[w]e need a biographical lens that looks inward as well as outward, to focus on the constitutive elements of human subjectivity as well as its external determinants' (Taylor, 'Separations of Soul', 651).

[29] The key text here, foundational to the Jesuit identity is the *Spiritual Exercises*.

left with a similar model of self-cultivation, moderated by the effects of individual personality.

While it was always expected that a member of the order followed the peculiarly Jesuit *modo de proceder*, this did not amount to a slavish attachment to an image or example of the ideal Jesuit.[30] It was Ignatius himself who prescribed accommodatio as the heart of Jesuit pastoral practice. The particular demands of the pastoral or missionary field dictated how missionaries translated their inner commitments into practical action and self-presentation.[31] This pastoral activity, which demanded careful management of their external selves to be successful, was also intimately related to their sense of interior self-cultivation. The process of self-cultivation and discipline necessitated by accommodatio ultimately bore fruit within the Jesuit himself, in ensuring his own salvation and consolation, as much as that of his neighbour.

Despite the conscious ways in which these missionaries fashioned themselves in the colonies, this is not a model in which the pristine agency of the European drives the motor of history. While Europeans came to missions abroad with a set of tools through which to present and cultivate themselves, the context itself imposed unexpected and unintended consequences. In adapting to these imperial locations, however strategically, the European changed, becoming something else entirely, becoming an 'imperial' man with very different perceptions and motivations to the earlier self who first sailed from the shores of Europe to the 'Indies'. Acting in the imperial theatre, the European undoubtedly adopted masks; but these masks were

[30] On critiques of slavish imitation in the period, see Pigman, 'Versions of Imitation'. Herdt argues that the mimesis of Christ is predicated on the perfection and inexhaustibility of the pattern he provides. Exemplary characters such as saints point beyond themselves to Jesus as the original exemplar, thus securing their ability to serve as models of character. See Herdt, *Putting on virtue*, 67, 112.

[31] As O'Malley notes, accommodatio was 'one of the principles characteristic of Jesuit ministry ... In practice, of course, it might be separated by only a hair's breadth, or less, from opportunism'. This latter trait may explain in part the vitriol directed to the most radical examples of Jesuit accomodatio (O'Malley, *The First Jesuits*, 81).

internalized, becoming integral parts of the European imperial self, sometimes despite precautions against cultural contamination. This is not, it must be emphasized, a history of the Janus-faced, strategic European.

The practice of accommodatio depended crucially on the cultural encounter in the non-European world, which is at the heart of this genealogy of an imaginaire of European empire. In other words, this is not an intellectual history of imperial ideas projected from the metropole onto the peripheries; it is instead a history of empire written from the margins. Methodologically, this requires a double reading of encounter, which considers the 'implicit ethnography'—the unstated assumptions regarding the nature of personhood, self and other, identity and alterity, which underpins perceptions of social reality—of *both* interlocutors.[32] Thus, for each encounter our missionary protagonists report—with a brahmin priest or an Amerindian shaman, with untouchable village headmen in Tamil Nadu or indigenous children in the Bahian backlands—this book will reconstruct the encounter from the perspective of these interlocutors too, through an eclectic mix of textual sources in European and non-European languages and scholarly advances in anthropology. Moreover, it will situate these interlocutors, and hence these encounters, in the full complexity of the hierarchies and tensions of their own societies. Even if the conclusions offered are speculative, the value of such an exercise is in making empire strange again. The goal is to displace the Eurocentric modes of thought that are empire's legacy, and to which, as scholars working in imperial archives and European traditions of history-making, we are still vulnerable.

The historiography of cultural encounters with Europeans in both America and India is vast, rich, and complex. Nonetheless, these fields may be schematized according to three dominant approaches. The first denies to some extent the very possibility of genuine encounter in the chasm of cultural incommensurability.[33] The European, in this model, is caught perpetually in 'a hall of distorting mirrors in which each individual sees himself, as he thinks, truly reflected, while those about

[32] See the introduction to Schwarz, *Implicit Understandings*.

[33] Pagden, *European Encounters*, 238.

him are disquietingly altered into grotesques, as familiar gestures and expressions are exaggerated, parodied, even inverted'.[34] The other, often demonic, is a construct against which to articulate a sense of identity.[35] At work here is a more or less unconscious emphasis on the problems of human communication.[36] Even where the European succeeds in reading the signs of native culture for the instrumental purposes of colonial activity, the possibility of genuine exchange is precluded.[37] This historiographical strand assumes the colonial actor's cultural embeddedness, which remains, sometimes despite his own best efforts, ultimately insurmountable in the encounter with the other.

The second approach to the history of colonial encounter has centrally employed the trope of the gaze. Strongly influenced by the theoretical apparatus bequeathed by Michel Foucault, Edward Said's *Orientalism* is the cornerstone of this field of research for its polemical call to demystify the relationship between European representation and rule of others. Here, the eye itself is not innocent, but deeply implicated in a politics of domination. As one might imagine, this historiography has focused heavily on domains of ritualized observation: travel and ethnography.[38] Understandably, much of this literature has been centrally concerned with a political

[34] A classic formulation of this metaphor of colony as European mirror is Elliot, *The Old World and the New*.

[35] See, for example, Mello e Souza's application of Michel de Certeau's notion of heterology in discursive constructions of colonial Brazil in *Inferno Atlântico*.

[36] Clendinnen speaks of the metaphor of 'the confusion of tongues' in the characterization of colonial situations (*Ambivalent Conquests*, 127).

[37] Todorov, *The Conquest of America*. As Clendinnen notes, Todorov's semiotic analysis remains part of a broad colonial historiographical tradition based on 'proving', in whatever domain, the superiority of European culture in explaining its colonial mastery Clendinnen, 'Fierce and Unnatural Cruelty', 66.

[38] The classic text in this vein is Pratt's *Imperial Eyes*, which relies heavily on a particular, almost Saidian, interpretation of the great Cuban anthropologist Fernando Ortiz's notion of transculturation for its theoretical framework.

project to decolonize knowledge.[39] This historiography has evolved from understanding contact as a one-way relationship between the seeing eye and the observed, to a model of dialogic, if unequal, interaction between the colonizer and the colonized.[40] Nonetheless, this literature, despite allowing for the possibility for genuine mutual recognition, does not escape from the metaphor of the mirror: the self and the other stand beholding each other, as if each were gazing into a looking glass, in a 'mirror dance'.[41]

The third approach to cultural encounter pivots from an emphasis on sight, observation, and representation to a focus on action. This agent-centred approach focuses on colonial actors who move back and forth between separate but at least partially porous cultural spheres.[42] For the case of Brazil, this approach has been employed particularly in the history of Bandeirantes and Mamelucos, whose familiarity with indigenous and Portuguese culture allowed them to play a crucial role in the making of colonial Brazil.[43] Frontiersmen were not the only agents capable of traversing cultural boundaries between indigenous and European society and acting as transactional go-betweens.[44] Histories of merchants, soldiers, and mercenaries, as well as of indigenous agents in the employ of the imperial bureaucracy, often cast these actors in similar terms.[45] Despite the wide range of peoples

[39] Pompa, in *Religão como tradução*, reflects on the persistence in current scholarship of the terms Europeans originally elaborated to understand Tupí culture, while Tupí efforts to 'translate' Europeans has been largely forgotten.

[40] Pratt, 'Arts of the Contact Zone', 33–40.

[41] Pratt, *Imperial Eyes*, 137.

[42] The term 'agent' captures both the flavour of individual actors and their role as cultural double-agents, evoking the stigma of inauthenticity or disloyalty such movement across cultural boundaries can inspire, both in history and in historiography. See, for example, Vainfas's study of the Mameluco Jesuit-turned-apostate, Manoel de Moraes, in *Traição*.

[43] The classic statement of this thread in Brazilian historiography is Vianna Moog's *Bandeirantes e pioneiros*. On their role in the creation of a slave society as well of frontier expansion in Brazil, see, for example, Metcalf, 'The *Entradas* of Bahia'.

[44] The term is from Metcalf, *Go-betweens*.

[45] Cohn, *Colonialism and Its Forms of Knowledge*.

studied, this historiographic strand is characterized by a certain tendency towards instrumental interpretations, where cultural fluidity is primarily a comparative advantage in the imperial transactional economy, an explanatory variable rather than a locus of explicit investigation. Moreover, this approach typically takes as its point of departure the existence of persons capable of traversing cultural spheres; the process by which this capacity is generated, including the extent to which it is the direct result of conscious self-fashioning rather than biological or circumstantial accident, has been relatively understudied. This is particularly true of those individuals who altogether jumped cultural ship, that is those infamous Europeans who went unapologetically native, or those indigenous people whose cultural fluency in the linguistic and religious practices of Europeans drew both scorn and approbation.[46]

Like all heuristics, this attempt to schematize an enormous body of scholarship is at best a gross generalization and at worst unfair caricature. It points, however, to a deeper current in historiography to underestimate the capacity of historical actors to understand the terms of cultural encounter. The approach to the analysis of interaction across cultural barriers adopted in this book is different. First, I reject any notion of insurmountable cultural incommensurability or the absolute inability of interlocutors to communicate or understand each other across cultural barriers. This is not to say that some measure of opacity and misunderstanding did not play a crucial role in structuring these encounters, particularly in the very beginning. Second, I take seriously the possibility that the historical actors in this exchange could gain fluency over time with the cultural vocabulary of the other and use this mastery to fashion themselves in suitable ways. Thus, the ability to traverse cultural boundaries is not taken as a given but is rather considered an acquired skill, central to both the

[46] On the European side, this lacuna is a reflection of the limitations of archives. Such figures as Gonzalo Guerrero, Diogo Álvares, and João Ramalho left little in the way of primary testimony. Perhaps the most poignant example of the *indio ladino*, an indigenous person with European cultural and linguistic fluency, is Felipe Guamán Poma de Ayala, whose indictment of the Spanish colonial system lay forgotten in the Danish royal library till 1908. See Adorno, *Guaman Poma*.

missionary practice of accommodatio and the indigenous adoption of Christianity.

Last, I do not assume an immediate imbalance of power in favour of the Europeans in understanding encounter. As this history of accommodatio clearly shows, cross-cultural fluency was not made incumbent solely on the indigenous to survive in the disciplinary structures of the colony. The imbalance of power between European would-be colonizers and indigenous societies implied by this assumption simply did not exist in the sixteenth and seventeenth centuries.[47] To the extent that the European imperial enterprise in this period had to rely on negotiation as well as coercion, on persuasion as much as power, European actors had to learn the dynamics and symbolic structures of local cultures and self-consciously play roles suited to them.[48] Indeed, when other forms of authority proved sufficient, accommodatio as a strategy could be and was abandoned.

Nonetheless, accommodatio, forged as a practice in the crucible of cultural encounter in the non-European world, was crucial to the development of the imperial imaginaire at the heart of this book. It required the individual missionary to fashion a self suited to the local mission context, without losing sight of either his role as representative of the universal Church or the vagaries of global politics to which Portuguese rule was always vulnerable. It is also the unifying thread of the various biographical studies that make up this book.

The Old World and the New

Since this book investigates the development of an imperial imaginaire that encompasses the local and the global, it resists a national or regional delimitation of scope. In focusing on the Portuguese empire in particular, the historian is also afforded a rare opportunity

[47] On the tendency of historians to overstate the capacity of past imperial states to acquire and sustain dominance, see Hopkins, 'Back to the Future'. See also Pagden, *Lords of All the World*.

[48] Subrahmanyam notes that an accommodationist attitude towards local context was exhibited by a variety of colonial actors as late as the early nineteenth century in southern India (Subrahmanyam, 'Profiles in Transition').

to bring together into a single frame the history of European imperial engagement in the old world and the new.[49] Specifically, this book intertwines the histories of South Asia and Latin America, two fields that have rarely been brought into historiographical conversation.

The interpenetration of South Asian and Latin American historiography remains in its infancy. Empirically grounded historical studies that consider these regions simultaneously are conspicuous largely by their absence.[50] The limited engagement between the two fields has been confined to the search for common methodologies and the realm of theory.[51] Moreover, many scholars of Latin American history, not without reason, have been cautious about a form of engagement which they see as homogenizing disparate (post)colonial experiences.[52]

The rise of comparative studies of settler colonialism seems only to confirm this fundamental historical difference between Latin America and South Asia. The experience of British colonialism in India was paradigmatic of a mode of colonialism characterized by the material domination of a numerically greater indigenous population by a foreign minority, acting in the name of an explicitly articulated ideology of racial and cultural superiority.[53] Canonical thinkers of decolonization and their intellectual inheritors have largely hailed from such

[49] In the field of Portuguese imperial history, studies generally focus on one region of the far-flung empire. See Coates, 'The Early Modern Portuguese Empire', 83–90.

[50] New attempts to connect Latin American and Asian history include Seijas, *Asian Slaves*. Scholars of Jesuits have also been pioneers in this regard: see Bailey, *Art on the Jesuit Missions*; Clossey, *Salvation and Globalization*; Hosne, *The Jesuit Missions*.

[51] See the pioneering efforts of Gilbert Joseph and Floencia Mallon to found a Latin American school of Subaltern Studies: Joseph, 'On the Trail'; Mallon, 'The Promise and Dilemma'. The beginning of the postcolonial turn in Latin American scholarship was heralded by the 1993 special issue of *Latin American Research Review* (vol. 28, no. 3). South Asianist engagement with Latin American history has been negligible.

[52] See, for example, Klor de Alva, 'Colonialism and Postcolonialism'; Moya, 'A Continent of Immigrants', 24.

[53] This seminal definition of colonialism derives from Balandier, 'La situation *colonial*'.

(post)colonies in which the indigenous population could ultimately become the inheritors of their own earth. The Cabo Verdean and Guinea-Bissauan nationalist leader, Amílcar Lopes da Costa Cabral, expressed this view most succinctly in his 1970 lecture at Syracuse University. In his analysis of what he termed 'foreign domination', Cabral dismissed outright the choice of genocide as a practicable solution to indigenous cultural resistance, on the grounds that it would create 'a void which empties foreign domination of its content and its object: the dominated people'. Instead, unable to 'harmonize economic and political domination of these people with their cultural personality ... imperialist colonial domination has tried to create theories which, in fact, are only gross formulations of racism'.[54]

Latin America, by contrast, is a world 'made by conquest'; the settler colonial state relied on a (juridically) marked distinction 'between conquerors and conquered, settlers and natives', which in turn formed 'the basis of other distinctions that tend to buttress the conquerors and isolate the conquered, politically'.[55] As Patrick Wolfe puts it, 'settler colonies were (are) premised on the elimination of native societies ... The colonizers come to stay—invasion is a structure not an event. In contrast, for all the hollow formality of decolonization, at least the legislators generally change colour'.[56] These definitions of settler colonialism, by a scholar of southern Africa and Australia respectively, also capture starkly the catastrophic demographic collapse, however unintended, of indigenous populations in Latin America following contact and its subsequent trajectory. It only seems to affirm the gulf between the historical experience of a non-settler (post)colony like South Asia, and the settler colonial societies of Latin America.

Yet, this gulf depends on two fallacies. The first is a selective reading of South Asian history, in which the long history of European presence in the subcontinent is reduced to the British Raj. It is not incidental that the vast majority of the essays published in the volumes of *Subaltern Studies* focus on the late nineteenth and twentieth centuries; postcolonial scholarship has also generally fallen within

[54] Cabral, 'National Liberation and Culture'.

[55] Mamdani, *When Does a Settler Become a Native?*

[56] Wolfe, *Settler Colonialism*, 2.

this narrow temporal focus. The early modern era, during which the Portuguese pioneered European imperialism in the subcontinent, is still largely overlooked. Taking into account this early history of European imperial intervention in South Asia avoids altogether the uncomfortable projection of the theoretical insights from nineteenth-century British India onto the history of the early modern Iberian empires in Latin America, and vice versa.

The second fallacy—and this is more subtle but equally pernicious—is the notion that European imperialism in the old world and the new followed separate and disconnected trajectories, leading inexorably to the ideal types of non-settler and settler colonialism in these regions. Rather, as this book will demonstrate, the epistemic structures of what Aníbal Quijano calls the coloniality of power was a result of circulation and comparison of European experiences in both regions.

In Quijano's view, the Eurocentric structure of global power, which allows resources to accrue to a small minority of Europeans and their descendants even after the end of formal rule, depends crucially on regimes of social discrimination. These, in turn, evolved from a project of knowledge originating in the colonial period. These regimes evolved from the complex ways in which Europeans came to know and hierarchically classify others, even as they appropriated and delegitimized indigenous forms of knowledge, thus producing what Partha Chatterjee calls the rule of colonial difference.[57] Whereas Quijano suggests that this was the singular product of the Latin American encounter with Europe, this book instead demonstrates that this process played out on both sides of the globe.[58] European observers in these lands drew on a great variety of conceptual tools to grapple with their 'discoveries' in *both* the old and new worlds.[59] Moreover, unlike the secular view of this history advanced by Quijano, the contention here is that in the development of the ideology of European superiority, which eventually underpinned empire, religion played a crucial part.

This book, therefore, considers the foundational moment of early modern European engagement in both South Asia and Latin America

[57] Chatterjee, *The Nation and Its Fragments*, 19, 33.

[58] Quijano, 'Colonialidad y Modernidad/Racionalidad'.

[59] Randles, '"Peuples sauvages"'.

in a comparative *and* connected manner. This is not to suggest that these regions in the sixteenth century were somehow essentially similar or equivalent, thus leading inexorably to their absorption within the matrix of empire. Though these regions could occupy the same plane within the symbolic structure of the 'Indies' for European observers, in reality they could hardly present a greater contrast as imperial theatres. If pre-colonial Brazil was characterized by stateless societies, centred on shamanic cosmologies, where indigenous societies suffered dramatic mortality rates after contact, South Asia was bristling with indigenous polities and empires, with many competing forms of religion, in a similar disease ecology as Europe. Far from suggesting any essential similarity between Brazil and South Asia, this book hopes to investigate why their manifest *disparities* as political and cultural terrain could eventually be subsumed by the logic of empire.

The protagonists of this history follow precisely this arc: when Francis Xavier and Manuel da Nóbrega arrived in India and Brazil in the 1540s, they encountered a series of local contexts to which they had to tailor their missionary strategies. In the localized nature of their geographical imagination, they were no different from the men of their time. Caught between the past and the future in its debt to Ptolemaic classical cosmography and in its anticipation of new knowledge and the still-germinating imperial projects of conquest in the 'age of discoveries', as Frank Lestringant has shown, cosmography was equally contradictory in its spatial dimensions. The field, with its 'aesthetics of varietas' and its obsessive detailing of the singular, was nonetheless committed to the notion of totality implied by the very term 'cosmography'. As Lestringant puts it,

> to plunge into the minute diversity of the world, to recognize its fundamental and inexhaustible heterogeneity, paradoxically joined up with the project of accounting for its totality ... Even if he might lose himself among the [field of singular things], this encyclopaedist of the disparate ... managed to recover in his project the 'delectable,' shimmering unity of the Creation.[60]

What is important to note for our purpose here is this brief moment to which Lestringant repeatedly draws attention, a moment in which

[60] Lestringant, *Mapping the Renaissance World*, 35.

the world was a concatenation of singularities bound mostly by the notion of a unitary Creation—and not by the later heuristic of empire.

A century later, by contrast, Baltasar da Costa and António Vieira as imperial missionaries inhabited very different roles from their pioneering forbears. They instead visualized these far-flung and completely different mission-fields in one frame, simultaneously and in a relationship of subordination to Europe—in other words, as an empire, albeit one in peril. In Costa's case, though his mission was located in the lands of indigenous kings, he nonetheless understood his activities as the work of a Portuguese vassal in imperial space. From specific and strikingly disparate mission-fields, India and Brazil had come to signify colonial outposts, interchangeable in as far as they bore a relationship of possession with Portugal, which thus emerges as the centre to the imperial periphery.

Chapter Outline

The following chapter sketches the world that the Portuguese 'discovered' upon their arrival in South Asia and Brazil from the viewpoint of the indigenous peoples they encountered. It thus serves as an introduction to the methodology adopted in this book in approaching the history of cultural encounter. It also tracks Portuguese efforts to establish a foothold in these arenas, and the political situation by the 1540s, when the first Jesuits arrived on the scene.

The book is then divided into three parts, tracing roughly three different stages in the development of this religious imaginaire of empire. The first section explores the foundation of the Jesuit enterprise in India and Brazil by the pioneers, Francis Xavier and Manuel da Nóbrega. Tracing the different trajectories in the east and west of these missionaries in relation to the geography of Portuguese power, I show the conceptual boundaries of Jesuit missionary space in the Indies that they would bequeath.

The next chapter compares the ethnological frameworks Xavier and Nóbrega developed to understand the peoples they encountered. Through his troubling encounter with brahmins, Xavier came to elaborate a hierarchical ethnological schema, in which peoples were classified according to a ladder of civility. Adopting an Augustinian framework, Nóbrega instead insisted that the Tupí be viewed not as the bottom rung of an ethnological ladder, but rather as inherently equal to all other peoples in their capacity to become Christians.

For all their differences, Nóbrega and Xavier were most alike in their ambivalence towards the value of a humanistic approach to learning about the other for evangelism. Their successors, however, devoted themselves to the particular form of accommodatio for which the Jesuit missions came to be known. The next section of the book is devoted to the literary corpus of two non-Portuguese missionaries: the Spaniard José de Anchieta in Brazil and the Englishman Thomas Stephens in India, which married the skills, sensitivity, and intellectual proclivities of the European humanist to the imperatives of imperial political calculation and indigenous conversion.

The fourth chapter explores the effects of Anchieta's early experience in the Tupí village of Piratininga as well as the turbulence caused by the French–Tamoio alliance on his poetic corpus. A significant portion of this corpus was in the standardized form Anchieta gave the *lingua geral*, the coastal indigenous lingua franca.[61] His poetic works also encompassed various European vernaculars and even Latin. This corpus used the very terms of Tupí orality to mount a powerful assault on the *fait social total* of Tupí culture, namely warfare. It replicated and reinforced the emerging social project of Jesuit custodial control of the Amerindians in the *aldeias* instituted as part of the pacification campaign of Mem de Sá.

The first English Jesuit in India, Thomas Stephens, rejected the forcible conversion strategies of the Portuguese in Salcete in favour of humanistic accommodatio. Yet, like Anchieta, Stephens's corpus in Marāṭhī and Kōṅkaṇī, which adapted admirably the generic conventions of local literature, was ultimately directed at creating a Christianized (if brahminical) convert community. Accommodatio was less an index of cultural convergence or tolerance than a strategy adopted in the face of the manifest failure of coercion.

[61] Though published only in 1595, the second published text on the indigenous languages of the Americas, Anchieta's *Arte de Gramática da lingua mais usada na costa do Brasil* (Art of the Language Most Used on the Coast of Brazil) was composed between 1555 and 1556. On language ecology in colonial Brazil, see Lee, 'Conversing in Colony'.

The emphasis on the specificities of the local missionary context by these non-Portuguese missionaries must be read in light of the changing circumstances of Portugal, which lost its autonomy to Spain in 1580. As a result, the Portuguese empire was increasingly exposed to the imperial ambitions of Spain's greatest antagonists of the period: the Dutch and later the English. As relative outsiders within the Portuguese empire, Anchieta and Stephens's desire to set aside the increasingly fractious ethnic and imperial rivalries that had begun to plague the empire and the Jesuit order to focus instead on local conversion is understandable. Yet, a few years after Stephens's death in 1619, the crisis of the Portuguese empire became undeniable. The particular combination of temporal dominion and religious jurisdiction, enshrined in the Padroado, which undergirded the Jesuit missions in Portuguese Brazil and India, began to falter.[62]

It was in response to this crisis that a genuinely imperial imaginaire developed among Portuguese Jesuits of the day. The final section focuses on the careers of António Vieira and Baltasar da Costa. I first explore how millenarian visions of the Portuguese empire developed in the Portuguese conquests, to make comprehensible in local terms the vicissitudes of global politics originating in Europe and to imbue these events with meaning. For Vieira, in particular, serving as a colonial missionary and a metropolitan political agent, the need to render the colony as politically and religiously meaningful in itself was acutely felt. Costa, equally committed to the local mission to which he had been assigned, adopted in the course of his career in Madurai an extreme mimetic practice in the name of acommodatio. His many 'faces', however, were a pragmatic result of his attempt to find a unity of purpose in the contradictory demands of his particular location in Madurai, his adherence to a notion of the universal Church, and his sense of his responsibilities and aspirations as a vassal of the Portuguese empire.

The last chapter considers the discursive parameters of this imaginaire of empire. Through various genres, particularly historical prophecy, this vision circulated amongst Portuguese Jesuits,

[62] The Padroado, literally meaning patronage, was the arrangement between the papacy and the Portuguese Crown that ceded to the latter the right to administer various aspects of the church in its domains.

affirming the divine destiny of the Portuguese empire in the teeth of its obvious disintegration. This imaginaire underpinned the eventually unsuccessful attempts by Vieira and Costa, among others, to found a company to save the Estado da Índia. As travel became safer, unlike their forbears, Baltasar da Costa and António Vieira could circulate freely between the metropole and the imperial outposts. This very mobility allowed them to inhabit a multitude of roles, negotiating both the colonial mission context and the complex political landscape of the metropole. What is remarkable here, however, is the extent to which, even in the metropole, they remained 'imperial' men, their commitment to the conquests a marker of identity. In turn, this allowed them to view the world they inhabited within the framework of empire, understanding their travels and negotiations as structured by the relationship of imperial colonies and metropolitan kingdom. In the story of these two men, the various strands of this book—the Jesuit struggle to find appropriate means of conversion in local mission through strategies of self-cultivation and presentation, their intimate implication in Portuguese imperialism, and their attempts to safeguard universal Catholicism—come full circle.

I

FROM CONTACT TO 'CONQUEST'

Dispatches from the Pepper-Land

> It was in the year 904 AH the Portuguese made their first appearance in Malabar ... On this occasion, they did not engage themselves in any trade. The main purpose of their trip to Malabar, according to their own accounts, was to seek information about the pepper-land and to establish trade in that commodity, for at that time they were buying pepper from other traders who export pepper from Malabar.[1]

This is how Sheikh Zainuddīn Ma'abari II described the arrival of the Portuguese on the shores of his homeland in present-day Kerala. The banal, almost matter-of-fact tone is suggestive of the kind of reception these newcomers may have received upon their arrival in the busy ports of Malabar, where strangers seeking to make their fortune in pepper were hardly unusual. If this was the beginning of the age of discoveries, the thrill appears to have been sensed only by the Portuguese (see Figure 1.1).

When Vasco da Gama rounded the Cape of Good Hope, he stumbled into a world webbed by various networks predicated on certain cultural attitudes towards the Indian Ocean. Very quickly, the Portuguese, who brought with them wholly new legal and cultural

[1] Ma'abari II, *Tuhfat al-Mujāhidīn*, 49. The hereditary judges of Ponnani are often referred to with the honorific Makhdūm, meaning master or one worthy of service.

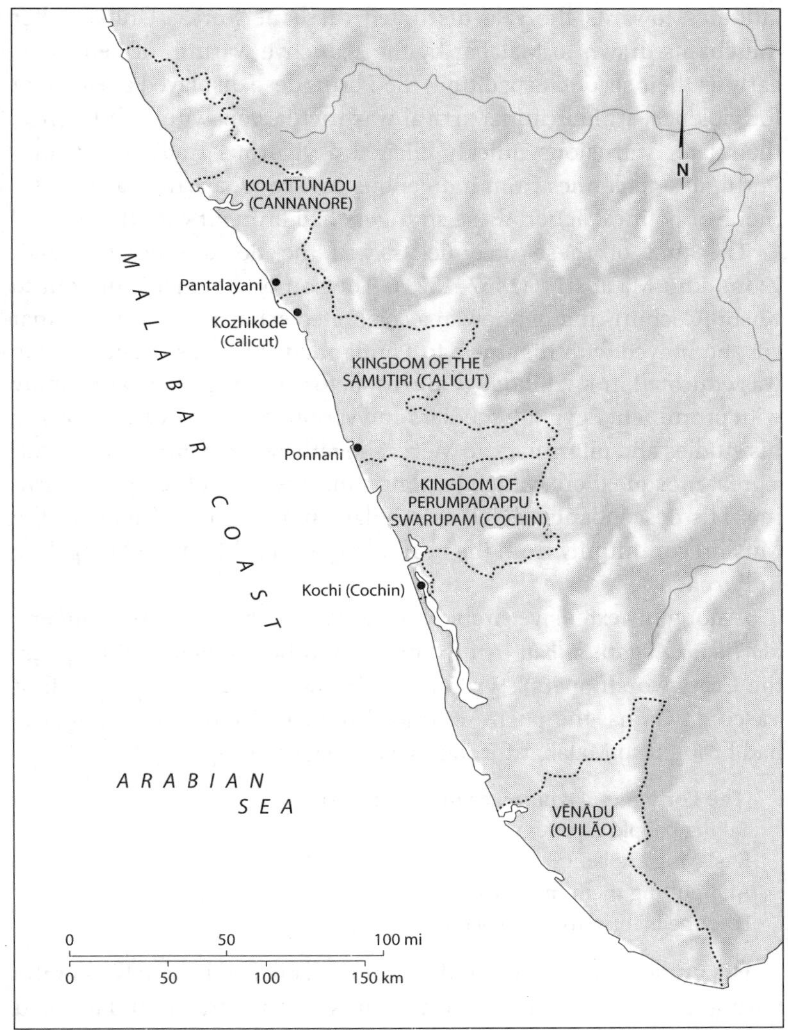

Figure 1.1 The Malabar Coast in 1498
Source: The author (drawn by William Nelson).

attitudes towards the sea, disrupted these networks. Unlike other merchants drawn to Malabar by the seductive warmth of pepper, as early as their second expedition, the Portuguese displayed a penchant for violence. If their initial arrival was met largely with indifference, their later intrusions quickly elicited a vigorous tradition of anti-Portuguese polemics from indigenous observers, alarmed at the new mode of political action these strangers had brought with them.

The first of these polemicists was the noted scholar Sheikh Zainuddīn Ma'abari I (1467–1521). The son of a Yemeni migrant to Kochi (Cochin), and nephew to a celebrated scholar and judge of that city, he moved with his uncle to Ponnani after he was orphaned. He was educated in Kozhikode (Calicut), before leaving Malabar to study with prominent Egyptian scholars and various Sufi masters. Following his studies and pilgrimage to Mecca, he returned to Ponnani and built a great mosque there, which became a major centre of religious learning. His descendants served as scholars and religious leaders of the Muslim community from the pearl coast of Tamil Nadu to Mangalore in Karnataka.

Among his extensive Arabic corpus was the poem *Tahrīd Ahlilmān ala Jihādi Abdati Sulbān* (An Exhortation to Believers to Fight against the Cross-worshippers). Written within two decades of the arrival of Vasco da Gama, the poem described the conditions the Portuguese had brought to Malabar through vivid images of captivity:

> [The Portuguese] tyrannized [us] in Malabar ...
> Taking people captives ...
> Enslaving the believers ...
> And putting them into narrow quarters
> Like sheds for senseless sheep.[2]

His grandson, Zainuddīn Ma'abari II, deepened his analysis of the Portuguese intrusion and continued this polemic tradition. Educated at his family's famous madrasa in Ponnani, the sheikh also studied in Mecca and Medina with important jurists and Sufi scholars. Upon his return to Malabar, he taught at Ponnani and kept up his scholarly connections in the Arab world. Aside from his academic life, the sheikh was a statesmen of import, cultivating relationships

[2] Ma'abari I, *Ahlil Iman*, 92–3.

with the rulers of Bijāpur and serving as the envoy of the Samūtiri of Kozhikode on diplomatic missions to Egypt and Turkey, in part to garner military support against the Portuguese. Among his extensive writings is an Arabic text entitled *Tuḥfat al-Mujāhidīn fī ba'ḍ al-akhbār al-Burtughāliyyīn* (Gift of the Holy Warriors in Matters Regarding the Portuguese). Composed in Malabar in the 1570s, the book was dedicated to 'Ali 'Ādil Shāh, the ruler of the Deccan sultanate of Bijāpur, to mobilize a Muslim military response to the Portuguese.

In his explication of *jihād* (holy war), the sheikh mentions two sorts of obligations towards two sets of unbelievers. The first is the group that dwells permanently in the land of Muslims, the second those who invade Muslim territories. The latter is what the sheikh claims Malabar is experiencing. This is intriguing in that he essentially classifies the territory of Hindu rulers as Muslim land. As he explains:

> It is well known that the Muslims of Malabar do not have a leader ... All of them are subjects of the rulers who are non-believers. Notwithstanding, [these rulers] kept on fighting their foreign enemies who were trying to dominate [the Malabari Muslims]. They have already spent their wealth to the extent of their means in the cause of this struggle, with the generous help from the Muslim-friendly [Samūtiri].[3]

In Sheikh Ma'abari II's analysis, the category of the other is a complex enmeshing of the separate categories of foreigners (to Malabar) and unbelievers (to Islam). The Portuguese, as foreign unbelievers, are unquestionably the other, the interloper, and the antagonist of this text. But the non-Muslim rulers of Malabar, and particularly his patron, the Samūtiri of Kozhikode, known to the Portuguese as the Zamorim of Calicut, are contrasted favourably with foreign believers, the sultans and emirs of the Muslim world who had ignored the plight of Malabar's Muslims.

The cross-cutting ways in which belonging to the diasporic world of the *ummah* (the community of Muslims) and to the locality of Malabar mark Sheikh Ma'abari II's own relationship to Malabar is evident in his description of the peoples of the land. He describes his Hindu neighbours, among whom his family had lived for generations, with the ethnographic detachment of a foreigner,

[3] Ma'abari II, *Tuhfat al-Mujāhidīn*, 15.

not unlike the tone of sixteenth-century Portuguese chroniclers like Duarte Barbosa. In the chapter devoted to the 'very strange and unique customs ... prevalent among the Hindus in Malabar, such as not seen anywhere else in the world', he noted that the local matrilineal custom

> of denying inheritance to male children [had] crept into the families of the Muslim community in Kannur (known as Cannanore to the Portuguese) and the neighboring places. They read the Qu'ran; they learn it by heart; they recite it beautifully; they acquire religious learning; they perform prayers and other forms of worship; yet it is extremely strange and surprising that this custom prevails among them.[4]

Belonging in the Indian Ocean world was thus inherently multilinear, interlacing diasporic and local relationships to space and people. Yet, before the Portuguese the open structure of Indian Ocean port cities allowed such modes of being to flourish, without a sense of internal contradiction. The sheikh's history of Malabar prior to the arrival of the Portuguese is instructive in this regard:

> A party of Jews and Christians with their families arrived in a big ship in Kodungallur, the port city of Malabar ... They secured from the king grants of lands, plantations and houses and thus they settled there. Some years later, there arrived at Kodungallur a party of Muslims, who were poor, with a sheikh ... on their way to visit the footprint of our father Adam in Ceylon. When the king heard about their arrival, he sent for them ... [T]he sheikh informed the king about Prophet Muhammad and the religion of Islam ... [T]he king asked the sheikh and his companions to call on him on their return journey [so] he might go with them.[5]

He then recounts how the king went to Shāhar al-Mukalla and perished there, after instructing his Muslim emissaries to bring back a letter in Malayalam outlining his testamentary desires. This included provisions for land grants to his emissaries, who built mosques in Kollam, Ezhimala, Barkur, Mangalore, and other places.

The event was remembered by both Hindus and Muslims in Malabar, in garbled mythic forms, both of which the sheikh dismisses. These myths, however, reflected a process of fragmentation that gave the Malabar coast its particular political landscape. The first Malayalam

[4] Ma'abari II, *Tuhfat al-Mujāhidīn*, 40.

[5] Ma'abari II, *Tuhfat al-Mujāhidīn*, 29.

chronicle, *Kēraḷōlpatti*, reflective of a Nambūtiri brahmin perspective, identifies this legendary king as Cēramān Perumāḷ, the last of the line of Cēra kings. His disappearance precipitated the supersession of Cēra rule, lasting roughly between the ninth and twelfth centuries, by a host of competing successor states, including that of the Samūtiri of Kozhikode; the Porḷātiri and the Kurumbiatiri, whose lands lay on the outskirts of the dominion of the Samūtiri; the Kōlatiri of Kannur, and the chiefs of Kochi and Valluvanad.[6] The *Kēraḷōlpatti* reports a striking injunction given by Cēramān Perumāḷ to Manavikraman, the governor of Eranad and future Samūtiri, to 'conquer by courting and conferring death'. Symbolically, the chronicle reflected an understanding that the dissolution of the Cēra state ushered in a process of political fragmentation and competition among its erstwhile feudatories.

The Sheikh's account too reflected this process: he recounted that the Samūtiri, who arrived late to the meeting in which the partition of Malabar was effected, was only bequeathed a sword by Cēramān Perumāḷ, along with the instruction to 'grab power fighting with this'.[7] He noted that the rulers ranged from chieftains ruling over territories as small as three and a half square miles with troops as meagre as a hundred soldiers, to those who commanded extensive lands and armies numbering a hundred thousand or more. Coalition rule was not uncommon. The principal players, according to the sheikh, were the Tiruvadi, the ruler of the territories between Kollam and Kanyakumari (whom the Portuguese identified as the king of Quilão); the Kōlattiri, ruler of Kannur, and the Samūtiri. The sheikh, ever loyal, contended that the last was the greatest of the Malabari rulers, in part because of his treatment of Muslims, especially foreign Muslims.[8] He also described the rules of political contest in Malabar,

[6] Gundert, *Keralolpatti*. On the *Kēraḷōlpatti* as early indigenous 'history', see Veluthat, *The Early Medieval in South India*, 129–46.

[7] Ma'abari II, *Tuhfat al-Mujāhidīn*, 34.

[8] The symbiotic relationship between Muslim courtiers and the Samūtiri had old roots: Veluthat notes that the hereditary Muslim nobleman in charge of the port city had first advised and assisted the Samūtiri to acquire the right to preside over the major festival at the temple of Tirunāvāya, increasing the legitimacy of the ascendant ruler (Veluthat, *The Early Medieval in South India*, 261).

where the subjugation of weaker rulers would traditionally cause the vanquished to accept a tributary relationship with the conqueror or, occasionally, forfeit his kingdom entirely. Nonetheless, the sheikh noted, 'If the subdued king does not give, he would not be forced to do so though a long time may lapse in waiting.'[9]

The sheikh's history and description of pre-contact Malabar is instructive for our purposes for two reasons. First, the internal world of Malabar was characterized by a continual contest for sovereignty through territorial control and tributary recognition, mainly between the principalities of Kochi and Kozhikode. Moreover, as the founding mythology of the post-Cēra world suggests, this continual struggle was never marked by an ambition for total and final conquest—in other words, of imperial dominion in a European key.

By contrast, the coastal world of Malabar was remarkably peaceful, its cosmopolitanism maintained through mercantile and pilgrimage networks. Port cities in the early modern Indian Ocean often escaped the normal rules of state sovereignty internal to South Asia.[10] The economic reasons for this are clear: as the sheikh noted, the governments of Malabar exacted one-tenth of profits from trade as tax and did not tax land. Maintaining the open structure of these port cities, in part through religious tolerance, was thus crucial to the economic survival of these polities.

The Portuguese newcomers did not respect this formula. The sheikh made this clear when he described their second advent into Malabar, in stark contrast to the ways in which Islam arrived there. He noted that they approached the Samūtiri's officers 'with a request to stop the Muslims from their trade and trade voyages to Arabia, promising to pay double the loss' that would be incurred. When the Samūtiri responded with an order to capture and kill 'the Portuguese invaders', they moved to his rival's port in Kochi and built their first fort. They also 'demolished a mosque ... and built a church in its place'.[11]

9 Ma'abari II, *Tuhfat al-Mujāhidīn*, 35.

10 Pearson, *Merchants and Rulers*.

11 Ma'abari II, *Tuhfat al-Mujāhidīn*, 49–50.

Despite their ostensible mandate to enter the spice trade, the second Portuguese convoy, led by Pedro Álvares Cabral, clearly harboured religious ambitions. As the sheikh explained, with each successive wave of Portuguese arrivals, they increased not only their volume of trade but also their political influence, exploiting the rivalries of Malabar's polities to their advantage and engaging in violence to assert their will. Over time, as their own trade grew, from their base in the *feitoria* (fortified trading-post), the Portuguese instituted a system of licences for sea travel, thus cementing the opposition of the Samūtiri and his supporters.

Sheikh Ma'abari II's text, though couched in the language of religious jihād, is actually a call to defence of the older form of sovereignty and openness that characterized the Indian Ocean port cities before Portuguese arrival.[12] He speaks on behalf of his non-Muslim rulers, as well as his Hindu, Jewish, and Christian neighbours, in calling Muslim foreigners to come to the defence of Malabar's imperiled coastal world. As Eng Seng Ho puts it,

> From the European perspective, what was strange about this rich world of the Indian Ocean and its international economy was that no one state controlled it, or even had the idea of doing so. The Portuguese ... were the first to think of this ocean as a unity and to thereby dream up a systematic strategy to monopolize the means of violence within it ... The marriage of cannon to trading ship was the crucial, iconic innovation.[13]

Yet, for all their novelty, for much of the subcontinent, far from being the harbingers of a new Euro-centric world order, these interlopers were minor characters in the dramatis personae of political life. The *Kēraḷōlpatti*'s description of the early battles of the Portuguese with Kozhikode focuses not on these foreigners, but on the origin of the adoption of Vettakkorumakan as the lineage deity of the Kurumbiatiri

[12] Europeans were aware of the cosmopolitan nature of these cities. See, for example, the description of Calicut and other Indian ports in the Syrian Christian Priest Joseph's account, widely circulated in Europe (*The Voyage of Pedro Álvares Cabral*, 109).

[13] Ho, 'Empire through Diasporic Eyes', 218.

and subsequent struggles over temple lands and ritual offices.[14] From the viewpoint of the brahmin authors of the chronicle, such internal politics were of far greater consequence than the (mis)deeds of the foreigners. Beyond those communities such as the Muslims and, later, the Syrian Christians, whose religious lives depended upon access to the Indian Ocean, as Veluthat notes, 'Portuguese pretensions of an overseas empire did not have any effect on the people of Kerala.'[15]

Waving from the Beach

> Affonso Lopez ... captured two well-built natives who were in a canoe ... One of them caught sight of the captain's collar, and began to signal with his hand towards the land and then to the collar, as though telling us there was gold in the land ... Then food was given them; bread and cooked fish, comfits, cakes, honey, and dried figs. They almost would not eat anything, and if they tried some things they threw them out ... One of them saw some white rosary beads; he signalled that they should give them to him ... He made a sign towards the land and then to the beads and to the collar of the captain, as if saying they would give gold for that. We interpreted it so, because we wanted to. But if he meant that he would take the beads and the collar too, we did not wish to understand because we did not intend to give it to him.[16]

This is how Pero Vaz de Caminha, secretary to Pedro Álvares Cabral, described the first meeting with the indigenous inhabitants of what Caminha called the island of Vera Cruz in his iconic letter of 1 May 1500 to D. Manuel. Following in the wake of Vasco da Gama, Cabral had made landfall on the coast of Brazil on his diplomatically disastrous expedition to Malabar, where a riotous mob would later kill Caminha. The letter would bequeath a series of powerful tropes that came to structure European beliefs about Brazil: from the mirage of the land as an El Dorado, to the idea that the gentiles of Brazil were denizens of a nearly Edenic nature. Fittingly, from his perspective,

[14] Gundert, *Keralolpatti*, 85–7.

[15] Veluthat, *The Early Medieval in South India*, 267–8.

[16] Caminha, 'A Carta'.

these gentiles were innocent of the trappings of known civilization such as clothing, organized religion, a state capable of monumentalizing itself, or even significant internal social differentiation. The image was of lasting appeal precisely for the reason Caminha himself suggested: '[a]ny stamp we wish may be easily imprinted upon them', such that the indigenous inhabitants of Brazil were not so much people, as clay to be moulded in the image of the Christian European.

Caminha also bequeathed perhaps the most lasting idea of the method by which to begin this process of 'imprinting', of 'taming' these peoples: their purported love of European things. From the white rosary beads to the 'other trifles of little value' exchanged most cunningly for gorgeous indigenous artifacts like the feather capes that Cabral sent to D. Manuel, Caminha noted time and again the indigenous fascination and desire for European things. This was especially marked for the iron tools they observed the Portuguese carpenters using, for, 'they have nothing of iron'. This belief in the indigenous love for European things as crucial to contact and its inevitable corollary, 'pacification', has persisted into the present day, with missionaries, state functionaries, and even anthropologists continuing to treat this as an article of faith.[17]

Yet, as Caminha himself acknowledged when he revealed that they chose to interpret their interlocutors' actions as *they* wished, the letter is a testament to European wishfulness and a projection of their own predilections. That Caminha chose to read every interaction as an index of the indigenous amenability to barter or conversion reveals much about the *Portuguese* understanding of contact, but not much about how their interlocutors themselves experienced it. Caminha reacted with contempt when the enticements of European things failed to produce the desired effect upon their indigenous guests: 'The other two, whom the captain had had on the ships and to whom he had given those things already mentioned, did not appear here again—from which I gather them to be bestial people, of little knowledge and thus timid.'

[17] On the belief in progress propelled by limitless desires among missionaries and state officials in contemporary Amazonia, see Hugh-Jones, 'Yesterday's Luxuries, Tomorrow's Necessities'.

Lacking indigenous textual evidence, the rich body of contemporary ethnographic work from Brazil provides us with interpretive clues. It might elucidate the seeming contradiction between Caminha's belief in the irresistible allure of European things and the apparent indigenous indifference to it. As Fernando Santos-Granero argues in his survey of contemporary Amazonian sociality, beyond the two poles of convivial consanguinity and the common practice of turning enemies into affines, one of the modes in which indigenous peoples seek out relationships with potentially predatory strangers is through trading partnerships. Inter-tribal trade in the ecology of lowland South America, however, cannot be reduced to product differentiation, economic self-interest, or even political alliances, since trading partnerships rarely culminate in marriage exchanges. Given the fact that even headmen were not distinguished from other villagers by economic privileges, the logic of profit through trade was irrelevant. Therefore, the exchange of goods to maintain trading partnerships was less important for the goods acquired than for the formalized friendships they helped facilitate, a reversal of the value system Caminha exemplifies.[18] This might explain why, once indigenous needs for iron tools were satisfied for subsistence and cultural needs, Portuguese attempts to barter labour for such material enticements failed. As Stuart Schwarz brilliantly observes, indigenous peoples steadfastly refused to respond to the 'market' conditions the Portuguese attempted to create.[19]

Moreover, far from encountering these strangers with the guileless receptivity of innocent children, the indigenous peoples of Brazil approached contact with a judicious mix of curiosity and caution. Perhaps the most telling sign of this caution was the reaction to strange food. Commensality is both fraught with danger and rich with significance—and not just in Brazil, as any student of caste in South Asia can attest. In the particular case of Amazonia, '[f]ood consumption appears less as an activity directed towards the production of a generic physical body, and more as a device for producing related bodies'.[20] In other words, the act of eating together is

[18] Santos-Granero, 'Of Fear and Friendship', 3.

[19] Schwarz, 'Indian Labor and New World Plantations'.

[20] Fausto, 'Feasting on People', 500.

often constitutive of kinship. Moreover, ethnographic studies of indigenous lowland traditions across Brazil attest to a particular view of the body as constantly open to transformation.[21] In this context, eating the food of foreigners carried the risk of the physical transformation of oneself.[22] The refusal of Portuguese food indicated that the indigenous men Cabral and his crew 'captured' were far from uncritically receptive to the foreigners. The same caution was apparent in their refusal to allow the Portuguese to spend the night at the longhouses in their villages, a space of domesticity and kinship.

In maintaining their boundaries, the indigenous actors in this encounter nonetheless proved to be curious and open-minded. Nowhere was this more apparent than in their reaction to the performance of the mass. On Friday, as the friars and priests led a procession, singing and chanting ahead of those who carried the cross, a group of over two hundred indigenous people gathered to observe the ritual. Many of them copied the liturgical gestures performed by the Portuguese, kneeling in silence with hands lifted in a manner that Caminha found exemplary. After communion, however,

> [o]ne of them, a man of fifty or fifty-five years ... gathered those who had remained and even called others. And walking among them, he talked to them, signaling with his finger to the altar, and afterwards he pointed his finger towards the Sky, as though he were telling them something good; and we took it thus.

For Caminha, their pious behaviour during the mass and their acceptance of little tin crucifixes were proof that 'these people lack nothing to become fully Christian except to understand us, for whatever they saw us do, they did too, thereby appearing to us all that they have no idolatry, nor worship'. The trope was remarkably resilient: as we shall see, Manuel da Nóbrega repeated this notion, verbatim, over half a century later. More importantly, Caminha missed the significance of the shaman's oral performance to his people: an attempt, it

[21] Vilaça, 'Chronically Unstable Bodies'; Viveiros de Castro, 'Cosmological Deixis'.

[22] For a striking account of how the consumption of foreign foods renders one physically foreign, such that one is unrecognizable to one's kin, see Oakdale, 'The Commensality of "Contact"'.

seems, to come to terms with the discovery of a new source of cosmological knowledge.

In his seminal 1627 history of Brazil, Frei Vicente do Salvador characterized this encounter as the indigenous recognition of white men 'as divine, and more than men, and thus called them Carahibbas, that is to say in their language something divine'.[23] The classic colonial trope of the indigenous misidentification of white men as gods is hardly unique to the history of encounter in the New World.[24] Frei Vicente do Salvador was correct in his assessment that the indigenous interest in these strangers was in part centred on their status as strangers conveying new cosmological knowledge—not as gods, but as *karaíba* or travelling shaman-prophets. Even the manner of procession to the mass, led by a singing priest, lent itself to this indigenous interpretation, akin to how karaíba would enter enemy territory.

Missionaries would later emulate precisely these indigenous religious figures, adopting their practices to better accommodate the Christian message to indigenous tastes. Yet, this indigenous openness to others rarely translated into uncritical and unwavering faith, as they continued to test the efficacy of the Portuguese shamans and their strange gods.[25] Still, Caminha's belief in the simplicity and malleability of indigenous belief systems persisted. Blinkered by their expectations of what 'religion' looks like, European observers failed to appreciate the thickness and resilience of indigenous cosmologies, to their enduring frustration.

If Caminha failed to observe the intricacies of indigenous cosmology, he had even less access to the demographic complexity of coastal

[23] Salvador, *História do Brasil*, 5.

[24] The classic debate between Gananath Obeyesekere and Marshall Sahlins on this issue was based on the Pacific encounter. Obeyesekere views this trope as self-aggrandizing European myth-making, while Sahlins challenges his defence of indigenous 'rationality' as based upon a mistaken and problematic universalization of Eurocentric standards of thought. See Obeyesekere, *The Apotheosis of Captain Cook*; Sahlins, *How 'Natives' Think*.

[25] Lévi-Strauss, in his work on indigenous mythology and the encounter between Amerindians and whites, noted this openness to alterity, as opposed to the European emphasis on identity. Other anthropologists, most notably Eduardo Viveiros de Castro, have continued to document the other-centric cosmology of Brazil's indigenous peoples (Lévi-Strauss, *The Story of Lynx*).

Brazil. Far from being an 'island' peopled by undifferentiated gentiles, the Brazil Caminha and his compatriots had wandered into was a deeply politically fragmented world (see Figure 1.2). By one recent estimate, the peoples of Brazil, coastal and inland, comprised some 2,000 distinct groups, representing 40 or more language families broadly categorized into Tupí, Macro-Gê, and Arawak languages.[26]

Moreover, though most of the coastal societies shared broadly similar cultural attributes, including a common language known as the *língua geral da costa*, the peoples who came to be known as the Tupí did not exhibit any formal, stratified political unity above the village level. They were as likely to consider inimical competing segments of Tupí society as non-Tupí, usually Gê-speaking groups, who came generically to be known as the Tapuía.[27] While multi-family village units might temporarily agglomerate, the networks of alliance and kinship that bound several villages were inherently contingent and mutable and did not imply the development of larger political units.[28]

Neither diversity nor political fragmentation was unique to the New World. What was new, however, was a particular attitude towards territorial sovereignty, different again from the regime the Portuguese had encountered and disrupted on the coast of Malabar. Advances in archaeology and anthropology from the 1960s onwards have uncovered fascinating patterns of Amerindian occupation of land and dispelled the long-standing trope, originating with Caminha himself, that the peoples of Brazil, lacking monumental states and settled agriculture, left no mark on the untouched nature of the land.[29] Indeed, in their own dichotomous classification of the peoples of the coast as Tupí or Tapuía, the Portuguese noted among the former greater degrees of sedentary settlement, including horticultural activity, as one of their distinguishing features.[30] Even the Tupí, however, showed a relationship to land use predicated first and foremost upon mobility,

26 Langfur, 'Recovering Brazil's Indigenous Pasts', 9.

27 Monteiro, 'The Crises and Transformations of Invaded Societies', 973–4.

28 Monteiro, 'The Crises and Transformations of Invaded Societies', 982–3.

29 On the archaeological evidence of a rich and thriving pre-contact civilization, see Roosevelt, 'The Rise and Fall of the Amazon Chiefdoms'.

30 Monteiro, 'The Crises and Transformations of Invaded Societies', 975.

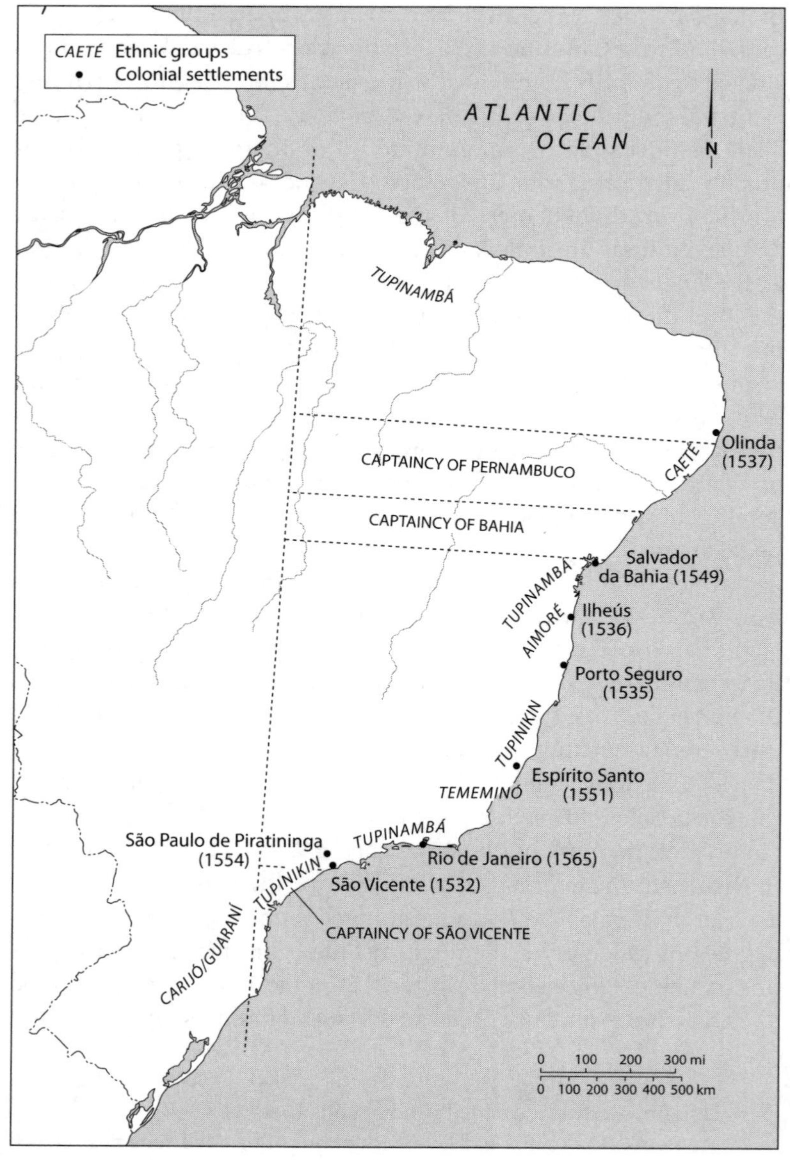

Figure 1.2 Coastal Brazil, Mid-Sixteenth Century
Source: The author (drawn by William Nelson).

undergirded by cosmological imperatives.[31] In short, sovereignty was not tied to continuous occupation of land.

If indigenous use of land did not conform to European notions of territorial kingdoms, indigenous headmen were not local equivalents of kings. The status conferred no particular economic privilege. Leading largely by consent, their responsibilities included mobilizing warriors against enemy villages, and organizing social and material life, including the contracting of strategic marriages and deciding when and where to resettle a village community. Headmen operated at the level of the multi-family unit, or *maloca*, the village and occasionally pan-village alliances, cobbled together usually for the purposes of war. Authority subtended from their prowess and reputation as warriors, but equally from their charisma and ability as orators. These rhetorical skills were used as much to galvanize warriors, as to impart knowledge of the history and traditions of the community in organizing daily life.[32]

The other figures of authority within the village, to whom even headmen acquiesced, were shamans or *pajés*. Following long apprenticeships with experienced shamans, pajés were considered gifted healers. Their ability to transcend their own species perspective allowed them to mediate between the world of men, spirits, and animals. The pajés, unlike the wandering prophets or karaíbas, were resident in their communities.

The karaíbas, able to traverse enemy territory, used their rhetorical skills to exhort villagers to seek the land without evil, whose spatial coordinates were new lands of spiritual and material revival, and whose temporal axes were both the abode of dead ancestors and the future destiny of warriors who had killed and eaten human flesh.[33] In other words, their function was to maintain an enemy-centric cosmology, in which the attainment of personhood depended upon one's status

[31] Monteiro notes the frequent references to *taperas* or abandoned settlements in the colonial archive as evidence of the temporary nature of indigenous settlements. See Monteiro, 'The Crises and Transformations of Invaded Societies', 983. On land use, mobility, and cosmology, see Chakravarti, 'Invisible Cities'.

[32] Monteiro, 'The Crises and Transformations of Invaded Societies', 983–5.

[33] Fausto, 'Fragmentos de história e cultura Tupinambá', 381–96.

as a warrior and the successful accomplishment of anthropophagic and sacrificial rituals. They also lubricated the constant mobility that shaped spiritual, material, and political life. In this world, European notions of territorialized sovereignty were absurd.

The trope of a people without faith, law, or king that crystallized around the indigenous inhabitants of Brazil reflected the European inability to imagine other kinds of cosmology and sovereignty.[34] Viewing them in this light, untouched by the corruptions of either power or idolatry, Caminha saw only boundless opportunity. He urged the king to send priests to baptize the peoples of this new 'island', who would by then be better prepared by the two convicts remaining behind to receive the faith. He closed his letter to D. Manuel by indicating that in Brazil the greatest opportunity afforded was religious; even if it remained only 'a rest-stop for this voyage to Calicut', the conversion of the indigenous people would suffice as sufficient reason to invest in this new land.

In light of the zeal Caminha demonstrated upon the shores of Brazil, perhaps it is unsurprising that by the time they made landfall in Calicut, he and his compatriots were willing to risk violent conflict to pursue their exclusionary religious aims. Still, for the first three decades, the Portuguese impact on indigenous society was mostly negligible. An early extractive trade in brazilwood was successful, in so far as it did not unduly stress Tupí social structures and norms.[35] Beyond occasional exploratory missions and this trade, indigenous society had little interaction with Europeans.

Girding the Earth, Binding the Ocean

Upon his return to Portugal, Pedro Álvares Cabral presented the first accurate assessment of Portuguese prospects in India. His travails had raised doubts among several notable figures in the court

[34] The *locus classicus* of this trope was Pero de Magalhães Gândavo, who claimed that the Tupí lacked the letters 'f', 'l', and 'r' in their language, 'a thing worthy of awe for thus they have neither *fé* (faith), nor *lei* (law), nor *rei* (king), and thus live in a disorderly manner without justice' (Magalhães Gândavo, *Tratado da Terra do Brasil*, chapter 7).

[35] Schwartz, 'Indian Labor and New World plantations', 43–79.

regarding the usefulness of 'a conquest so remote and of such dangers'.[36] Thus, before dispatching a second fleet under the command of Vasco da Gama, D. Manuel convened several councils. The chronicler João de Barros informs us that the discussions centred on whether or not to undertake commerce in India with arms or to focus on trade with Guinea and Ethiopia, where the natives had proved themselves to be peaceful. Dispelling Vasco da Gama's misconception of the Christian faith of the Samūtiri, Cabral impressed upon the king and his counsellors that, between Goa and Kochi alone 'there were more Moors than all those facing us on the coast of Africa between Ceuta and Alexandria'.[37] Downplaying his own misbehaviour, Cabral emphasized the implacable hostility of these Moors. Fearing the loss of their trade, they stood as the chief obstacle to the conversion of and commerce with gentiles. Referring to his experience, Cabral claimed that not only did the Portuguese not 'have the hand of the gentiles of the land, but had to rely on their large number of ships and many soldiers, more than any other commodity' to further their purpose.[38] Cabral's belligerence carried the day, aided by D. Manuel's desire to fulfil the destiny of his lineage in expanding his kingdom. When Vasco da Gama returned to Malabar, he came as an aggressor.

While the Portuguese experiences in the north Atlantic islands off the coast of Africa were an early experiment in colonization, this was not the blueprint of the experiment in the Indian Ocean.[39] From the beginning, this new enterprise was marked by a deep, though often productive, tension. Despite the Crown's desire to monopolize the seaways, noblemen and captains—foremost among them Vasco da Gama and his family—viewed this oceanic space as a playground for private profiteering and raiding.

The sporadic skirmishes with Moorish ships and indigenous kings did not crystallize into a systematic project of power until the governorship of Francisco de Almeida. Appointed in 1505, he was

[36] Barros, *Décadas*, 2.

[37] Barros, *Décadas*, 5.

[38] Barros, *Décadas*, 3.

[39] Fernández-Armesto, *The Canary Islands*. For a seminal interpretation of the impulses to expansion in the mid-fifteenth century, see Thomaz, *De Ceuta a Timor*, 1–41.

instructed to secure and fortify several east African ports, including Kilwa and Mombasa, strategic points in the Arabian Gulf, as well as Ceylon and Melaka, to provide a series of safe harbours for Portuguese ships traversing the Cape route across the Indian Ocean. This early plan would come to fruition a few years later when the governor Afonso de Albuquerque conquered key chokepoints of the Indian Ocean trade (Goa, Melaka, and Hurmuz), between 1510 and 1514. Holding these fortified ports, the Portuguese were able to tax and control the Asian trade through the mechanism of the *cartaz* (sea licence or pass).[40] (It was precisely this system of licensing and control that had drawn the ire of Sheikh Ma'abari I, who accused the Portuguese of penning his people in like 'senseless sheep'.)

These developments went neither unnoticed nor unanswered: potentates across the Indian Ocean were galvanized to resist the Portuguese assault on the status quo of their trading world. Yet, the complexities of diplomatic relations among indigenous powers made it difficult to coordinate efforts to dislodge the Portuguese.[41] In 1509, when the joint forces of the Samūtiri, the Mamlūks of Egypt, and the Sultan of Gujarat, supported by both the Ottomans and Venice, were defeated at Diu, the Portuguese had established their naval dominance in this new arena decisively.

The following year, Albuquerque established what would become the spoke in the wheel of the Estado da Índia: the imperial city of Goa. Given the precarity, however unintentional, of the hospitality of their ally in Kochi, the need for a permanent and sovereign foothold was increasingly apparent. Goa, a lightly defended port of the sultanate of Bijāpur, whose military strength was largely directed towards the Deccan interior, was an attractive prize, not least because of its importance as a trading entrepôt for war horses from the Arabian Gulf. Following the death of Yūsuf 'Ādil Shāh, while his successor was occupied with fending off challenges in the interior, Albuquerque seized the town, aided by the Hindu merchant Timayya (known in

[40] Bulhão Pato, *Cartas de Affonso de Albuquerque*, I, 1, 269–71; 370–1; II, 311; III, 206, 268–76.

[41] On the diplomatic high-wire act of the Sultan of Gujarat, caught between the Mughals, the Ottomans, and the Portuguese, see Alam and Subrahmanyam, *Writing the Mughal World*, 34–89.

Portuguese sources as Timoja). For the next two years, Albuquerque vigorously defended Goa from Bijāpur's attempts to retake their territory, in which enterprise the 'Ādil Shāh was nearly successful. From these dubious beginnings, Goa became the centre of the vast networks of the Estado da Índia, with the capital moving officially from Kochi to Goa in 1530.[42]

The coastal region of Goa, prior to the arrival of the Portuguese, had not been the seat of a major polity itself. As an area that had existed at the edges of the great kingdoms and empires of the interior, local life was left mostly untouched by ruling regimes. Villages were dominated by *gāunkār*s or the male patrilineal descendants of those considered the original inhabitants of a village. Gāunkār lineages, hailing from upper castes, held land in common. Labour, organized along caste lines, was divided such that lower castes served subservient ritual and productive functions to the gāunkārs. Gāunkārs administered the villages, including standing surety for tax payments due to the ruling regime. They also reserved for themselves ritual privileges at most village festivals and in the general functioning of the temple. Lower castes received at best subsistence plots or, more usually, shares in harvests; temple lands, by contrast, reserved for the maintenance of the village cult and those who performed ritual functions, were often the most fertile. While larger temple cults may have been dedicated to a pantheon of brahminical gods familiar across broader swathes of South Asia, lineage and village deities bound to each locality were of prime importance. These deities protected an agricultural society, in which the careful maintenance of village lands and boundaries was of prime material and symbolic import.[43]

This basic structure, it seems, had persisted through different regimes, although there is evidence that the Bijāpuri regime had begun a more interventionist policy, focused on displacing the local gāunkārs with their own military functionaries.[44] This may explain, perhaps, why the Portuguese found willing allies among the local population when they seized Goa. Accordingly, the 1526 Foral,

[42] For a seminal analysis of this process, see Madeira-Santos, *Goa é a Chave.*

[43] Kosambi, *Myth and Reality*, 156–71.

[44] Kosambi, *An Introduction to the Study of Indian History*, 333.

Figure 1.3 South and Central India, Mid-Sixteenth Century
Source: The author (drawn by William Nelson).

Portuguese Goa's foundational fiscal charter, was at pains to document the nature of village administration and the gāunkār system and to maintain it largely untouched, while extracting as much revenue as possible.[45] It was not till 1649 that the state would deem itself the direct owner of all communal lands, thus rendering the gāunkārs tenants.[46]

In these lands, formerly marginal to the great polities of central India, Goa rose as a Portuguese imperial city, marked by a closed structure quite unlike earlier Indian Ocean ports. In addition to the militarization of trade shipping, the institution of heavy fortifications, and the licensing of seaways, in Goa a systematic attempt to impose a religious monopoly was effected, including through judicial discrimination against non-Catholic resident. Harsh rules of escheat allowed the Crown to seize the property of Hindus who died without male heirs and public celebrations of non-Catholic rituals were increasingly curtailed.[47] Over time, particularly after the 1540s, the push towards evangelization became more militant; inducements were replaced by more coercive measures, including a systematic campaign to destroy the temples of the region.

There were costs to this policy of religious exclusion in Portuguese port cities. The later history of Melaka is instructive here. While the Portuguese initially tried to retain the original social structure of the city, over time, they increasingly fortified it and imposed religious restrictions, first and foremost by increasing tax rates for non-Christian traders exorbitantly. The exodus of various ethnic and religious mercantile communities not only led to the decreased profitability of their own trade, but it also nourished the rival sultanates of Johor and Aceh, who welcomed these immigrants. These sultanates then increasingly posed credible military threats to the Portuguese.[48]

Nor was this imperial model embraced universally by the Portuguese—*casados* or private traders not only resisted the centralizing impulses of the Crown and its representatives, but themselves

[45] Cunha Rivara, *Archivo Portuguez Oriental*, 118–33.

[46] See 'Assento do Conselho da Fazenda declarando o Estado senhorio directo das terras aldeanas e prohibindo doação dellas, July 5, 1649', 236–7.

[47] Derrett, *Essays*, 131–65.

[48] Sousa Pinto, 'Purse and Sword'.

emigrated, living in *bandéis* as part of the ethnic mosaic of various Indian Ocean port cities.[49] These settlements, far from being formal extensions of the Estado, were considered explicitly illegal and were often at direct odds with the empire—though scholars have contended that their actions too furthered the Portuguese imperial project.[50]

Nonetheless, at this early stage, the establishment of Goa was the culmination of a remarkably rapid rise to power for the Portuguese in the theatre of the Indian Ocean and the beginnings of an explicitly imperial project. While the Venetians scrambled to find alternative routes, the Portuguese monopoly of the spice trade in Europe proved very lucrative, and their naval dominance stood unparalleled.

By the mid-1520s, significant threats began to emerge in the maritime sphere as other powers sought to break this monopoly.[51] Combined with chaotic internal power struggles, such was the condition of the Estado by 1529 that D. Jaime, the Duke of Bragança, was advocating the abandonment of Portuguese holdings in Asia in order to consolidate their limited strengths in North Africa.[52]

Perhaps unsurprisingly, the 1530s saw efforts to extend the fledgling imperial project in new directions. Attention again swerved towards the new world, in part because of the worrying presence of French corsairs along the Brazilian coast, threatening the monopoly of the oceanic route to India. The Spanish discovery of silver in Potosí also reignited the desire to find another El Dorado in Brazil.[53] In December 1530, Martim Afonso de Sousa embarked from Lisbon for an exploratory expedition to Brazil. Erecting *padrões* (large stone crosses erected by Portuguese explorers as a claim of Portuguese sovereignty) along the coast and capturing French ships laden with brazilwood,

[49] *Bandéis* (plural of bandel, a Portuguese corruption of the Persian bandar, meaning port or harbor) could refer to any ethnic settlement in a locality (*bandel dos guzerates, bandel dos portugueses*).

[50] Thomaz, 'Portuguese Control on the Arabian Sea'; Subrahmanyam, 'The Tail Wags the Dog'; Bernardes de Carvalho, 'A "Snapshot" of a Portuguese Community in Southeast Asia'.

[51] See, for example, Casale, 'The Ottoman Administration of the Spice Trade'.

[52] Subrahmanyam, 'Making India Gama'.

[53] On these complex motivations, see the classic work by Buarque de Holanda, *Visão de paraíso*.

the expedition signalled the Crown's newfound intent to assert its sole sovereignty over the land. After founding the key southern coastal settlement near Piratininga, the expedition returned to assure D. João III of the favourability of the conditions in Brazil for colonization.[54]

Over the next few years, the Crown established donatory captaincies across Brazil to stimulate the colonization and development of the region. In a pattern perfected in the Atlantic islands, these captaincies were constituted by the *carta da doação*, a quintessentially medieval mechanism for the devolution of political sovereignty, which allowed the captain to govern beyond the jurisdiction of royal officials. He could found towns and appoint local officials, exercise extensive jurisdiction in criminal and even civil cases, and make individual land grants or *sesmarias* at his discretion. Monopolies in salt, grain, and sugar pertained to the captain. He received a portion of revenues collected for the Crown, could enslave a certain number of indigenous people and was exempt from personal taxes. This was, in effect, a blueprint for the notions of individual autonomy and sovereignty that came to define the colonial planter class.

The captaincy was also governed by a *foral*, which set out the rights of settlers and the Crown's prerogatives. The Crown retained monopolies in brazilwood and spices, and the royal fifth for any precious metals or gems that might be mined. Treasury officials sent to each captaincy safeguarded the Crown's interests. The foral also provided incentives to stimulate colonization, including immunity for settlers from crimes committed before coming to Brazil; the right to trade with the indigenous population; the right to receive sesmarias and obtain titles after five years of cultivation, and exemption from various taxes.

Despite these inducements, the Crown's push towards colonization was stymied, partly due to the difficulty of governing a group of settlers freed from the strictures of metropolitan law. Of the twelve donataries, only São Vicente and Pernambuco truly prospered, and the lives of the remaining band of settlers remained precarious. They were vulnerable both to the depredations of the French and to indigenous enemies, provoked to understandable hostility by Portuguese attempts to enslave them. Nonetheless, Martim Afonso de Sousa had

[54] For an account of the expedition, see Sousa, *Diario de Navegação*.

laid the groundwork for the nascent colony of Brazil before leaving for India.

In the search for profit, the Portuguese attempted to compel indigenous labour for the colonial project. Increasingly, this required forcible enslavement, because of 'the divergent outlooks of Portuguese and Indians toward the nature of labor and production'.[55] Though enslavement of the indigenous population did not solve the problem of unreliable labour, even after the large-scale importation of African slaves after the establishment of the sugar industry in the 1580s, the practice continued. As the coast was denuded of indigenous peoples through a combination of devastating epidemics and flight, regular expeditions into the interior, often facilitated by mixed-race Mamelucos, 'descended' indigenous slaves from the backlands of the *sertão* to coastal plantations. As Alida Metcalf puts it, this sixteenth-century trade was 'the first manifestation of a phenomenon that would repeat itself in later centuries in São Paulo, Minas Gerais, Goiás, and Amazonia'. Though the dramatic influx of African slaves added yet another element to this evolving society based on frontiers and plantations, this *bandeirismo* or informal expansionist movement in the backlands 'would make Indian slavery an integral part of the colonial Brazilian economy and society'.'[56]

Even as efforts were made to penetrate the interior of Brazil, the 1530s was a period of territorial consolidation around Goa, including the establishment of the *província do Norte* centred on Chaul, Bassein, and Bombay. Under the leadership of Martim Afonso de Sousa, who had overseen a similar process in Brazil, the Estado da Índia took what Sanjay Subrahmanyam characterizes as a limited terrestrial turn, with the piecemeal establishment of a system of *aforamento*s or land grants. The shift was timely, for *renegado*s (renegades) had begun to accept land grants from rival Asian states, and soldiers and noblemen voiced their fatigue at constantly having 'one foot in the water'.[57]

Nonetheless, large-scale territorial ambitions at the expense of continental states in the east were rightly seen as beyond the realm of possibility. The Portuguese instead functioned as a regional player in

[55] Schwartz, 'Indian Labor and New World Plantations', 47.

[56] Metcalf, 'The Entradas of Bahia', 375.

[57] Subrahmanyam, 'Holding the World in Balance'.

an indigenous theatre of power.[58] By the early 1540s, they were observing carefully the changing balance of power in the Deccan heralded by the death of Achyuta Deva Raya, the emperor of Vijayanagara. The Portuguese were unable to capitalize upon this opportunity, however. The resultant political turmoil culminated in the battle of Talikota in 1565, when the Vijayanagara empire was crushed by the combined force of the Deccan sultanates. The ensuing transformation of the Vijayanagara Nāyakas from imperial functionaries to petty kings in their own right further complicated the power dynamics of the region.[59]

Not only was the Deccan and its southern Indian neighbourhood the site of intense and complicated political competition, but the region also witnessed a remarkable flowering of the rituals and symbolism of power and state building, drawing on local religious traditions and ideologies.[60] Further north, the upheavals of Humayun's reign would give way in the next decade to the rise of the Mughal empire under Akbar. In this environment, the Portuguese were at best minor players, embroiled in but unable to set the terms of local politics. The crisis of the mid-sixteenth century—when the Portuguese recognized their inability to enforce a spice monopoly in Europe to counteract the mounting costs of their Asian possessions—led to a strategy focused on exploiting Asian trade networks, further cementing their status as regional players.[61] Not only did they find themselves in an environment that boasted many models of power, statehood, and empire, the Portuguese were often directly dependent upon the goodwill of indigenous polities in the Indian Ocean system.

[58] Subrahmanyam, 'Holding the World in Balance', 1372.

[59] Here, Burton Stein and Noboru Karashima's otherwise very different interpretations coincide: both see the growing power of the Nāyakas as local feudal lords as crucial to this final period in Vijayanagara history (Stein, *Vijayanagara*; Karashima, *A Concordance of Nayakas*).

[60] See Stein's *Vijayanagara* on the use of architecture in representing power in the empire. On the indigenous evolution of rituals of power and strategies of state building amongst the Nāyakas, see Rao, Shulman, and Subrahmanyam, *Symbols of Substance*. On the relationship of religion and power in indigenous state building in the Deccan, see Eaton, *Sufis of Bijapur*.

[61] Subrahmanyam, *The Portuguese Empire in Asia*.

By contrast, in Brazil, after the intermittent French and Dutch attempts to establish colonies in the region and the later extraordinary kingdoms of Palmares, there was no sustained rival to the Portuguese mode of state building. This is not to say that the colonial state was omnipotent—far from it. As in the Estado da Índia, the Portuguese were internally divided and the mounting private authority of the planter class could and did pose a serious obstacle to the Crown. This dynamic in part explains a mode of settlement that Richard Morse described as occurring in 'an archipelago pattern', such that the frontiers of the colony should be read 'more as interpenetration than as advance'.[62]

By the 1540s, therefore, when the first Jesuits arrived on the scene, the Portuguese Crown had limited capacity to exert its will in both Brazil and South Asia, albeit for very different reasons. Moreover, despite the responsibilities towards the spread of the Catholic faith made incumbent upon the king by the Padroado with the final papal confirmation of the arrangement in 1514, the institutional infrastructure of the Church in these locations remained scanty: as late as 1700, the vast territory of Brazil would be the seat of only three bishoprics.

In this context, the arrival of newly minted missionaries of the Society of Jesus, full of activist zeal, would have profound effects for the Portuguese project of temporal and spiritual dominion. They came to terrains marked by a dual difference. In South Asia, they faced a landscape of complex indigenous polities and a disease ecology that rendered contact benign to the indigenous population. Brazil, by contrast, was a land of stateless indigenous societies facing demographic collapse through contact. In these vastly different environments, Francis Xavier and Manuel da Nóbrega sought to forge a lasting Christian community.

[62] Morse, *The Bandeirantes*, 30–1.

I
IN SEARCH OF THE INDIES

2

OTHER INDIES

Lord, send me where you will, except the Indies.[1]

The European (re)discovery of the Old World and the New begins with two iconic, almost slapstick, moments of confusion: Christopher Columbus's insistence that he had landed on the shores of India in 1492, and Vasco da Gama's Christian thanksgiving at a Hindu temple in 1498. These moments encapsulate the provenance of the confused geography of the 'Indies'. Yet, long before these moments of disorientation, the Indies was already the focus of a tradition of Christian utopian promise. As the apostolic domain of St Thomas and the land of the legendary Christian king Prester John, the cartographic particulars of the Indies evolved throughout the medieval era. Nonetheless, its meaning as a land of evangelical opportunity and eschatological significance remained constant.[2]

For missionaries, and particularly the fledgling Society of Jesus, the new vistas of the Indies glimpsed through Iberian seaways offered tantalizing opportunities. The careers of the first Jesuits in the Indies *por allá* (over there) would have profound implications for the locus of the order's work in the New and Old Worlds. This chapter follows the different trajectories of Francisco Xavier and Manuel da Nóbrega in the east and west. It traces too their very

[1] Jacopo Voragine, *Legenda Aurea*.

[2] Ramos, *Essays in Christian Mythology*.

different relationships to the geography of Portuguese power, which would come to shape the boundaries of Jesuit missionary space in the Indies.

The facts of Xavier's life are largely beyond dispute and long-standing.[3] Born in 1506 of aristocratic Navarrese stock, Xavier lived through the tumultuous annexation of Navarre by Ferdinand. After receiving the tonsure, he left in 1525 for the Collège Sainte-Barbe. During the next eleven years at the university, he was largely untouched by the stirrings of the humanist and, above all, the burgeoning Protestant movement. In Paris, Xavier met Ignatius of Loyola, his college mate, who effected in him a conversion that changed the course of his life. Leaving the sure path of scholarly achievement and an ecclesiastical benefice, he joined the band of companions that formed around Ignatius to make a pilgrimage to Jerusalem. Thwarted by the Venetian–Ottoman war, the companions preached in various cities in Italy. As the Society struggled to receive recognition from the Pope in Rome, their fame spread till the Portuguese Crown sought their members. When Ignatius's original choice, Nicolás Bobadilla, fell ill, Xavier was chosen instead to go to the Indies. Thus began the missionary career that took Xavier all along the eastern coast of Africa, western and south India, Southeast Asia, Japan, and, finally, the outskirts of the Chinese empire.

Xavier's image as the wandering missionary is enduring, as much among Catholic hagiographers as scholars who have discerned in the contours of his 'peripatetic life ... something of the geography of early Jesuit activity'.[4] Yet, this itinerancy was neither instinctual, nor inevitable, but rather a result of his time in southern India. Here, Xavier's early faith in the Portuguese imperial apparatus as a vehicle of conversion was finally eroded. Despite his experiments in (re)founding a Christian society through convert children, we find here the genesis of Xavier's never-ending quest for subjects culturally and socially more amenable to conversion than those he encountered in India.

[3] See Georg Schurhammer's monumental four-volume biography, *Francis Xavier.*

[4] From Alam and Subrahmanyam, 'Frank Disputations', 459.

Manuel da Nóbrega, Xavier's pioneering counterpart in Brazil, was born on 18 October 1517 to a magistrate from northern Portugal.[5] Nóbrega completed his humanistic studies, most probably in Porto, before commencing a scholarship under royal auspices. After some years in Salamanca, he graduated from the Faculty of Canon Law in the University of Coimbra in 1541. In 1544, two years after Simão Rodrigues and Xavier had come to Portugal, Nóbrega joined the company, taking part in the scandalous public demonstrations of self-mortification as a novice in Coimbra.[6] Though Ignatius would proscribe such activities as part of his famous dicta on obedience, this simple but burning zeal marked Nóbrega's entire missionary career, from a brief but distinguished period in Portugal till his death in Brazil in 1570.

Though Nóbrega was well aware of Xavier's career in India—and would be confronted repeatedly by its shadow in Brazil—the political and social landscape he had to navigate was radically different. Accordingly, the geography of Jesuit mission space and of Portuguese imperial power in Brazil remained, if not identical, then at least a palimpsest, in which one underwrote and extended the other. In the early careers of these two men, one can see a blueprint of the Jesuit Indies in the east and west, with profound implications for the development of the order's missions and for the Portuguese empire.

The chapter begins with Xavier's vision of the Indies as a utopian space for conversion before departing to the east and its transformation through the exigencies of the Fishery Coast mission. The second half considers Nóbrega's nascent attempts to draw Brazil into the geography of Christian space, and the contradictions that the realities of the Brazilian mission presented to the already normative example that Xavier had set in India. In these different circumstances, they would forge very different relationships with Portuguese imperial authority.

[5] The best biography of Nóbrega is still Leite's *Breve itinerário*. The details given in the chapter are gleaned from this work.

[6] Leite, *Breve itinerário*, 30. His sympathies for such demonstrative piety continued in Brazil, despite the society's strictures against it.

Solos Gentiles, Sin Mixtura De Moro Ni Judíos

While at court in Lisbon, Xavier's confidence in the prospects for conversion in the Indies was bolstered by the reports of those who had spent many years there. He urged his confreres to arrange for Jesuit missionaries to join him within two years.[7] Xavier's enthusiasm was in part due to the favour of the Portuguese imperial apparatus, evident in the patronage of the king afforded to the Society. Furthermore, Xavier's conversations with the newly appointed viceroy, Martim Afonso de Sousa, who Xavier reported was held in great esteem by Portuguese allies in the Indies, gave him confidence in the mission abroad.[8] It was from these interactions that Xavier came to imagine the Indies as a land of religious opportunity, 'inhabited solely by gentiles, with no admixture of either Moors or Jews'.[9]

The attraction of a land where evangelism could be pursued without the interference of Jews and Moors was profound. After the establishment of the Portuguese Inquisition in 1536, the first *auto-da-fé* (ritual of public penance) had been held mere months before, inaugurating a long, although not exclusive, campaign of persecution of New Christians and Judaizers in Portugal. The threat of Islam was even more palpable.[10] Unlike the Jews, who remained largely an internal religious taint in Catholic Iberia, Islam functioned as a religious and a political antagonist, beyond and within Iberia: thus, in Portugal, while Jewish converts as *cristãos novos* (New Christians) were subject to a policy of integration, the Muslim community was viewed with clear hostility.[11] The piecemeal process

[7] Xavier to Ignatius and Jean Codure, Lisbon, 18 March 1541, *Epistolae* I, 82.

[8] Xavier to Ignatius and Jean Codure, Lisbon, 18 March 1541, *Epistolae* I, 80–1. On the king's favour to Xavier, see Dom João III to Antonio de Ataide, Almeirim, 14 February 1541, *Documenta Indica* I, 3. On the viceroy's standing in Xavier's eyes, see Xavier to Claude Jay and Diego Laínez, Lisbon, 18 March, 1541, *Epistolae* I, 89.

[9] Xavier to Ignatius and Jean Codure, Lisbon, 18 March 1541, *Epistolae* I, 80.

[10] Xavier to Claude Jay and Diego Laínez, Lisbon, 18 March 1541, *Epistolae* I, 85.

[11] Marcocci, 'La coscienza di un impero', 28.

of purging Islam from Iberia during the *Reconquista*, as well as the rise of the Ottomans, hardened confessional boundaries in the Mediterranean world.[12] Moreover, these boundaries were stretched to the newly discovered lands of the world: while Jewish converts could receive licences to emigrate to the New World, Moriscos were proscribed.[13] In this context, the promise of a land inhabited only by gentiles, without the competing interference of the Jewish and Islamic faith, was a tempting one. This was itself a long-standing trope of the Indies: the Jewish Gaspar da India, who acted as interpreter for Vasco da Gama and Pedro Álvares Cabral, deliberately portrayed the Indies as largely free of Muslims so as not to dissuade potential travellers.[14] Later, in Socotra, Xavier's views were dramatically confirmed. Unable to cross the confessional boundary between Muslims and Nestorian Christians on the barren island, itself under constant Ottoman threat, Xavier's belief in the implacable obstacle to conversion represented by Islam hardened. So too did his faith in Portuguese imperial patronage as a bulwark against this obstacle.[15]

Xavier's first impressions of Goa were largely positive.[16] Both ecclesiastical and temporal elites seemed committed to conversion. Prime among their efforts was the foundation of the College of Goa, built with revenues from lands reclaimed from destroyed temples. With the patronage of the bishop and the secretary of the treasury, Cosme Eanes, the vicar general Miguel Vaz founded the college in November 1541. Within six years, Xavier averred, the college would have more than 300 students, of different languages, countries, and races, who would go forth and spread Christianity in their lands. He was particularly impressed by the new governor's attitude towards the College and its mission.[17]

[12] Hess, *The Forgotten Frontier*, 207.

[13] García-Arenal, 'Moriscos and Indians', 42.

[14] Bouchon and Thomaz, *Voyage dans les deltas du Gange et de l'Irraouaddy*, 17–18.

[15] Xavier to Simão Rodrigues, Cochin, 20 January 1549, *Epistolae* I:I, 40–1.

[16] Xavier to Simão Rodrigues, Cochin, 20 January 1549, *Epistolae* I:I, 121–2.

[17] Xavier to Ignatius, Goa, 20 September 1542, *Epistolae* I, 132–3.

Xavier observed a happy alliance of those dedicated to the work of the Padroado and those charged with defending the temporal interests of the Portuguese Crown. Yet, the structure of the church and the state in the Indies created peculiar hardships. In another letter, Xavier described to Ignatius the vast vineyard in which he laboured. He reported that 'the Portuguese in these parts are the lords of the sea' and their dominion included coastal fortresses, which were 'settlements of Christians, inhabited by Portuguese casados'.[18] Xavier then listed the leagues separating Goa from outposts such as Malacca, Hormuz, Diu, and Sofala, emphasizing the huge distances involved (see Figure 2.1). To allow his confreres in Rome to make sense of the amorphous geographical mass of the Indies, Xavier sketched a radial map, emanating from the Portuguese imperial capital.

Though the Portuguese imperial network provided a backbone and structure to the Indies, the mission field was fraught. Xavier noted, for example, that though the bishop had appointed vicars in all the nodes of this network, because of the physical distance between them, he was unable to visit and confer the sacrament of confirmation. Accordingly, Xavier wrote, the governor sought permission to delegate the right to confer the sacrament to vicars.[19] This sacrament was vital 'because of the great commerce, captivity and conflict that we have continually with infidels'.

These potentially polluting relations, the physical distance between imperial outposts, and the thin episcopal structure presented a major obstacle to the work of Christ in the Indies. Still, at this stage, the essential elements of Xavier's template of the Indies as a mission field remained untouched: an imperial and episcopal structure, unified by the common goal of Christian conversion under the terms of the Padroado, and the threat of Muslim infidels to this structure.

Within this mission field, Xavier's particular charges were the recently converted fishermen of the Parava caste on the Fishery Coast of southern India. By the time the Portuguese arrived, the peoples of the Coromandel lived in separate settlements based on labour specialization afforded by the natural diversity of the coast. Each group was held together by distinctive polities, closed marriage networks,

[18] Xavier to Ignatius, Goa, 21 September 1542, *Epistolae* I, 141–2.

[19] Xavier to Ignatius, Goa, 21 September 1542, *Epistolae* I, 141–2.

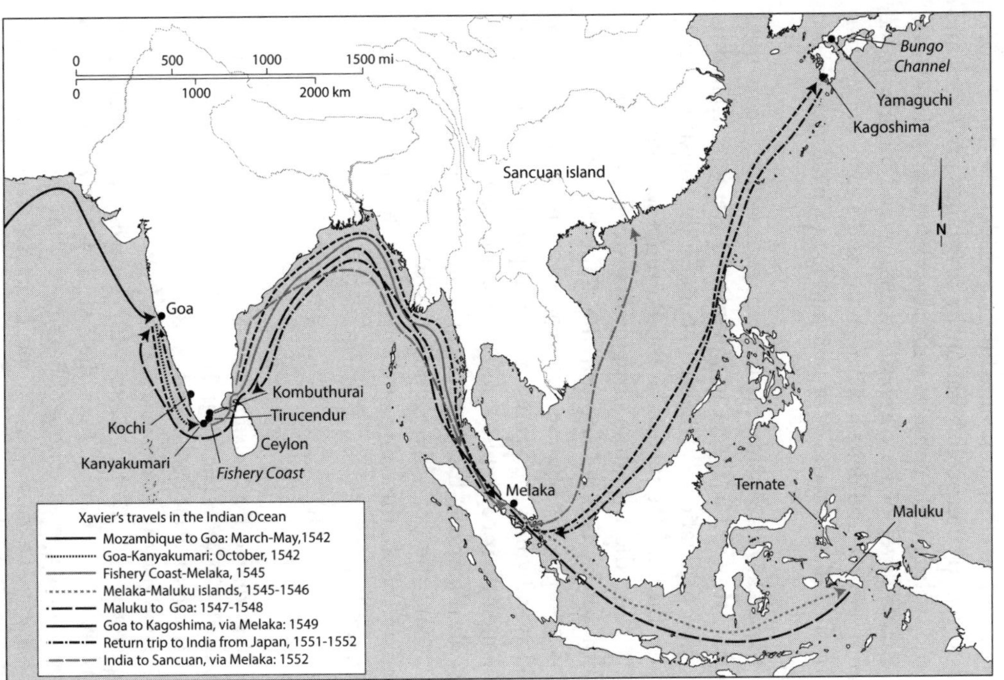

Figure 2.1 Xavier's Travels in the Indian Ocean
Source: The author (drawn by William Nelson).

separate temples, and exclusive norms of intercourse. The Paravas, who had developed rights in pearl and chank fishing, which had become 'the hallmark of the *jāti* (caste)', were spread out in thirty villages.[20] Occupational specialty, especially one as lucrative as pearl diving, lent itself to consolidating caste identity. Local rulers attempted to secure their collaboration by providing privileges and honours, and vesting caste notables with new rights and titles.[21] Over time, the Parava developed a corporate structure and identity based on a common temple and deity at Tirucendur and a caste polity characterized by the village assembly of *urāṛ* and led by headmen known as *paṭṭaṅkaṭṭi*.[22]

When Maraikkāyar Muslim fishermen encroached upon their fishing rights, it posed a 'threat to this pivotal element upholding Parava social organization'.[23] Unable to contain the threat militarily or politically, the Paravas turned to the Portuguese. Between 1527 and 1539, during the maritime struggles between the Portuguese and Muslim forces centred around the Samūtiri of Kozhikode, the Paravas secured Portuguese patronage and protection against the Maraikkāyar diving groups and their local patrons. In return, the Paravas pledged their conversion and a large monetary tribute. The Portuguese thus gained a tributary client group, a lucrative foothold in the coast and the pearl-diving trade, as well as an opportunity for evangelism.[24] Still, the contractual nature of the conversion was beyond dispute.[25]

[20] Roche, *Fishermen of the Coromandel*, 36–8.

[21] Bayly, *Saints, Goddesses and Kings*, 323.

[22] Roche, *Fishermen of the Coromandel*, 36–8.

[23] Roche, *Fishermen of the Coromandel*, 38.

[24] Albuquerque and Costa, 'Cartas de "servicos" da Índia', 329; Subrahmanyam, 'Noble Harvest from the Sea', 134–72. On the foothold gained by the Portuguese for control of the straits of Sri Lanka, see Flores, *Os Portugueses e o Mar de Ceilão*. On the desire for Parava conversion, see D. João III to Pedro Mascarenhas, December 1537, in Schurhammer, *Gesamelte Studien*, 245.

[25] On gift exchange in contracting Parava conversion, see João da Cruz to D. João III, Cochin, 15 December 1537, in Schurhammer, *Gesamelte Studien*, 260–2.

The political opportunism underlying the event only cemented Xavier's faith in the support of the Portuguese imperial system.[26] Moreover, his initial assessment of the mission was very positive: Xavier, moved by the poverty, ignorance, and enthusiasm for baptism of his charges, was confident that the Parava could become good Christians.[27] Ensconced within the arms of the Portuguese imperial apparatus, the Parava held out hope for the particular fruit of the Indies: 'gentiles, without admixture of Jews and Muslims', ripe for the Christian harvest.

Qui Non Est Mecum, Contra Me Est

Xavier's personal charisma and reception as a spiritual figure in the indigenous mould played a large role in the process of Christianizing the Parava.[28] Yet, Xavier also seemed to have found socially novel sources of support for his authority through Parava children:

> I hope in God ... that the boys may become better men than their fathers ... They abhor greatly the idolatries of the gentiles, so much so that many times they fight with the gentiles and reprove their own parents when they worship idols and denounce them, by coming to tell me about it ... The boys take the idols and smash them to bits as small as ashes, and then spit on them and tread on them with their feet, and other things which, although it seems better not to name them, are an honor to the boys who do them against [the devil] who has the temerity to be worshipped by their fathers.[29]

Xavier gave no indication that the violence in which the boys engaged was driven by anything other than fervent devotion. He did not reflect on the use to which the boys put his own authority in the village, sanctioning reversals of existing social hierarchies such as age.[30]

[26] Xavier to Ignatius, Tuticorin, 28 October, 1542, *Epistolae* I, 150–1.

[27] Xavier to Ignatius, Tuticorin, 28 October, 1542, *Epistolae* I, 147–8.

[28] See Županov, 'Prosélytisme et pluralisme religieux', 41.

[29] Xavier to the Society, Cochin, 15 January 1544, *Epistolae* I, 164.

[30] There is cultural precedent in south India for the political significance of defying one's own parent at the behest of another authority in order to secure one's own power under the overlordship of this authority. See, for example, Dirks's analysis of Visvanātha Nāyaka's capture of his rebellious father, Nagama Nāyaka, at the command of Vijayanagara (Dirks, *The Hollow Crown*, 98–101).

Yet, implicitly, he relied upon this very possibility for the re-creation of this society in a Christian pattern—the possibility that 'the boys may become better men than their fathers', and lay the foundations for their own Christian society. His interest in this possibility was apparent in the relationship he developed with a bright Parava boy, Matheus, who Xavier sent to aid Francisco Mansilhas, when he joined him on the Fishery Coast. Xavier instructed Mansilhas to remind Matheus to 'be a very good son since [Xavier] would do more for him than his relatives would'.[31] Xavier also impressed upon Mansilhas the need to treat the boy with kindness: the boy was 'free' and could thus leave. In converting, therefore, the boy had been freed from the coercive ties of pre-Christian sociality, even biological kinship. The very notion of virtue was recast in terms of a new, elective kinship with the Christian priests: as Xavier told Mansilhas, 'Tell Matheus to be a good son, that is to say, a good man.'[32]

The focus on children and the use to which Xavier put these boys, soldiers in his campaign, attested to his belief that genuine Christian conversion could not be overlaid upon existing social foundations. It depended instead upon an entirely new generation of Christian children to lead their brethren to the faith. The belief accounted in part for a missionary policy that was focused primarily on baptism and the instruction of infants. Xavier wished to save as efficaciously as possible the *massa damnata* (the condemned mass), in preference to those truculent adults who resisted the faith.[33]

Though the power of the paṭṭaṅkaṭṭi had compelled the mass conversion of the community, Xavier remained deeply suspicious of these indigenous headmen, even when their authority was deployed towards interests he shared.[34] The paternalistic attitude he adopted with the children took on a harder edge with the adult converts, like

[31] Xavier to Francisco Mansilhas, Manapar, 27 March 1544, *Epistolae* I, 196; Xavier to Francisco Mansilhas, Manapar, 14 March 1544, *Epistolae* I, 192.

[32] Xavier to Francisco Mansilhas, Virapandyanpatanam, 11 June 1544, *Epistolae* I, 205.

[33] Xavier to Francisco Mansilhas, Virapandyanpatanam, 11 June 1544, 205. See also Xavier to Francisco Mansilhas, Manapar, 14 March 1544, *Epistolae* I, 192

[34] Xavier to Francisco Mansilhas, Manapar, 30 June 1544, *Epistolae* I, 209.

'a good father with bad sons'. Xavier relied upon the secular power of the Portuguese, threatening the headmen with the *meirinho*, or justice of the peace, who could fine, imprison, or permanently displace them, effectively divesting them of office.[35]

Still, Xavier's relationship with the Portuguese had become significantly more complex. He now distinguished between the local representatives of Portuguese power and the higher imperial authorities. Xavier was scrupulous in his financial dealings with the former, rejecting the generosity of local officials and insisting on access to the legitimate monies afforded him by the Crown or the patronage of indigenous converts.[36] The effect was to distance himself and his mission from these officials who so often treated the low-caste converts no better than their erstwhile Hindu brethren, with no regard to their status as fellow Christians.[37] To associate with local Portuguese officials, who were often arbitrary and oppressive towards indigenous converts, would have undercut Xavier's standing amidst his new charges.

Equally worrying was the murky role the Portuguese played in local politics. In 1544, the rulers of Kollam and Vēnādu found themselves embroiled again in a conflict with the Pāndya Vettum Perumāl, a subject of the Vijayanagara empire. Invading Telugu *vaḍuga* forces terrorized the Fishery Coast, their incursions into the Tirunelveli region testifying to the coalescence of military power around the Madurai Nāyakas.[38] The Parava community, spread between the lands of the rival factions, was attacked by all sides, left destitute

[35] Xavier to Francisco Mansilhas, Manapar, 14 March 1544, *Epistolae* I, 191–2.

[36] Xavier to Francisco Mansilhas, Punicale, 23 February 1544, *Epistolae* I, 189–90; Xavier to Francisco Mansilhas, Manapar, 16 June 1544, *Epistolae* I, 207; Xavier to Francisco Mansilhas, Cochin, 18 December 1544, *Epistolae* I, 244–7. He repeated and expanded this advice in the widely circulated Instruction to Gaspar Barzaeus upon his departure for Ormuz, Goa, April 1549, *Epistolae* I:I, 99.

[37] Xavier to Francisco Mansilhas, Manapar, 27 March 1544, *Epistolae* I, 195.

[38] Rao, Shulman, and Subrahmanyam, *Symbols of Substance*, 32–40; see also Dirks, *Hollow Crown*, 96–106.

and starving, and forced to abandon their villages and flee to barren reefs off the coast.[39] Xavier interceded with the Portuguese governor on behalf of Unni Keralā Tiruvadi Varman, the ruler of Kollam, to resettle the Paravas solely in his lands.[40] This arrangement was akin in some ways to the *reducciones de indios* (system of indigenous mission villages in the Spanish world) in the New World in that it would have brought together the dispersed converts more firmly under Portuguese religious and political control. In the political turmoil of this period, Xavier saw an opportunity to ease the way towards such a social reorganization.[41]

As he conducted these delicate negotiations, Xavier was thwarted and embarrassed at every turn by the Portuguese, particularly the captain of the Fishery Coast, Cosme de Paiva. Despite his support for the Kollam ruler, the captain persisted in his profitable trade in horses with Vettum Perumāl, supplying the rival king with beasts for warfare. The antagonism of the captain for the Jesuit padre was such that 'God and the whole world [knew] that he [could] not write to [Xavier] without scandal'.[42]

[39] Xavier to Francisco Mansilhas, Manapar, 16 June 1544, *Epistolae* I, 207; Xavier to Francisco Mansilhas, Manapar, 30 June 1544, *Epistolae* I, 209–10; Xavier to Francisco Mansilhas, Manapar, 1 August 1544, *Epistolae* I, 211–12; Xavier to Francisco Mansilhas, Manapar, 3 August 1544, *Epistolae* I, 213–15; Xavier to Francisco Mansilhas, Manapar, 19 August 1544, *Epistolae* I, 216–17. This episode has received several, somewhat contradictory interpretations, often relying heavily upon Xavier's letters (Heras, *The Aravidu Dynasty*, 99–130; Schurhammer, 'Iniquitriberim and Beteperumal, Chêra and Pândya Kings in Southern India, 1544', 255–62).

[40] Xavier to Francisco Mansilhas, Manapar, 3 August 1544, *Epistolae* I, 213–15; Xavier to Francisco Mansilhas, Manapar, 19 August 1544, *Epistolae* I, 216–17.

[41] Xavier's extreme warnings to the paṭṭaṅkaṭṭi not to resettle the Parava in their old village grounds following the cessation of fighting may indicate this deeper purpose. See Xavier to Ignatius, Tuticorin, 28 October 1542, *Epistolae* I, 150–1; Xavier to Francisco Mansilhas, Manapar, 1 August 1544, *Epistolae* I, 212.

[42] Xavier to Francisco Mansilhas, Alentalai, 5 September 1544, *Epistolae* I, 225.

Yet, at a critical juncture in the negotiations with the king of Kollam, Xavier was forced to turn to the same captain. A prince and nephew of the king had been won over by Xavier's efforts, allowing provisions to pass unhindered to the Parava and conferring titles amongst them.[43] Suddenly, a Portuguese man seized and imprisoned a servant of this prince, carrying him off to the capital of Vettum Perumāl himself. Xavier wrote to Mansilhas in barely suppressed panic to ask the captain to free him, complaining bitterly about the unjust nature of local Portuguese rule, which he compared unfavourably to the earlier Pāndya administration.[44] The pejorative comparison of Portuguese authority with previous indigenous regimes was startling. His condemnation of the immorality of Portuguese rule, which held no regard for either justice nor the etiquette of sovereignty, was a far cry from Xavier's optimistic appraisals when he first arrived. Such was the sense of frustration that, for the first time, Xavier expressed a desire to abandon his mission: 'So that I should not hear these things and also to go where I desire, to the land of the Preste, where so much service can be done for God our Lord without having someone persecute us, it would not be much to take a *toni* (a type of Tamil boat) here in Manapar and take myself off to India without delay.'[45] Portuguese India was thus manifestly distant from the utopian Indies of Prester John.

Despite this wistful desire to labour in a utopian land 'without having someone persecute us', Xavier did not lose hope. He exhorted the paṭṭaṅkaṭṭi to show respect to the emissary of the prince and asked the captain to ensure that the subjects of the king of Kollam be left unmolested.[46] The king of Kollam even contributed to the building of

[43] Xavier to Francisco Mansilhas, Manapar, 12 September 1544, *Epistolae* I, 236–8. Following Dirks, the conferring of titles, in the political language of little kingship in old regime south India, indicated the absorption of these Parava into the sovereignty of the king.

[44] Xavier to Francisco Mansilhas, Manapar, 11 September 1544, *Epistolae* I, 234–5.

[45] Xavier to Francisco Mansilhas, Manapar, 11 September 1544, *Epistolae* I, 235.

[46] Xavier to Francisco Mansilhas, Manapar, 11 September 1544, *Epistolae* I, 235.

a church, a significant gesture in south Indian polity-formation, and he and Mārtanda Varman, the king of Vēnādu, allowed the conversion of the Makkuva fishermen.[47]

Still, Xavier's efforts eventually came to naught.[48] Due to Vijayanagara's political pressure, the Portuguese did not cement the alliance Xavier attempted to broker with the kings of Kollam and Vēnādu. Moreover, another affront, for which he had solicited the intervention of the Portuguese, went unavenged: the martyring of several hundred new converts by the king of Jaffna, an event which had been marked by a miraculous apparition of a cross in the sky. Despite the governor's zeal and Xavier's tireless efforts, a punitive expedition was made impossible when the king of Jaffna captured the Portuguese ships returning from Burma and held them hostage.[49]

Xavier's increasing sense of isolation and frustration became palpable.[50] Too many, it seemed, were implacably hostile to him and to his cause. One index of this was a recurring emphasis on the notion of punishment, a striking departure from his earlier attitude. The mission field was defined by a famine of punishment—whether of the paṭṭaṅkaṭṭi by the meirinho, of the king of Jaffna by the Portuguese governor, of the corrupt converts by the priest, or of the renegade captain by various episcopal and secular authorities. Thus, even though God would 'ultimately give each his pay', this sense of a final accounting remained absent, not just amidst the local elites with whom Xavier had to deal, but even in the court of the Portuguese king. As Xavier boldly told him, the Portuguese king had forgotten the

[47] Xavier to Francisco Mansilhas, Negapatam, 7 April 1545, *Epistolae* I, 284–8. On the relationship of the temple and polity, see Appadurai and Breckenridge, 'The South Indian Temple'.

[48] Even the requests Xavier sent from Goa on behalf of the governor were yet to be honoured. Interestingly, the reason for this helplessness was, according to Ignatius, rampant suspicion in Rome that the society wanted 'to rule the world'. See Ignatius to Simão Rodrigues, written by Polanco, October 1546, *Monumenta Ignatiana* I, 43.

[49] Xavier to the Society, Cochin, 27 January 1544, *Epistolae* I, 275.

[50] Xavier to Francisco Mansilhas, Punicale, 29 August 1544, *Epistolae S. Francis Xaverii* I, 220–2.

fundamental reason for his great dominion in the Indies: that, among all the Christian kings, God had granted him rule over the Indies, not to enrich the royal treasury, but to send 'devoted missionaries to ... the gentiles of these lands'. Xavier warned the king that on his death bed:

> You may then hear from an irate God: why did you not punish those, who were authorized by you and subject to you and were opposed to me in India, though you punished severely those who were found negligent in caring for your taxes and finances? Your Highness should initiate an exact and complete accounting of all the fruits and temporal gains which, by the grace of God, you obtain from the Indies ... [B]etween your realm and the heavenly kingdom of God, divide these revenues ... since you confer from your vast revenues only a small part for its gravest spiritual needs.[51]

In the moral calculus of empire, therefore, Xavier saw a crucial deficit in the Portuguese commitment to the missionary enterprise, which was both the purpose and the justification of empire. At the heart of his recommendation was a preoccupation with a phrase from the gospel of Luke: 'Give an account of your stewardship!'[52] At every turn, in the workings of the Portuguese empire, he found no sense of such an accounting, seeing instead base corruption and rampant looting. As he warned, 'Do not consent that any friend of yours should come to India with charges or offices of the king, since of them it can be properly said: *they should be deleted from the book of the living and not written with the just.*'[53]

By the first months of 1545, Xavier thus turned decisively away from the Fishery Coast, away from the political difficulties in India, and towards the promise of two princes from Makassar, who had expressed a desire to convert and were, moreover, 'very far from Goa'.[54] Though this mission too proved a disappointment, Xavier

[51] Xavier to João III, Cochin, 20 January 1545 (Latin text of Possinus), *Epistolae* I, 248–54. See also Xavier to João III, Cochin, 20 January 1548, *Epistolae* I, 417.

[52] Xavier to the Society, Cochin, 15 January 1544, *Epistolae* I, 175. 'Redde rationem villicationis tuae!' from Luke 16.2.

[53] Xavier to Simão Rodrigues, Cochin, 27 January 1545, *Epistolae* I, 281–2. The quotation is from Psalms 68.29.

[54] Xavier to the Society, Malacca, 10 November 1545, *Epistolae* I, 298–301.

continued to seek new pasture further afield, provoking controversy in India.[55] In response, Xavier wrote to Ignatius privately. He described the difficulties of India as a mission field where 'the troubles of spirit and body are so great in dealing with a people of such quality that it is a marvel and ... the dangers of *both lives* [spiritual and physical] are many and difficult to avoid'.[56] Apart from the poor character of the people, Xavier reported that 'the Portuguese in these parts do not rule over anything but the sea and the villages which are along the seashore; therefore, they are not lords of *terra firma* [dry land] but only of the villages where they live'. Even in those places where they ruled, their ill-treatment of the converts dissuaded many from the Christian path. Gone was the belief in the extent and goodwill of Portuguese power: from the extensive radial map in which much of the world emanated from Goa, to this dismissive description of a network of sea-hugging villages, Xavier's vision of the Indies had grown beyond the flimsy tendrils of Portuguese power.

Accordingly, Xavier wrote of his desire to go to Japan, 'because all those in Japan are gentiles and there are neither Moors nor Jews and the people are very curious and desirous of learning new things, both of God and of other natural things, I determined to go to this land'.[57] Japan thus represented a new ideal of the Indies: a land only of intelligent and curious 'gentiles', without Moors or Jews, but also, this time, a land removed from the unreliable representatives of Portuguese government in India, from whom he was 'almost fleeing'.[58]

In leaving India, the peripatetic nature of his later career and the end of his reliance on the formal Portuguese empire was definitively established. From the beginning of Xavier's journey in Lisbon to its end in China, the Indies shifted constantly, functioning at times as a purely missionary category, at other times as a geopolitical referent, and at still others as a symbolic realm. Before he travelled there, the Indies was first a landscape defined only by the absence of the

[55] Nicolò Lancilotta to Ignatius, Quilon (Kollam), 25 January 1550, *Documenta Indica* II, 10–11.

[56] Xavier to Ignatius, Cochin, 20 January 1549, *Epistolae* I:I, 5–9.

[57] Xavier to Ignatius, Cochin, 20 January 1549, *Epistolae* I:I, 10.

[58] Xavier to João III, Cochin, 26 January 1549, *Epistolae* I:I, 60–1.

troubling realities of Mediterranean Europe—a land untouched by Protestant heresy, Islam, and Judaism, undergirded by the goodwill and power of the devoutly Catholic Portuguese Crown. Once in India, the complexity of indigenous society, but more significantly the profane realities of Portuguese imperial power, forced Xavier to rethink this assumption. Escaping from India, beyond the pollution of Portuguese colonial officialdom, Xavier spent the rest of his life in search of a people better suited to becoming Christian subjects. As he roamed, from the Spice Islands to Japan, till his death on the fringes of China, there remained the possibility of a more propitious mission field, just beyond the known extent of the Indies.

This was manifestly not the image of the Indies that operated in Europe. For one, the scope of the Indies was difficult to imagine from Rome: thus, Bartolomé Ferrão, writing about Peter Favre's appointment at the Council of Trent, could deem that '[Favre] is not born to be in one place as Master Francisco in the Indies, Master Simon in the court of Portugal, the licenciate Araoz in that of the prince and our Father Ignatius here in Rome'.[59] The Indies, in this estimation, was constituted as an undifferentiated and singular mission field, no different from the court of Portugal or Spain or the Society's headquarters in Rome. Crossing the Indies was different from traversing the confessional and political boundaries entailed by Favre's travels between Iberia and Germany.

Moreover, the Indies was a description of the difficulty of the mission field and of the relative merit of the missionary's labour. It was also, therefore, a name for the tracts of imperfectly civilized and Christianized areas in Catholic Europe, of the gulf of culture that existed between the Jesuit missionary and those amongst whom he laboured.[60] As Peter D'Agostino puts it, '"Indies" became a fluid symbol of any place where the gospel could be preached and souls won to Christ, and where a missionary felt assured his work in Basilicata or Calabria was as important and difficult as his confreres' efforts in China or Brazil.'[61] The Indies, in Europe, thus

[59] Ignatius to Martin Santacruz, rector of college at Coimba, written by Bartolomé Ferrão, 19 February 1546, *Monumenta Ignatiana* I, 362.

[60] Prosperi, '*Otras Indias*'.

[61] D'Agostino, 'Orthodoxy or Decorum?'

functioned as a chasm, a vantage point from which to notice and express estrangement.[62]

The Indies, as Xavier understood it, was instead a horizon: a land known through hearsay, which, when attained, however asymptotically, proved always a disappointment. By the same token, the Indies, precisely because it was a horizon, retained an element of utopia: it always held open the possibility of a better version of itself. In this regard, Xavier maintained the essence of the medieval tradition of Prester John's India. The Indies was a land constantly to be sought.

Ignatius decreed that the mission should have a provincial stationed permanently in Goa shortly after Xavier's death, making Xavier's peripatetic method unavailable as a model for later Jesuits.[63] He did, nonetheless, configure the Indies for the audience in Europe in an essentially utopian way, thus parting the oceans for future waves of missionaries to fan across its expanse to spread the Christian message.[64] The frustrations he expressed in his private missives of the difficulty of the terrain remained—in accordance with Ignatius's own directives—tactfully confined to a chosen few.

As Índias Chamada Brasil

If Xavier had come to an Indies already riven by the familiar boundaries of Islam and Christianity, his pioneering counterpart in Brazil came to a very different world. On 1 February 1549, Nóbrega sailed alongside the new governor of Brazil, Tomé de Sousa, who came with the tools to build a Portuguese city of man and God in the wilds of Brazil. Nóbrega's companions included some 400 *degredado*s, or exiles, and an additional 600 men, including civil and military functionaries, soldiers, a surgeon, an architect, carpenters, stonemasons, blacksmiths, shipbuilders, and other skilled artisans. He came too with five confreres, the fathers Leonardo Nunes, João de Azpilcueta Navarro, and António Pires, and two brothers, Vicente Rodrigues and

[62] This latter point is indirectly noted in Ginzburg, *Wooden Eyes*, 1–24.

[63] Ignatius to Miguel de Torres, Provincial of Portugal, Rome, 21 November 1555, *Documenta Indica* III, 303–11.

[64] See Girolamo Imbruglia's study of *litterae indipetae*, submitted by missionaries seeking to be sent abroad (Imbruglia, 'Ideali di civilizzazione').

Diogo Jácome. Arriving in Bahia on 29 March, they found a peaceful town of some fifty inhabitants.[65]

Nóbrega quickly began to build the infrastructure of the Jesuit mission. Vicente Rodrigues taught catechism to indigenous children each day in the 'school of reading and writing' to prepare them for baptism.[66] In Bahia, the enterprise of learning the indigenous language was aided greatly by the access the fathers had to the villages led by Diogo Álvares Caramuru, the infamous Portuguese turned indigenous chief.[67] If the European inhabitants, long removed from the matrix of Portuguese civility, had become wayward, the indigenous peoples seemed promising, especially Rodrigues's young charges who were eager to learn how to read and write.[68] Nóbrega, Navarro, and Pires meanwhile directed their efforts to bringing back to a proper Christian life the Portuguese inhabitants who had lapsed from long years in Brazil.[69]

These early letters hinted at a fundamental division in Nóbrega's conception of the mission space, which was crystallized by the time he wrote his first lengthy missives in August 1549. One pole, centred on the Portuguese residents, was familiar from his formative experiences as a missionary in Beira, Portugal, where he had first distinguished himself in the service of the Society.[70] This was the imperfectly Christianized Portuguese town in embryonic form, whose residents, though baptized, did not observe the sacraments. The problem posed by such a town to the Jesuit missionaries was one of discipline, basically alike to that faced by their confreres in the Indies *por acá* (over here) of Europe. Here too, the Jesuit had to

[65] Nóbrega to Simão Rodrigues, Bahia, 10 April 1549, *Cartas do Brasil*, 18–19.

[66] Nóbrega to Simão Rodrigues, Bahia, 10 April 1549, *Cartas do Brasil*, 20.

[67] Nóbrega to Simão Rodrigues, Bahia, 10 April 1549, *Cartas do Brasil*, 21–2.

[68] Nóbrega to Simão Rodrigues, Bahia, 10 April 1549, *Cartas do Brasil*, 20.

[69] Nóbrega to Simão Rodrigues, Bahia, 10 April 1549, *Cartas do Brasil*, 23–4.

[70] Melchior Nunes Barreto to P. Martinho de Santa Cruz, Coimbra, 27 September 1547, ARSI, *Hist. Soc.* 170 I, ff. 6r–9v; Nóbrega to P. Manuel Godinho, São Fins, 18 June 1548, *Cartas do Brasil*, 10–16.

correct the errors of men living in flagrant sin or engaging in public blasphemy.[71] Of course, the fledgling nature of the civilizational apparatus posed problems: Nóbrega commented on the undesirability of colonizing the land with exiles instead of respectable householders, as well as the logistical problems created by the inadequate numbers of skilled workers and public officials.[72] Similarly, the lack of episcopal authority in the figure of a bishop or at least a vicar general created ritual and disciplinary difficulties, as there was no one to consecrate the unguents or confirm the new Christians, much less to chastise the secular and episcopal clergy who lived in sin or heresy.[73] Still, Nóbrega saw here in recognizable if rudimentary form the same civilizational matrix familiar to him from Portugal.

The second type of mission space encompassed the indigenous world. In Nóbrega's view, this turned on a dichotomy between a resplendent nature and a barbaric culture. Writing to his friend, the renowned doctor Martín de Azpilcueta Navarro in Coimbra, Nóbrega wrote that it was 'very shocking that such a good earth has been given for so long to a people so uncultured, and that know so little, for they have no certain God and whatever they are told, they believe'.[74]

Nóbrega's sense of the jarring incongruity between the people and land of Brazil was based on a tradition deriving from a Stoic view of natural order, reflected in Pliny the Elder's famed natural history. While Pliny had averred that the antipodes did exist and that it was peopled, he also held that there was a direct relationship between the type of a nation and the nature of the part of the world it inhabited. In the middle of the earth could be found a salutary mix of heat and cold, such that the land was fruitful in all ways; the people of these lands bore physical traits that were a median of those found among the savages who inhabited the lands of the extremes of heat and cold.

[71] Nóbrega to Simão Rodrigues, Bahia, 9 August 1549, *Cartas do Brasil*, 29–31.

[72] Nóbrega to Simão Rodrigues, Bahia, 9 August 1549, *Cartas do Brasil*, 37–9.

[73] Nóbrega to Simão Rodrigues, Bahia, 9 August 1549, *Cartas do Brasil*, 35–6.

[74] Nóbrega to Dr Martín Azpilcueta Navarro, Salvador, 10 August 1549, *Cartas do Brasil*, 47–8.

Their manners were gentle, their intellects clear, their societies complex, boasting empires that could not be found in remote extremes of the earth. The Brazil of Nóbrega's acquaintance seemed to directly contravene the relationship Pliny posited between the nature of man and the nature of his habitat.[75]

Nóbrega's own contribution to the European cosmographical tradition was the oft-published 'Informação das Terras do Brasil' (Information of the Lands of Brazil), a far more systematic and neutral account than the musings he sent in a private letter to Martín de Azpilcueta Navarro. After a brief description of the land, in which he again stressed the cool, temperate, and humid climes and the natural abundance, Nóbrega turned to the 'the gentiles [who were] of diverse castes', mentioning in particular those called 'Goaianases' and the Carijós. Despite this seeming attentiveness to internal diversity, in Nóbrega's nascent ethnographic schema, the peoples of the Brazilian coasts were of two categories: those who communicated with Christians—broadly, the Tupí, which included the Goainás and the closely related peoples known as Guaraní to the Spanish or Carijó to the Portuguese—and those who did not. These latter groups were called 'Guaimurés, and these are a people who live in the forests'. He noted that these people were shocked by the Christians but also that 'they say that we are their brothers'. Though they were willing to consider the Portuguese brothers, Nóbrega made clear he saw no physical similarities with them, beyond the practice of maintaining beards: 'They bore their lips and nostrils, and place some bones in them, so that they seem demons.' These people were like giants and made formidable enemies due to their skill with bows and clubs and their ability to quickly flee into the forest after an attack.[76]

Nóbrega depicted the members of the second category, who did not communicate with Christians, in a mould derived from Pliny: the Aimoré were antipodal peoples, giants, who, in an appropriately

[75] Pliny the Elder, *The Natural History*, in particular Book II, chapter 65; Book II, chapter 80. On the ways in which the contradictions of ancient learning and empirical observations jarred European observers of the Americas, see Grafton, *New Worlds, Ancient Texts*.

[76] Nóbrega, 'Informação das Terras do Brasil', August 1549, *Cartas do Brasil*, 61.

Christian twist on classical knowledge, were demonic in aspect and belligerent towards Christians. This dovetailed with a Tupí world view, as shown by the Portuguese adoption of the pejorative Tupí name, meaning thief, for the Gê-speaking groups who served as outsiders in their schema. Still, even in Nóbrega's antipodal classificatory blueprint based in part on the Tupí construction of Gê alterity, there is the mark of veracity in his observation that the Aimoré considered the bearded Portuguese, the others of their Tupí others, to be brothers of sorts. As Manuela Carneiro da Cunha describes it, Gê thought proceeds through complementarities and negations, so that personhood is stated in the negative: 'I am that which I am not is not.'[77]

If the nomadic forest-dwelling Aimoré were antipodal others, those who had relations with the Portuguese were divided into two 'castes ... called Tupeniques and the other Tupínambás'. In contrast to the Aimoré, both groups lived in communal fashion on the coasts, in palm houses in which some fifty families would reside, and displayed an appropriate fear of demons.[78] Nóbrega took pains to make clear that the Tupí were not bestial and lived in many ways according to natural law. They held and shared everything in common, particularly food, and did not save things for another day, nor strive to accumulate riches. They were hospitable to any Christian who came to their community and the women were faithful to their husbands.[79] The best of them, the Carijó, had already proved themselves capable of the highest rigours of segregated, almost ascetic, Christian living under Franciscan care, an experiment that only ended through the brutal rapacity of the Portuguese settlers, when 'the demon carried there a boat of [Portuguese slave] raiders and they captured many of them'.[80]

In Nóbrega's vision, Brazil provided a space in which the twin strands of the evolving Jesuit vision for religious reform found

[77] Carneiro da Cunha, *Os mortos e os outros*, 143.

[78] Nóbrega, 'Informação das Terras do Brasil', August 1549, *Cartas do Brasil*, 61.

[79] Nóbrega, 'Informação das Terras do Brasil', August 1549, *Cartas do Brasil*, 65.

[80] Nóbrega, 'Informação das Terras do Brasil', August 1549, *Cartas do Brasil*, 61.

fruitful ground. It was a world that encapsulated both the Indies por acá, characterized by the need to discipline and educate the baptized but imperfect Christians of Europe, and the Indies por allá, in which the missionary's task was to convert the gentiles untouched by the Christian word.

In such a dichotomous schema, the cross-contamination of the European and indigenous worlds in Brazil was troubling. Thus, in promoting a Christian family life among the Portuguese residents in Bahia, as he had done in Beira, Nóbrega found that he had to contend with the ubiquity of Portuguese men keeping not only their indigenous slaves as mistresses, but also their adoption of the custom of taking free indigenous women, perhaps as a way to cement ties with indigenous groups.[81] To convert these domestic arrangements into a family based on Christian monogamy entailed many difficulties, not least the thorny question of which of the women in a household could lay legitimate claim to marriage. Nóbrega's solution was to bring women who would otherwise have little opportunity for marriage in Portugal to Brazil.[82]

An even more troubling way in which the European and indigenous worlds intersected was the illegal capture and enslavement of the indigenous peoples by the Portuguese. The ill effects could be seen in the destruction of the Franciscan mission to the Carijó by slave-raiders.[83] Writing to Simão Rodrigues, Nóbrega clarified that Portuguese were to blame: pretending to behave peacefully with the Tupí and luring them to trade, they would capture the indigenous illegally. This was particularly disheartening, given that one of the chief attractions for the Tupí of intercourse with the Christians was the trade in foreign objects, particularly iron goods.[84]

By comparison with the duplicitous Portuguese, the converted Tupí were actually morally superior, as they kept natural law even

[81] Nóbrega to Simão Rodrigues, Bahia, 9 August 1549, *Cartas do Brasil*, 29–30.

[82] Nóbrega to Simão Rodrigues, Bahia, 9 August 1549, *Cartas do Brasil*, 30.

[83] Nóbrega to Simão Rodrigues, Bahia, 9 August 1549, *Cartas do Brasil*, 32–3.

[84] Nóbrega to Simão Rodrigues, Porto Seguro, 6 January 1550, *Cartas do Brasil*, 77.

better than the Christians. Nóbrega even recommended allowing converted slaves to return to their indigenous lands accompanied by a priest, who would then be able to access remote communities with greater ease. Thus, Nóbrega asked Rodrigues to intercede with the Portuguese king to direct the governor to free the slaves.[85] In Xavier's mould, Nóbrega came to identify the importance of the mission to the Indies, not with the pastoral needs of the Portuguese, but primarily with the prospect of converting the gentiles:

> This land, and the rest of the gentiles of the world, is our enterprise ... Everything that is done there [in Portugal] is misery, [for] at most they win a hundred souls, although they cover the whole kingdom; here there is a great handful [of souls].[86]

The New India in Brazil

Everywhere in the Jesuit letters of these early days of the mission in Brazil one is struck by the bustling sense of building a new world. For Nóbrega, much like Xavier, this meant a particular interest in the youngest members of Tupí society. When he applied to the governor Tomé de Sousa for a certain allotment of land known as the Água dos Meninos, Nóbrega argued that the lands were needed for the sustenance of the Jesuit house, 'because of the intention of the King and the fathers of the Company to bring up and teach in it children of the gentiles, so that in time they may carry the name of the Lord to all the peoples'.[87] This notion was similar to the original mission of the College of St Paul, of which Xavier had approved.

It was for the education of Tupí children that Nóbrega devised his most innovative mission, that of Portuguese orphans, who, as playmates, would be better able to attract the Tupí to a Christian life. Accordingly, devout children in the care of Jesuits in Portugal were sent to save their Tupí neighbours in Brazil. In an echo of the hagiography of St Anthony of Padua, ignoring the entreaties of relatives

[85] Nóbrega to Simão Rodrigues, Bahia, 9 August 1549, *Cartas do Brasil*, 80–1.

[86] Nóbrega to Simão Rodrigues, Bahia, 9 August 1549, *Cartas do Brasil*, 34.

[87] Donation of 'Água dos Meninos' by Tomé de Sousa to Nóbrega, Bahia, 21 October 1550, in *Monumenta Brasiliae* I, 195.

and friends, these children were reportedly determined to follow his footsteps to spread the Christian word outside Europe. The children showed a remarkable unwillingness to make a distinction between Brazil and Portugal as fitting sites for God's work, reflecting a general enthusiasm for the foreign missions among their custodians in the Society of Jesus.[88]

Once there, the boys quickly became an integral part of Nóbrega's ambitious plans to expand the mission into the hinterlands of Brazil, dovetailing with Portuguese imperial interest in penetrating these parts. In this project the aim was 'to teach well the children [for they] well-indoctrinated and accustomed to virtue, [would] be firm and constant'. Thus, the missionaries divided themselves across the various captaincies and, accompanied by interpreters, prepared themselves 'to enter the *sertão*, where Christians still have not reached'. Nóbrega specifically ordered that the children, both indigenous and Portuguese, be collected and taught. The orphans from Lisbon were of particular help, for their songs 'attract to themselves the sons of the gentiles and edify greatly the Christians'.[89]

Pero Doménech, writing to Ignatius a year later about the foundation of the college of orphans in Lisbon, boasted of the successes of the seven orphans sent to Brazil 'to teach the gentile children'. The orphans drew hundreds of gentile children, who would come to play with them and be led to catechism; in turn, they would instruct their families.[90] The villagers had 'made an hermitage there in their territory', where the indigenous children gathered for prayers and to learn the catechism taught to them by the Portuguese orphans.[91] The Tupí were willing to consider these foreign children as potentially powerful shamans, particularly when their passage occurred in

[88] Pero Doménech to the Society in Coimbra, Lisbon, 27 January 1550, *Monumenta Brasiliae* I, 171.

[89] Nóbrega to Simão Rodrigues, Pernambuco, 11 August 1551, *Monumenta Brasiliae* I, 268.

[90] Pero Doménech to Ignatius, Almeirim, 17 February 1551, *Monumenta Brasiliae* I, 214–15.

[91] Pero Doménech to Ignatius, Almeirim, 17 February 1551, *Monumenta Brasiliae* I, 214–15.

conjunction with contagion caused through contact.[92] By the same token, the orphans proved adept students of Tupí: 'Since they are children, they learn immediately, so that our children understand many things of their language.'[93] The orphans' mission also had the particular advantage of generating support for Nóbrega's expansion of the mission's activities.[94] The exemplary behaviour of the orphans induced the goodwill of the Portuguese so that, as Nóbrega informed D. João III, 'the residents of these Captaincies help with what they can to make these houses for the children of the gentiles to grow up in them, and will be the great means, and quickly, for the conversion of the heathen'.[95]

The orphans were also key to the re-inscription of the landscape of Brazil in an apostolic mould, since they led a successful pilgrimage to the site at which, Nóbrega believed, the footsteps of St Thomas were preserved. This belief came from one of the indigenous myths in which Nóbrega found evidence of Brazil's place in Christian geography and history. He had reported the myth to his brothers almost immediately upon his arrival in Brazil.[96] In Nóbrega's retelling, St Thomas the Apostle, whom the indigenous called Zomé, had passed through Brazil. This fact had been passed on through the sayings of their ancestors and was attested to by four footprints preserved near a river, which Nóbrega had since seen with his own eyes. The Tupí claimed that when Zomé had left the footprints, he was fleeing indigenous archers, and had parted the river and passed through it, untouched by the water. From the other bank, Nóbrega claimed, he

92 Vicente Rodrigues, through commission of the governor Tomé de Sousa to Simão Rodrigues, Bahia, May 1552, *Monumenta Brasiliae* I, 320; Pero Doménech to Ignatius, Almeirim, 17 February 1551, *Monumenta Brasiliae* I, 216.

93 Pero Doménech to Ignatius, Almeirim, 17 February 1551, *Monumenta Brasiliae* I, 216.

94 Pero Doménech to Ignatius, Almeirim, 17 February 1551, *Monumenta Brasiliae* I, 216.

95 Nóbrega to D. João III, Olinda, 14 September 1551, *Monumenta Brasiliae* I, 293.

96 Nóbrega to D. João III, Olinda, 14 September 1551, *Monumenta Brasiliae* I, 66; He reported the legend first in Nóbrega to Simão Rodrigues, Bahia, 15 April 1549, *Cartas do Brasil*, 27.

had then left for India, an addition to the local myth that allowed it to be subsumed into the well-known narrative of St Thomas's apostolic career. The Tupí also said that the arrows aimed at Zomé turned on the archers and killed them in their tracks. The Tupí believed that Zomé had promised them that he would return and they would see him in the sky; being their intercessor to God, through whom would come knowledge of God, Nóbrega believed that they would convert.

Nóbrega's account, involving a nearly Mosaic parting of waters as well as the miraculous survival of a barrage of arrows in the fashion of St Sebastian, seemed almost a potpourri of Christian elements. Swayed undoubtedly by the striking parallel between the Tupí name of the deity (Zomé) and the Portuguese name of the apostle (Tomé), Nóbrega subsumed the myth into the narrative of St Thomas. Nóbrega's appropriation centred on another element of the indigenous myth, mentioned in an earlier letter: Zomé had given the Tupí the manioc root, from which they made bread. In the context of Tupí anthropophagy, the giving of food Nóbrega deemed proper to humans was significant: Zomé/Tomé functioned as a giver of culture, bringing the Tupí into the human fold. Such an interpretation was unwarranted in Tupí terms: the nearly universal Amerindian mythic structure posited an original state in which animals and humans were not differentiated and in which all beings shared and recognized personhood or 'humanity'. Thus, as Vivieros de Castro argues in indigenous originary myths, it was not man who acquired culture but rather animals who lost their 'human' qualities.

The choice to assimilate Zomé into the narrative of St Thomas had precedent in the New World.[97] This identification allowed Nóbrega to subsume the second type of Brazilian mission space, encompassing the Tupí world into the larger category of the Indies, whose extent and sweep was circumscribed by the apostolic wanderings of St Thomas. Jesuits in the Indies—whether Xavier in Asia or Nóbrega in Brazil—understood themselves to be following in his footsteps, metaphorically and literally.

The pilgrimage led by the orphans to the site of these footsteps was thus of crucial import in sacralizing antipodal land. The child preachers, holding aloft a cross and singing a catechism translated

[97] See the classic study by Lafaye, *Quetzalcoatl and Guadalupe*, 177–206.

into Tupí, entered the village neighbouring the site. Some villagers greeted them welcomingly. Others pleaded with them not to do them harm or even burnt salt and pepper to keep them away, harbouring doubts about the intention of these young foreign prophets. Still, the procession was well received by the chiefs, who promised to make them a house near the footsteps of the saint. In the morning, after preaching from house to house, the procession continued, accompanied by the chiefs. They sung a litany to the saints with the Tupí singing the refrain, 'Ora pro nobis' (Pray for us). The footsteps, which were covered in full tide, were visible on the stone, which had 'given way to [St Thomas's] feet as if it were clay, as if it had humbled and humiliated itself'. To honour the claiming of this land by the Christian God, the pilgrims erected a cross in the hallowed spot.[98]

The pilgrimage reified the cosmography Nóbrega had begun to elaborate, in which Brazil could take its place in biblical geography and history. Yet, Nóbrega was aware that such a pilgrimage was fundamentally different from pilgrimages in India, where the tradition of St Thomas was the subject of neither doubt nor translation, let alone invention. As Nóbrega explained to the Portuguese settlers of Pernambuco, the sacralization of the land of Brazil depended ultimately not on apostolic tradition, but on the devotion and labour of the Christians. The fire of the Holy Spirit, which had originally set alight the tongues of the twelve Apostles, who 'kindled all Europe and Asia and Palestine and Africa, and nearly all the world', had never burned in Brazil. It was, therefore, vital, Nóbrega cautioned, that those who possessed this fire should not lose it, which required 'great care of the senses and even more of the heart, which is not reason'. Through such spiritual care, Nóbrega hoped that the fire of the Holy Spirit would burn 'in charity in such a manner that even the woods burn with it'.[99]

Nóbrega's elaboration of the notion of charity, or neighbourly love, through which the Brazilian woods would burn, bears clearly the stamp of Augustine, in which the heart, not reason, was primary.

[98] Letter of the orphans, written by Francisco Pires, to Pero Doménech, Bahia, 5 August 1552, *Monumenta Brasiliae* I.

[99] Nóbrega to the residents of Pernambuco, Bahia, 5 June 1552, *Cartas do Brasil*, 109–10.

The Augustinian influence became even more apparent when he chastised the settlers to not focus their energy on the false desires of the world, the fires of lust and pride, but to burn instead in the fire of the Holy Spirit. As he reminded the planters:

> You are the plants, the new seed, which the Lord placed and planted in these parts. Who holds you back that you do not give fruit worthy to present at the table of the Celestial King? These are the principal plantations that you have to make in Brazil.[100]

Brazil, inhabited by exiled men and the indigenous ignorant of God, held a promise far greater than India or the rest of the Old World, which had heard, forgotten, and rejected the word of God. Brazil held open the possibility to remake the city of man in the image of the city of God. In this project of a new world, unsullied by the mundane concerns of adults, the importance of children—both as preachers and as students but also as models for the inherent malleability of the perfect subject of conversion—was paramount.

The City of Man in Bahia

Nóbrega's increasing emphasis on the newness of the world of Brazil was a relatively later development in his missionary career. Like others of the first generation of Jesuits in Brazil, he had sought out and delighted in the remotest of connections with Xavier's India. Writing to Dr Navarro, he had flatteringly written that if India had Xavier, then the lands of Brazil had Navarro's nephew, Juan de Azpilcueta, also belonging to Xavier's family.[101] Azpilcueta himself named a boy he had taken from the Tupí after Antonio Criminali, the first Jesuit martyr of India, killed in 1549.[102]

Interest in the eastern missions was far from idle: there was a belief that the lessons gleaned there could be fruitfully applied in

[100] Nóbrega to the residents of Pernambuco, Bahia, 5 June 1552, *Cartas do Brasil*, 110–11.

[101] Nóbrega to Martín de Azpilcueta Navarro, Salvador, 10 August 1549, *Cartas do Brasil*, 52.

[102] Jõao de Azpilcueta to the Society in Coimba, Pernambuco, 15 September 1551, *Monumenta Brasiliae* I, 283.

Brazil. Pero Correia wrote to his confrere in Africa, urging him to share information, for the Brazilian gentiles were 'like the Moors, as much in having many women, and in preaching in the morning at dawn, and in the sin against nature [homosexuality] which is said to be very common there, [and which] is the same here in this land'. In this regard, Correia mentioned 'some women, who even in arms as in all other things, follow the office of men, and have other women with whom they are married [and for whom the] greatest injury that can be done to them is to call them women'.[103] In this stew of rumour, stereotype, and myth, in which the sodomizing Moors are compared with the gender-bending Amazons of Brazil, what is worth emphasizing is Correia's belief that the lessons of missionaries working among the infidels of northern Africa was of direct relevance to their confreres in Brazil. This was particularly remarkable given Correia's extensive experience in Brazil, who had lived there since 1534, long before the arrival of the Jesuits.[104] Despite his familiarity with this land, its peoples, and the language, as a mission space Correia still imagined Brazil within the larger rubric of the Indies, subordinating its specificity to the parameters of that category.[105]

Yet, the comparability of Brazil and India also instilled something of a sense of subtle rivalry, as the missionaries of the former sought to prove that both their zeal and the difficulty of their task were as great as that of their confreres in the east. Nóbrega wrote: 'India is a great thing, and the fruit of it [too], and I too have much that will be done here. There, many kingdoms will be converted and here, many souls will be saved, [of those who are] the most lost to God in all the nations (*gerações*).'[106] Similarly Leonardo Nunes compared the 'awe (*espanto*) and fervor' in his heart inspired by the Carijó to that caused by 'the

[103] Pero Correia to P. Jõao Nunes Barreto (in Africa), São Vicente, 20 June 1551, *Monumenta Brasiliae* I, 224.

[104] Pero Correia to Simão Rodrigues, São Vicente, 10 March 1553, *Monumenta Brasiliae* I, 434.

[105] Thus, Ignatius termed the region 'the India called Brazil'. Ignatius to Simão Rodrigues, Rome, 7 July 1550, *Monumenta Brasiliae* I, 192.

[106] Nóbrega to the Society in Coimbra, Olinda, 14 September 1551, *Monumenta Brasiliae* I, 289.

things which our Lord, through those of the Company, has worked in the Indias, in Hormuz, Japan etc.'[107]

The most dramatic confrontation between the missionaries in Brazil and the anxiety of influence of Xavier's India occurred through the person of the first bishop of Brazil, Pero Fernandes Sardinha. He had replaced the formidable Miguel Vaz as vicar general in 1545.[108] Xavier had once personally entrusted Sardinha to argue that the civil jurisdiction of converts be transferred from local Portuguese captains either to Simão Rodrigues, should he come to India, or to the Bishop.[109]

Sardinha's time in India had crystallized a rigid view of the best ways to convert the gentiles, laid out most clearly in a long memorial to the king on the spiritual and temporal needs of India.[110] The dominant note in this memorial was the need to separate the Christians, particularly the converts, from the gentiles, including relatives and especially the brahmins. He advocated for strict discipline to ensure the religious purity of the Christian city of Goa, to which matters of state, including the crucial trade in horses that sustained the city, must be subordinated.

In Goa, this attitude had proven controversial. Cosme Eanes, one of the architects of the College of Goa, wrote mildly, 'Master Pero who goes there and who served in this charge is ill-disposed and not for this land. He is a man who lived virtuously ... and is not suitable here.'[111] Garcia de Sá, the governor, was particularly aggrieved that, in keeping with Xavier's aversion to local officials, Sardinha had exceeded the bounds of his charge and habit, 'for he took [to task]

[107] Leonardo Nunes to Nóbrega, São Vicente, 29 June 1552, *Monumenta Brasiliae* I, 339.

[108] On his reverence for Miguel Vaz, see Sardinha, 'Papel sobre as couzas q se hão de prover na India para reformação dos costumes e bem da Christandade e serviço de El-Rey'.

[109] Xavier, 'Lembrança pera ho vigario geral das cousas que ha de negocear com el Rey pera bem dos Xraos da Imdia, 1549', *Monumenta Xaveriana*, 858.

[110] Xavier, 'Lembrança pera ho vigario geral das cousas que ha de negocear com el Rey pera bem dos Xraos da Imdia, 1549', 858.

[111] Eanes, 'Carta de Cosme Eanes'.

bailiffs (*meirinhos*) throughout this land with a rod'.[112] It was only the more devout Portuguese townsmen and artisans of Goa who approved of the vicar general.[113]

Despite this reception in Goa, the bishop showed no sign of abandoning his high-handed style, his strict commitment to Christian discipline, and his aversion to religious contagion. Though Nóbrega had thought him friendly upon his arrival on 22 June 1552, he was quickly disabused of this notion.[114] Sardinha launched a frontal assault upon all the innovations underpinning the Brazilian mission, prohibiting in his very first sermon that any 'white man should use the gentile customs'.[115] He spoke in particular of the use of songs, associated with the worst indigenous practices: he noted that 'the orphan children before I came had the custom of singing every Sunday and feast-day the songs of our Lord in the gentile tone, and ringing certain instruments that these barbarians chime and sing when they wish to drink their wine and kill their enemies'.[116] He attributed the origin of this innovation to a certain Gaspar Barbosa, who had come to Brazil as a degredado, or exiled criminal, and had continued in his bad ways, before eventually inserting himself '*like a wolf in sheep's clothing* with these your Fathers, more zealous in virtue than experienced in malice'. Gaspar Barbosa's conversion, effected through the administration of the spiritual exercises, was genuine: he eventually died fighting in the final conquest of Rio de Janeiro against the French.[117]

[112] Sá, 'Carta de Garcia de Sá'.

[113] 'Carta dos mestres do Povo da Cidade de Goa'. The group included from internal evidence a barber, a shoemaker, a leather-dresser (*surador*), and a tailor.

[114] On his initial good impression, see Nóbrega to Simão Rodrigues, Bahia, 10 July 1552, *Monumenta Brasiliae* I, 349–50.

[115] Pero Fernandes Sardinha to Simão Rodrigues, Bahia, July 1552, *Monumenta Brasiliae* I, 358.

[116] Pero Fernandes Sardinha to Simão Rodrigues, Bahia, July 1552, *Monumenta Brasiliae* I, 359. The bishop was not mistaken in making this connection, as the following chapter will explore in greater length.

[117] Pero Fernandes Sardinha to Simão Rodrigues, Bahia, July 1552, *Monumenta Brasiliae* I, 359fn6. I rely on Leite's identifications, which appear plausible.

Yet, for Sardinha, like the formerly renegado priest whom he prevented from going to India despite the bishop's request, Barbosa was fundamentally tainted. Whereas Nóbrega in Pernambuco had called upon the degredados to build a city of God in Brazil, Sardinha denied that such masons could lay the foundation of the church in this new land.

Sardinha also objected to the orphans wearing their hair in the manner of the Tupí children, 'for they seem like monks'.[118] The use of mestiça women as interpreters during confessions was unacceptable even if 'three hundred Navarros and six hundred Caetanos' approved it, a cutting reference to Nóbrega's friend, the theologian Dr Martín de Azpilcueta Navarro, and his ally, Cardinal Caetano.[119] He disapproved too of the public demonstrations of religious fervour and discipline that Nóbrega had allowed to thrive in Brazil, calling for a return to the norms established by Ignatius; he conveniently forgot that Xavier had introduced similar practices in the Moluccas.[120] He also disliked the building of hermitages amongst the Tupí and their burial in 'the gentile mode', presumably a reference to the wailing practices that continued after conversion, as part of the death rites of the Tupí.[121]

Sardinha did not resort to a simple appeal to ecclesiastical hierarchy or canonical correctness or even the emerging ideas of Catholic discipline at the coeval Council of Trent. Rather, he insisted upon the correctness of his positions on the basis of his experience in India: 'And thus I told him that this land was to take the path it had [taken] in India in the making of Christians, and what Father Master Francsico [Xavier] and the other fathers of the Company hold there.' Claiming that 'since I have much experience in India', Sardinha brooked no

[118] Pero Fernandes Sardinha to Simão Rodrigues, Bahia, July 1552, *Monumenta Brasiliae* I, 360.

[119] Pero Fernandes Sardinha to Simão Rodrigues, Bahia, July 1552, *Monumenta Brasiliae* I, 361.

[120] Pero Fernandes Sardinha to Simão Rodrigues, Bahia, July 1552, *Monumenta Brasiliae* I, 363.

[121] Pero Fernandes Sardinha to Simão Rodrigues, Bahia, July 1552, *Monumenta Brasiliae* I, 364.

dissent: he explained to Nóbrega that he upbraided him privately 'for following thus his opinions in public'.[122]

The conflict quickly escalated over the financial necessities of Nóbrega's project to establish houses for the teaching of Tupí children.[123] Nóbrega had already acquired lands through the governor's intercession, and had bought twelve cows and was beginning to acquire African slaves for the college. Apart from royal grants for the sustenance of the ten Jesuit fathers, he was relying on tithes in fish, among other things, to maintain the children.[124] Disgruntled observers grumbled that the Jesuits were acquiring land and slaves without a concomitant gain in conversion.[125] Underlying these complaints was resentment at Jesuit interference in the illegal capture and enslavement of indigenous people, particularly the Carijó. To quell these rumours, Nóbrega determined that the Jesuits themselves should eat only once a day on the charity of the governor and rely on alms for their support.[126] Still, the bishop lent a sympathetic ear to these complaints.[127]

If Nóbrega was attempting to drum up support in public in Brazil, to the bishop's ire, he was not slow to defend his mission to his confreres in Europe. To Simão Rodrigues, he sent a point-by-point refutation of the bishop's objections, relying not only on the exigencies of Brazil, but also on theological opinion.[128] He noted that it was the

[122] Pero Fernandes Sardinha to Simão Rodrigues, Bahia, July 1552, *Monumenta Brasiliae* I, 360, 364–5.

[123] Manuel de Nóbrega to Simão Rodrigues Bahia, August 1552, *Monumenta Brasiliae* I, 401–2.

[124] Manuel de Nóbrega to Simão Rodrigues Bahia, August 1552, *Monumenta Brasiliae* I, 402–4.

[125] Manuel de Nóbrega to Simão Rodrigues Bahia, August 1552, *Monumenta Brasiliae* I, 404.

[126] Manuel de Nóbrega to Simão Rodrigues Bahia, August 1552, *Monumenta Brasiliae* I, 404.

[127] Manuel de Nóbrega to Simão Rodrigues Bahia, August 1552, *Monumenta Brasiliae* I, 405.

[128] In justifying the use of indigenous boys as interpreters during confession as a practice, which did not violate the sigil of confession, he referred to Martín de Azpilcueta Navarro's published works on canon law, who himself relied on Cardinal Caetano, just as the bishop's cutting remarks suggested (Nóbrega to Simão Rodrigues, Bahia, July 1552, *Monumenta Brasiliae* I, 370).

custom to permit gentiles in the churches to hear mass alongside the Christians and not leave them outside for fear of scandalizing them.[129] Presumably because the bishop had insisted on the kind of radical separation of gentiles from Christians that he had tried to enforce in Goa, Nóbrega asked if this policy should continue. He also asked if they could continue to embrace some local customs that were neither contrary to the Catholic faith nor idolatrous, such as the singing of songs, which Sardinha had so vociferously condemned.[130] He explained that allowing these practices made it easier to root out those customs that were irredeemably bad such as cannibalism. Thus, the Jesuits went 'preaching in their manner in a certain tone, walking wandering and beating [their] chests'. They also allowed the boys in their houses to have their hair shorn in their traditional manner 'because similarity is a cause of love'.[131] Here, finally, was Nóbrega's reasoning for these experiments in accommodatio, and one that would come to hold such sway in certain quarters of the Society. By cultivating 'similarity' with their charges, Nóbrega hoped to persuade them to the Christian faith. It is another matter, that in the context of the other-centric cosmology of the indigenous peoples, this strategy may well have had limited efficacy.[132]

The final issue he raised was the most important: whether or not it was licit to make war against the indigenous and capture them because they did not follow natural law.[133] Given his steadfast criticism of the slaving practices of the Portuguese from his earliest days in Brazil, the fact that Nóbrega raised this issue suggested that the bishop and his supporters had disagreed with the Jesuit position. Nóbrega asked

[129] Nóbrega to Simão Rodrigues, Bahia, July 1552, *Monumenta Brasiliae* I, 370.

[130] Nóbrega to Simão Rodrigues, Bahia, July 1552, *Monumenta Brasiliae* I, 407.

[131] Nóbrega to Simão Rodrigues, Bahia, July 1552, *Monumenta Brasiliae* I, 408.

[132] See the difficulties faced by Nóbrega and Anchieta in negotiating a peace in chapter 4; Amerindian chiefs were unimpressed by these foreign shamans who were unable to procure enemies.

[133] Nóbrega to Simão Rodrigues, Bahia, July 1552, *Monumenta Brasiliae* I, 408.

that these doubts be placed before the College of Coimbra and that the learned opinions of the principle literati of the university should be sent to him, for 'as much for here, as for India and the other parts of infidels'.[134]

Nóbrega's requests came upon the heels of the Valladolid controversy on the treatment of the indigenous of the New World.[135] It is unclear if he was already apprised of the course that debate had taken, but certainly the tenor of his sympathies within the debate was clear. Yet, the bishop's criticisms, made partially upon the basis of his superior theological and canonical knowledge, led Nóbrega towards a certain anti-intellectualism in his later career. Regardless of Coimbra's theoretical opinions on the issues he raised, in practice, Nóbrega's experience in Brazil had made these questions moot.

The emerging convergence between the settlers and the bishop made Bahia an increasingly inhospitable place for Nóbrega. Moreover, it solidified his nascent alliance with the representatives of the king in Brazil, helped by his fast friendship with the first governor, Tomé de Sousa. As early as 1551, Nóbrega had written to the king, arguing that, regardless of the qualities of the owner of the captaincy, for the good administration of justice, it was necessary that 'the jurisdiction of the whole coast should be of Your Highness'.[136] Moreover, he wished the College of Bahia to pertain to royal jurisdiction. While this strategy was useful as a countervailing force against the settlers, the episcopal authority represented by the bishop, even under the terms of the Padroado, was another matter. It is no coincidence that Nóbrega sought increasingly to shift the centre of the mission away from the meddling influences in Bahia, and to seek new pastures in the south. Even here, the bishop's agents continued to exert influence

[134] Nóbrega to Simão Rodrigues, Bahia, July 1552, *Monumenta Brasiliae* I, 408.

[135] For a superb reconstruction of this debate, see Pagden, *The Fall of Natural Man*.

[136] Nóbrega to D. João III, Olinda, 14 September 1551, *Monumenta Brasiliae* I, 291. These calls would only get stronger. See, for example, Nóbrega to Luis Gonçalves da Camara, São Vicente, 15 June 1553, *Monumenta Brasiliae* I, 496.

in the coastal areas of Portuguese settlement, leading Nóbrega to turn to the sertão.[137]

Unfortunately, the sertão also represented a retreat from the authority of the Portuguese king, as the governor's own objections to Nóbrega's reorientation suggests.[138] Unlike in India, where Xavier had sought to avoid Portuguese imperial dominion, this was a form of authority that the Brazilian Jesuits welcomed, not least because of an emerging discourse concerning the obstacle to conversion created by the lack of recognizable sovereignty among the Tupí.[139] Yet, the Jesuit missions would soon become an indispensable part of the expanding web of Portuguese imperial power into the hinterland.

By August of 1553, Nóbrega had arrived in Piratininga, the Tupí village in the sertão of São Vicente, which would come to be a major propulsive node for the expansion of the mission henceforth.[140] Here, the methods Nóbrega had devised could find full flower. In the absence of Portuguese force, they also represented the best strategy for evangelization, in direct contravention of the views of the bishop. Moreover, in almost a re-enactment of the earliest days of European contact with Brazil, Nóbrega discovered that the inducements to intercourse and exchange were not solely of the order of cultural accommodatio. Older modes of interaction, involving the trade in iron particularly, were as important as the innovations which allowed the Jesuits to enter the sertão like karaíba, the indigenous stranger-prophets. Here, again was a chance to build a new society, unsullied by the competing claims of others who could define the terms of Christian civility. Here was a place in which labour, physical and spiritual, was primary and

[137] Nóbrega to Simão Rodrigues, São Vicente, 12 February 1553, *Monumenta Brasiliae* I, 421.

[138] Tomé de Sousa to D. João III, Salvador, 1 June 1553, *Monumenta Brasiliae* I, 485. He referred to the incursion of the Spanish from Asunción and their jurisdictional violations as part of his reasons for not allowing the Jesuits to enter the sertão without permission from the king.

[139] See, for example, Pero Correia to Simão Rodrigues, São Vicente, June 1551, *Monumenta Brasiliae* I, 231.

[140] The mission of Piratininga will be discussed at length in chapter 4 and Nóbrega's own experiences will be briefly touched upon therein.

in which interactions with the Tupí involved neighbourly charity, not slavery.

Thus, Nóbrega wrote proudly that they made their living 'by the labor of our hands, like the Apostle St. Paul', and were careful not to burden the converts. The converts themselves were won through the labour of the ironsmith, Brother Matheus Nogueira, who forged tools for the indigenous villagers in exchange for foodstuffs and handicrafts. The fruits of this barter system were supplemented by alms.[141] Still, despite Nóbrega's idyllic view, these were far from Christianized indigenous villages, but rather 'Jesuit-controlled Indian communities (*aldeias*) situated near white settlements, models of European civilization and Catholicism as well as markets for Indian-produced goods and Jesuit-supervised Indian labour.'[142]

It was not till the governorship of Mem de Sá that Nóbrega's project of instituting the aldeias as model missionary space could come to full fruition, indicating its dependence on Portuguese imperial power. Following the cannibalization of Bishop Sardinha and his brutal retaliatory pacification campaign, the governor authorized a project of Jesuit custodial control over the indigenous at Nóbrega's own suggestion. Accordingly, by the beginning of 1562, some eleven aldeias with a population comprising some 34,000 indigenous peoples had been established.[143] These aldeias, in which Jesuit and Portuguese imperial control coincided, stood in sharp contrast to the interior, the sertões, in which indigenous peoples retained their sovereignty, and from where they were 'descended' to be placed in aldeias.

The importance of Portuguese imperial authority in constituting the aldeias can be seen in a letter penned by Rui Pereira in 1561. He began by acknowledging that all, gentiles and Christians, 'keep the law of the Christians', albeit 'some because they were obliged'.[144] This was due to the exemplary zeal of Mem de Sá, who, in Pereira's

[141] Anchieta, 'Quadrimestre May-September 1554', in Anchieta, *Cartas*, 75. Note that Matheus Nogeuira was the subject of Nóbrega's '*Diálogo sobre a Conversão do Gentio*', discussed in the following chapter.

[142] Alden, *The Making of an Enterprise*, 73.

[143] Marchant, *From Barter to Slavery*, 108.

[144] Letter of Rui Pereira, Bahia, 15 September 1560, *Monumenta Brasiliae* III, 291.

opinion, short of joining the Society of Jesus, could do no more for the business of conversion.[145] Due to his pacification campaign, not only were whites safer but even an Indian could traverse the territories of former enemies by claiming to be 'a friend of the whites' and threatening them with death should he be harmed. Moreover, the governor paid due attention to the Jesuits: Pereira claimed that when an indigenous chief was found guilty of a transgression and begged the governor's mercy, clemency was made conditional upon the forgiveness of the fathers. Within the aldeia, Mem de Sá had created a special office, where an indigenous person in each village was 'in charge of holding in stocks those who do anything to hinder conversion and this [only] when [the Jesuits] tell him. And there is so much fear of these stocks that, after God, they are the [things] which cause them to follow the path and costumes in which we place them.'[146]

The tools of imperial dominion and missionary discipline were cast as entirely legitimate mechanisms of conversion, which made moot the question of choice in conversion. If choice arose, it was only in negative terms: Pereira lamented that the aldeia of São João was now no more, because 'after the departure of the Governor ... all are gone forever, fleeing for the hinterland so secretly that Leonardo do Vale, who was with them, did not sense a thing till they were almost all gone'.[147] Despite Pereira's attempt to soften the blow rhetorically, the point was clear: following the withdrawal of imperial authority, the indigenous peoples had exercised choice, if only with their feet, and conversion had *not* been the outcome.

* * *

The aldeia reflected the striking differences between Nóbrega's conception of the Indies and that of Xavier. Whereas Xavier sought to escape the corruptions of Portuguese officialdom, mired in the politics of the competing sovereigns of south India, Nóbrega cleaved to

[145] Letter of Rui Pereira, Bahia, 15 September 1560, *Monumenta Brasiliae* III, 292.

[146] Letter of Rui Pereira, Bahia, 15 September 1560, *Monumenta Brasiliae* III, 292–3.

[147] Letter of Rui Pereira, Bahía, 15 September 1560, *Monumenta Brasiliae* III, 299.

a very different machinery of imperial power in Brazil. While Xavier came to see the Portuguese casados as a fitting ally in his missionary enterprise, for Nóbrega the settlers came to represent an implacable enemy, who viewed indigenous people only as slave labour and not as potential Christian subjects. As a result, in Brazil, the geography of Jesuit missionary space and Portuguese power would coincide; in the east, however, the Jesuit missions exceeded the boundaries of the Padroado and the underlying temporal domain of the Portuguese Crown. These spatial patterns would persist, with important implications for Jesuit politics in the Portuguese world.

3

THE LIVING BOOKS

For both Xavier and Nóbrega, the rubric of the Indies proved inadequate to comprehend the sociopolitical complexity of the spaces they encountered. The bitter disappointment which drove Xavier to dream of taking himself 'off to India without delay' from the Fishery Coast was an index of the chasm which separated the utopian lands of Prester John from the mundane realities of sixteenth-century south India.[1] The failure of the Portuguese imperial apparatus to conform to his strict standard of evangelical commitment contributed to this disappointment. No less disconcerting was the shattering of the other element of the image of the Indies with which he had departed from Lisbon: that the 'gentiles' to whom he would minister, sheltered from the influence of Judaism or Islam, would be particularly amenable to conversion. His encounter with religious others on the Fishery Coast, particularly the brahmins, would cast doubt both upon his implicit assumption of the cross-cultural transparency of the notion of Christian conversion and the inability of 'pagan' cosmologies to mount effective resistance to his faith. Similarly, despite the radically different missionary terrain Nóbrega encountered in Brazil, his initial belief in the amenability of indigenous peoples to be persuaded by the Christian faith would also come under revision. He too would be forced to confront that, in the moment of encounter, the cultural

[1] Xavier to Francisco Mansilhas, Manapar, 11 September 1544, *Epistolae* I, 235.

opacity of the Catholic notion of conversion invited local interpretations of 'conversion'.

Yet, Xavier and Nóbrega would craft divergent responses to the challenge posed by the thickness of indigenous cosmologies. For Xavier, the encounter with the brahmins would lead him on a lifelong quest across the Indies for more amenable subjects of conversion. The hierarchical ethnological schema that he would come to elaborate would have long-standing implications not only for the structure of the order in the east, but for the missions in the New World too. By contrast, Nóbrega strongly resisted this project of categorizing the gentiles of the world on a civilizational ladder, turning instead to an Augustinian anthropology to assert the universal capacity of all humans, regardless of culture, to receive the Christian message.

This chapter will first demonstrate the challenge posed by indigenous cosmologies to both Xavier and Nóbrega, focusing particularly on their early encounter with indigenous religious specialists. Despite some important similarities in their outlook, including a suspicion of humanism as a vehicle for the Christian message, the two missionaries articulated opposite ethnological projects in response to this challenge.

De Gente Non Sancta, Ab Homine Iniquo Et Doloso Eripe Me

In an important letter written to the society from Cochin in January 1544, Xavier began by recounting his successes amidst the Parava, particularly among the children. While he had succeeded in creating a demand for his ministrations amidst the community, so severe was the shortage of instructors that Xavier was forced to enlist the very children he was instructing.[2] One reason for this shortage of teachers was his inability to convert the religious elite of the realm—the brahmins. He described them as 'the most perverse people in the world', liars who cheated 'the poor, the simple and the ignorant', demanding ritual offerings which were 'nothing but those things which the brahmins feign and desire for the support of their wives and children and homes'.[3] Xavier claimed that the brahmins were willing to admit to him in secret that there is but 'one God' but truculently refused to convert in public.

[2] Xavier to the Society in Rome, Cochin, 15 January, 1544, *Epistolae* I, 165.

[3] Xavier to the Society in Rome, Cochin, 15 January, 1544, *Epistolae* I, 165.

Thus, the proliferation of idols and their worship by brahmins was the crudest hypocrisy. To Xavier, this attitude could only be explained by the manipulations of a corrupt, ignorant but shrewd clergy.[4]

The caricature of the theologically or philosophically ignorant ritual practitioner may have rankled in Hindu estimations too. Indigenous legal injunctions to revere the brahmin, regardless of his learning or his undesirable actions, suggest a widespread recognition of the failings of brahmins.[5] Xavier, labouring amidst the low-caste Paravas, was undoubtedly exposed to their views of brahmins, expressed perhaps more frankly by converts who were no longer bound by the strictures of caste society. Moreover, in his vitriolic characterization, Xavier drew upon the tropes of European anti-clericalism: the brahmins resembled the priests who 'are greedy and avaricious and care more for their own bellies than for the souls entrusted to them', a topos of anticlericalism that had permeated much of late medieval European culture.[6] Xavier drew subtly upon these very tropes in exhorting his colleagues at the university in Paris to come to the aid of his mission, accusing them of being more interested in a commerce in benefices than with the labour of conversion.[7]

Nonetheless, his interactions with the brahmins were profoundly unsettling. The first of these involved the Śaiva Siddhānta brahmins of Tirucendur, the famous Murugan temple of the region and the centre of Parava life before their conversion. A public disputation here would have carried immense weight, in particular with those adults among the Parava community who continued their idolatrous practices.[8] When Xavier demanded that the brahmins explain their path to salvation (*la gloría*), the brahmin representative provided two elements of Hindu orthopraxy: the prohibition upon cow slaughter and the injunction to give alms to brahmins. The offering of orthopraxy in

[4] Xavier to the Society, Cochin, 15 January 1544, *Epistolae* I, 170–1.

[5] Olivelle, *The Law Code of Manu*, 317–19.

[6] Graus, 'The Church and Its Critics', 65–81. See also Benassar, *The Spanish Character*, 97–102.

[7] Xavier to the Society, Cochin, 15 January, 1544, *Epistolae* I, 167.

[8] As Roche puts it, 'The jati shifted its attachment from Subhramanya [Murugan] and Tirucendur to ... Catholicism' (Roche, *Fishermen of the Coromandel*, 49).

response to a demand for orthodoxy is a move that Richard F. Young reads as deliberately provocative, critiquing infamous Portuguese practices of beef-eating and the loss of financial donations to the temple represented by the conversion of the Paravas.[9]

Xavier, moved by the extent to which 'demons rule over our neighbors', rose and, 'in their language', 'in a loud voice', 'pausing at each Commandment', recited the Creed and the laws. After this, Xavier claimed, 'all the brahmins rose and embraced me, saying that truly the God of the Christians is the true God, since his commandments are in conformity with natural reason'. Despite the tourist's perennial belief in the power of loud, slow speech, Xavier's discourse must have been largely incomprehensible to his brahmin interlocutors, even through interpreters. Nonetheless, as Young contends, the affective nature of Xavier's performance was received positively.[10] On Xavier's part, these most 'deceitful' of men were now cast as neighbours, who, confronted with the Christian message, were immediately won over through the use of 'natural reason'. The attribution of natural reason to the brahmins was important in itself, indicating Xavier's appraisal of their capacity to receive Christian knowledge.

Still, Xavier's opinion of the brahmins' capacity for theological speculation was poor: 'The reasons, which must be made with this idiotic people, do not have to be as subtle as those which exist in the writings of very Scholastic professors.'[11] Nonetheless, the brahmins interrogated him to discern his sectarian identity in the complex landscape of indigenous philosophical debates. To their first question, regarding the immortality of the soul, Xavier's response proved satisfactory, since the denial of the soul was the foundation of heresy in Hindu thought.[12] They then asked Xavier where the soul goes after death. Though Xavier had answered this in his earlier discussion of heaven and hell, even if the brahmins had understood him, they may not have been receptive to a cosmology that precluded the Pelagian

[9] Young, 'Francis Xavier', 64, 79.

[10] Young, 'Francis Xavier', 71–2.

[11] Xavier to the Society, Cochin, 15 January 1544, *Epistolae* I, 171–2.

[12] Xavier to the Society, Cochin, 15 January 1544, *Epistolae* I, 171–2. On the question of heresy in Hindu thought, see Doniger, 'The Origins of Heresy in Hindu Mythology'.

heresy of universal salvation and introduced the idea of an eternal hell: Śaiva Siddhāntins, like almost all Hindu sects, believed in universal salvation. The third question, regarding where the soul goes during dreams, Xavier left unanswered in the letter, a query requiring reasons perhaps as 'subtle as those that exist in the writings of very Scholastic professors'. The final question the brahmins asked him was perhaps most perplexing to European ears: they asked if 'God were black or white'. It is unclear if Xavier fully understood its import—an attempt, it seems, to classify the newcomer as a Vaiṣṇava or Śaiva devotee. Xavier, whose image of brahminical religion did not extend to admitting internal differentiation, explained this question as a corollary to the varieties of peoples in the world, a fact of which he was freshly cognizant through his travels in the Indies. Misunderstanding the abstract nature of the question, he offered a folk psychology in which the literally benighted people of this land preferred to imagine god in their own image. This rationalization gave way to frank revulsion at the product of this religious imagination—a most frightful idol, in stench and countenance.

Xavier impressed upon his confreres that he had satisfied his audience in Tirucendur. This may have been true, to the extent that the brahmins had determined that Xavier was not a materialist, the bête noir of Hindu thought. Yet, the conclusion to which Xavier came—that they should convert—was clearly premature to his listeners. Their refusal to convert, based partly on fears of societal disapprobation, Xavier heard in a familiar key of self-serving clerical corruption.

This particular image of the brahmin is developed further in the final encounter—no doubt mediated again by an invisible interpreter—that Xavier recounted in the same letter. He claimed that he had found 'only one brahmin in a village of this coast, who knows anything ... as he had studied in some famous schools'. The brahmin, despite an injunction against revealing the teachings of these schools, told Xavier the secrets he had learnt at these schools 'for the friendship he had with me'.[13]

Although Xavier did not explicitly note this taxonomy, the report of this final meeting completed, almost in ranked order, an ethnography

[13] Xavier to the Society, Cochin, 15 January 1544, *Epistolae* I, 173–4.

of the various kinds of brahmins commonly distinguished: those who officiate as priests for non-brahmins, those who serve as temple priests, and the scholastic brahmins devoted to the study of the *śāstras* (treatise or text on a specific field of knowledge).[14] Unlike the brahmins who had attempted to bribe Xavier so that he would not 'uncover their secrets', this brahmin broke his own oath to admit Xavier into the secrets of the 'famous schools'. Of these secrets, the most important was an admission of what Xavier took to be a commitment to monotheism: the brahmin told Xavier that 'they should never reveal that there is only one God, Creator of the heavens and the earth, he who is in the heavens; and that he should adore this God and not the idols, who are demons'.[15]

In his encounter with this scholar, Xavier confirmed his earlier, inchoate suspicions of the perfidy of the brahmins: not only did they know that there was only 'one god'—distinct from his own creation, much like the Christian God—they were also fully aware that it was only to him that they should direct their devotion. Worse, here was incontrovertible proof that the brahmins conspired, through their training and their oaths, to keep this knowledge from the uninitiated. Aware neither of the esoteric and exoteric structure of Hindu religiosity and society, nor of the particular philosophical school to which this brahmin belonged, Xavier had few resources to interpret the nature of these 'secrets' or their contents.

Still, Xavier and his interlocutor genuinely sought to understand each other's religious frameworks. For Xavier, at least, the brahmin's religious universe appeared remarkably familiar. The language of brahmin universities was 'like the Latin used in ours', in which they also 'preserved their commandments'. (This may have been a reference to the Vedas, of whose textual and ritual status Xavier seemed unaware. While Xavier notes that the brahmin explained these 'commandments' well, the content of Vedic injunctions is not reported to his confreres.) 'Natural law' prevented them from

[14] André Béteille notes that these three categories of brahmins are of unequal rank, with the last considered the highest. Technically, non-brahmins could serve as temple priests, which is not uncommon among the Śaiva Siddhānta. See Béteille, *Caste, Class and Power*, 15.

[15] Xavier to the Society, Cochin, 15 January 1544, *Epistolae* I, 173–4.

having many wives. The brahmin revealed that 'in their writings' it was said that there would come a time when 'all must live under one law', a description of the coming of Kalki that might have puzzled Vaiṣṇava theologians but which would evoke Christian eschatology for Xavier's readers.

Two months or so after writing this letter, Xavier corrected the faulty Tamil of the rudimentary catechisms he had had translated, suggesting that this 'friendship' may have aided him in his missionary work in concrete ways.[16] For his part, it remains unclear what the brahmin gleaned from their relationship. He offered to keep what Xavier taught him of the Christian law secret, to which Xavier responded by insisting that the brahmin should make what he learnt from Xavier public.[17] If Xavier had taken the brahmin's revelation of esoteric knowledge as a sign of friendship, in offering to keep Christian doctrinal knowledge secret, the brahmin made a gesture of reciprocal respect. Uncomfortable with the culture of Nicodemism, Xavier refused to traffic in such secrets.

If, as Schurhammer contends, this brahmin was a follower of Madhva, Xavier's non-esoteric knowledge may not have been automatically excluded from serious consideration.[18] Madhva had a notoriously open-ended view of the sacred corpus, or what he terms *sarvavidyājāta*, in which extra-Vedic local influences, including from competing religious constituencies, can be absorbed into an exegetical reformulation of the corpus predicated upon the exegete's personal charisma. Thus, even though all theist traditions had to reconcile revelation with the narrowly construed Vedic textual tradition, the tradition from which this particular brahmin came had a particularly open-minded attitude towards sources of knowledge.[19] In this light,

[16] Xavier to Francisco Mansilhas, Manapar, 27 March 1544, *Epistolae* I, 196.

[17] Xavier to the Society, Cochin, 15 January 1544, *Epistolae* I, 174.

[18] Given the incompatibility of a monistic philosophy with a Catholic world view, one must wonder if the strongly dualistic reading of the brahmin's philosophy is fully reliable. This caveat aside, the following reading will assume this identification, since it is at least a historically plausible alternative amongst the Vaiṣṇava schools in the region.

[19] This open-mindedness elicited bitter criticism: the sixteenth-century scholar Appayya Dikshitar claimed in the *Madhavatantramukhamardana*

one can understand why the brahmin wrote down the Creed and commandments recited to him by Xavier.[20]

Xavier was satisfied with what he had managed to convey to the brahmin, leaving him optimistic that he might convert in the future:

> He said to me that one night he dreamed with great pleasure and joy that he was to become Christian and to be my companion and accompany me. He asked me to make him a secret Christian ... Since [his conditions] were neither honest nor licit, I refused.[21]

Given the different traditions of the dream in Christian and Hindu thought, perhaps the brahmin was commenting, playfully, upon the nature of their relationship: that, by contemplating and even studying the other, one could become him, (if) only in the realm of the dream.[22] For him, conversion as a public confessional declaration was meaningless if he could accompany Xavier and learn his teachings without 'converting' as such in his waking, socially bound caste life. His conditional request to convert while preserving his status within Hindu society attests to this possibility, while indicating that he considered Xavier a teacher of some interest.

For the Paravas, who had 'to say that they are Christians' according to their agreement with the Portuguese, conversion did not threaten the integrity of their jāti and indeed, cemented it.[23] By contrast, for a sole brahmin to convert publicly would have entailed great social loss, not least because of the close association with the Portuguese

---

[The Slap on the Face of Madhva Tantra] that Madhva transgressed the boundaries of Vedicness in his exegetical choices, particularly through the use of unknown and perhaps even fake *śruti* texts (Mesquita, *Madhva's Unknown Literary Sources*, 32).

[20] Xavier to the Society, Cochin, 15 January 1544, *Epistolae* I, 174.

[21] Xavier to the Society, Cochin, 15 January 1544, *Epistolae* I, 174.

[22] This is precisely the lesson of the story of the hundred Rūdras in the seminal medieval philosophical text *Yoga Vāsiṣṭha*. See *The Concise Yoga Vāsiṣṭha*, 318. For a sustained discussion of the distinction between Western and Hindu notions of the dream, see Doniger, *Dreams, Illusions and Other Realities*.

[23] Roche, *Fishermen of the Coromandel*, 44.

and the Paravas it would have necessarily foisted upon him.[24] As a *dvaita-vādin* (dualist), this brahmin would have followed a theology that preserved the importance of caste in spiritual as well as social life.[25] Thus, conversion in Xavier's terms, as a public declaration of allegiance to a religion that did not attend to the linkage between social and spiritual paths, would have been a particularly troubling proposition.

To Xavier, the dream indicated the changes he had begun to effect in his friend's heart and thus, the brahmin's conditional request to convert was doubly frustrating, an epistrophe halted, even subverted. The idea of a secret conversion could only compare to the most timid Nicodemism of post-Reformation Europe.[26] Yet, what the brahmin meant by secrecy—the ability to inhabit a certain set of behavioral codes, while maintaining theological commitments that are logically independent of them—would not have been dissemblance in indigenous terms.[27]

The encounter ends at the same fundamental impasse he found at Tirucendur—Xavier requested the brahmin to teach the people the truth regarding the existence of 'one god', and again the brahmin demurred. Perhaps, Xavier really had no sense of the deep theological difficulties involved in the notion of a single god. Certainly, it is not clear that he was aware that for the two schools

[24] Xavier turned his sole brahmin convert to instructing Parava children in the faith (Xavier to the Society, Cochin, 15 January 1544, *Epistolae* I, 171). On pollution by association with the Portuguese, see Bayly, *Saints, Goddesses and Kings*, 388–9.

[25] On the ways in which Madhva innovatively maintained a socially hierarchical theology while admitting a certain degree of flexibility in appealing to other religious constituencies in his time, see Stoker, 'Conceiving the Canon in Dvaita Vedānta'.

[26] On the prevalent anxiety in post-Reformation Europe regarding the emergent culture of dissemblance, as men professed to different confessions from those their hearts followed, see Zagorin, *Ways of Lying* and Snyder, *Dissimulation*.

[27] On the issue of how brahmins can maintain orthopraxic behaviour while departing from the doctrinal and normative framework of orthodox brahminical tradition, see Sanderson, 'Purity and Power among the Brāhmans of Kashmir'.

of brahmins he had met, this proposition would not be interpreted equivalently. For the Śaiva Siddhāntins of Tirucendur, god (*pati*, literally lord), soul (*paśu*, literally domestic animal), and worldly bonds (*pāśa*) exist logically distinctly, although this does not imply strict difference between them. The entire system thus subtends from the relationship of differences between these three ultimate categories, thus existing outside the framework of a strictly dualist philosophy. By contrast, the dvāita-vādin scholastic brahmin would consider himself a witness (*sākṣin*) to his own being, separate from both god and world, despite his dependence upon the former. At the level of worship, though both sects admitted the worship of god as personality, they identified him differently and mutually exclusively, as Śiva and as Viṣṇu respectively. Thus, the understanding of god, let alone the question of his personality or forms, differed even among the brahmins of Xavier's acquaintance.[28]

These troubling encounters shook Xavier's belief in the transparency of the Christian message and its invitation to conversion. In this light, Xavier's repeated insistence on the notion of 'one god' throughout the report is significant, in that it explicitly evaded the difficulties of the concept of the Trinity. It is worth remembering here the short catechism that Xavier composed upon arriving in Goa, translated soon after into Tamil, and which undoubtedly formed the basis of his instructions to the brahmin.[29] Among the changes that Xavier made in adapting João de Barros's original version was the addition of several short sections that repudiated idolatry, prompted by his troubling encounters in southern India.[30]

> And you, my God, made me in your likeness, and not the *pagodes*, which are the gods of the pagans in the form of animals and beasts of the devil ... O pagans, how great is your blindness to sin that you make god out of

[28] On the Śaiva Siddhānta, see Sivaraman, *Śaivism in Philosophical Perspective.* On the Dvāita view, see Siauve, *Le Doctrine de Madhva.*

[29] There are echoes of the language of the catechism in Xavier's report on the brahmins, including the repeated reference to 'God, Creator of the heavens and earth', an epithet he does not generally use.

[30] Xavier, 'Doctrina Christiana', May 1542, *Epistolae*, 106–16. Schurhammer provides Barros's text for easy comparison.

beasts and demons, since you adore [the Devil] in his forms. O Christians, let us give thanks and praise to God, three and one.[31]

One may speculate that what must have appeared a self-evident dichotomy between God as Trinity, and the Devil and his attendant forms when Xavier first composed the catechism, did not remain so in light of his encounter with the brahmins. Perhaps, Xavier gleaned enough from his conversations with the brahmins to realize the difficulty of distinguishing the Christian Trinity from the indigenous distinction between a single God and his forms.[32] Moreover, Hindu mythological, but not necessarily theological, frameworks may also have been more open to the notion that God and Jesus stood simultaneously in a relationship of equivalence and filial kinship, given Purāṇic traditions where divine fathers could also be the sons of their own progeny. Precisely because the concept of the Trinity may have seemed less alien in this theological landscape than elsewhere in the Indies, the need to focus on philosophical difference was imperative.[33]

Xavier thus presented his encounter with the brahmins in the baldest of terms, as one between the straightforwardly monotheistic and the deceitfully polytheistic. Thus, even the brahmin who most closely approached the horizon of friendship, if not Christian fellowship, was ultimately reduced in Xavier's report to the familiar topoi of Christian notions of idolatry: a combination of priestly conspiracy and genuine devil worship.[34]

These musings regarding the extent to which Xavier understood the theological content of his conversations with brahmins are

[31] Xavier, 'Doctrina Christiana', May 1542, *Epistolae*, 114–15. The term *pagode* here properly refers to 'idol' and not 'temple' as the Portuguese were wont to use it.

[32] It may have been this experience of explaining the creed to this brahmin and the confusions the exchange highlighted which led Xavier to compose his extended explanation of the creed in Ternate during August–September 1546. See *Epistolae* I, 355–69.

[33] For an instructive comparison on the obstacles presented to missionary work by the concept of the Trinity in two radically different contexts, see Tavárez, 'Naming the Trinity' and Alam and Subrahmanyam, 'Frank Disputations', 483–5.

[34] Pau-Rubíes, 'Theology, Ethnography and the Historicization of Idolatry'.

necessarily speculative. Still, incontrovertibly, the brahmins deeply disturbed Xavier. This was partly due to his failure among them: his attempts to enlist these traditional religious teachers to his cause, to teach Christian doctrine to Parava converts, had found only one instance of success.[35] The rest, despite his efforts to convert them and his exhortations for them to teach the truth of one god, remained unmoved.

The troubling effect that this encounter had upon Xavier may be gauged through the biblical provenance of the epithet he chose for the brahmins: 'From the unholy nation, from the iniquitous man and the deceitful, rescue me.' The brahmin stood as the single greatest obstacle to conversion. As Xavier himself put it, 'If there were no brahmins, all the pagans would convert to our faith.'[36] For the first time, Xavier was forced to contend with the thickness of 'pagan' beliefs and of the challenges that it could present to Christian conversion, even without the interference of Islam. The brahmin and all he stood for could not be dismissed out of hand: he possessed natural reason, believed in the precepts of natural law and was even capable of extending the hand of friendship. Xavier's original assumption—that the gentiles of the Indies would readily convert if the Moors were kept away by Portuguese imperial force—was no longer tenable. In his person, the brahmin combined the worst religious villainies—the truculent hostility of the Moor, the corruptions of the Christian clergyman, the hypocrisy of the Nicodemite or Judaizer, and the idolatry or the 'pagan'.

The Opacity of Conversion

The brahmins of India, with their idols and temples and religious texts, seemed far removed from the peoples of Brazil: in his earliest reports, Nóbrega insisted that they worshipped nothing, including God, except the thunder, which they called Tupana and which was a way to refer to something divine in their tongue.[37] This impoverished

[35] Xavier to the Society, Cochin, 15 January 1544, *Epistolae* I, 171.

[36] Xavier to the Society, Cochin, 15 January 1544, *Epistolae* I, 171.

[37] Nóbrega, 'Informação das Terras do Brasil', August 1549, *Cartas do Brasil*, 62.

religious vocabulary meant that the Jesuits resorted to referring to the Christian God as Father Tupana. Nonetheless, if Nóbrega's understanding of Brazil had been framed by classical geography and anthropology, it was also conditioned by tropes that his forbears had developed in the other Indies. Borrowing terminology developed in the descriptions of early Portuguese explorers of India, such as Duarte Barbosa, Nóbrega described the various castes (*castas*) of gentiles (*gentios*) of Brazil. Further, in identifying and focusing upon a class of indigenous ritual practitioners who were 'the greatest opponents' of the Jesuits, Nóbrega was following a precedent set by Xavier himself.

Nóbrega described how the 'sorcerers' (*feiticeiros*) came intermittently from distant lands, 'pretending to bring *santidade* (holiness)'.[38] This was a reference to the stranger–prophet or karaíba, who was received with great festivities. In honour of his coming, the women engaged in a form of public penance, confessing the faults they had committed against their husbands and begging for forgiveness. Nóbrega then described how the 'sorcerer' would enter a dark house and place 'a gourd, which he brings, in human form'. Changing his voice into that of a child, he would speak through the gourd, telling the villagers not to work or go to the fields, for food would grow by itself. Instead, they should return home, since their digging sticks and hunting arrows would find their marks for their masters. He extolled them to kill and capture their enemies for food, promising them longevity, and, to the old women, a return to youth. When he finished speaking, the villagers would start to tremble, especially the women, lying on the ground and foaming at the mouth, a rite that Nóbrega saw as demonic possession. The 'sorcerers' convinced their followers that evil would befall those who did not enter the santidade. Further, these 'sorcerers' were consulted during wars.[39]

Though Nóbrega insisted to Dr Navarro that these wars were fought not out of greed but in cycles of hatred and vengeance, from the 'Informação' it was apparent that the warfare played some part

[38] Nóbrega, 'Informação das Terras do Brasil', August 1549, *Cartas do Brasil*, 63.

[39] Nóbrega, 'Informação das Terras do Brasil', August 1549, *Cartas do Brasil*, 64.

in the ritual cycle and cosmology of the Tupí.[40] Given that he had also admitted privately to Navarro that one of the two greatest challenges to conversion faced in Brazil was warfare, and its associated anthropophagy, the role of the sorcerers in this process indicated their importance as religious rivals.[41]

The 'sorcerers' were also healers. Nóbrega described how, as 'the greatest opponents of the Jesuits', they would convince the sick that the Jesuits placed knives, scissors, and other things in their bodies, causing their illnesses and killing them.[42] Though he did not include it in the 'Informação', as he wrote to Doctor Navarro, such charges were deeply damaging: 'Only one thing frightens us, that almost all those we baptize fall ill ... and their sorcerers have occasion to say that we, with the water with which we baptize them, give them illness and, with the creed, death.'[43] In omitting this from the public 'Informação', Nóbrega betrayed how troubling this accusation was to the mission in the context of the devastating epidemics ravaging indigenous populations.

The need to defeat indigenous shamans was thus acutely apparent to Nóbrega. In an inversion of Matthew's account of the cleansing of the temple of Jerusalem, in which the priests had questioned the basis of Jesus's authority, Nóbrega once asked a famous shaman, 'the greatest of this land', by whose authority he acted. The very framing of the question implied that he viewed the shaman as a priest, who derived his authority from supernatural forces, either divine or demonic. The shaman instead neatly sidestepped Nóbrega's question:

> He responded to me with little shame that he was god and had been born god and presented to me there one to whom he had said to have given

[40] Nóbrega, 'Informação das Terras do Brasil', August 1549, *Cartas do Brasil*, 64. Compare Nóbrega to Dr Martín Azpilcueta Navarro, Salvador, 10 August 1549, *Cartas do Brasil*, 48–9.

[41] Nóbrega, 'Informação das Terras do Brasil', August 1549, *Cartas do Brasil*, 64.

[42] Nóbrega, 'Informação das Terras do Brasil', August 1549, *Cartas do Brasil*, 64.

[43] Nóbrega to Dr Martín Azpilcueta Navaro, Salvador, 10 August 1549, *Cartas do Brasil*, 55.

health, and that the God of the Heavens was his friend, and appeared to him in the clouds and thunder, and in lightning, and in many other things.

The significance of the shaman's claims may be best understood in light of the nature of Amerindian perspectivalism.[44] Beings in the world—human, animal, spirit—see themselves as persons and view other beings from this perspective. Thus, a jaguar would view itself in anthropomorphic terms, such that its own traits and habits would constitute culture: blood to a jaguar would be the manioc beer so central to Amerindian social and religious life; its fur and claws would be bodily decorations; and its interaction with other jaguars would be organized along the lines of 'human' institutions of kinship, ritual ceremonies, chieftainship, and so on. By analogy, the jaguar would consider humans, as prey, to be animals. In such a view, the body proper to each type of being is a 'clothing' that conceals a person, that is, a 'human' form with a subjectivity formally identical to human consciousness. This form can be recognized as such by members of that particular species or by shamans who can transcend the limits of species-being and adopt the perspectives of other types of beings. In this sense, the shaman was indeed a god, in that he was able to adopt the perspective of a (godly) spirit; from this ontological ground, he conversed with other gods on 'human' terms, as friends he met in the sky, in thunder or in lightning.

The shaman's claim to be a god and to have conversed in the sky with the gods was a direct response to Nóbrega's question regarding the basis of his claim to authority. In indigenous terms, he asserted his direct, experiential access to cosmological knowledge, that is, his unique ability to inhabit the perspectives of the gods, without mediation.[45] The ability to claim this privileged viewpoint, marked linguistically in the Tupí distinction between the narration of events personally experienced by the speaker and those heard from others, was precisely the source of the shaman's authority.[46]

[44] Viveiros de Castro, 'Exchanging Perspectives'.

[45] Viveiros de Castro, *Araweté*, 564–71. See also Viveiros de Castro, *A inconstância da alma selvagem*, 215.

[46] This linguistic feature is common in Amerindian cultures (Viveiros de Castro, *A inconstância da alma selvagem*, 215).

Nóbrega, coming from a tradition of Christian revelation in which belief was predicated upon the unseen, heard this as gross blasphemy. Like Xavier before the priests of Tirucendur, 'in a raised voice and with signs of great sentiment', Nóbrega contradicted the shaman at length—through an interpreter. The shaman, in turn, 'became confused' and in the gathered audience, Nóbrega saw that 'some youths and women were astounded' at his performance. His greatest affirmation came afterwards, however, when the shaman himself asked to be baptized and became a catechumen.[47]

Nóbrega missed, however, the key significance of the mediated nature of his own performance. To those listening to the interpreter reporting what he had heard from Nóbrega about the Christian God, it was possible that the Jesuit appeared, like a shaman, to have direct knowledge of that god. The astonishment of some listeners, who may have contemplated revising what they knew of the cosmos according to this new foreign shaman, would have contributed to the indigenous shaman's own subsequent 'conversion'.

From this privately reported and dimly understood fragment, Nóbrega seemed to perceive that the shaman's relationship to divinity was not that of a priest to a worshipped entity. Still, his representation of the shamans in the 'Informação'—who were decidedly not gods, a blasphemous proposition—cast them in the familiar trope of 'pagan' priests. They used deception and demonic sorcery in equal measure, and were the counterpart and foils of the Jesuits.

Still, Nóbrega would not impute idolatry to the Amerindians. He held instead that they did not worship (*adorar*) anything, unlike the gentiles of India who were defined by their idolatry.[48] He refused to label the gourd used in santidade as an idol, despite noting its humanoid form. Thus, not only did Nóbrega refuse to use idolatry as a generic term for all manner of gentile ritual and belief; he also perceived that the *relationship* between the shaman and the gourd in the rite of santidade was not one of worship. Nóbrega's insistence that the central if not the sole rite involved possession underlined that

[47] Nóbrega to Dr Martín Azpilcueta Navarro, Salvador, 10 August 1549, *Cartas do Brasil,* 56.

[48] Nóbrega, 'Informação das Terras do Brasil', August 1549, *Cartas do Brasil,* 62.

indigenous cosmologies in Brazil, unlike India, were not marked by the worship of false gods or inert objects.

Still, as Nóbrega approvingly reported, the Tupí would huddle around the fire at night in fear of demons, a reference perhaps to the Tupí fear of the inimical spirits of the dead. They showed an imaginative capacity for religion in their relationship to thunder. While the vocabulary available to express 'the things of God' was impoverished, Nóbrega made clear in his discussion of Tupana that there was some indigenous concept of the supernatural and the divine.[49]

That this conception was very different from the Christian one was apparent to Nóbrega, not least because of the seeming centrality of the body: Tupí rituals appeared to focus on the body, whether during the possession of santidade, or in the carefully orchestrated series of anthropophagic rituals that involved sating, cleaning, cutting, and cooking the imprisoner warrior's body.

The indigenous concern with the relationship of the body to divinity may have been particularly troubling to Nóbrega, given the fraught nature of this question within the Christian fold itself. The ontological status of Christ as both fully human and divine, and the place of his body in what Fenella Cannell describes as the 'highly unstable syntheses which Christian orthodoxies themselves represent', has generated theological diversity, if not controversy, throughout Christian history.[50] Indeed, Luther had rejected the scholastic formula of the soul as the substantial form of the human body, eventually leading to his challenge of the Catholic notion of transubstantiation.[51]

Nóbrega's suspicion of the emphasis on the body led him to dismiss indigenous attempts at eliciting the nature of the Christian God. The Tupí would often ask 'if God had a head, and a body, and a woman, and if he ate, and in what he was clothed, and other such things'. Nóbrega cited these questions as a sign that the Tupí were 'very attached to sensual things', denying these questions the legitimacy of theological

[49] There is a long historiographical tradition on the imputation of 'religion' to the Tupi by early European observers, perhaps best exemplified by the first chapter of Hélène Clastres's landmark work on Tupí-Guaraní millenarianism (Clastres, *The Land without Evil*).

[50] Cannell, 'The Christianity of Anthropology', 352.

[51] Luther, *A Prelude to the Babylonian Captivity*, 2:26–2:27.

debate.[52] Yet, in light of Amerindian perspectivalism, they appear to be an attempt to test Nóbrega's own authority: if he could 'see' God as a human, 'wearing' a human body and enmeshed in 'human' social relationships such as marriage, Nóbrega was indeed a shaman, capable of transcending the perspective proper to his human body. As a shaman, his cosmological knowledge would then have been credible, allowing them to acquiesce, in distinctly indigenous terms, to 'conversion'. These questions regarding the ability of the Jesuit shaman to 'see' God on common ontological ground were thus fundamental to the Tupí process of conversion to Christianity. They were not, as Nóbrega thought, the seemingly inane queries of sensuous beings unable to imagine an unseen god.

In adopting practices of the shamans, such as the musical processions used to enter the sertão, Nóbrega's mission implicitly depended on the authority commanded by these figures in indigenous society. Yet, he failed to perceive the centrality of the Jesuit as a shaman in the Tupí reception of Christian knowledge: the credibility of cosmological knowledge depended upon the authority of its speaker. As Eduardo Viveiros de Castro has shown, the Tupí proved perfectly willing to abandon the Jesuit shamans and their teachings, an inconstancy that puzzled and obsessed their European observers, who attributed it to an essential defect of their character.[53] The Tupí readiness to mimic the practices of the Jesuits, to 'become like them', and to follow their ritual prescriptions and modes of knowledge had raised hopes of their susceptibility to conversion. What 'conversion' meant to the Tupí, however, was vastly different from the Catholic understanding of it as a process of profound, possibly irrevocable confessional change. For the Tupí, it was instead a contingent acceptance of an alternative source of cosmological knowledge.

If Xavier encountered the cross-cultural opacity of the Christian notion of conversion through failure in India, Nóbrega confronted it through apparent success in Brazil. The brahmin willingness to entertain Christian precepts had raised false hopes in Xavier, much as the Tupí readiness to mimic was cause for similar optimism in

[52] Nóbrega, 'Informação das Terras do Brasil,' August 1549, *Cartas do Brasil*, 66.

[53] Vivieros de Castro, *A inconstância da alma selvagem*, 181–264.

Nóbrega. Yet, Xavier's incomprehension of the brahminical possibility of adopting new theological commitments while maintaining orthopraxic behaviours that were independent of them would lead him to see brahmins as implacable enemies of the Christian faith. Similarly, Nóbrega failed to see the importance of the shaman in authorizing cosmological knowledge among the Tupí. In both cases, a particularly European notion of conversion, which they took to be universally accessible and obvious, hampered their ability to understand their interlocutors.

Os Vivos Livros

Following Xavier's disappointments in India, the Spice Islands seemed to promise a people more amenable to conversion: 'They have neither houses of idols, nor people to move them to idolatry. They adore the sun when they see it, and there is no more idolatry amongst them.'[54] After the troubling experience with brahmins, an animist people without an indigenous clergy to contend with must have seemed particularly attractive. In his public *carta particular* (public letters) he extolled the great prospects of the islands, where the pagans outnumbered the Moors and where the Moors themselves would be easily converted due to their great ignorance.

Privately, however, Xavier wrote of an infernal, apocalyptic landscape.[55] The islanders, Xavier wrote, were extremely barbarous and treacherous, indulged in cannibalism of enemy warriors and other 'abominable sins' of the flesh. The people were deeply ignorant, largely illiterate, with writing being purely an artifact of the Arab presence. Each of the islands had its own language, a living example of the confusion of Babel. So disturbing was this experience that afterwards Xavier remained constantly watchful for the devil, the language of hell and diabolism permeating his later letters.[56] Again, his failures were

[54] Xavier to Society, Malacca, 10 November 1545, *Epistolae* I, 298–301.

[55] Xavier to the Society, Amboina, 10 May 1546, *Epistolae* I, 328–9. In part, the volcanic, earthquake-prone nature of the islands contributed to this impression.

[56] See, for example, Xavier's extended meditation on the work of the devil and hope (Xavier to the Companions in Goa, Kagoshima, 5 November 1549, *Epistolae* I:I, 181–4.

confined to private messages, while his publicly circulated letters continued to paint the Indies as a land of religious promise.

Xavier once again sought more propitious subjects for conversion, this time in the unknown land of Japan, of which he had heard from the convert Anjiro. This time, his optimism was not baseless: the Japanese occupied the apex of the ethnology he had begun to elaborate after leaving India, as they were 'the best that has until now been discovered'.[57] The society adhered to a system of honour and nobility that transcended Iberian aristocratic conventions, tainted as they were with hierarchies based on wealth.[58] Xavier found amidst the Japanese good evidence of natural law and reason, and, conveniently, a single language that was not difficult to understand.[59] Further, the political circumstances were propitious: the captain of Malacca aided Xavier's voyage, in returning for acting as a commercial ambassador and informant on behalf of the Portuguese in Japan, and Xavier quickly found sympathetic allies among the territorial lords of Japan.[60]

Nonetheless, in Japan, unlike in the Spice Islands, Xavier had to contend with an indigenous clergy, the Buddhist monks. In describing these bonzes, as with the brahmins, Xavier resorted to familiar anti-clerical tropes: they were, he said, busily employed in finding means to part the laity from its wealth, and engaging in sodomy and illicit intercourse with nuns, resulting in many casual abortions.[61] As with the brahmins, his report was riddled with tensions. Despite their licentiousness, he also mentioned that they were respected precisely

[57] Xavier to the Companions in Goa, Kagoshima, 5 November 1549, *Epistolae* I:I, 186.

[58] Xavier to the Companions in Goa, Kagoshima, 5 November 1549, *Epistolae* I:I, 186.

[59] Xavier to the Companions in Goa, Kagoshima, 5 November 1549, *Epistolae* I:I, 187–8, Xavier to the Society, Cohin, 29 January 1552, *Epistolae* I:I, 254.

[60] Xavier to Dom Pedro da Silva, Kagoshima, 5 November 1549, 229–30; Xavier to the Companions in Goa, Kagoshima, 5 November 1549, *Epistolae* I:I, 210–11.

[61] Xavier to Ignatius, Cochin, 29 January 1522, *Epistolae* I:I, 288; Xavier to the Companions in Goa, Kagoshima, 5 November 1549, *Epistolae* I:I, 204; Xavier to the Society, Cochin, 20 January 1552, *Epistolae* I:I, 267–8.

for their continence, both in their abstemious eating and in matters of sex.[62] The bonzes, like the brahmins, were implacably hostile to the Christians, planning their verbal and even physical persecution.[63] Their hostility, as with the brahmins, was roused because Xavier disclosed their secrets.[64]

Unlike the brahmins, Xavier saw the bonzes as worthy intellectual opponents: he asked the society repeatedly for those skilled in rhetoric [*artes*] and philosophy to be sent to Japan so they could defeat the bonzes in disputation.[65] Here too, Xavier made the close acquaintance of one learned monk. Though he remained unable to decide upon the immortality of the soul, in keeping with the central Buddhist tenet regarding no-self, Xavier counted this monk as a good friend.[66] His failure to convert his Japanese friend did not arouse the same anger in Xavier as it did with the brahmin in India.

For all their virtues, the Japanese were still marked by one crucial defect: the people were extremely bellicose and constantly at war, despite having an emperor.[67] This situation was dangerous for the missionaries. Xavier described in detail a battle instigated by the 'demon' in Yamaguchi, the land of the territorial lord of the Ōuchi clan, whose hospitality Cosme de Torres and Juan Fernández had been enjoying at that moment. The defeat of this particular lord did not change the political equation as far as the Christians were concerned, as a new lord was found from the Ōtomo clan based in Bungo, which was friendly to the Portuguese and where Xavier had been working when the revolt broke out.[68] Still, it was clear that the constant warfare made any political allies at best temporary security for the missionaries and

[62] Xavier to the Companions in Goa, Kagoshima, 5 November 1549, *Epistolae* I:I, 203–4.

[63] Xavier to the Companions in Goa, Kagoshima, 5 November 1549, *Epistolae* I:I, 204.

[64] Xavier to the Society, Cochin, 20 January 1552, *Epistolae* I:I, 267.

[65] See, for example, Xavier to Simão Rodrigues, Cochin, 30 January 1552, *Epistolae* I:I, 298.

[66] Xavier to the Companions in Goa, Kagoshima, 5 November 1549, *Epistolae* I, 188–91.

[67] Xavier to the Society, Cochin, 29 January 1552, *Epistolae* I:I, 254–5.

[68] Xavier to the Society, Cochin, 29 January 1552, *Epistolae* I:I, 272.

their new converts. Xavier also harboured doubts about the political strength of the lords with respect to the religious establishment: the lord at Kagoshima, their first port of call and the site of their first success in Japan, was eventually convinced by the Buddhist monks that allowing Christians in his land would threaten the stability of his polity. Subsequently, conversion to Christianity was banned under pain of death in the realm.[69]

Xavier now justified his next major project: to establish a mission in China. It was, like Japan, a land of 'white people', full of riches and a people endowed with acuity, skill, and intelligence, greatly devoted to the scholarly life. Xavier noted that the religious and scholarly culture of Japan had come originally from China, although he could not complete this historical arc and identify the birthplace of the Buddha with the India he had since abandoned. Most importantly, China was a very peaceful land of uncompromising justice, with only one king who commanded genuine obedience.[70] The favourable contrast with Japan was obvious: China had all of Japan's virtues, being in large part historically responsible for its culture, as well as the added advantage of a stable political structure. It was in pursuit of the mission to this land that Xavier would finally end his days.

Xavier's initial disappointment with the peoples of India, after he had to contend with the resilience and complexity of their cosmologies, had led him to seek ever more suitable subjects of conversion across Asia. In doing so, he evolved a hierarchical ethnology, in which the more closely the indigenous culture resembled European modes of civility—literacy, a form of state sovereignty concentrated in a single person, a hierarchically ordered society—the greater their capacity for conversion.

Xavier's ethnographic attentiveness was also part of a strategy of protecting his own soul. Ultimately, Xavier's programme was a conservative one, based on saving the massa damnata through the baptism of infants, the care of established Christians, and, only lastly, after all the disappointments of his career, the attempt to convert

[69] Xavier to the Society, Cochin, 29 January 1552, *Epistolae* I:I, 258–9.

[70] Xavier to the Society, Cochin, 29 January 1552, *Epistolae* I:I, 277; Xavier to Ignatius, Cochin, 29 January 1552, *Epistolae* I:I, 291.

pagans.[71] As Xavier repeatedly emphasized, the care of one's own soul was indispensable if one were to help one's neighbour. The Indies provided both the opportunity for this endeavour, and the most terrible hindrances to prevent it.[72]

Thus, his instruction to Gaspar Barzaeus, which Xavier circulated to other missions in the Indies, began with an injunction to care for one's own soul. Xavier recommended conversing with everyone as if they may become an enemy and to keep abreast of all that happened in the missionary's location. Further, he warned the missionary to 'speak as little as possible from the authorities in your sermons'. Instead, to produce fruit in oneself and one's neighbours, it was necessary to 'converse with sinners'. These were 'the living books' that must be studied. While Xavier did not proscribe 'written books', he recommended them only 'to find authorities to authorize through Scripture those remedies against the vices and sins that you read in the living books'.[73]

The primacy Xavier gave to his nascent ethnology was thus vital and theological—upon it, in the Indies, depended the salvation of both one's own soul and that of the neighbour. It was a knowledge gleaned through intercourse, through conversations and disputations, rather than passive observation or academic study. The former magister—who wrote disparagingly of the scholars he had left behind for being unequal to the physical and spiritual dangers of the Indies—had found a new branch of knowledge with which to understand and transform this environment:[74]

[71] See, for example, Xavier to Francisco Mansilhas, Negapatam, 7 April 1545, *Epistolae* I, 284–8; Francis Xavier, Instruction for the Society on the Fishery Coast and Travancore, Manapar, February 1548, *Epistolae* I, 426–35; Francis Xavier, Instruction to Gaspar Barzaeus upon His Departure for Ormuz, Goa, April 1549, *Epistolae* I:I, 86–101.

[72] The need to attend to one's own soul first before turning to the conversion of pagans is first expressed in Xavier to Simão Rodrigues, Cochin, 20 January 1548, 419. See also the previous note.

[73] Francis Xavier, Instruction to Gaspar Barzaeus upon his departure for Ormuz, Goa, April 1549, *Epistolae* I:I, 99.

[74] For one example of the many exhortations and doubts Xavier expressed about his former colleagues at the University in Paris, see Xavier to the Society, Malacca, 22 June 1549, *Epistolae* I:I, 150.

> This is the principal study that helps to advance souls. This is to read [them] as books which teach things that you cannot find in dead written books, nor will they help you as much in fructifying souls as it would help you to know well these things through living men who walk in the same tract, for always I have done well with this rule.

As Xavier wrote to Ignatius after returning from Japan, it was through the knowledge of others that he had come to truly know himself, 'for, being outside of myself, I did not know how many evils existed within me, until I saw myself amidst the labors and dangers of Japan'.[75] In this classic moment of estrangement, of being outside of oneself and then seeing oneself through and amidst an alien culture, one may detect perhaps another prehistory of the ethnographic stance, its peculiar self-consciousness.

This was knowledge that Xavier directly opposed to the humanism embraced by the new generation of Jesuits arriving in India who increasingly departed from his own experience and methods.[76] Though university-educated humanists were superior linguists and useful against sophisticated indigenous priests like the bonzes, for Xavier, erudition was not an essential qualification of the missionary. Rather, he emphasized the need for an attentiveness to others, based not on antiquarian tradition but on experience and on a Catholic understanding, derived from Augustine, of mutual knowledge and salvation of oneself and one's neighbour.[77] Xavier valued the simple zeal of a humble Barzaeus more than the erudition of a Jesuit such as António Gomes, who purged all the indigenous students from the college of Goa, transforming it from a tool of conversion to an Asian outpost of the University of Coimbra.

[75] Xavier to Ignatius, Cochin, 29 January 1552, *Epistolae* I:I, 287.

[76] Examples include Antonio Gomes, whom Xavier dismissed for expelling all indigenous students from the College of Goa, and Nicolò Lancilotto, who arrived at the College to teach a syllabus that included Erasmus. See Nicolò Lancilotto to Ignatius, Goa, 5 November 1546, *Documenta Indica* I, 136.

[77] On the evolution of anthropology from the antiquarian strain of the humanist movement, see Momigliano, *The Classical Foundations of Modern Historiography*, especially chapters 2 and 3; Momigliano, 'The Place of Herodotus', 1–13.

The City of God in the *Sertão*

Nóbrega shared Xavier's predispositions towards humanism, as can be seen in the *Diálogo sobre a conversão do Gentio* [Dialogue on the Conversion of the Gentile]. The text, written in Bahia in 1556–7 after his return from a three-year stay in the south, marked a sharp departure from the epistolary genre to which he confined himself in writing from Brazil.[78] Like the 'Informação', the shift in genre signalled a distillation of his views and demarcated the importance of the *Diálogo* compared to the quotidian letters he sent to the society. The *Diálogo* dramatized the debates swirling amongst the missionaries in Brazil for a distant audience, while clarifying Nóbrega's stance.

The protagonists were based on two missionaries of Nóbrega's acquaintance. This first was Gonçalo Alvarez, a lay brother who, through marriage and long years in Brazil, had acquired a great command of the local language and preached to the Amerindians in service of the Jesuits.[79] His interlocutor was Matheus Nogueira, the blacksmith who had fought against indigenous groups in Espírito Santo and was admitted to the society by Leonardo Nunes. The protagonists were thus representatives of the rank and file of Brazil's missionaries.

The dialogue begins with seeming accord between the two interlocutors: Alvarez, complained of the useless labour of attempting to convert people who were 'so bestial, that nothing of God enters their heart', 'so inflamed with killing and eating each other' that 'to preach to them is to preach in the desert to stones'. Nogueira concurred, pointing wistfully to their lack of a notion of sovereign kingship and of worship as obstacles to their conversion.[80] Like Xavier, Nóbrega had come to believe in the need for the proper subjection of the indigenous to a recognizable, if not European, form of sovereignty.

As the choice of protagonists suggests, however, the *Diálogo* was less concerned with the question of the nature of the Amerindians

[78] Cohen, *The Fire of Tongues*, 26–7.

[79] On interpreters like Alvarez, see Maria Cândida D.M. Barros, 'The Office of *Lingua*'.

[80] Nóbrega, 'Diálogo', 219–20.

than the means of their conversion.[81] These means could range from preaching, through the help of gifted linguists like Alvarez, to the trade in iron objects, which required the skill of artisans like Nogueira.[82] Despite the difference in the nature of their activities, Nóbrega sought to establish parallels between the preacher and blacksmith, who not only shared his initials with the author but was his mouthpiece in the dialogue.[83]

The *Diálogo* begins on a pessimistic note, showing the apparent uselessness of missionary labour among the Amerindians in light of their inconstancy.[84] Alvarez echoed the theme of inconstancy raised by Nogueira: if the conversion of the Amerindians could be done and undone by the fish hooks of blacksmiths, they were equally inconstant and hypocritical with regard to the words of the preachers.[85] In his harangue, Alvarez repeatedly drew upon imagery of John the Baptist: from the very first lines comparing his mission to preaching to stones in the desert, Alvarez seemed to give voice to those priests who saw themselves preaching, like the prophet, in a moral and political wilderness. It was thus fitting that he should repeat the dashed hopes of those priests who saw the mission to the Amerindians as involving little more than mass baptism by an austral River Jordan. As Alvarez' epithet for the Amerindians as sons of vipers suggested, these priests were suspicious of the capacity of the inconstant indigenous inhabitants of Brazil to receive baptism: John the Baptist originally used the epithet for the Pharisees and Sadducees, hypocrites and experimenters in matters of religion.

In the face of such doubt of the value of the mission to the Amerindians, Nogueira asked, what was the meaning of their work?[86]

[81] Cohen reads the *Diálogo* as 'a long memorandum to Nóbrega's fellow Jesuits', while Sturm reads it as part of the contemporaneous European debate on the intellectual and spiritual potential of Amerindians (Sturm, ''Estes Têm Alma como Nós?' 72–82).

[82] The echo of Caminha's observations regarding the relative attractions of iron and faith for the Tupí are apparent.

[83] Nóbrega, 'Diálogo', 219.

[84] Nóbrega, 'Diálogo', 221.

[85] Nóbrega, 'Diálogo', 223.

[86] Nóbrega, 'Diálogo', 225.

Alvarez's response centred on the missionary self, comparing his fruitless labour to the sacrifice of the holocaust under the Old Law, the divine benefits of which would accrue to the sacrificer. Nogueira, however, compared it instead to the charitable self-sacrifice for the other, represented by the Passion. The rebuke was unmistakable and echoed a theme that runs through the work, in which Alvarez consistently refers back to pre-Christian antiquity and the time of the Old Law, while Nogueira's stance is founded upon a Christ-centric theology.

If the object of missionary labour was in contention, so was its method. Nogueira questioned if the silver-tongued skill of the preacher was truly necessary for evangelizing to the Amerindians, since the forge was as much use as the tongue.[87] In a land where the reason of the people was in question and, thus, where a missionary's intelligence and rhetorical sophistication was of dubious use, the preacher's tongue was of no greater value than the blacksmith's forge. The blacksmith's work was not merely an abstract metaphor for apostolic labour. As the text itself revealed, the making of iron tools was quite literally a means to attract the Amerindians to the Christian faith. For Nóbrega, both the speech-act of preaching and the activity of ironwork were equally legitimate concerns of a Christian *vita active* (active life). It was a literary reflection of the author's respect for the work of missionaries such as Nogueira: Nóbrega elevated the blacksmith to the office of temporal coadjutor in 1560.

When Alvarez insisted that their offices were different 'for mine is to speak, and yours is to make', Nogueira responded that their ends were not different: 'charity or the love of God and of one's neighbor'.[88] When Alvarez asked if the Amerindians were neighbours in this schema, Nogueira responded affirmatively, 'for I never find myself except among them, and with their sickles and axes'.

> *Gonçalo Alvarez*: And for this you call them neighbors?
> *Nugueira*: Yes, because neighbors, that is to say those who come near [*chegados*], and always they come near [*se chegão*] to me in order to make what they need, and I make it for them as neighbors, taking care to fulfill

[87] Nóbrega, 'Diálogo', 226.
[88] Nóbrega, 'Diálogo', 226.

> the precept of loving the neighbor as myself, so doing for them what I would want them to do for me, if I had the same need.[89]

Nogueira's argument, though made in rustic language, had long theological precedent, beginning with Augustine's *De Doctrina Christiana*. This posited not only the idea of charity as neighbour-love, but also that this love was not an abstract, idealized love that encompassed equally and universally all mankind, but was instead contingent: 'Since one cannot do good to all, we ought to consider those chiefly who by reason of place, time or any other circumstance, by a kind of chance, are more closely united to us.'[90] Trained in canon law, Nóbrega would have been familiar with this argument, as it had been foundational to Aquinas's discussion of whether one should love one neighbour more than another in the sixth article on the order of charity in the *Summa Theologiae*.

Nogueira thus applied Augustine's precept literally to the Brazilian context: since he found himself surrounded by Amerindians who were drawn to him by the sickles and axes he forged, they qualified as neighbours. They were thus worthy objects of charity and love. In this light, the earlier discussion on the fruit and use of missionary labour in the *Diálogo* also becomes more understandable. Augustine's *De Doctrina Christiana* turns upon a crucial distinction between things that are 'enjoyed' (*frui*) or loved for their own sake, and those that are 'used' (*uti*) or loved for the sake of another object. The former category was proper to God alone; the latter encompassed the neighbour, who was to be loved for the sake of God, that is, benevolently in order to direct him towards God. Such love was an active process imitative of Christ himself, who had transformed himself through his act of charitable self-sacrifice into a means for the salvation of all humanity.[91] Accordingly, Nogueira was correct in asserting that the end of his labour as a blacksmith and that of the preacher were indistinguishable, in that these activities were done for the sake of God and were meant to direct their neighbours, the Amerindians, towards God. Moreover, Nóbrega/Nogueira made it clear that in such

89 Nóbrega, 'Diálogo', 227.

90 Augustine, *De doctrina Christiana* I, 28.

91 On this issue, see Baer, 'The Fruit of Charity'.

work was to be found one's own salvation, as much as that of the neighbour. Again, the similarities with Xavier are striking.

Nogueira's elegant formula was not enough to appease Alvarez, who raised prevalent doubts about the Amerindians, not only regarding their status as neighbours, but even as men. Nogueira, nonetheless, insisted that man was 'all the same nature', thus admitting all mankind into the fold of the neighbour. Moreover, he asserted that his views were 'proven in the Gospel of the Samaritan, where Christ our Lord says that he who makes use [*usa*] of mercy is the neighbor'.[92] The interpretation of the parable of the Samaritan offered in Nogueira's speech reinforced the Augustinian notion of the neighbour at work in the text. In his sermon on the parable, Augustine explained that in the Samaritan, a member of a community most reviled by the Jews, Christ had wished his disciples to understand Christ himself. Like the Samaritan, a true neighbour, Christ had helped all humanity, left for dead, out of mercy.

The underlying principle of Nogueira's view and this notion of the neighbour was the central tenet of Augustinian anthropology: the unity of mankind in diversity. Due to the common origin of man from the protoplast, Adam, all men, composed of souls and bodies, regardless of differences in colour, movement, sound, or other qualities, shared a common nature.[93] Thus, Augustine did not deny the divisions between the Samaritans and the Jews; rather, he insisted that these differences should not prevent members of one community from seeing those of another as neighbours deserving of their mercy.

It was for this reason that Nóbrega had been so taken with a Tupí originary myth concerning a flood since his arrival in Brazil. The myth, in Nóbrega's judgement, was nothing less than a confused memory of the biblical flood, in which the Tupí remembered a primordial couple, who survived the flood by climbing atop a tree. This memory, despite its inaccuracy with regard to the biblical deluge, placed the Tupí in

92 Nóbrega, 'Diálogo', 227.

93 This latter point is made repeatedly in Book 16 of the *The City of God*. For one example, see the argument in the chapter entitled, 'Whether certain monstrous races of men are derived from the stock of Adam or Noah's sons'.

the lineage of Noah and, thus, Adam.[94] Accordingly, Nogueira argued that if Christ wished the Jews to see the Samaritans as neighbours, by the same token, it was incumbent upon the Portuguese to see the Amerindians as neighbours.

Throughout the piece the rustic speech of the blacksmith was directed against both the humanistic preoccupation with rhetoric as well as scholastic theologians, who were more interested in debating the Aristotelian subtleties of the nature of the Amerindians than in effecting their conversion. At stake, again, was Nogueira's peculiarly Augustinian view of the nature of their task. He rebuked Alvarez for his preoccupation with the logical reasons underlying the Jesuit fathers' belief in the mission to the Amerindians: 'It seems to be that is right that where there is overvaulting zeal, at times one must break away from reasons or use them little.'[95] The hard distinctions of reason would be melted, like iron, by the fire of charity. Moreover, truth could not be discerned by human reason, since it was only intelligible to God; nor was the will, to which charity belonged, to be subject to reason. Thus, Nogueira argued, the zealous man should not cleave to the prideful belief in the power of reason to guide the will, but should rather direct his activities to conform to divine will.

The debate encapsulated the tensions between a Stoic belief in human reason as a divine spark in man and the Augustinian rejection of the notion that man, as a created being, could contain within himself even such a small measure of divinity.[96] Here was the ground on which Nóbrega rejected entirely the notion that the value of the Amerindian mission could be found through the sorts of scholastic reasoning favoured by learned theologians. If human reason itself were fallible, how could one rely solely upon the counsel of theologians ensconced in the universities of Europe and who eschewed missionary labour in matters relating to the conversion of Amerindians in distant Brazil? In this context, Nóbrega gave the clearest outline of the Augustinian anthropology that was the linchpin of this faith, using Nogueira as his mouthpiece:

[94] Nóbrega, 'Informação das Terras do Brasil,' August 1549, *Cartas do Brasil*, 65.

[95] Nóbrega, 'Diálogo', 231.

[96] On the characteristic Renaissance tension between Stoicism and Augustinianism, see Bouwsma, 'The Two Faces of Humanism'.

> I shall tell you what I often remember while hammering on the hard iron and which I have often heard from my Priests. It seems that Christ, who is listening to us, could say: Oh fools and those tardy of heart to believe! I am imagining all the souls of men to be human and made of the same metal, made in the image and likeness of God, all capable of salvation and created for it; and before God, by its nature the soul of the *Papa* [Pope] is worth as much as that of your slave, Papaná.[97]

In this view, an insistence on reason presented an obstacle to the heart, central to the Augustinian vision of human virtue. To Christ, the blacksmith of souls, all humans were made of the same metal, all malleable to his will and thus capable of salvation.

Alvarez pounced upon Nogueira's almost scandalous play on words and seized on the potential problem of asserting the equivalence of the soul of the Pope and that of an Amerindian slave. Still, Nogueira insisted that Amerindians had souls like theirs, since they possessed the three potentialities of the soul distinguished in Augustinian philosophy—understanding, will, and memory.[98] Moreover, the reason for this could be found in the genealogy of all men, from their fallen father Adam. His original sin had made him 'similar to the beasts, so that all of us, from the Portuguese, to the Castilians, to the Tamoios, to the Aimurés, remain similar to beasts because of our corrupt nature and in this we are all equal'.[99] Adapting an Augustinian account of creation, Nogueira showed that due to the sin of a common protoplast, all men, whether Iberian or Amerindian, had fallen into the same bestial state, their souls resembling in their common condition cold, useless iron. Yet, through the fire of Christian conversion, these souls could be transformed and bent to divine will.

The parallelism in Nogueira's speech between the traditional rivalry of the Portuguese and Castillians and that of the Tupí peoples like the Tamoio against the Gê-speaking Aimoré served to underscore the

[97] Nóbrega, 'Diálogo', 232–4.

[98] Nóbrega, 'Diálogo', 232–4. This tripartite schema of the mind, reflecting the divine trinity, was established in Book 10 of *De Trinitate*. Augustine emphasized that analogous to the unity of the three persons of the Christian God, these three elements were not three lives or minds, but constituted one single life and mind.

[99] Nóbrega, 'Diálogo', 235–7.

unity of all humanity in their fractious baseness. The Amerindians, who believed there was a god and identified him with thunder, were far more correct than those who worshipped idols, no matter how sophisticated their culture.[100] Reflecting Augustine's exhortation in *De Civitate Dei* for Christians to orient themselves to the city of God instead of towards the city of man, Nogueira made clear that the trappings of complex civilizations did not distinguish these pagans in their fatal error from the Amerindians.

Alvarez, unwilling to give up a scholastic respect for the intellectual achievements of pre-Christian antiquity, contended that the stark difference in cultural achievements between the great civilizations of the pagan past and the Amerindians suggested an unequal level of understanding amongst these people. Rebuking Alvarez for suggesting that there existed different types of souls, Nogueira offered an explanation of these civilizations disparities based on differences of upbringing.[101] This difference had its roots, like everything else within Augustinian thought, in biblical history: although as descendants of Adam the Amerindians possessed the same sort of nature shared by all humans, their particular lineage traced back to the accursed Ham, who had shamed his father by uncovering his nakedness, thus condemning his descendants to go naked. The other peoples, descendants of Seth and Japheth, were sons of blessing. Much like two brothers of equal intelligence brought up separately in the village and city, so that one would know how to make plows and another how to be a courtier, the apparent difference of the Amerindians was a reflection of their difference in upbringing, not some essential defect in their understanding.[102]

If Augustinian anthropology would not admit a substantial difference between the humans of different places, the appeal to biblical history did allow for their apparent difference in their civilizations. Still, Nogueira argued, this did not necessarily lead to a positive valuation of the achievements of sophisticated pagan civilizations. After all, Christians had faced the staunchest resistance from the most learned of ancient civilizations, the ones of whom St Paul had said:

[100] Nóbrega, 'Diálogo', 237–9.

[101] Nóbrega, 'Diálogo', 239.

[102] Nóbrega, 'Diálogo', 240–1.

'We preach Christ crucified, to the Jews a scandal and to the gentiles [Greeks] a foolishness.'[103] In this regard the simplicity, not to mention the credulity, of the Amerindians was their great advantage: 'As the most essential matters of the faith, such as the Holy Trinity and God making himself into man and the mysteries of the sacraments, cannot be proven by demonstrative reason, and are indeed beyond all human reason, it is clear that it is more difficult for a philosopher, who is founded upon the subtleties of reason, to come to believe, than one who believes in simpler things.'[104]

Nogueira thus vociferously denied Alvarez's claims regarding the insufficiency of the Amerindian capacity for belief, attributing their apparent deficiencies instead to the failings of the priests who ministered to them. Again, the history of the early Church allowed Nogueira to assure Alvarez that the mission to the Amerindians was not hopeless: if the infidels of antiquity had eventually been converted, there was no reason to doubt the possibility of the conversion of the Amerindians.[105] Still, despite these encouraging signs, ultimately their conversion was a matter of divine will.

Alvarez objected, claiming that even if conversion was 'on God's part ... on the part of the gentiles there must also be the necessary preparation, since I have heard said that St. Augustine said that God who made me without me will not save me without me'.[106] Alvarez's appeal to Augustine was specious, if not perilously close to heresy, since it imported Augustinian soteriology into a discussion on the conditions for conversion. As was apparent in Augustine's account of his own conversion in Book VII of the *Confessions*, conversion depended entirely on divine providence and all men were potentially deserving of it. By contrast, as Augustine established in his conflict with Pelagius, salvation involved both the proper orientation of the human will as well as divine justification, and was *not* universal. Nogueira, as the true Augustinian in this dialogue, made the distinction between conversion and salvation clear: 'Regarding the gentiles, I say that they and all others are cold iron, and when

103 Nóbrega, 'Diálogo', 241.
104 Nóbrega, 'Diálogo', 242.
105 Nóbrega, 'Diálogo', 244–8.
106 Nóbrega, 'Diálogo', 244–8.

God wishes to place them in the forge, they will be converted; and if in the furnace of God they remain to place themselves in the final fire, the true blacksmith, the lord of iron, will know there why; but their disposition is no worse than that possessed by all other nations.'[107]

The *Diálogo* ends upon a peculiarly unresolved and pessimistic note: for all the clarity with which Nogueira laid out his vision of the conversion of the Amerindians and responded to his interlocutor's many doubts, ultimately he was unable to sway him. This vaguely discomfiting end was perhaps a reflection of Nóbrega's pessimistic appraisal of his ability to sway his opponents (including the bishop) in their opinion of the Amerindians.

The *Diálogo* marked a fundamentally new orientation to the people of Brazil than that encapsulated in the 'Informação': the ethnographic sketches of the former had given way to the Augustinian anthropology of the latter. Much more importantly, Nóbrega's appeal to an Augustinian anthropology sidestepped the vexed debate over the nature of the Amerindians, which had raged among the theologians of Europe since the discovery of the New World. In insisting upon a common human nature, Nóbrega obviated the Aristotelian distinctions that had animated this debate, particularly with regard to their status as natural slaves. It was a stance in keeping with his ongoing conflict with the planters and the governor over the intrinsic liberty of the Amerindians.

Even the shocking cannibalization of the Bishop Sardinha by the Caeté in 1556 did not undo this conceptual framework. The incident did further crystallize for Nóbrega a belief that had become widespread among the Jesuits working in the sertão: that the mobility and lack of sovereign authority among the Tupí was an insurmountable obstacle in their conversion. Thus, Nóbrega, like other Jesuits, threw themselves wholeheartedly behind Mem de Sá's pacification of the Tupí, undertaken as just war in retaliation for the bishop's sacrilegious end.[108] Moreover, it was Mem de Sá's campaign that allowed

[107] Nóbrega, 'Diálogo', 249.

[108] On this shifting view, see Alden, 'Changing Jesuit Perceptions of the Brasis'.

Nóbrega to begin the project of the aldeias proper, bringing the Tupí under Jesuit custodial care, an enduring cornerstone of their missionary strategy in Brazil.

The desire for custodial control over the Tupí, however, was decidedly not the same as enslavement in his eyes. Thus, in the very last extended piece of writing Nóbrega left before his death, he mounted a vociferous attack against Quirício Caxa's allowance for the sale of Tupí children in extreme circumstances by their father.[109] He allowed that those taken in captivity after Sardinha's cannibalization were justly enslaved, but he insisted that any one sold after 1560 could not be a slave. As befitting such a polemic, the argument was made in a formal style, with plenty of support from theological and scriptural sources to supplement his own knowledge of the intricacies of the first years of the mission in Brazil. However, its spirit was that of the *Diálogo*: it claimed no intrinsic value in such disputation but sought only to uphold Nóbrega's most cherished principles regarding the Tupí. According to his schema, the Tupí were best understood not under the hierarchical classificatory schema of Aristotelian scholastics but under the universalizing anthropology of Augustine, in which all descendants of Adam have an intrinsic capacity for conversion. Nóbrega's project to make room for the India called Brazil within the conceptual rubric of the Indies refused the possibility of creating a hierarchical civilizational schema in which the Amerindian would inevitably be placed at the bottom. He insisted instead on a fundamental anthropological unity. Differences were a matter of historical accident. To Nóbrega, the Tupí, sophisticated pagans like the brahmins and bonzes of Xavier's acquaintance, and the Portuguese were intrinsically equal in their capacity to become citizens of the city of God.

* * *

The two pioneers of the Jesuit missions in India and Brazil arrived at radically opposite ways of understanding the nature of the Indies and its inhabitants. Xavier's career was characterized by a continuous search for 'better' subjects of conversion, such that he constructed a hierarchical ethnology in which he placed the Japanese (provisionally) at the apex. Implicit in this schema was the notion that members of complex civilizations untouched by the taint of Islam, familiar with the literate and philosophical arts, and under the jurisdiction of a stable central polity would be the most amenable to the Catholic faith. Nóbrega instead sought to do away with the classificatory debates that had coalesced around the Amerindians altogether. He insisted on a fundamental anthropological unity, in which the Tupí were as inherently capable of conversion as the gentiles of Xavier's acquaintance, or even the Portuguese.

Xavier and Nóbrega also arrived at opposite conclusions regarding the role and importance of the Portuguese imperial apparatus in facilitating their missions. Xavier, disillusioned by the corruption of the local officials he had encountered in South India and by the paltry power of the Portuguese in the vast political landscape of Asia, left Portuguese jurisdiction and sought instead the patronage of indigenous overlords for the fledgling missions. Locked in a bitter struggle with local colonizers over control of indigenous peoples, Nóbrega cleaved instead to the representatives of the Crown as a countervailing force. This strategy was only reinforced by the hostility of the episcopacy, after the controversy with Bishop Sardinha. Little wonder then that the Jesuits were heavily invested in the violent enterprise of extending Portuguese control over the entire coast of Brazil. The pacification campaign of the Amerindians undertaken by Mem de Sá as retaliation for the cannibalization of the controversial bishop only served to affirm the logic of this alliance, since the governor awarded the Jesuits custodial control of the Amerindians, encapsulated in the Jesuit institution of the aldeia.

For all their differences, there are nonetheless intriguing points of convergence between these pioneers. Xavier came to devalue the dry knowledge of the European universities he had left behind for the practical education of the mission field. He trusted far more in the 'living books' of his acquaintance than written knowledge, and preferred the humble but zealous Barzaeus to the arrogant humanists who flocked to the college in Goa.

The underlying attitude was identical to that expressed by Nóbrega in his famous dialogue. When Alvarez asked if it was not enough

[109] Nóbrega, 'Se o pai pode vender a seu filho e se hum se pode vender a si mesmo', *Cartas do Brasil*, 397–429.

for a missionary to be a good linguist and know how to speak well, Nogueira vociferously denied this, appealing to the biblical apostles as the exemplary models for those who wished to convert the Indians. The Apostles, burning with zeal, had been able to light a divine fire in the hearts of the people. The need for priestly virtue, particularly among the lay brotherhood, was especially important in Brazil, where the bad behaviour of the Christians had already harmed the mission to the Amerindians.[110] In other words, linguistic or rhetorical skill was no substitute for zeal and vocation in missionary activity. Much like Xavier, Nóbrega proved suspicious of the over-reliance on the arts of rhetoric or the reasons of scholastic philosophy in the task of conversion. He was more concerned with the zeal and practical value embodied by the humble blacksmith Nogueira than the greater sophistication but dubious fervour of preachers such as Alvarez. The goal of the missionary was not to debate Aristotelian classifications of the Amerindians or to acquire a mastery over their language in order to pen grammars; it was to labour, out of obedience and neighbourly love, for their conversion.

This attitude was opposed neither to careful observation of other cultures nor to accommodatio in missionary praxis. Both Xavier and Nóbrega had shown themselves to be willing to adapt their practices and modes of living to the peoples to whom they ministered, whether this entailed an adoption of vegetarianism in Buddhist Japan or the use of Tupí musical traditions in Brazil. Yet, increasingly, among the ensuing generation of Jesuit missionaries, accommodatio took a distinctly humanist turn, in which the mastery of the language and literary arts of the indigenous culture came to be seen as the most powerful weapon in the missionary's arsenal. It is to two remarkable representatives of this new mode of accommodatio that we now turn.

[110] Nóbrega, 'Diálogo', 243–4.

II

ACCOMMODATIO AND THE POETICS OF LOCATION

4

JOSÉ DE ANCHIETA AND THE POETICS OF WARFARE

While their second beatitude is to be singers, the first is to be slayers.[1]

In his very first letter from Brazil, Manuel da Nóbrega had written hopefully of an exemplary student in the new school, a chief who had mastered the alphabet within two days. He wanted 'to be Christian and not eat human flesh'. He also averred, however, that he would still have to go to war and 'sell and make use' of those he captured, 'for those of this land are always at war with others and thus ... all is in disorder, eating one another'.[2] Nóbrega was not overly concerned with the chief's reluctance to give up the custom of warfare, seeing it then as a minor obstacle to Christian civility for such a willing and able subject.

Over half a century later, the French missionary Yves d'Évreux recounted a conversation with an indigenous slave he met in Maranhão. He demanded to know of the slave if he was not pleased to be with the missionary, 'first, for I had taught him to fear God, second, [because] he was assured of never being eaten'. While the convert was pleased on the first count, he was anguished 'not to die in the way of the chiefs, amidst dances and drink, and not to avenge myself before dying upon those who would eat me'. Remembering

[1] Jacomé Monteiro quoted in Leite, *História da Companhia*, vol. VII, 415.

[2] Nóbrega to Simão Rodrigues, Bahia, 10 April 1549, *Cartas do Brasil*, 20.

his status as a fearsome chief's son, and seeing himself now 'as a slave, without paint, without feathers ... like the sons of the chiefs of our parts', the convert wished he were dead. Particularly painful was the knowledge that he would never avenge his mother, who had been killed and eaten.

This remarkable speech, accompanied by 'a great abundance of tears', moved d'Évreux as proof of 'how tender are these savages in their love for their relatives'. The convert also added that after his mother was killed and eaten, his captors 'adopted him as a son and he called them with the name of father and mother; and when he spoke, it was with an unspeakable affection, even though they had eaten his own mother, and had considered eating him, a little before we arrived on the Island'. Moreover, d'Évreux added, this same couple came regularly to the mission, traversing the distance of more than 50 miles from their village to see their erstwhile captive and adopted son.[3]

Nóbrega and d'Évreux recounted these stories as testimonials of the Amerindian disposition for the Christian life. Separated by over sixty years, however, both converts recoiled at abandoning their roles as Tupí warriors. The intransigence of the sixteenth-century chief in Bahia facing only the prospect of this loss became a howl of despair in the mouth of the enslaved son of a chief in seventeenth-century Maranhão, who had forfeited in fact, and without remedy, his role as a warrior.

For both Nóbrega and d'Évreux, the mechanism through which this attachment to warfare was understandable was vengeance, similar to European chivalric codes of honour. Yet, the phenomenon they observed clearly exceeded European notions of vengeance: the very people d'Évreux's slave wished to avenge himself upon, the ones who had killed and eaten his beloved mother and threatened him with a similar fate, were also his adoptive parents. He was bound to his enemies through ties of affection, as much as fictive kinship and captivity. To d'Évreux, the Tupí practice of turning 'enemies into affines, the better to eat them'[4] was decidedly not intuitive; in this light, the slave's sentimental attachment to warfare and his undeniable trauma at a life of enforced Christian peace seemed even more remarkable.

[3] d'Évreux, *Voyages dans le nord du Brésil*, 55–6.

[4] Viveiros de Castro, *From the Enemy's Point of View*, 182.

The slave's suicidal lamentations at the loss of a warrior's life were no hyperbole: since only the dead were insensate, he lived in his mother's wake, without painting himself or adorning himself with feathers, in itself a marker of mourning. His grief was twofold, social and personal. First, in consonance with European assumptions about vengeance, the slave had been deprived of the possibility of correcting the terrible wound he and his community had suffered through his mother's death. Second, he had lost the possibility of becoming a full Tupí person, capable not only of marriage and thus social reproduction, but also of immortality in the afterlife through ritual anthropophagy—privileges reserved for warriors. If the padres had saved him from the Christian devil, añánga the demon would nonetheless take his cowardly (non-killer) soul.[5] Tupí warfare constituted a Maussian *fait social total* (total social fact); its loss, through conversion, enslavement, and forced pacification, entailed the Catholic undoing of Tupí society.[6]

The Tupí predilection for warfare, objectionable in itself, was particularly unpalatable to European tastes by its association with ritual cannibalism. Yet, if cannibalism represented one polarity of Tupí culture, the second pole centred on song and discourse. The Huguenot Jean de Léry witnessed the performance of such songs during a santidade, similar to that described by Nóbrega, in which the karaíba had sequestered the women (and Léry with them) while the men sang.[7] His revulsion at the possession ritual, which Léry considered diabolic, could not diminish his admiration for the sweetness of the singing. The ravishing songs, which haunted him long after his departure from Brazil, included a lamentation for ancestors and the millenarian lore of the Tupí quest for the land without evil, as well as the recitation of foundational myths such as that of the flood (which both Léry and Nóbrega had taken to be a garbled version of the

[5] Métraux, *A religião dos Tupinambás*, 11.

[6] Fernandes, *A função social da Guerra*, 357. Death through warfare for Fernandes is essentially a reactive, not a productive mechanism, unlike Viveiros de Castro, who writes: 'Against death, the Tupinambá adopted the best defense: attack ... [W]arfare vengeance was a method of instituting society.' See *From the Enemy's Point of View*, 286–7.

[7] Léry, *Histoire d'un voyage*, 68.

biblical deluge). It also included the ritualized declaration of enmity against a rival group, and prophesies regarding the impending eating of their enemies through successful warfare.[8] Despite Léry's judgement of the difficulty of retaining 'things in purity' without writing, Tupí song appeared from his own account to be a remarkably rich repository of cultural knowledge. Moreover, it was not merely a mode of retaining and retelling cosmological knowledge, but clearly played an important ritual role with regard to warfare.

The connection between ritualized discourse and warfare was a more generalized feature of Tupí oral culture, one that was most visible in the rites surrounding the sacrifice of the prisoner. As Eduardo Viveiros de Castro puts it, 'The cannibal anthropophagy was preceded and prepared by a dialogical anthropophagy, a solemn battle of words between the protagonists of the ritual drama of execution. The captive and his killer undertook a verbal duel that crowned the numerous discourses exchanged between the enemy and his captors ever since his arrival in the village.'[9]

In this central ritual, the twin poles of Tupí orality, cannibalism and song/speech, were clearly intertwined. Nonetheless, despite their revulsion at the first of these elements of Tupí culture, the Jesuits came to value their reverence for the mastery of speech. In the dramatic confrontation with a shaman whose conversion he effected through a public war of words, Nóbrega had learnt the value of shamanic discourse in Tupí political and religious life. Moreover, as *senhores de fala* (masters of speech), travelling shamanic prophets and Jesuit missionaries—the old and new karaíba alike—could pass safely through villages that would have ordinarily viewed them as enemies. Little wonder then that the *entradas* of the Jesuits routinely used processions of orphans and children, singing and playing instruments, as an advance guard.[10]

[8] Léry, *Histoire d'un voyage*, 72–3.

[9] Viveiros de Castro, *From the Enemy's Point of View*, 290–1. It was this aspect of the cannibal complex that most attracted Montaigne in his famous essay 'On Cannibals'.

[10] *Entradas* were expeditions into the interior to 'descend' indigenous peoples to the coastal Portuguese plantations.

Still, expedience alone could not justify the missionary adoption of Tupí song and discourse. As early as 1550, Nóbrega wrote of José de Azpilcueta's pioneering efforts to replace traditional forms of Tupí oral discourse with those more suited to a Christian purpose. Possessing a facility with the local tongue, nightly he sang 'some prayers to the boys that he teaches them in their language, instead of certain lewd and diabolical songs that they previously used'.[11]

In many ways, therefore, one could see the poetic corpus of the Jesuit José de Anchieta as the culmination of Jesuit attempts to replace the content of the 'lewd and diabolical songs' of Tupí orality, while retaining their form. In the context of a Tupí cosmology peopled by warriors and singers, this corpus—its dramatis personae bristling with Portuguese and Tupí soldiers, incorporating Portuguese canticles and Tupí dances—seems a particularly sensitive example of Jesuit accommodatio.

Recent historiography on early colonial missions in Brazil has focused on the role of language learning, translation, and writing. Andrea Daher, for example, following in the interpretive footsteps of Michel de Certeau, notes that the systematic description of indigenous languages through dictionaries and grammars was an operation that exceeded practical expedient: it expressed instead the theological and ethnographical assertion of the 'convertability' of the indigenous peoples of Brazil by missionaries.[12] As Adone Agnolin notes, in the process of creating the *língua geral da costa* (the lingua franca of the coast) through Latin grammatical structure and the Iberian catechetical tradition, 'the missionaries ended up turning the indigenous language itself into a material—presupposed to be inert—upon which to found a meaning external to it'.[13] This linguistic project, in other words, was more than a process of translation of Christian doctrine: missionaries came to understand that catechizing in the Brazilian context required the absorption of elements of indigenous cosmology.[14]

[11] Nóbrega to Simão Rodrigues, Porto Seguro, 6 January 1550, *Cartas do Brasil*, 72.

[12] Daher, *A Oralidade Perdida*.

[13] Agnolin, *Jesuítas e Selvagens*, 21.

[14] Agnolin, *Jesuítas e Selvagens*, 51.

Yet, as I will argue, Anchieta's *poetical* corpus is more than a reflection of European catechetical or literate traditions with some elements of indigenous cosmology judiciously absorbed into it. Precisely because it spoke to the very foundations of Tupí cultural life, this corpus represented a powerful assault on the world of Tupí orality. The danger José de Anchieta's corpus posed did not stem from the supposed fragility of a non-literate culture in the face of the technological and semiotic resources of European literate culture.[15] The corpus drew upon his profound understanding of Tupí culture as well as the popular traditions of European Catholicism, with its own relationship to orality, piety, and violence. In doing so, Anchieta sought to destabilize the fundamental cultural equations of the Tupí warrior's world and subordinate it to a Christian ideal of permanent peace.

This corpus reinforced and replicated the emerging social project for the isolation and confinement of the Tupí under Jesuit custody, the profane and colonial corollary to the Christian notion of a state of permanent peace.[16] In his corpus one finds a conceptual geography of colonial coastal Brazil, characterized by the dichotomy between the European *vila* (incorporated Portuguese town) and the Amerindian aldeia. The European world was oriented outwards: towards Europe and its imperial concerns beyond the seas, and towards the sertão as the site for its future expansion. Meanwhile, the world of the Tupí shrank and fragmented into isolated, highly controlled aldeias.

This chapter will begin with a brief outline of Anchieta's life and career, focusing on his early experience in Piratininga and the conflicts surrounding the Portuguese foundation of Rio de Janeiro. These formative experiences provided the basis of his deep understanding of Tupí culture. The latter part of the chapter is devoted to an analysis of his poetic corpus in light of this working ethnography.

[15] My reading, therefore, departs sharply from that forwarded by Todorov in *The Conquest of America*.

[16] For an excellent study of the full flowering of the Jesuit aldeia as a social, economic, and political project at the end of Anchieta's life, see Castelnau-L'Estoile and Zeron, 'Une mission glorieuse et profitable'.

Civility and Conflict in a Tupí Village

José de Anchieta was born in São Cristóvão da Laguna on the island of Tenerife in 1534, to a new Christian mother and an old Christian father. At fourteen, he went to Coimbra for his humanistic studies and joined the Society in 1551, already having established a reputation for linguistic and scholastic talent. In 1553, Anchieta joined the third group of missionaries to leave for Bahia, under the leadership of Luis da Grã, in the company of the second governor Duarte da Costa.[17] Soon after his arrival, Anchieta was sent to the Tupiniquin village of Piratininga on the southern Brazilian coast, seen as a gateway to converting the peoples of the interior.[18] He devoted himself to the school for children, who could already 'read and write and abhorred the customs of their fathers'.[19]

In his first significant consideration of the new land and people to whom he administered, Anchieta wrote to Ignatius of the cultural intransigence of the indigenous, who had in them 'so ingrained the custom of drinking and singing their gentile songs, that there is no remedy to dissuade them'. These habits were most apparent after their return from war, which Anchieta acknowledged was an opportunity to escape from Jesuit scrutiny. The detriment to the missionary enterprise caused by Tupí song was most apparent in the case of an indigenous villager, who had once been baptized but withdrew from Portuguese influence 'to live according to his will'. Anchieta reported that 'one day he came, with two women, singing through the village, according to the gentile custom, and inciting the others to do the same', leading many to revert to drink and song.[20] In Anchieta's estimation, song in the Tupí idiom was not merely associated with drunken revelry and warfare; it marked clearly the limits of Jesuit

[17] Anchieta has been the subject of biographies in both Portuguese and English, most notably Dominian, *Apostle of Brazil* and Abranches, *Anchieta o apóstolo do Brasil*. For an early biography, which recounts the various legends important to his hagiographical reception, see Rodrigues, *Vida do Padre José de Anchieta*.

[18] Anchieta, Quadrimestre, May to September, 1554, *Cartas*, 70.

[19] Anchieta to the brothers in Coimbra, Piratininga, 15 August 1554, *Cartas*, 59.

[20] Anchieta to Ignatius, Piratininga, end of August 1554, *Cartas*, 62.

control. In such a context, the control and reorientation of Tupí song was imperative.

It was no accident, therefore, that the indoctrination of children, which Anchieta identified as the mission's primary task, included the teaching of singing, a responsibility Anchieta himself shouldered. The strategy bore fruit: 'Almost all the nights, they gathered to sing songs of God in their language, as opposed to their parents, for which *out of the mouths of babes and infants His praise has been perfected by means of his enemies.*'[21] If Tupí song adumbrated a particular relationship between enmity, piety, and orality, the Christian tradition offered its own model for such a relationship, as Anchieta's appropriation of Psalm 8 indicates. The Tupí convert who sang in praise of the Christian God was transformed from a state of enmity, such that his own brethren, as 'pagans', would now be enemies to him. This was precisely the intended effect: Anchieta insisted that their principal task was the catechism of the children to keep them 'under [their] hands', so that afterwards they would come to 'take the place of their parents', 'forming a people of God'.[22] In these sentiments, one can hear echoes of Xavier's call to the Parava children to become better men than their fathers.

Despite his bacchanalian representation of Tupí song, the underlying cultural institution of which these feasts of song and wine were objectionable manifestations was warfare. In 1555, when many villages gathered for war, Anchieta saw for the first time the challenge posed by this institution to Christian civility, newly instilled in the converts and carefully regulated within the confines of the village. Warfare drew the Tupí outside the village, turning their attention to the networks of enmity that webbed the surrounding world and embroiled the village within the same cultural system. Anchieta was thus dismayed at the willingness of the Tupí to go to 'feasts of their miserable songs and wine' in a neighbouring village, in honour of the

[21] Anchieta to Ignatius, Piratininga, end of August 1554, *Cartas*, 62. The biblical quotation reads: 'Ex ore infantium ac lacentium perficiatur laus propter inimicos ejus.'

[22] Anchieta to Ignatius, Piratininga, end of August 1554, *Cartas*, 62.

imminent death of an enemy.[23] Anchieta saw an 'obstinate hardness' in the Tupí, 'who, except for a few, it seems wished to return to the vomit of their ancient customs', a metaphor that would remain like a leitmotif throughout his letters.[24] So powerfully entrenched was this cultural system of warfare that it came to involve even the Portuguese residents of São Vicente: they 'approved and praised' the festivities held in town for the killing of an enemy, thus encouraging the catechumens to leave in search of war captives.[25]

From the frank report Anchieta sent privately to Ignatius, it was obvious that the Jesuits prevented their catechumens from participating in warfare only through coercion. In 1555, the villagers took two men, members of the much-feared, forest-dwelling Gê Papaná (alternatively, the Maromomi), with whom they returned to the village in order to kill them.[26] The chief Tibiriçá, of whom the Jesuits harboured great hopes, immediately called for the preparation of ropes, swords, and other things necessary for the sacrifice of one of the captives.[27] Hearing this, the villagers, including the catechumens, gathered happily, to call in one voice for the captive's death. The scandalized Jesuits acted swiftly, grabbing by force the ritual implements for the sacrifice so it would not reach the hands of the chief.[28] Tibiriçá, angered by the interference, asked for a scythe with which to kill the prisoner even without the traditional ritual implements and heaped abuse upon the Jesuits for not defending the village against enemies. Nonetheless, the Jesuits, aided by

[23] Anchieta, Quadrimestre September–December 1554/Trimestral January–March 1555, São Vicente, end of March 1555, *Cartas*, 92–3.

[24] Anchieta, Quadrimestre September–December 1554/Trimestral January–March 1555, São Vicente, end of March 1555, *Cartas*, 92–3.

[25] Anchieta, Quadrimestre September–December 1554/Trimestral January–March 1555, São Vicente, end of March 1555, *Cartas*, 102–3.

[26] Anchieta, Quadrimestre September–December 1554/Trimestral January–March 1555, São Vicente, end of March 1555, *Cartas*, 103.

[27] Anchieta, Quadrimestre September–December 1554/Trimestral January–March 1555, São Vicente, end of March 1555, *Cartas*, 103.

[28] Anchieta, Quadrimestre September–December 1554/Trimestral January–March 1555, São Vicente, end of March 1555, *Cartas*, 103.

women of the chief's household, managed to wrest the prisoner from Tibiriçá.[29]

This private account of the behaviour of the villagers of Piratininga during the warfare of 1555 was at odds with letters intended for widespread consumption. In these latter epistles, in accordance with Ignatius's prescriptions to present the missions in the best possible light to European audiences, Anchieta took pains to make it appear that even in the conduct of their warfare, the catechumens had retained something of their Christian training. Thus, he wrote that the catechumens did not participate when, on the day before combat, 'those who came from elsewhere (as is custom among them) began to offer a sacrifice to their sorcerers'.[30] Asked 'if they wished to give credit to these lies' of shamans, the catechumens had responded that they did not, and that they carried God in their hearts', showing every confidence that with his assistance, 'they would achieve greater victory than those with their filthy sacrifices'.[31] Anchieta was keenly aware of the severity of the taunts the catechumens had withstood, since 'their happiness is above all in being taken for valiant men and in not showing fear': to 'attribute to them such ignominy serves as the most powerful way to move them'.[32] Indeed, to dissuade Tibiriçá from participating, the Jesuits resorted to 'the examples of the [Christian] martyrs' as an alternative model of bravery to that of the 'pagan' warrior.[33]

The catechumens rejected the notion that to be the unresisting victim of violence could be an act of bravery. Still, Christianity could be put to use in the conduct of indigenous war: when the villagers 'began to lose their courage and soul (*ânimo*)', a baptized wife of a chief

[29] Anchieta, Quadrimestre September–December 1554/Trimestral January–March 1555, São Vicente, end of March 1555, *Cartas*, 103.

[30] Anchieta, Quadrimestre May–September 1554, São Paulo de Piratininga, 1 September 1554, *Cartas*, 72.

[31] Anchieta, Quadrimestre May–September 1554, São Paulo de Piratininga, 1 September 1554, *Cartas*, 72.

[32] Anchieta, Quadrimestre September–December 1554/Trimestral January–March 1555, São Vicente, end of March, 1555, *Cartas*, 94.

[33] Anchieta, Quadrimestre September–December 1554/Trimestral January–March 1555, São Vicente, end of March, 1555, *Cartas*, 94.

exhorted them on the battleground that 'losing their fear, they should make the sign of the cross upon their foreheads'. Anchieta reported that the only casualties were the two who failed to do so, while the enemy was forced to flee. He further claimed that those taken captive by the catechumens 'were killed and buried in a Christian fashion', instead of being eaten 'with utmost joy and great vocalizations and songs'.[34]

In sharp contrast to the private report Anchieta had sent to Ignatius, the villagers here were represented not as Tupí warriors, but as Christian crusaders fighting beneath the symbol of the cross. Moreover, while he had tactfully hidden the circumstances associated with the capture and attempted sacrifice of the Papaná enemy, Anchieta attempted to show how the catechumens had observed Christian customs even in the aftermath of battle, taking care to bury the dead.[35]

Certainly, the intrusion of Christianity affected the traditional benefits of warfare. Anchieta reported that a man returned from battle only to find that a woman, to whom he expected to lay claim based on his status as a warrior, had rejected him and was in the church, attending catechism. He 'grabbed her by the hair in sight of everyone with punches and slaps', so that the captain arrested him, desisting only when he begged forgiveness and blamed his outburst upon the evil counsel of others.[36] To Anchieta, this submission was remarkable in a people who recognized 'no law, no authority, nor did they obey the rule of any one'. Yet, he ignored the obvious coercion that had induced the apology, as well as the changing power dynamics that allowed a woman to reject and humiliate a warrior. Even the shamans proved vulnerable to the shifts in authority induced by these Christian karaíba.[37]

Much as Xavier's ministry to the Parava children allowed them to challenge traditional hierarchies, the intrusion of the Jesuits effected

[34] Anchieta, Quadrimestre May–September 1554, São Paulo de Piratininga, 1 September 1554, *Cartas*, 72.

[35] The Tupí horror of burial did not seem to be fully understood at this early stage. See Anchieta, Quadrimestre, May to September, 1554, *Cartas*, 71.

[36] Anchieta, Quadrimestre, May to September, 1554, *Cartas*, 72–3.

[37] Anchieta, Quadrimestre, May to September, 1554, *Cartas*, 73.

profound changes in the nature of relationships between men, women, and children. As the mission matured, Anchieta commented on the particular devotion of the women, attending church as much as twice a day, as well as the children, who attended school twice a day before leaving to hunt or fish.[38] The men, by contrast, required far greater labour on the part of the missionaries.[39] Undoubtedly, the tepid reaction of the men to the Jesuits stemmed from their unsettling assault on the privileged position of both warriors and shamans in Tupí society. Anchieta perceived as much when he reported that the catechumens resisted the calls to warfare, 'as if they were women and not men, in order to obey [the Jesuits] and because they wished to adopt [their] customs'.[40]

The resistance of these key groups—young men and shamans—to the intrusion of Christian notions of civility in Tupí village life could be fierce. The most common sort of violence caused by the interference of the missionaries revolved around marriage: men who bitterly resented Jesuit attempts to impose monogamy often unleashed their anger upon the baptized women, of whom the Jesuits were now self-appointed custodians. The Jesuits, as religious practitioners protected by the chief, were comparatively safe from such open physical assaults, though irate, thwarted lovers would regularly threaten them with death.[41]

Shamans, on the other hand, could and did mount more effective challenges to the Jesuits. At the end of 1556, Anchieta noted with dismay that many of the villagers had left for other places, 'where they can live freely, as they used to', taking with them the majority of the children.[42] This was particularly upsetting since they would 'necessarily

[38] Anchieta, Trimestral, May to August 1556, São Paulo de Piratininga, August 1556, *Cartas*, 109–10.

[39] Anchieta, Trimestral, May to August 1556, São Paulo de Piratininga, August 1556, *Cartas*, 110.

[40] Anchieta, Quadrimeste September–December 1554/Trimestral January–March 1555, São Vicente, end of March 1555, *Cartas*, 94.

[41] Anchieta to Society in Portugal, São Paulo de Piratininga, end of April 1557, *Cartas*, 119.

[42] Anchieta to Provincial of Portugal, Piratininga, end of December, 1556, *Cartas*, 114.

have to imitate' their parents, without the countervailing influence of the Jesuits, thus destroying his most cherished hopes for creating a new Christian society.[43] The reason for this sudden wave of movement was because 'they were now persuaded by a diabolical imagination that the church is made for their destruction, in which we may enclose them and there, aided by the Portuguese, kill those who are not baptized and make the baptized our slaves'.[44] This rather perspicacious set of charges came from a pajé, who was travelling through the sertão, who 'all now followed and venerated as a great saint'. Anchieta had also heard from two catechumens that this particular pajé exhorted his followers to go to war and to destroy the church.[45]

Anchieta gave one particularly egregious example of the disorder the shaman caused, when a man invited his younger brother, a catechumen, to follow the 'great sorcerer'.[46] The catechumen refused, angering his older brother who, 'taking a hatchet, injured him gravely and left him wounded for dead'. Their mother, herself a catechumen, began to quarrel with the wife of the eldest son who had begun the fight. A boy who interceded was wounded in the melee by the old woman and died by daybreak. The woman, firebrand in hand, made to flee but soon returned to tell her children that she would not leave them, sad and alone, but would sooner kill them all. The following day, her eldest son made a pit in which to inter the dead and taking his mother by the hand, he placed a rope around her neck, buried her, placing above her the corpse of her victim. Anchieta marvelled that 'none of the people impeded him, nor did anyone say a word to him, for this is how they are used to avenge such homicides, for the relatives of the dead do not make war and eat each other'. This was punishment meted for violence outside the context of warfare. Though the Jesuits took some advantage of the situation by healing

[43] Anchieta to Provincial of Portugal, Piratininga, end of December, 1556, *Cartas*, 114.

[44] Anchieta to Society in Portugal, São Paulo de Piratininga, end of April 1557, *Cartas*, 119.

[45] Anchieta to Society in Portugal, São Paulo de Piratininga, end of April 1557, *Cartas*, 120.

[46] Anchieta to Society in Portugal, São Paulo de Piratininga, end of April 1557, *Cartas*, 121.

the wounded and preparing him for baptism, the episode highlighted how Tupí ways still superseded Christian norms. It also showed the violent upheaval Jesuit intervention could cause in village life.

Warriors, Crusaders, and Martyrs

The interference of other groups in indigenous life, particularly those who served as cultural and linguistic intermediaries, also fomented unrest against the missionaries. The village of Maniçoba, for example, had to be abandoned because the Mamelucos had encouraged the villagers to kill and eat the missionaries. 'Demoralized by them', the villagers refused to listen to the priests.[47] As Anchieta explained, 'the Christians born of Portuguese fathers and Brazilian mothers are so hard and blind, that they grow each time in the living hatred' they bore towards the Jesuits.[48] This was the culmination of Anchieta's growing disillusionment with the mestiço population of Brazil, in whom he had originally seen 'the greater part of the edification or destruction of the land', since as interpreters they could aid the conversion of the gentiles.[49]

While the Mamelucos, raised in Brazil and of mixed parentage, caused him disappointment, the treachery of those born in Europe was even more shocking. In the sertão, Nóbrega's cherished ambitions for the conversion of the Guaraní received a severe blow with the martyrdom of Pero Correia and his companion at the instigation of a Spanish interpreter. Countering Correia's message to the Guaraní to make peace with their enemies, the 'Castilian (who had spent much time amidst the Carijó adopting their customs, but exceeding them in corruption, so that he had much authority among them) counseled them to make war....' Such behaviour, Anchieta averred, was 'customary among these interpreters, agents of iniquity, precipitating the perdition of the Indians with such lies'.[50]

[47] Anchieta to Society in Portugal, São Paulo de Piratininga, end of April 1557, Cartas, 121.

[48] Anchieta, Quadrimestre May to September, São Paulo de Piratininga, 1 September 1554, *Cartas*, 93.

[49] Anchieta to Ignatius, Piratininga, July 1554, *Cartas*, 55–6.

[50] Anchieta, Quadrimeste September–December 1554/Trimestral January–March 1555, São Vicente, end of March 1555, Cartas, 98.

The palpable danger posed by the intercession of such unreliable intermediaries hardened Anchieta's resolve to learn the local language. As early as 1555, Anchieta noted the great strides he had made linguistically. He claimed that although he had understood the structure of the language, there was nobody to make use of a grammar, except himself and those missionaries who came from Coimbra.[51] His rueful acknowledgement of the level of education of the missionaries in Brazil stood in contrast to the anti-humanist stance Nóbrega would eventually adopt. Nonetheless, the dangers of humanistic education without its appropriate harnessing to a missionary purpose was also clear to Anchieta. These dangers were only underscored by the French Calvinist convert João de Bolés or Jean Cointa, who gained safe passage from Rio de Janeiro to São Vicente through the help of Tamoio warriors. Boasting both of his aristocratic birth and his deep knowledge of the liberal arts, Greek and Hebrew, as Anchieta noted in fascinated horror, he soon 'began to vomit from his stomach his fetid errors'. The erudite heretic eventually faced the Inquisition.[52]

Anchieta's humanistic pursuits were constantly interrupted by a nearly permanent state of war, waged between indigenous factions and a fractious group of European interlopers. The shifting contours of conflict involving the increasingly Christianized settlement of Piratininga was again crucial to Anchieta's understanding of the Tupí world of war.[53] The enemies faced by Piratininga were the Tupiniquin of the interior, beyond the sway of the Portuguese as well as the coastal Tupinambá Tamoios, who were allied with the French.[54] While

[51] Anchieta to the ill brothers of Coimbra, São Vicente, March 20, 1555, *Cartas*, 85, 87.

[52] Anchieta to Diogo Laínes, São Vicente, 1 June 1560, *Cartas*, 166. On Cointa's remarkable career, which led to his execution for apostasy in Goa in 1572, see Révah, 'Jean Cointa'.

[53] The transformation of the Piratininga was accelerated once the governor ordered the Portuguese settlement of Santo André to merge with Piratininga, at the intercession of the provincial Luis de Grã and Nóbrega, who wished to unite the ministries of the Colegio de São Paulo for their Amerindian and European charges.

[54] Anchieta to Society in Portugal, São Paulo de Piratininga, end of April 1557, *Cartas*, 120.

governor Mem de Sá's campaign of 1560 against Villegaignon's France Antartique had subdued French imperial pretensions, the Tamoio themselves were far from quelled. The following year, Anchieta wrote of the precarious position of Piratininga, 'which is often ruined for the little fear [the enemies] have of the Christians'.[55] While Portuguese *fazendas* (estates or plantations) and slaves suffered attacks from nominally friendly Tupiniquin, Piratininga was especially vulnerable to attacks by land and sea from the Tamoios.[56]

In response, the Portuguese inhabitants, with some Mamelucos, decided to wage war upon these 'frontier enemies'.[57] The war party, accompanied by a priest and a brother interpreter 'to carry forward the flag of the cross', headed towards a Tamoio stronghold by the River Paraíba.[58] As befitting Christian warriors, the men had confessed and taken communion before reaching the enemy, 'making these untamed and frightening woods a church'.[59] The Tupí warriors, as much as the Portuguese, proved their bravery, 'with the help of the royal flag of the cross'.[60] Back in Piratininga, the Jesuits served the cause with public orations, while devout mestiça women kept vigil. These disciplines coincided with the holiest time of the Christian calendar, Easter. The whole church, Anchieta reported 'was one voice and lamentation, which could not fail to penetrate the heavens and move the Lord to have mercy on us and our warriors, who were then fighting for his love....'[61]

The campaign, presented here as a veritable New World crusade, stood in contrast to the conflicts of 1555, when Anchieta had struggled to represent Tupí warfare in a Christian light. This was not gentile violence but just war. It was waged not as an economic expedient for the illegal enslavement of the indigenous, but for reasons which fulfiled the Thomist conditions of *jus ad bellum* (just war).[62]

[55] Anchieta to Diogo Laínes, São Vicente, 30 July 1561, *Cartas*, 180.
[56] Anchieta to Diogo Laínes, São Vicente, 30 July 1561, *Cartas*, 180.
[57] Anchieta to Diogo Laínes, São Vicente, 30 July 1561, *Cartas*, 180.
[58] Anchieta to Diogo Laínes, São Vicente, 30 July 1561, *Cartas*, 180–1.
[59] Anchieta to Diogo Laínes, São Vicente, 30 July 1561, *Cartas*, 181.
[60] Anchieta to Diogo Laínes, São Vicente, 30 July 1561, Cartas, 181.
[61] Anchieta to Diogo Laínes, São Vicente, 30 July 1561, Cartas, 181.
[62] The relevant articles on war in *Summa Theologiae* for the following discussion are: Second part, part II, section 40, articles 1, 2, 4.

The civic body that constituted the inhabitants of Piratininga was a proper sovereign authority by whose command war could be waged. The war party manifestly had just cause to attack the Tamoio in accordance with Augustine's precept that a just war avenges wrongs and is a punitive action. Anchieta took pains to show that the campaign was pursued with the right intention, in that they intended the advancement of a good by seeking to open 'some path, so that the Gospel can be preached'. The conduct of the war too fulfiled Thomist criteria. The priests who led the campaign as the flag-bearers of Christ did not actively participate in the fighting, restricting themselves to the proper activities of confessing warriors and providing spiritual aid. The timing of the conflict, during Lent, was no hindrance to its classification as a just war, according to Aquinas. Nonetheless, if the soldiers who left Piratininga formed a Christian crusade in one sense, they were also simultaneously a Tupiniquin war party, occupied not with the defence of a Christian village but engaging in a form of inimical sociality.

The victory achieved by these crusaders galvanized the Christians: war was declared across the captaincy against the Tamoio, to force them to submit to Portuguese sovereignty in the spirit of Mem de Sá's contemporaneous campaigns in Bahia. From a missionary viewpoint, these skirmishes were productive: not only were the gentile enemies defeated, but they also created local Christian martyrs, whose actions were a model of bravery and violence that could be used as an alternative exemplum to indigenous warriors for Tupí converts. Foremost among these martyrs was Tibiriçá, who had formerly so disappointed Anchieta, but who was now the baptized Christian, Martim Afonso. Before the impending war of 1563, 'he did nothing more for the five days that we were waiting for combat but admonish and exhort [his people] ... preaching continually night and day through the streets (as is the custom of the Indians) to defend the church [and] that God would grant them victory against their enemies....'[63] Though some villagers stayed behind and one even joined the enemy, Tibiriçá gathered his people from three villages, 'raising the banner ... and a sword of wood, all painted and ornate with feathers of various colors, as a signal of war'.[64] When the enemy arrived, they came adorned in much

[63] Anchieta to Diogo Laínes, São Vicente, July 30, 1561, *Cartas*, 181.
[64] Anchieta to Diogo Laínes, São Vicente, July 30, 1561, *Cartas*, 181.

the same fashion as Tibiriçá's men. Anchieta marvelled at how ties of kinship meant little on the battlefield.[65] The chief's actions allowed Anchieta to cast Martim Afonso in terms of Christian pious warfare: he was one 'who had made an enemy of his own brothers and relatives, for love of God and his church and afterwards to whom God had granted victory over his enemies'. Later Anchieta would report that his devout deathbed confessions and declarations were made 'with so much understanding and maturity that he did not seem a Brazilian man'.

Anchieta's univalent gloss of these events is noteworthy. It was true that Martim Afonso the convert had served his faith well. Nonetheless, the Tupiniquin chief Tibiriçá had also performed his role as a warrior with ritual and social precision, from the exhortation 'in the custom of the Indians' before the battle to the act of killing with the ceremonial sword, to finally dying the 'handsome death' of a Tupí warrior through battle. Anchieta's descriptions of these wars of Piratininga were clothed in a Christian vocabulary of pious violence that translated and sanctioned local, non-Christian modes of warfare, without recognizing them as such. Nonetheless, his account could not erase the cultural multivalence of these skirmishes.

Making Peace in Brazil

Though war could occasionally be productive, by and large it was profoundly detrimental to conversion. In 1565, Anchieta wrote despairingly of the incessant violence that plagued the land and made evangelism impossible: the Tamoios of Rio de Janeiro continually raided 'the slaves, women and children of Christians, killing and eating them without ceasing'. Yet, this violence, in Anchieta's judgement, was divine punishment for the earlier wrongs of the Portuguese against the Tamoios, 'who before were our friends, assaulting them, capturing and killing them, many times, with many lies and deceptions'.[66] The cycle of violence required dramatic intervention. Accordingly, Nóbrega, accompanied by Anchieta in the role of interpreter,

[65] Anchieta to Diogo Laínes, São Vicente, July 30, 1561, *Cartas*, 195.

[66] José de Anchieta to Diogo Laínes, São Vicente, 8 January 1565, *Cartas*, 210.

offered to negotiate a peace with the Tamoios on behalf of the Portuguese settlers. Such a peace was increasingly attractive in light of the growing hostility of the Tupí surrounding the Christian kernel of Piratininga.

In 1563, Nóbrega and Anchieta left for Iperuí, where some Tamoios came to receive them: 'because they feared that if they entered the ships [the Europeans] would attack them (as [they] have done many other times)', the Tamoios suggested an exchange of hostages.[67] The Jesuits offered themselves as part of the European contingent, and were protected somewhat by the good opinion of the people who had heard of the missionaries. The testimonial of one woman in particular aroused enough interest that the Tamoios wished to take them to their villages.[68]

Anchieta prepared the way for their entry into the Tamoio village, in the manner befitting visiting karaíba, promising them the sorts of spiritual goods to which they were accustomed from their own shamans:

> Speaking in a loud voice through their houses as is their custom, I told them that they should be happy with our coming and friendship, that we wished to stay among them and teach them the things of God, so that He would give them an abundance of foodstuffs, health and victory over their enemies and other similar things ... [69]

As a captive, it was the Jesuit who had to adapt to the cultural expectations of the Tamoio, transforming himself into a Christian karaíba. It was an inversion of the process of cultural translation at play in Piratininga, where Tupí modes of being and acting were increasingly dominated by Christian systems of meaning.

In Iperuí, Anchieta made clear the terms within which the Tamoio would consider an offer of 'peace':

> And the principal reason that moved them to wish for peace was not the fear they have of Christians, to whom they always brought defeat ... nor the necessity they have of their things, for the French with whom they

[67] José de Anchieta to Diogo Laínes, São Vicente, 8 January 1565, *Cartas*, 211–12.

[68] José de Anchieta to Diogo Laínes, São Vicente, 8 January 1565, *Cartas*, 212.

[69] José de Anchieta to Diogo Laínes, São Vicente, 8 January 1565, *Cartas*, 212.

> treat give them those in such abundance ... but the great desire they have to war with their enemy Tupís ... [U]ntil now [the Tamoios] have done us much ill, with their continuous assaults, for we obstructed their passage to their enemies.[70]

For the Tamoio, to accede to peace was merely another means to continue warfare with their traditional enemies. As his performance of the role of karaíba suggests, Anchieta understood that cosmologically, as much as socially, the Tupí aspired not to peace but rather to continued victory over ever-present enemies. This contrasted with a Christian eschatology and society, oriented towards an ideal state of peace following the final triumph over an (evil) adversary. It was only due to the Tamoio's relative disinterest in the Portuguese as enemies, as opposed to their indigenous allies, that a space for negotiation could be created.

It was a marvel that they could negotiate at all with 'people of such a kind that each is a law unto himself, and gives nothing for the pacts and contracts others make'.[71] The fragmentary nature of authority among the various groups of Tamoio complicated process of making an enforceable peace. The Jesuits did find unexpected allies. The first Tamoio chief in whose house Anchieta and Nóbrega boarded had been captured and enslaved by the Portuguese once. He thus 'had reason due to this to have great hatred of us'. Yet, he was 'determined to forget and convert in all love, showing himself to be one of the principal authors of the peace'.[72] Another early ally in their cause was the chief Pindobuçu, who had initially spurned rudely their advances of friendship. Yet, the space for dialogue opened by the peace negotiations allowed him to engage with these strange visitors, so that Pindobuçu came to respect the Jesuits as powerful sorcerers. When another Tamoio, unhappy with these developments, stole the bell

[70] José de Anchieta to Diogo Laínes, São Vicente, 8 January 1565, *Cartas*, 212–13.

[71] José de Anchieta to Diogo Laínes, São Vicente, 8 January 1565, *Cartas*, 213.

[72] José de Anchieta to Diogo Laínes, São Vicente, 8 January 1565, *Cartas*, 214. His goodwill seemed all the more remarkable considering the tepid interest the men of the villages showed towards the teachings of the Jesuits, particularly when compared to the women.

with which the Jesuits called the Tamoios to catechism, Pindobuçu himself intervened. He demanded its return in the streets, calling out: 'If we fear our sorcerers, how much more should we fear the fathers, who must be true saints, and have the power to bring us bloody stools, coughs, headaches, fevers and other infirmities of which we would all die.'[73] The threats were effective, probably because contagion and devastating loss of life regularly followed contact with the Jesuits and other Europeans.

Yet, many remained unmoved by the mission for peace. The most resistant were the Tamoios of Rio de Janeiro, closely allied to the French. Anchieta himself could not deny the legitimacy of their suspicions: the chief Aimbiré 'showed himself incredulous and hard to all we told him, bringing to memory how many ills we had done to them, and how he himself had been taken [captive] in another time on the pretext of peace....'[74] He proved himself especially sceptical of what Anchieta had termed their 'first and principal condition for peace': the inclusion of the Jesuit's Tupiniquin disciples in the peace treaty. Aimbiré insisted that they had to kill and eat the chief of these Tupí, just as they had done to the Tamoio in another time. When the Jesuits claimed they had nobody to give him, since God did not wish it, Aimbiré replied: 'Enemies are not God, you are the ones that treat of the things of God and must hand them over to us.'[75] Since the Jesuits were short of enemies to give to him, the Tamoio could not have peace with them.

Aimbiré's speech reinforces what Anchieta's account already suggested: peace was only to be entertained as a means to warfare. Moreover, as Eduardo Viveiros de Castro's work among the Araweté might suggest, if enemies were not gods, gods could certainly be enemies. It was the shamans, bearing the sole responsibility of the management of 'the things of god', who were tasked with negotiating an enemy-centred cosmology and ensuring victory over enemies.

[73] José de Anchieta to Diogo Laínes, São Vicente, 8 January 1565, *Cartas*, 218.

[74] José de Anchieta to Diogo Laínes, São Vicente, 8 January 1565, *Cartas*, 219.

[75] José de Anchieta to Diogo Laínes, São Vicente, 8 January 1565, *Cartas*, 221.

Aimbiré's rebuke of the Jesuits, as shamans unable to procure, let alone help in, the defeat of enemies, was sharp indeed.

If Tupí shamans formed one axis of comparison for the Jesuits, the other was the host of European intermediaries in these delicate negotiations, including Aimbiré's French son-in-law. The most disturbing, to the Jesuits, was the French Lutheran interpreter who accompanied Aimbiré, of whom Anchieta wrote with horror and fascination.[76] The Frenchmen cheerfully spoke of Rio's 'faithfuls', or non-papists, who did not have mass. He also recounted the history of some missionaries from the Order of St Bernard: though they were kindly received by the 'savage and cruel Indians', the Protestants burnt down their subsistence plots and church, eventually causing the Catholic brothers to return to France, where many of them were killed. From his conversations with the Frenchmen, Anchieta concluded that the French in Rio de Janeiro were not only cut off from the Church, but were now 'savage'.

> They live in conformity with the Indians, eating, drinking, dancing and singing with them, painting themselves with their black and red inks, adorning themselves with the feathers of birds, walking nude at times ... and finally, killing enemies, according to the rite of the same Indians, and taking new names with them, such that they only lack in eating human flesh for their life to be the most corrupt ... [G]iving [the Indians] all manner of arms, inciting them always to make war and helping them in this, they are yet the worst.[77]

In abandoning the precepts of Christian civility and adopting instead indigenous practices of warfare, the French Lutherans represented the very worst of European life in Brazil. They also dramatized what was at stake for the Jesuits in seeking peace. Peace was not merely a necessity for the survival and prosperity of the Portuguese settlements of the coast; peace represented the very bedrock of Christian civility as the antithesis of Tupí warrior culture. If war in Brazil could allow a representational idiom of double entendres, equivocally Christian

[76] José de Anchieta to Diogo Laínes, São Vicente, 8 January 1565, *Cartas*, 221–2.

[77] José de Anchieta to Diogo Laínes, São Vicente, 8 January 1565, *Cartas*, 222.

and Tupí, the language of a permanent peace was unmistakeably Christian, rather than Tupí.[78]

Aimbiré was eventually placated by a grand reception at São Vicente, followed by a joint captive-taking campaign against the Tupiniquin, in which the Portuguese participated as a sign of good faith. Aimbiré's desire for access to enemies and the willingness among the Portuguese to enslave indigenous warriors taken in 'just' war coincided to create the necessary conditions for peace.[79] Nonetheless, in Iperuí itself, the lives of the negotiators depended on the shifting sands of personal whim and internal Tamoio politics. If Pindobuçu was favourable, his son was barely prevented from sacrificing the hostages. A particularly frightening moment occurred when Cunhambebé (a son of the chief immortalized in Hans Staden's account) took Anchieta to his village. Though he warned the guests at his feast not to harm the negotiators, a Tamoio told the Jesuits, 'Do not enrage me, for I have killed and eaten one of you.' His wife then brought forth a shin-bone of the escaped slave he had slain, saved 'to make flutes'. The others began to gnaw this bone 'like dogs', although they did ask for manioc flour as a condiment, fastidious in their dining habits.[80]

Anchieta's fear and isolation, particularly after Nóbrega departed for São Vicente to aid in the negotiations, was palpable. Nóbrega's departure affected the balance of power: not long after, a slave of one of the Portuguese hostages was ceremonially quartered and devoured. After 'the night passed with bitter wings', the women of the house in which the hostages lived publicly denounced the killing, 'saying that the bones knew and would wreak vengeance'.[81] Their warnings backfired, as the killers began to feel that the Portuguese were so merged with the dead slave that it would be incumbent upon them to avenge him. As fear spread, Anchieta disavowed the women's words, proclaiming that the Portugese would not make the death of a slave their cause. The incident, as he himself admitted, shook him profoundly. Still, even as various Tamoios conspired to kill him, others believed in

[78] Contrast this with the fluid temporality of revenge in Tupí cosmology: see Carneiro da Cunha and Viveiros de Castro, 'Vingança e temporalidade'.

[79] Anchieta to Diogo Laínes, São Vicente, 8 January 1565, *Cartas*, 223.

[80] Anchieta to Diogo Laínes, São Vicente, 8 January 1565, *Cartas*, 227.

[81] Anchieta to Diogo Laínes, São Vicente, 8 January 1565, *Cartas*, 230.

him as a shaman, a figure of power who could ensure animals in the hunting traps and cure illness at will.[82]

These harrowing experiences as a captive among the Tamoio came to an end when news of the peace effected in Piratininga between the Tupiniquin, the Tamoios, and the Portuguese reached Anchieta. Still, peace was not to last for long: Estácio de Sá, nephew of the governor, came to São Vicente with the express intention of dislodging the French once and for all from the Brazilian coast. After five months of preparations, the campaign began, with Anchieta playing an active role as interpreter and surgeon. War ended only in 1567 with the death of Estácio de Sá, the defeat of the French and the ushering in of a new city in Rio de Janeiro.

Anchieta's career in Brazil would continue for some thirty more years: he served as a visitor and in other administrative capacities in São Vicente, before becoming provincial of the mission in 1577. When ill-health forced him to relinquish this post in 1585, he moved to Reritiba, where he served as superior of Espírito Santo, and where he died in 1597. His career as provincial coincided with the most important transitional moment of early colonial Brazil, when the sugar plantation and the concomitant trade in African slaves became the dominant economic formation of the colony, displacing earlier labour and trade arrangements centred on the indigenous population. His forty-four years in Brazil thus spanned the twilight of the Tupí world, as the balance of power shifted towards the colony, not least due to the pacification and resettlement campaigns Anchieta had so enthusiastically embraced.[83] He also witnessed from Brazil the Spanish captivity, when the autonomy of the Portuguese Crown was lost to the Hapsburgs in 1580. Yet, his early years in Piratininga had provided an unsurpassed linguistic and cultural education in Tupí ways. This shaped the poetic corpus that has been his most vaunted, if understudied, legacy.

[82] Anchieta to Diogo Laínes, São Vicente, 8 January 1565, *Cartas*, 230–5.

[83] On this shift, see Monteiro, *Negros da terra*. The *santidade de Jaguaripe* of 1583 represented a last gasp of an era in which the indigenous could set the terms of coexistence, an experiment that was crushed decisively by the first visitation of the Inquisition in Brazil. See Vainfas, *A Heresia dos Índios*.

The *Aldeia* in Words: Anchieta's Poetry of Confinement[84]

In a detailed catalogue of the natural history of São Vicente, Anchieta included this description of the demons that populated the forests of that land:

> As to what often frightens the Indians, the nocturnal specters or demons ... which the Brasis call *corupira*, which often afflict the Indians in the woods ... Therefore, the Indians go to the top of the highest mountain, on a path which goes to the *sertão* through the harsh woods and steep hills, usually leaving feathers, fans, arrows and other similar objects, begging them not to do them ill.[85]

As Anchieta's account made clear, missionaries believed in the efficacy of these local entities and viewed them as manifestations of the Christian devil. Still, what is most particular here is the relationship to space the demons circumscribed for the Tupí.[86] If venturing into the woods could lead to affliction, placating these spirits also required an excursion away from the village, into the mountains, which occupied such an important place in Tupí cosmological thought. Encounters with demons were intimately associated with Tupí habits of mobility.

This letter was penned shortly after Mem de Sá instituted the aldeia, a formation that explicitly sought to curb the nomadism seen as inimical to the conversion of the Tupí.[87] These villages were sanctioned at the behest of the Jesuits, as a means to gather and settle the Amerindians under their custody. If the demons that had peopled the Tupí world before conversion marked their relationship to the sertão, Anchieta's reimagining of these demons instead circumscribed them in the aldeia.

[84] On the reconstruction of Anchieta's works, see the critical introductions to Cardoso, *Teatro de Anchieta* and Martins, *Poesia*. I rely on Cardoso's and Martins's translations into Portuguese from the Tupí.

[85] Anchieta to Diogo Laínes, São Vicente, 31 May 1560, Cartas, 144–5.

[86] Susana Viegas's work on contemporary Tupinambá in Olivença is suggestive here (Viegas, 'Ethnography and Public Categories'). I am grateful to Christina Toren for referring me to Viegas's work.

[87] Anchieta himself had come to see in the itinerant habits of the Tupí one of the greatest obstacles to conversion in Piratininga. See Anchieta to Provincial, Piratininga, end of December 1556, *Cartas*, 113.

One example of this reimagining can be seen in the piece Anchieta wrote on the occasion of the raising of the image of the Assumption of the Virgin in Reritiba, an aldeia he founded in Espírito Santo and where he wrote much of his corpus.[88] The opening dialogue takes place on the road, where an angel is praying, 'Come, Virgin Mary, mother of God, visit this village and expel from it the demon.' The devil in turn countered: 'No, you come to remove me from the village in vain. All, in tobacco, like me and preserve me. Turn back on your path; I do not consent that you enter. Like these Amerindians of the mountain, I am here in my home and they do not sympathize with you.' The angel remained unmoved, and referring to himself as 'custodian of the village', warned the devil of the arrival of the Virgin. The devil, in rather anti-climactic fashion, dissolves into self-pity, declaring the Virgin to be his enemy, the one who would 'liberate' the land from him, and turning to his companion demons, urged that they should flee, carrying away their sins.

Variations and elaborations of this schematic exchange can be found throughout Anchieta's corpus.[89] The skeletal nature of this dialogue clarifies its intention. The angel as 'custodian of the *aldeia*' approximated the role in which the Jesuits served and saw themselves with regard to the Tupí. The devil, as indicated by the reference to tobacco, central to shamanic rituals, was a particularly Tupí instantiation of the Christian antagonist. Yet, as the conspicuous absence of a Tupí human in this roadside scene indicated, the Tupí convert was no longer to encounter the demon or placate it in the sertão: rather he remained confined to the aldeia, under custodial care, while his spiritual 'liberation' depended on the displacement of the demon by Christian holy entities.

[88] Anchieta, 'Dia da Assunção, quando levaram sua imagem a Reritiba', *Poesia*, 578–85.

[89] The most famous example is in the first dialogue of the *Pregação Universal*, Anchieta's first piece and one performed repeatedly across the Brazilian littoral. The device is also used in the piece Anchieta penned for the occasion of the reception of the relics of the 11,000 virgins in Espírito Santo as well as that for the arrival of the Provincial Marçal Beliarte around 1587 in Guaparim. This dialogue and its variations were performed in both Tupí and Portuguese.

The confinement of the Tupí within the aldeia in Anchieta's schema became apparent in the following act, involving 'six savages' dancing the *machatins* (see Figure 4.1).[90] These 'sons of the forest' declared that they lived 'like savages', but in honour of the visit of the Virgin

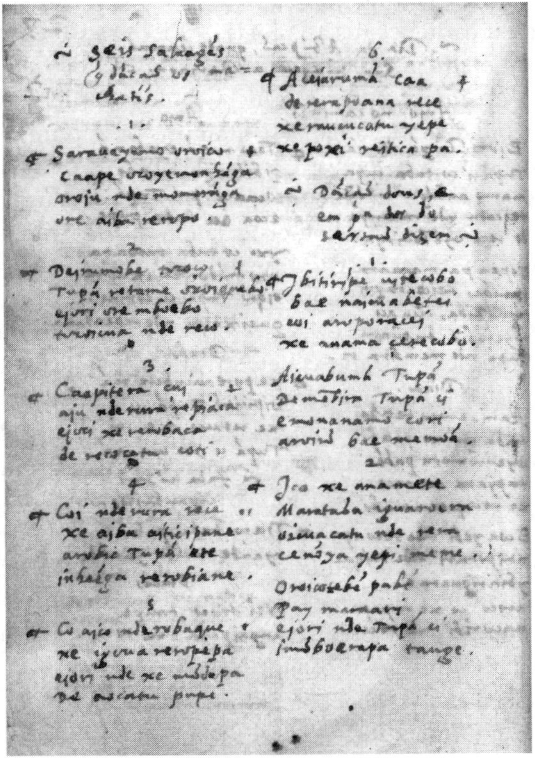

Figure 4.1 Manuscript of Poem Describing Six Savages Dancing, *Os Machatins*

Source: Anchieta, *Poesia*, Archivum Romanum Societatis Iesu, Rome, Italy, MS OPP NN 24, f. 27V.

[90] The term appears to be derived from the Portuguese word for hatchet and refers to a form of sword dancing involving choreographed fencing (Anchieta, 'Dia da Assunção, quando levaram sua imagem a Reritiba', *Poesia*, 582).

they had repudiated their faults. Thus, one of them declared: 'I am here before you, I, who was a rebel! ... I left the forest in your honor ... Living in the mountain, I did not know many things. I dance here in the way of my own [people]. I now know God, your son, Mistress.'[91] Conversion thus required not only that the Tupí remove themselves from the wilderness, though they were its 'sons', but also that they renounce their earlier status as 'rebels'. In doing so, they transformed the savagery of their earlier warfare and its associated feasts and dances into an almost pastoral pastiche, not unlike Iberian traditions of linked sword dancing, a pious pantomime of warfare.

The indigenous warrior was literally demonized in the longest and most intricate play in Anchieta's corpus written exclusively in Tupí, *Na aldeia de Guaparim.*[92] Another variation of the dialogue between the devil and an angel over the custody of an aldeia, this particular work was set in the eponymous village in Espírito Santo, and dated most probably to the last few years of Anchieta's life. The piece is notable for the richness and variety in which the devil and his minions are depicted through the four antagonists: Añhangaçu, the great demon; Tatapytéra, the one who throws flames; Kaú mondá, the thief of wine; and finally Moroupiaroêra, which translates roughly to 'the old and feared enemy too accustomed to fighting'.

Añhangaçu complained that the priest had caused him to leave the tobacco and had expelled him, while teaching the Christian faith to the villagers who earlier had 'lived under his dominion'.[93] He then called his infernal companions. Tatapytéra told Añhangaçu he would be able to change the hearts of the old women, a group Anchieta routinely described as the most bloodthirsty and the primary instigators of cannibalistic rituals in his early letters. Añhangaçu was pleased and conferred upon Tatapytéra an honour reserved for warriors who had killed successfully: he gave him a new name, Arongatu, the good protector.[94]

[91] Anchieta, 'Dia da Assunção, quando levaram sua imagem a Reritiba', *Poesia*, 582–3.

[92] Anchieta, 'Na Aldeia de Guaraparim', *Poesia*, 612–47.

[93] Anchieta, 'Na Aldeia de Guaraparim', *Poesia*, 614.

[94] Anchieta, 'Na Aldeia de Guaraparim', *Poesia*, 616.

Still, Añhangaçu lapsed into a depression, remembering that the mother of the Christian God was coming to liberate the villagers from his thrall. Kau mondá then arrived, describing himself as one who had once been a Tupinambá, but had shot them all, taking, binding, and catching them for prey. In other words, he had become their enemy, using their weakness for drunken feasts to lure them away from the churches. Given his success amidst the Tupinambá, he was certain that the Temiminós, who lived in Guaparim, would not resist him for long.[95]

Yet again, Añhangaçu's spirits flagged and was only revived by the arrival of the fourth demon. Moroupiaroêra brought with him the *ingapema*, the war club used to break the heads of prisoners.[96] The group began preparations for the attack upon the village, looking around in almost comic fashion for their tobacco. Tatapytéra chose the old women, who remained obstinately attached to the pajé and constantly invoked death; Kaú Mondá chose drunks, randy youths and dishonest women in the village; Moroupiaroêra, whom Añhangaçu referred to as 'our hero', chose 'to capture the Indians with attacks of words', hoping to restart the cycle of violence through threats and taunts, until the spirit of cannibalism took them again.[97] The demons thus represented a catalogue of Tupí cultural traits/Christian sins, with the warrior as the most exalted example in both senses.[98] As the parable of the weeds exemplified, the devil in Christian thought was the progenitor of disorder and warfare. Nonetheless, the detailed descriptions of the ways in which Moroupiaroêra fomented warfare suggest a deliberate demonization of Tupí warfare.

As the demons hid themselves for the ambush, the soul of a villager, Pirataráka, appeared on the path. He wondered if he had somehow been deceived by Jesus or had committed some sin, since he could not find his way to the promised kingdom of God.[99] He looked around

[95] Anchieta, 'Na Aldeia de Guaraparim', *Poesia*, 618–19.

[96] Anchieta, 'Na Aldeia de Guaraparim', *Poesia*, 620.

[97] Anchieta, 'Na Aldeia de Guaraparim', *Poesia*, 625–9.

[98] For another interpretation of the worst of Tupi traits, see McGinness, 'Transforming Indigenous Vice to Virtue'. I am grateful to the author for sending me this article.

[99] Anchieta, 'Na Aldeia de Guaraparim', *Poesia*, 632.

for his guardian angel but spied the demons. They pursued him, as Moroupiaroêra assured Añhangaçu that he would bring Pirataráka's soul for him to eat.[100] The centrepiece of this section is a dialogue much like that which preceded the sacrifice of the warrior, in which the captors taunted and insulted their victim.

Anchieta's profound understanding of Amerindian cosmology is clear in this scene. The representation of the demons as warrior enemies was appropriate: the term 'añánga', identified as the devil by the missionaries, had an association with the wandering souls of the dead, so that 'this spirit of death is a mixture of images of savagery, bellicosity, rottenness and cadaverous appearance'.[101] Moreover, the ontological status of Pirataráka's soul as *aña*, spirit, made possible precisely the cannibalism the demon-warrior threatened it with.

Pirataráka's soul countered Moroupiaroêra's charge that he kept his old names and ways: he insisted that he was a Christian, giving the name of his patron saint and his baptismal names.[102] However, he acknowledged that he had 'abandoned the *aldeia*', thus failing to maintain the sacraments and keep the holy days. The implication was clear: for the convert to leave the aldeia was to leave a realm of spiritual security and enter a space of moral danger.[103] The piece ends upon the familiar theme of the confrontation between the demons and the Jesuit-like angel. The angel freed the captive soul and forced the demons to withdraw from the aldeia, saying, 'Our Lord charged me to keep custody of this village.'[104]

The figure of Pirataráka's soul as the captive in need of liberation reinforced the theme of the spiritual and physical confinement deemed essential to the Tupí convert. Though the soul defended itself against the verbal onslaught of the demons, it was not in a manner befitting a Tupí captive taken in war, who would meet his captors with grandiose threats affirming the cycle of vengeance of which his death

[100] Anchieta, 'Na Aldeia de Guaraparim', *Poesia*, 635.

[101] Viveiros de Castro, *From the Enemy's Point of View*, 248.

[102] Anchieta, 'Na Aldeia de Guaraparim', *Poesia*, 632.

[103] Anchieta, 'Na Aldeia de Guaraparim', *Poesia*, 638. This was the primary pedagogical theme of the piece regarding the need to confess fully and not hide any infractions.

[104] Anchieta, 'Na Aldeia de Guaraparim', *Poesia*, 646.

was a part. Instead, the confusion of Piratarákas's soul, its recognition of the demons and eventual repudiation of them were reminiscent of the interiorized drama of Ignatian discernment of spirits.

Conversion thus entailed a radical translation of Tupí warfare, from the realm of social fact to that of metaphor. Warfare existed in the convert's world, but it was not he who fought: the demon-warriors, remnants of their earlier cosmology, battled the various Christian protectors of the Tupí soul. This soul, in turn, was to be 'liberated' from the captivity of the enemy-demons through the custody of the angels in the aldeias—whose mundane manifestations were the Jesuits themselves.

The Song of the *Vila*

For Anchieta, the isolation of the aldeia contrasted with the condition of the European town in Brazil. Compare the above works to *Na Vila de Vitória*, a play written in Portuguese and Spanish around 1584–6 and performed in the patio of the church of that Portuguese settlement. The play begins with a scene structurally similar to that found in the opening conversation between the demons in *Na Vila de Guaparim*. Whereas language and audience demanded a Tupí incarnation of the Christian devil and his minions in Guaparim, the devils of Vitória were of a different ilk. The Tupí Añánga of Guaparim were transformed (back) into Lucifer and Satan for the residents of Vitória. The play opens with Satan comforting Lucifer, assuring him that 'with Mahoma [Prophet Muhammad] and with Luther, with Calvin and Melancthon, you will cover all with such malediction that you will burn everything entirely....'[105] Satan boasted:

> If you knew what I did
> in Portugal and Spain!? ...
>
> I will stir up shortly
> Asia, Africa and Europe ...
>
> Any land of Brazil
> I swallow in a mouthful! ...

[105] Anchieta, 'Na Vila de Vitória', *Poesia*, 782.

Well these wars,
Waged throughout these lands
By those who call themselves 'Christians'
Against the pagan *brasiles*,
Through seas, rivers and mountains,
Where are they born?—From my hands.[106]

While Añhangaçu aspired only to the specific aldeia on whose outskirts he lurked, the Satan of the vila sketched a global imperial vision, in which Brazil was only a part of his campaign. The constant warfare of Brazil was as much a tool in his hands as the Muslim Prophet or the Protestant heretics of Europe.

Satan appeared here as a mirror and foil of Philip II of Spain, who had recently ascended the Portuguese throne. As the preeminent Catholic emperor, he led the charge not only against the Great Turk, but also heretic European forces. Unlike the residents of the aldeia, who were isolated in the custody of the Jesuits, the devils of Vitória reminded their audience of the larger world, and whose Catholic character they threatened both locally and globally. Fittingly, these imperious devils met their comeuppance not through the hands of a converted *índio* (Indian), but through the sword of St Maurice, patron saint of Vitória, leader of the Roman Theban Legion, who had been martyred for his refusal to kill Christians at the behest of Maximian.[107]

The second act gave concrete political substance to the cosmopolitan representation of the devils of Vitória. The town of Vitória introduced herself as 'old in Brazil'; her 'children and residents were always victorious, with manly effort, the swallowers of the Indians'.[108] The governor then asked with astonishment how, being Portuguese, she spoke in Spanish. Vitória replied in Spanish that it was 'because I wish to give glory to Philip, my lord'. She belonged to Philip, 'without strife,' the 'king of truth, to whom the supreme goodness wishes to give the monarchy of all Christianity'. The governor, continuing to speak in Portuguese, said this was why Vitória's people, 'with loyal hearts', wished to give her a new name along with a new government.[109]

[106] Anchieta, 'Na Vila de Vitória', *Poesia*, 783–5.
[107] Anchieta, 'Na Vila de Vitória', *Poesia*, 792–4.
[108] Anchieta, 'Na Vila de Vitória', *Poesia*, 797.
[109] Anchieta, 'Na Vila de Vitória', *Poesia*, 798.

Vitória rejected his proposition emphatically, implying that such a cosmetic change was unnecessary despite the circumstances of the Spanish takeover of the Portuguese Crown. In other words, Anchieta emphatically denied that the town of Vitória, as a Christian town, was changed by the transfer of sovereignty from one Catholic monarch to another.

The true problem lay in the disorder that had beset the town, the sins and vices that laid waste to her sons, who 'have to become captives of the world'.[110] Vitória was in turmoil after the traumatic loss of Portuguese sovereignty; ultimately, however, the disorder and weakness of the settlement was a reflection of the moral turpitude of its denizens. As the play made clear, the vigour of Catholic civility and its ability to withstand its enemies depended upon the obedience of its subjects to the precepts of natural law and the rule of a devout Catholic king, whether Spanish or Portuguese.[111]

The jingoistic sentiments of the Portuguese citizens were expressed by Ingratitude, who entered belligerently. She declared that she would never give up the bones of the martyr she held in her possession, a reference to the relics of St Maurice and the 11,000 virgins of St Ursula, given to the town by the Portuguese court in days past.[112] A Spanish-speaking ambassador accused Ingratitude of typically Portuguese vanity, and she in turn called him a 'Castilian devil'.[113] Eventually, two companions of St Maurice interceded on behalf of the ambassador. Though they spoke in Spanish, despite the ambassador's insistence they refused to identify themselves as being either Portuguese or Castilian. Instead, they claimed to speak for St Maurice, the 'royal lieutenant, patron of this town'.[114] The ambassador threatened either to take the relics over the river (to Paraguay) or to kill Ingratitude. The companions of St Maurice humbled the ambassador, reminding him of the many evils perpetrated by the Spanish in Paraguay, who had killed great numbers of the Guaraní unjustly and unrepentantly. When Ingratitude

[110] Anchieta, 'Na Vila de Vitória', *Poesia*, 799–800.

[111] Anchieta, 'Na Vila de Vitória', *Poesia*, 801.

[112] Anchieta, 'Na Vila de Vitória', *Poesia*, 806.

[113] Anchieta, 'Na Vila de Vitória', *Poesia*, 807–15.

[114] Anchieta, 'Na Vila de Vitória', *Poesia*, 816.

insulted the ambassador, the companions banished her. The mollified ambassador accepted the companion's request that he remain in Vitória, with their captain Maurice, for the benefit of the town.[115] The Portuguese governor then returned to the scene with Vitória to rejoice. St Maurice's helpers, the Fear of God and the Love for God, had restored peace.

Na Vila de Vitória allegorized the need Anchieta perceived in Brazil to set aside the political divisions caused by the Spanish takeover of the Portuguese Crown. In the Spanish king, Anchieta saw 'an inestimable help for extending and propagating the religion of Christ across the length and breadth of the New World'.[116] As a Jesuit whose native language was Spanish, such an argument may have appeared self-serving. His concern, however, was precisely to set aside such nativist squabbles; instead, he sought to unite his listeners under a Catholic banner, to defeat the various enemies of the Church and forge a lasting peace. (Perhaps, it was this that allowed Anchieta to be absorbed by the later tradition of Sebastianismo, whose adherents believed that the Portuguese Crown would be restored when the lost king Sebastião returned.[117]) This peace was the fundament of Christian civility, one that could not be enforced through isolation and vigilance by angelic Jesuit custodians as in the aldeia. Rather, in the Portuguese vila, it had to be brokered through diplomacy and through the willingness of its citizens to recognize and abide by the precepts of Christian moral and civic life.

Despite this crucial difference, there was an underlying conceptual unity at work regarding the nature of war and peace: here, as much as in the Tupí plays, the notion that conflict must always arc towards peace was paramount. Dramatically, this was expressed in a final celebratory act, much like those that ended the Tupí plays. In keeping with the setting, however, peace was not celebrated with a Tupí dance but rather with a procession of the relic of the head of St Maurice.

[115] Anchieta, 'Na Vila de Vitória', *Poesia*, 817–19.

[116] Quoted in Rumeu de Armas, 'Una carta inédita del Apostolo del Brasil', 7.

[117] See, for example, the Sebastianist appropriation of Anchieta in Balthazar Telles's influential seventeenth-century *Chronica da Companhia*, 297–8.

Martyrs and Warriors

The veneration of the relic of St Maurice, a Roman warrior but also a Christian martyr, is suggestive of the ways in which bravery was not equivalent in the Tupí and Christian worlds. In the former, bravery resided solely in the values of the warrior; in the latter, it comprehended the values of both martyr and warrior. In Anchieta's corpus, riddled with reflections on violence, martyrs figure in a large proportion of his poems, particularly those in Spanish, Portuguese, and Latin.

Martyrdom was of central importance in the poems Anchieta wrote in honour of various fallen priests of his acquaintance in Brazil. The majority of these related to the martyrdom of the members of the Jesuit Inácio de Azevedo's group at the hands of a French Huguenot corsair off the Canary Islands on 15 July 1570. Azevedo, whom Anchieta had accompanied during his visitations to the various missions to the south, was returning to Brazil with a group of new recruits for the mission. In a Spanish poem to Azevedo, Anchieta cast his death as *imitatio Christi* (imitation of Christ): 'God wished that life be given/ To the French enemy/ [By] the death of the Portuguese.'[118] The theme runs throughout the poem, not unlike the repetition of certain words at the beginning of psalms as a unifier for the whole composition.[119] The poem in honour of Azevedo invokes a particular Christology, made explicit in the last verse of the poem: 'As you had for a guide Jesus crucified, asking pardon for the people who had nailed him on wood, you beg, greatly inflamed, for your French killer.'[120]

The short poem revealed the key to the Christian valorization of martyrdom: it lay in the imitation of Christ crucified. This theme of imitatio Christi was the dominant note struck by the canticle Anchieta composed for the feast in honour of the forty martyrs, sanctioned by Rome to be held in Bahia.[121] It was also the key to the poem dedicated

[118] Anchieta, 'A Inácio de Azevedo', *Poesia*, 488.

[119] This figure in itself is significant: as Buber puts it, 'The recurrence of the key-words is a basic law of composition in the Psalms. This law has a poetic significance—rhythmical correspondence of sound values—as well as a hermeneutical one: the Psalm provides its own interpretation, by repetition of what is essential to understanding' (Buber, *Good and Evil*, 52).

[120] Anchieta, 'A Inácio de Azevedo', *Poesia*, 489.

[121] Anchieta, 'Cantiga', *Poesia*, 496.

to Pero Dias, the leader of a group of fourteen Jesuits who were martyred by French corsairs of Capdeville in September 1571.[122]

Yet, it was not the submission to violence that was important but rather the *willingness* to sacrifice oneself, out of love. The notion that the violence of martyrdom was ultimately an expression of the love of God was most explicit in a Latin litany, in which the violence suffered by each martyred figure was sublimated into love. Ventriloquizing St Francis, for example, Anchieta wrote: 'If the Lord Jesus imprints wounds upon you, profound love caused the injuries of both.'[123]

Still, it must be noted, that even in the representation of the forty martyrs so clearly destined for beatification, Anchieta did not entirely relinquish the image of the warrior. One notable poem in Spanish to the lay brother Manuel Álvarez, who had reportedly defended the group vociferously, began with this brief exchange, whose lines again served as the keywords and interpretive paradigm for the poem:

Shepherd,
From pastor made warrior,
You play well the drum!
—Now I play better
When, without fault, I die
With such force of pain.[124]

Like a shepherd beating a war drum, Álvarez in Anchieta's poem combined the martyr and the warrior in his person, such that his martyrdom was both self-sacrifice, a willing capitulation to violence without desire for revenge, *and* a hero's honourable death in battle.

The latter aspect of the martyr's death was particularly prominent in those poems dedicated to those killed during their efforts to convert the indigenous. It was key, for example, to Anchieta's representation of the martyrdom of Pero Correia and his companion, who had died at the hands of the Guaraní in 1554 at the instigation of a treacherous Spanish interpreter.[125] Comparing their life and death to the sacrifice

[122] Anchieta, 'A Pero Dias', *Poesia*, 505.

[123] Anchieta, 'Ladainha', *Poesia*, 549. St Francis here is referring to his stigmata.

[124] Anchieta, 'Ao Irmão Manoel', *Poesia*, 490.

[125] Anchieta himself recounted this incident, as mentioned above.

of the holocaust, Anchieta turned their martyrdom into an act of holy war: 'O, what a terrible army, by God so well commanded! By which was overthrown the satanic dragon and Jesus [was] highly exalted.'[126] Again, this interpretation had its roots in Anchieta's understanding of early Christian martyrdom, in which the martyr's death was the means of the victory of Christ in battle.[127]

Anchieta's most ambitious treatment of martyrdom is in his magnum opus, a trilingual Tupí–Spanish–Portuguese composition performed on 10 August 1583, on the occasion of the feast of St Lawrence. The play opens in Tupí, with the king of demons, Guaixará, speaking to his sons, Aimbiré and Saravaia.[128] Each of these names was of historical significance: Guaixará was the Tamoio chief who had led the assault in 1556 against the Portuguese town of São Sebastião; Aimbiré was the Tamoio chief Anchieta had encountered in Iperuí; and Saravaia, from internal evidence, referred most probably to a spy for the French.[129] While the demons prepared their assaults, the scene shifted to a song in Spanish, describing and commemorating the martyrdom of St Lawrence, which equated the violence he suffered with Christian love: 'For Jesus, my savior,/Who died for my defilements/I roast in these grills/With the fire of his love.'[130]

The second act reverts to Tupí, in which language Guaixará declared: 'I alone in this *aldeia* am [here] as its guardian, making it follow my laws. From here I will go far to visit other *aldeias*. Who [is there], like me? I am worthy, I am the great roasted demon, called Guaixará, famed all around.'[131] He presented himself in diametric opposition to St Lawrence: where the Christian martyr had been roasted through the fire of love, Guaixará was marked by the flames of hell.

Guaixará then described the content of his 'laws', which mandated smoking tobacco, drinking *cauim* to the point of vomiting,

[126] Anchieta, 'Dos irmãos mártires', *Poesia*, 508.

[127] See, for example, Anchieta, 'São Cristovão', *Poesia*, 511.

[128] Anchieta, 'Na festa de São Lourenço', *Poesia*, 686.

[129] Anchieta, 'Na festa de São Lourenço', *Poesia*, 686–7.

[130] Anchieta, 'Na festa de São Lourenço', *Poesia*, 688.

[131] Anchieta, 'Na festa de São Lourenço', *Poesia*, 689.

dancing, body adornment and 'in rage, walking around killing, eating each other, taking Tapúias....'[132] Guaixará boasted to his minions of the losses the Jesuits had suffered at his hands, including among the Tupinambás of Paraguaçu who had fled into the sertão.[133] Only the Temininós (under Jesuit care) detested his laws; thus, Guaixará now wished to attack them.[134] Riddled with doubt, Aimbiré reminded him that St Lawrence protected the Temininós.[135] The saint served as the foil of the self-appointed diabolic 'guardian' of the Tupí: whereas in Spanish he was a willing victim of violence, in Tupí St Lawrence was a terrifying warrior and 'valiant guardian'. Guaixará underscored the comparison: 'Which? This burnt Lawrence, roasted like us?'[136]

While Guaixará was encouraged by the sight of an iniquitous old Tupí woman, a stock antagonist in Anchieta's writings, Aimbiré and Saravaia spied the Christian guardians of the aldeia: 'burnt Lawrence', St Sebastian, and an angel.[137] Their appearance cowed Aimbiré and Saraiva. Guaixará instead proclaimed proudly: 'I am Guaixará, the drunk, great rattlesnake, jaguar, cannibal, aggressor, vampire bat who flies, demon (añánga) assassin.'[138] It was a masterful piece of Tupí discourse, reflecting the perspectival transformations necessary to make the eating of man possible: Guaixará would have 'to be' a jaguar, a rattlesnake, a vampire bat, or an enemy spirit (añánga) for whom man was properly prey, in order to eat another man. Yet, in the context of a Christian morality play, the speech was also and simultaneously an expression of the belligerence of the Christian devil, the Great Snake, towards the devout Christian.

The profoundly imposing figure Guaixará cut in this brief speech was necessarily undermined. After vainly attempting to convince St Lawrence of the incorrigibility of the Tupí, who should, therefore, be left to his dominion, Guaixará turned to the other demons in

[132] Anchieta, 'Na festa de São Lourenço', *Poesia*, 691.

[133] Anchieta, 'Na festa de São Lourenço', *Poesia*, 692. This escape was in response to Mem de Sá's declaration of their status as slaves, since they were related to the Caeté, who had cannibalized the Bishop Sardinha.

[134] Anchieta, 'Na festa de São Lourenço', *Poesia*, 693.

[135] Anchieta, 'Na festa de São Lourenço', Poesia, 693.

[136] Anchieta, 'Na festa de São Lourenço', *Poesia*, 694.

[137] Anchieta, 'Na festa de São Lourenço', *Poesia*. 696–700.

[138] Anchieta, 'Na festa de São Lourenço', *Poesia*, 700.

disgust. They began to adorn themselves for battle against the Tupí, arranging their teeth, putting on their claws, transforming themselves into predatory animals the better to prey on the Tupí.[139]

Quickly, the Christian saints took the Tupí warrior demons prisoner, who bemoaned their fate.[140] Their speech, defeated and cowardly, violated fundamentally the norms of discourse of a captured Tupí warrior, who would instead threaten his captors with the terrible vengeance awaiting them. In this rhetorical defeat, their Christian enemies had made vengeance impossible, consigning them to 'burn eternally'. In breaking the cycle of violence, a new state of lasting peace was established.

The angel now explained to the convert audience that God had entrusted them to his care, and that the martyr-saints would protect them.[141] Inverting all of Guaixará's earlier boasts, the angel explained that the lands the demon had claimed no longer existed, leaving only the corpses of its defenders floating in the river; their friends, the French, had also been defeated. The martyr-saints thus represented a new model of a warrior, one capable of defeating once and for all the Tupí warriors of yore.

Unlike the plays written purely in Tupí, this piece had a fascinating second half. Following an interlude of a song celebrating the imprisonment of the demons to the accompaniment of their weeping, the play returned to the scene of the original martyrdom of St Lawrence.[142] In front of his roasted corpse, the angel called Aimbiré and Saravaia to burn Decian and Valerian, the Roman emperors who had killed St Lawrence. The defeated Tupí demons then gathered several minions and armed themselves for the attack.[143]

In a direct parallel to the opening scene of Guaixará and Aimbiré, the Roman emperors were seated upon their thrones, oblivious to the impending assault of the Tupí demons against them, boasting to each other in Spanish.[144] The linguistic choice suggested a sly recognition

[139] Anchieta, 'Na festa de São Lourenço', *Poesia*, 708.

[140] Anchieta, 'Na festa de São Lourenço', *Poesia*, 710–14.

[141] Anchieta, 'Na festa de São Lourenço', *Poesia*, 716.

[142] Anchieta, 'Na festa de São Lourenço', *Poesia*, 719–20.

[143] Anchieta, 'Na festa de São Lourenço', *Poesia*.

[144] Anchieta, 'Na festa de São Lourenço', *Poesia*, 725–6.

that after Philip II's takeover of the Portuguese Crown, it was Spanish that was the true imperial language. In a clear homage to the Spanish monarch, Valerian reminded the boastful Decian that now it remained only to defeat Spain, since no other king had resisted him.[145] Like Aimbiré before him, however, Valerian also expressed fear that their comeuppance was upon them: 'Oh Decian, cruel tyrant! Now you pay and with you will I pay, for Christian Lorenzo, roasted, will roast us.'[146]

What follows is one of the most linguistically intriguing passages in Anchieta's oeuvre. While the Roman emperors spoke Tupí and even 'the language of the Carijó', the indigenous demon-warriors, now recruited to the cause of the Christian martyr-saints, spoke alternately in Spanish and Tupí. When the emperors realized that the Spanish-speaking Aimbiré had come to ensure that their 'imperial state will be confirmed in fire', Decian cried out in Tupí: 'Though I be a sovereign ... Ai! God roasts me, avenging his servant.'[147] The linguistic hall of mirrors made clear a series of identities between Tupí demons, the pagan Roman emperors of the ancient Christian past, the various antagonists of the Spanish emperor, and Satan. In doing so, it collapsed historical time into this exemplary moment of theatre. Brazil now took its place in Christian history, extending from the time of the early martyrs to the present moment of the ascendance of the Catholic monarch, Philip II.

The act ended with Aimbiré avenging Lawrence. Wearing the crown of the emperors, he then proclaimed: 'O! I, conqueror of terrible sinners, now a true chief, because of this will change my name to Cururupeba!'[148] As befitting a Tupí warrior who had felled his enemies, Aimbiré took a new name, in this case that of the chief of an eponymous island. The historical Cururupeba had once cannibalized many captives, including priests, in response to Mem de Sá's ban on anthropophagy. Once captured, however, and following a year of imprisonment, Cururupeba converted and became a good Christian.[149] Thus, Aimbiré's choice of name was revealing: once the

[145] Anchieta, 'Na festa de São Lourenço', *Poesia*, 726.

[146] Anchieta, 'Na festa de São Lourenço', *Poesia*, 727.

[147] Anchieta, 'Na festa de São Lourenço', *Poesia*, 729.

[148] Anchieta, 'Na festa de São Lourenço', *Poesia*, 735.

[149] Nobrega to Tomé de Sousa, Bahia, 5 July 1559, *Monumenta Brasiliae* III, 91–2.

most truculent of Tupí warriors, he had been transformed through Christian captivity in the hands of the angelic custodian of the aldeia. Without relinquishing his status as a warrior, he had changed from the demonic Tupí intent on destroying Christians into a soldier in a Christian holy war, through the intercession of St Lawrence. In the literary figure of Aimbiré, one may see a reflection of the brave chief Tibiriçá of Anchieta's acquaintance, who had died as the Christian martyr Martim Afonso.

The Christian tradition of the martyr-saint thus represented Anchieta's answer to the problem of the Tupí attachment to warfare. He held out to the Tupí convert the exemplary possibility of being a warrior, one driven not by vengeance or the 'vomitous' customs of the Tupí, but rather by the need to castigate the many enemies that continued to plague Christianity. He represented the twin poles of Christian belief, the fear and love of God. Anchieta represented this notion literally in the celebratory final act of this remarkable play, in which the body of St Lawrence was carried forth by the characters representing the Fear of God and the Love of God. Each of these characters gave a brief monologue, following the same psalm-like structure of repetition of an opening set of key lines which characterized Anchieta's poems on the martyrs. These key lines, juxtaposed, reveal the dual nature of Christ as princely warrior and Christ as loving self-sacrificer, the same duality that subtended the figure of the martyr.

Fear	Hell	*Love*	Love God, who created you,
of God	With its eternal fire	*of God*	Man, much loved by God!
	Awaits you,		Love, with all care,
	If you do not follow the flag		He who first loved you.
	Of the cross,		His own son he handed over
	On which died Jesus		To death, to save you.
	So that you may kill death.[150]		What more could he give you ... ?[151]

Much as in *Na Vila de Vitória*, where these characters also appeared at the end, the Fear and Love of God corralled the Christian subject behind the banner of Christ and within his loving care. The play thus brought together Anchieta's twin visions for aldeia and the vila,

150 Anchieta, 'Na festa de São Lourenço', *Poesia*, 737.

151 Anchieta, 'Na festa de São Lourenço', *Poesia*, 742.

models of Christian civility that had transcended the turbulence of various forms of warfare and violence, both indigenous and European, local and global.

Christian Word, Tupí Silence

Though Anchieta made the model of the martyr-saint available to the converts in this trilingual play, there was one last model of Christian violence in his oeuvre that was denied to the Tupí, both by virtue of its language and its genre. This was the early epic he wrote in Latin verse in honour of the governor Mem de Sá. The governor was the motive force of the crucial pacification campaigns of the early years of Anchieta's work. He sanctioned the creation of the institution of the aldeia, the linchpin of the Jesuit mission. *De Gestis Mendi de Saa*, the supreme expression of Anchieta's skill as a humanist literatus, was published anonymously in Coimbra in 1563.[152] Its opening describes the killing of Fernão de Sá in an uprising in Rio de Janeiro. This serves as the dramatic pretext for the series of campaigns undertaken by his father, Mem de Sá, in his pacification of the Tupí, including the campaign of 1560 against the French-Tamoio alliance that Anchieta had witnessed. The epic also staged an extended dramatization of the cannibalization of the Bishop Sardinha, which inspired the later pacification of Bahia. The work ends with the final expulsion of the French at the cost of his own life by the governor's nephew, Estácio de Sá.[153]

The epic reflected Anchieta's approval of the pacification of the indigenous, as they submitted, one by one, to the 'peace' Mem de Sá forged with an iron hand. Repetitively, the epic periodically rises to a crescendo of warfare, in which Mem de Sá, the Christian soldier-hero, or his surrogates prevail. This is followed by a brief interlude of peace marked by the triumphal return of the soldier and the celebrations within the Christian settlement. Lest one think that the orgy of

[152] Anchieta, *De gestis Mendi de Saa*.

[153] Although the events of the last book, which recounts the taking of Rio de Janeiro by Estácio de Sá, post-dated the publication, the philologist Armando Cardoso includes it as an authentic part of the work in his critical edition of the text.

warfare in the epic is regenerative in the manner of Tupí warfare, the final chapter ends with the coming of a decisive peace on the ruins of the French fortress, marked by a series of hymns of thanksgiving and praise to Christ. The simultaneity of discourse and warfare in the Tupí world, perhaps best exemplified by the rites surrounding the cannibalism of captured enemies, is precisely opposed to a Christian poetics, in which song and discourse can come only *after* warfare, in the context of peace.

It is difficult to ascertain what use the indigenous converts made of Anchieta's poetic corpus, or even their role in its creation. The profound cosmological understanding displayed in these texts certainly suggests their involvement; one may speculate that through the performance of these plays, indigenous converts could at least retain a memory of cultural traditions under profound assault. Regardless, from the Jesuit viewpoint, the conversion of the Tupí depended ultimately on the ability to bend (if not destroy) the two modes of their orality to a Christian will and purpose. If Mem de Sá's brutal campaign had ruptured the motor of warfare that underlay ritual cannibalism, Anchieta's corpus sought to reorient the terms of Tupí discourse, breaking its intimate links with warfare and thus anthropophagy. Through a form of ventriloquism, utilizing not only the tools of humanism but also popular traditions of European and indigenous orality, Anchieta's poetics of war imposed upon the Tupí a permanent peace. Their conversion was predicated upon this peace, which also represented the death of their own particular mode of orality. As much through coercion as through accommodatio, a strictly controlled Christian civility was ordained in the aldeias. Here, under the custody of the Jesuits, the convert was sequestered not only from indigenous cultural influence and the rapacious demands of colonial planters; he was also removed from the local European representatives of imperial rivals and Protestant heresy, which threatened a global Catholic order.

5

CHRIST IN THE *BRAHMAPURI*
Thomas Stephens in Salcete

> On the 4th of April [1579] five ships departed for Goa ... with trumpets and shooting of ordnance, you may easily imagine it, considering that they go in the manner of war. The tenth of the foresaid month we came to the sight of Porto Sancto, near unto Madeira, where an English ship set upon ours ... The English ship was very fair and great, which I was sorry to see so ill-occupied.[1]

Thus began the voyage of the English Jesuit Thomas Stephens, aboard a Portuguese ship, from Lisbon to Goa. The ambivalent juxtapositions of 'we' and 'they' indexed Stephens's oscillating sense of himself as an Englishman and as a Catholic escaping the persecutions of his homeland. For Thomas Stephens, the crossing to Goa signified not merely a missionary's journey to the Indies, but also an Englishman's passing into the domain of a foreign empire.

Ignatius had sought to circumvent the petty attachment to homeland among the Companions: he insisted on removing the reluctant Simão Rodrigues from his beloved Portuguese province precisely to demonstrate the precedence of obedience to the order above any sentimental call towards an ancestral land. Yet, the Society had changed significantly from his day. The rapid expansion of the order had created the possibility of factions based on homeland and language.

[1] Stephens to his father, 10 November 1579, in Hakluyt, *The Principal Navigations*, vol. IV, 234.

Moreover, the forays of the French, the Dutch, and the English into the Indies threatened its neat division between the Spanish and Portuguese Catholic monarchies at Tordesillas. In this increasingly complex interplay of European imperial rivalries, members of the Jesuit order were hardly immune from the prejudices and sentiments of their countrymen.

How then was an English Jesuit to conduct himself in the lands of the Padroado, even as the Portuguese monarchy slipped into Spanish hands? Stephens's solution was similar to José de Anchieta: a single-minded commitment to the creation of an indigenous Christian community through engagement with the alien culture amidst which he found himself. Stephens too was a liminal figure, not of New Christian ancestry like Anchieta, but, as an English Catholic, suspect both in his homeland and in the Estado da Índia.[2] If the avoidance of imperial politics in favour of local missions was important to the Spanish-speaking Anchieta in Portuguese Brazil, it proved of even greater import for Thomas Stephens in India. As the imperial ambitions of Holland and England eroded the Estado da Índia and the Jesuit order was riddled with ethnic divisions, Stephens set aside global concerns to devote himself to the difficult mission of Salcete, a border region of Goa.

Affected by his own experience of the paranoia and persecution that accompanied the confessionalization of states in post-Reformation Europe, Stephens rejected the violent tactics adopted by the Portuguese and their Jesuit allies to Christianize Salcete. Instead, he practised a form of accommodatio that the visitor Alessandro Valignano had sanctioned, in which the cultures of those peoples deemed worthy could be adapted for the purpose of converting them. Like Anchieta, for Stephens, this was a humanist enterprise, in which knowledge of the local language was crucial. Unlike Anchieta, however, Stephens's accommodatio, consonant with a hierarchical ethnological schema

[2] Such suspicion of Catholics in England was not entirely unfounded: see 'Algunos motívos y razones, que ay para favorever los Seminarios Ingleses', 1600, SC, Anglia, VI, MS 26; 'Las causas que han movido al Rey Catolico don Felipe II nuestro señor, para admitir y favorecer à los Seminarios de Clerigos Ingleses en los Reynos de España, y en sus Estados de Flandres', SC, Anglia, VI, MS 21.

au courant in the Society, would leave a lasting impact both on missionary practice and indigenous Catholic culture in Goa.

This chapter begins with a brief reconstruction of Stephens's early life in England and his evolving critique of the coercive forms of conversion practised in Salcete. I then trace Stephens's difficult position in the troubled local and global politics of the Jesuit order. Eventually, the brahmin convert community in Margão became his only consolation, for whom he composed the *Discurso sobre a vinda de Jesu Christo* (Discourse on the Coming of Jesus Christ). The final segment of this chapter is devoted to this remarkable work.

A Catholic Education in a Protestant Land

The early life of Thomas Stephens, like that of many English Catholics of the era, is difficult to reconstruct.[3] He was born around 1549–50 in Bushton, Salisbury, to a merchant of some prominence. This prominence was precisely the source of his vulnerability as a Catholic: commenting upon the martyrdom of Edmund Campion and his companions, Stephens wrote to his brother, the theologian Richard Stephens, that 'it is astounding that [our father], who having been so often vexed by heretics in a peaceful republic, should have evaded a carnage of citizens'.[4] Even so, the family, or at least those members willing to compromise their faith, maintained some influence within the English court.[5] Still, Stephens's religious career owed more to his acquaintance with Thomas Pounde, whom he met in 1572, than to his familial connections. Pounde, related to the Earl of Southampton, had once enjoyed the privileges of a courtier, before abandoning these 'very mermaid's allurements to perdition'.[6] In his petition to admit Pounde to the Society of Jesus, Stephens mentioned

[3] Schurhammer, 'Thomas Stephens', 368.

[4] Stephens to Richard Stephens, Goa, 24 October 1583, *Documenta Indica* XII, 817.

[5] Stephens to Richard Stephens, Goa, 24 October 1583, *Documenta Indica* XII, 817.

[6] Pounde, 'A Malicious Discourse of the Sufferings of a Recusant', in Foley, *Records*, 614. See also Stephens, 'Petitio Dni. Thomae Poundi ad Dom. R. Prem Societatis Jesu Prepositum Generalum, cum testimonis de ipsius vita et conversatione', SC, Collectio Cardwelli, vol. I, 16.

that though outdoors he assumed the persona of Pounde's servant, a position fitting Stephens's financial means and useful camouflage from inquisitive heretics, indoors he lived as his guest.[7] Stephens's friendship with the wealthier Pounde granted him a safe haven in which to hone his vocation. However, their subterfuges failed: while resting their 'blistered feet in Ludlow', the two were 'suspected forsooth for spies come to view the country' and briefly imprisoned.[8]

Pounde and Stephens did not lose their zeal for the Church, and, in particular, the Jesuit missions. Pounde resolved 'in consequence of reading letters of [Jesuits] from the Indies, and hearing the good fame of the Society', to join the order and Stephens too formed the same desire of going to Rome together and 'giving ourselves up to the Society.'[9] Ignatius's injunctions to missionaries to highlight their success, while demurring to speak publicly of their tribulations, clearly bore rich fruit in frigid England.

After prison, Pounde 'intended to pass two or three months in Flanders and France', to recruit more faithful young men for the order before making their way to Rome.[10] In preparation, he hoped to effect the conversion of 'a certain heretic in London'.[11] Not only did his exhortations come to naught, but Pounde was again imprisoned for six months.[12] He was only freed through the intervention of the Earl of Southampton.[13] Pounde again acted impetuously and, despite their hopes of serving the Society together, the careers of the two Thomases diverged.[14] Pounde spent his days in England's prisons, while Stephens joined the Society as a novice in October 1575, alongside Robert Persons, the future rector of the English College in Rome; Henry Garnet, who would be martyred in England

[7] Stephens, 'Petitio', SC, Collectio Cardwelli, vol. I, 18.

[8] Pounde, 'A Malicious Discourse', in Foley, *Records*, 614.

[9] Stephens, 'Petitio', SC, Collectio Cardwelli, vol. I, 17.

[10] Stephens, 'Petitio', SC, Collectio Cardwelli, vol. I, 17, 22.

[11] Stephens, 'Petitio', SC, Collectio Cardwelli, vol. I, 17, 22–3.

[12] Stephens, 'Petitio', SC, Collectio Cardwelli, vol. I, 17, 23. On this imprisonment, see also Pounde, 'A Malicious Discourse', in Foley, *Records*, 614–15.

[13] Stephens, 'Petitio', SC, Collectio Cardwelli, vol. I, 17, 24.

[14] Pounde retained a touching affection for Stephens more than forty years after their last contact. See Pounde, 'A Malicious Discourse', in Foley, *Records*, 614.

in 1606; and Petro Berno, who would sail along with Stephens to Goa. Stephens's self-effacing commitment to the Catholic faith was forged in the atmosphere of dissimulation and paranoia of the post-Reformation England: whereas Pounde courted imprisonment and indulged in flamboyant self-mortification, the unassuming Stephens played his servant till he could escape to Rome and begin his career in the Society of Jesus.[15] It was an important (and very Jesuitical) lesson on the need for political circumspection in pursuit of a religious life.

Journey to the East

In an age where the measurement of longitude was still an inexact art, Stephens's detailed description to his father of his journey from Lisbon to Goa and his unusual access to Portuguese navigation generated great interest in England.[16] Upon arriving in Goa on 24 October 1579, Stephens, who had completed his scholastic training in Rome, began his theological studies in the local college.[17] Due to the serious shortage of priests, however, he was quickly ordained and sent to the mission where he would spend the next forty years of his life—Salcete.

The trope of the hardships of the inhospitable climes of the Indies had underscored, from Xavier's day, the difficulty and nobility of the missionary enterprise; Stephens instead lavished praise upon the natural properties of his new home.[18] He seemed to posit the hospitability of the climate he found against the wisdom of earlier geographers such

[15] Pounde, 'A Malicious Discourse', in Foley, *Records*, 614. Admitting Pounde to the Society, Everard Mercurian admonished him to be cautious and moderate. Letter of General Mercurian to Thomas Pounde, 1 December 1578, SC, Collectio Cardwelli, vol. I, 29–30.

[16] Stephens to his father, 10 November 1579, in Hakluyt, *The Principal Navigations*, vol. IV, 235–6. On the English cosmographical interest in Stephens's letter, see John Newbery to Leonard Poore, 25 January 1584, in Hakluyt, *The Principal Navigations*, vol. V, 452. Jesuits also recognized Stephens's cosmographical skills: in 1595, at the Father General's behest, Stephens prepared and sent a detailed map of Goa, Salcete, and Bardez. See Thomas Stephens to Claudio Aquaviva, Margão, 19 December 1595, *Documenta Indica* XVII, 466–7.

[17] Stephens to Richard Stephens, Goa, 24 October 1583, *Documenta Indica* XII, 818.

[18] Stephens to Richard Stephens, Goa, 24 October 1583, *Documenta Indica* XII, 825.

as Pliny regarding the uninhabitable heat of the Torrid Zone. He was also struck by the natural abundance of Salcete, most clearly exemplified by the endless bounty of the palm tree.[19]

Salcete was also the setting of a rapid conversion process: when Stephens arrived in 1580, 'there were six churches in this place, to which were added three more [in 1582]'.[20] Nonetheless, for all its promise, Salcete was a difficult mission, not least because of its complicated political history. Ceded by Vijayanagara to Bijāpur along with Ponda and Bardez in 1520, the Portuguese attempted to incorporate these territories as a buffer zone against Bijāpur. Eventually, Nuno da Cunha successfully petitioned to build a fort in Rachol, in Salcete, under licence from Assad Khān, the Bijāpuri governor. Although this fort was destroyed in 1538 by Bijāpuri forces, by 1543 the Portuguese had formally acquired the territory from the 'Ādil Shāh.

Salcete, with its rich heritage of Hindu temples, was viewed as an important site for evangelism: Miguel Vaz, the famed vicar general and one of the original founders of the college in Goa, wrote to D. João III towards the end of 1545, urging him to destroy the rampant idolatry in Salcete and Bardez by placing it in the hands of reliable men rather than prominent brahmin agents, who would meddle in the business of conversion.[21] In 1560, Pedro Mascarenhas and his companion Manuel Gomes arrived in Salcete to found the Jesuit mission, centring their activities on the fortress of Rachol.[22] By the end of the year, there was already a core of 1,000 Christians. Living amidst some 50,000 Hindus in such close proximity to the Muslims of Bijāpur and lacking priests to cultivate them, they were hardly different from their unconverted brethren.[23]

[19] Stephens to Richard Stephens, Goa, 24 October 1583, *Documenta Indica* XII, 825. See also Stephens to his father, 10 November 1579, in Hakluyt, *The Principal Navigations*, vol. IV, 234–6.

[20] Stephens to Richard Stephens, Goa, 24 October 1583, *Documenta Indica* XII, 819–20. The churches were located in Cortalim, Rachol, Margão, Verna, Orlim, and Mormugão, with the later additions of Velção, Loutolim, and Colvá.

[21] Miguel Vaz to D. João III, 1545, *Documenta Indica* I, 70.

[22] Manuel Gomes to Society in Portugal, Rachol, 1 December 1560, *Documenta Indica* IV, 752–3.

[23] Luis Fróis to Society in Portugal, Goa, 1 December 1560, *Documenta Indica* IV, 742–3.

The ebb and flow of conversion in Salcete was marked by violence. The periodic invasions of the armies of Bijāpur left in their wake broken churches. Moreover, in 1567, Diogo Rodrigues, the captain of Rachol, began the systematic destruction of nearly 300 temples in the peninsula.[24] Still, the Jesuits made progress in the business of conversion.[25]

The Hindus of Salcete resisted their gains. One option, given the political geography of Salcete, was simply flight: the proximity with Bijāpur allowed recalcitrant gentiles to not only escape the confines of Portuguese rule and Jesuit vigilance; they could also remove their idols from destroyed temples and re-install them on the other side of the border.[26] The Jesuit correspondence from the 1560s and 1570s is full of references of plots to escape to the *terra de mouros* (land of the Moors), or of Christian converts being spirited away to these territories by their gentile or apostate relatives.[27] When Bijāpur did march against Salcete, their erstwhile subjects were often willing allies, aiding them in the destruction of the churches.[28]

Within the matrix of Portuguese power, the Hindu communities petitioned the governors and viceroys to grant them licences to continue their public festivities in exchange for large sums of money.[29] These attempts were stymied through strenuous Jesuit opposition, especially by the rector Afonso Pacheco, who carried his petition to Portugal.[30] When Philip II captured the Portuguese Crown, he continued the status quo: a series of royal decrees in 1580–1 confirmed

[24] On Bijāpur destroying churches during the war of 1571, see *Documenta Indica* VIII, L. Leitão, Goa, 5 Nov 1572, 586. For 1577–8, see *Documenta Indica* XI, 267, 552; for 1581, *Documenta Indica* XII, 68, 37, 110. For temple destruction, see *Documenta Indica* VIII, 387–96, 431.

[25] *Documenta Indica* VIII, 920.

[26] Axelrod and Fuerch, 'Flight of the Deities'.

[27] Chakravarti, 'In the Language of the Land'.

[28] The five villages of Assolna, Cuncolim, Verodá, Velim, and Ambelim, which had aided the 'Ādil Shāh's forces in 1577–8, remained rebellious. See Saldanha, *História de Goa*, vol. I, 141; *Documenta Indica* X, 808. On iconoclasm as a mode of asserting political sovereignty in South Asia, see Davis, *Lives of Indian Images*, 51–83.

[29] *Documenta Indica* XI, 262, 563–9, 692.

[30] *Documenta Indica* XI, 905, *Documenta Indica* XII, VI.

again that neither temples nor gentile festivities were to be tolerated in Salcete and Bardez.[31] Still, when Stephens arrived, Salcete was difficult missionary terrain:

> There are very few Christians and many gentiles, all bellicose and dangerous enemies of the Portuguese name and who abhor greatly the Christian faith, who for many years, partly by assaults, partly by conspiracies, have been doing great harm to the Christian republic. For, as in many other places subject to the Portuguese king, the gentile temples have been destroyed.[32]

Consoling his brother Richard, a theologian struggling against the Lutheran heresy in Europe, Stephens wrote: 'Do not say that the sun has set on you in the west while (as you say) it visits us from the east. For, while we enjoy prosperity, we too feel much of adversity.'[33]

A Massacre and a Parable: Two Approaches to Conversion

Of the 'adversity' Stephens had in mind, the most vivid and recent example was the infamous massacre in May 1583 of Jesuit missionaries and converts in Cuncolim.[34] Though the village was perennially rebellious, often refusing to pay tribute to the Portuguese king, the immediate provocation for the attack was the destruction and desecration of the local temple, an act that was at least partly a punitive

[31] 'Provisão dos Defenssores pera nas terras de Salcete e Bardez de que el Rey he Senhor não aver pagodes, Almeirim, 28 de Março de 1580', GSHA, Provisões a favour da cristandade, fl. 35v–36r; 'De Sua Magestade que não aja pagodes, nem ceremonias', 25 de Fevreiro de 1581 GSHA, Provisões a favour da cristandade, fl. 36v–37r. Philip also continued the settlement with village landholders or *gāunkārs* and with village scribes to retain their rights and offices. See 'Alvara de Sua Magestade para que se cumpre e guarda o foral de Goa, Bardes e Salcete acerca das gancarias', Lisboa, 2 de Abril de 1582, GSHA, Provisões a favour da cristandade, 48v.

[32] Stephens to Richard Stephens, Goa, 24 October 1583, *Documenta Indica* XII, 820.

[33] Stephens to Richard Stephens, Goa, 24 October 1583, *Documenta Indica* XII, 826.

[34] On the massacre, see Barreto Xavier, *A Invenção de Goa*, 333–79; Robinson, 'Cuncolim'.

measure for the villagers' rebellion against Portuguese dominion.[35] Rudolfo Aquaviva, newly returned from his mission to the Mughal court, had taken charge of the Salcete mission. To calm the angry villagers, Aquaviva visited Cuncolim, accompanied by the previous rector, Afonso Pacheco; Petro Berno, Stephens's companion in the novitiate and in the journey to Goa; Antonio Francisco, recently arrived from Portugal with Pacheco; and the brother Francisco Aranha. In their entourage, there were three brahmin converts: the collector of the rents of the temples, Francisco Rodrigues; his registrar, João da Silva; and Paulo Costa, the father and procurator of the new Christians. There were also two young brahmin boys, Domingo and Afonso, as well as two lay Portuguese brothers, Gonçalo Rodriguez and Domingo de Aguiar.

Stephens recounted what transpired in gruesome detail. The villagers did not spare even the brahmin converts hailing from Cuncolim. Rudolfo, 'at whom the most powerful Moghul king blushed, who among so many thousands of hostile Mahometans was safe', was killed 'near Goa by a few barbarians, who were subjects of the Catholic king'. Petro Berno, who had accompanied the Portuguese army and who had set fire to the temple and killed a cow upon its altar, was meted the worst violence: 'They plucked out one of his eyes, cut off the whole of his skull and committed other acts of atrocity that I balk at recounting.' While the villagers allowed the indigenous converts to be buried, only on the third day, 'with the permission of the seers (*arioli*), were [the Jesuit] bodies returned'.[36]

His account set the stage for the martyriological narrative surrounding the massacre that led eventually to the beatification of the Jesuit victims. Still, Stephens pointedly noted that the worst and most humiliating violence was meted out to those Jesuits held most culpable in the forced conversions: Petro Berno and Francisco Aranha, who had built the local church. As Stephens suggested, this conflict could not be interpreted as an indigenous uprising against Europeans. It was a religious conflict, of the kind usually analysed under the rubric of communalism in South Asian historiography. This much, however, was clear: Salcete, ostensibly in the hands of a Catholic monarch,

[35] *Documenta Indica* X, 808.

[36] Stephens to Richard Stephens, Goa, 24 October 1583, *Documenta Indica* XII, 820–2.

was far more dangerous to the missionaries and their flock than the realms of such infidel kings as Akbar.

Stephens's report on the massacre largely avoided the essentialist and derogatory epithets used by other Jesuit commentators about the villagers of Cuncolim. Instead, he was at pains to reveal the motivations behind the brutal attack. This willingness to impute reasonable motivations and sentiments to the people of his adopted land formed the basis of his own approach to conversion.

Stephens's critique of the violent strategies that led to the massacre was visible almost in parallax in an anecdote he relayed to his brother, immediately after recounting the events at Cuncolim. He invited explicit comparison between the two incidents, noting that the former had given 'an equal amount of trouble in the beginning, but ... resulted in a happier issue'. The anecdote, told almost in the manner of a parable, centred on a young brahmin convert, Bernard, who had been left in Stephens's care by his predecessor in the residence. His devotion rankled with his apostate brother, his obstinately gentile mother, and other relatives, who 'had been living as exiles in the neighboring country'. Upon learning that Bernard had received permission to go to Goa for humanistic studies, these relatives hatched a plan to kidnap the boy. The gentiles drugged him with 'a fruit called *Duttro*'. Bernard, raving and embracing 'shadows which he took for our Fathers, went about seizing the leaves of the trees glistening in the moonlight, thinking that they were the letters which he had received from us to be carried to Goa'. His cruelly mocking relatives carried him off into 'the territory of the gentiles' and imprisoned him. Upon regaining his senses, Bernard remained firm in his Christian resolve. Despite his mother's promises of gold and threats of torment, he refused to renounce the faith as his brother had done. Though they mixed sacred ashes in his food to change his mind, Bernard simply made the sign of the cross before eating.[37] After ten days of rigorous imprisonment, another apostate counselled Bernard's mother:

> You think of changing the mind of your son in one day, which you know can happen by no means ... Little by little he defected from us and little by little he must be recovered ... [E]ven the Fathers themselves do not persuade

[37] Stephens to Richard Stephens, Goa, 24 October 1583, *Documenta Indica* XII, 820–3.

> someone the first day, but attract people step-by-step ... Thus will it be with your boy, if you choose me as his counselor. First he will be released; then we must draw him gently by many enticements. For if you do him violence, you will certainly make him more obstinate.[38]

This was a view of the process of conversion that stood at odds with the violence of the temple-destruction campaigns, which had in turn engendered the violence at Cuncolim. The rhetorical device of using the apostate advisor as his mirror and foil allowed Stephens to articulate a critique of such evangelical strategies, without disrespecting recent martyrs like Petro Berno, who had embraced these violent methods.

In this key letter to his brother, there was a further clue to Stephens's evolving approach to conversion. The conspiracy to kidnap Bernard, in Stephens's view, had been a panicked response to his desire to go to Goa to study Latin. As Stephens put it, 'they began to reason within themselves, saying "If he masters the Latin language, it is to be feared that relying upon the support of literature he will greatly injure us and our sect".'[39] If Latin learning and the humanistic knowledge it entailed could be wielded as a weapon in the hands of a Christian convert, knowledge of local languages was equally important to the missionary's arsenal. Thus, Stephens described the linguistic landscape of Salcete with the same attentiveness with which he had described its natural features. The pronunciation of the many languages was 'not disagreeable'. More importantly, 'their structure is allied to Greek and Latin', and their phrases and constructions Stephens deemed 'wonderful'.[40] The seeds of Stephens's humanistic approach to conversion, which would flower in his literary legacy in Kōṅkaṇī and Marāṭhī, had been sown.

An Englishman in Salcete

Around the time of the massacre at Cuncolim, a merchant expedition led by the English adventurer John Newbery set off from London for the port of Hormuz. On 9 September 1583, five days after arriving in

[38] Stephens to Richard Stephens, Goa, 24 October 1583, *Documenta Indica* XII, 824.

[39] Stephens to Richard Stephens, Goa, 24 October 1583, *Documenta Indica* XII, 822.

[40] Stephens to Richard Stephens, Goa, 24 October 1583, *Documenta Indica* XII, 825.

Hormuz, the English traders were arrested at the instigation of local Venetian merchants, protective of their right to trade in Portuguese ports. The Englishmen were shipped to Goa, where they were imprisoned till December. Stephens, accompanied by the Flemish Jesuit Marke, supplicated to the viceroy on behalf of his compatriots. They had the support of the archbishop, swayed by the intercession of his servants Bernard Burcherts of Hamburg and Jan van Huyghen Linschoten of Enkhuizen.[41] When the merchants were unable to produce the requisite bail, Stephens and Marke procured sureties, on the understanding that they would not leave the country without the licence of the viceroy.[42] Allowed to set up shop in Goa, the Englishmen nonetheless escaped overland to Mughal territory.[43]

Ralph Fitch, the sole survivor of the expedition to return to England, acknowledged Stephens's kindness.[44] His account garnered sufficient fame that Thomas Pounde, still languishing in prison, could write in 1609: 'Father Thomas Stephens, these thirty-nine years since a famous preacher of the Society at Goa ... of whose great favors there showed to many of our English Protestants there sometimes arriving, they have in the history of their navigation given good testimony.'[45] By contrast, the Dutchman Linschoten in his infamous *Itinerario* imputed ulterior motives for the generosity of the Jesuits. They hoped, he claimed, to convert the good English Protestants and induce them to become Jesuits, thus securing for themselves their wares and skills. They were particularly interested in the painter Storey, since they needed decorators for India's churches. The Englishmen pretended to be convinced by the Catholics to gain their trust. Linschoten noted with satisfaction that once the three merchants had fled, Storey too abandoned the order, opening shop in town and marrying a local mestiça woman.

[41] John Newbery to Leonard Poore, 25 January 1584, in Hakluyt, *The Principal Navigations*, vol. V, 458–60.

[42] Ralph Fitch to Leonard Poore, 25 January 1584, in Ryley, *Ralph Fitch*, 65; Linschoten, *The Voyage*, 163.

[43] Linschoten, *The Voyage*, 164.

[44] Fitch thanked Stephens in his account and his descriptions of India were reminiscent of Stephens's famous letters, including an elegy to the palm tree.

[45] Pounde, 'A Malicious Discourse', in Foley, *Records*, 614.

It was Storey himself who had told Linschoten their tale. Since then, Linschoten claimed, no foreigners, other than the Italians plying their usual trade, had come to Goa.[46] Regardless of Linschoten's anti-Catholic prejudice, the English Jesuit and his Flemish confrere, as much as Linschoten and his German colleague, had aided the Englishmen to their own cost. As Linschoten reported, whispers arose in Goa that these advocates had counselled the Englishmen to escape.

The suspicion of foreigners in Goa would only increase over the next decade. When the Dutch rounded the Cape of Good Hope in 1595, they exposed the extent to which Portugal's fragile empire depended on the absence of rival naval powers in the Indian Ocean.[47] In the next six years, over sixty ships set sail for the east, and in 1602, the Vereenigde Oost-Indische Compagnie (VOC) was formed along the lines of the English East India Company. English efforts, after the successful voyage of James Lancaster in 1602, were not far behind. With prices of pepper and other spices plummeting in Europe and the high overhead costs of the Estado, the fragile financial basis of the eastern empire faltered. Private interests withdrew and the Crown was forced to resume its monopoly.[48] As Anthony Disney has shown, while the Portuguese were undoubtedly militarily weaker, it was ultimately an economic and organizational crisis that made their eastern holdings so vulnerable to the Dutch.[49] The metropolitan response to the Anglo-Dutch incursions was a truculent and increasingly hysterical attempt to keep all foreigners out. Nonetheless, by 1603, the Dutch began to build alliances with indigenous polities hostile to the Portuguese and to receive permissions to build factories and to trade in their dominions.[50] In such an atmosphere, foreign missionaries were viewed askance by the Portuguese, who sought increasingly to regulate their passage to the east.[51]

[46] Linschoten, *The Voyage*, 161–7.

[47] Heras, 'Decay of the Portuguese Power in India', 26.

[48] Boxer, *The Dutch Seaborne Empire*, 22–4.

[49] Disney, *Twilight of the Pepper Empire.*

[50] For agreements with Calicut, Golconda, and the Nāyaka rulers of Ginjee, see J.K.J. de Jonge, *De Opkomst, (1595–1610)*, vol. III, 204, 213, 294, 339, 348.

[51] See, for example, the document dated 31 January 1604, AHU, India 1, Doc. 43.

Yet, in 1609, when the French traveller François Pyrard de Laval was imprisoned alongside his French, Dutch, and English companions, he too found support amidst Jesuits of non-Portuguese descent. The group, comprising Stephens, Gaspar Schuren, Jean de Sein, Nicholas Trigault, and Etienne de la Croix secured their release from jail. Stephens showed particular consideration for his countrymen:

> The English also came by way of this good Father Thomas Stephens, who took much trouble: there were four who became Catholics, two of whom died there. And in truth the good fathers would have liked [to help] us [back] in our country; for all the trouble we gave them, they watched over us like their own brothers.[52]

The prisoners engendered empathy and fellow feeling amongst these Jesuits, whose origins made them outsiders to the Portuguese political order and the Society's own factions.

Perhaps the origin of the factionalism within the Jesuit order in this period can be traced to the career of Alessandro Valignano as visitor to the Indian province, where he tussled with the presumptive Portuguese control over the lands of the Padroado.[53] The visitor's vision centred on a codification of Xavier's incipient ethnology, in which the Japanese—classified as 'white people' of apparent rationality, possessing a lettered, refined honour-bound culture without idolatry—occupied the apex. In his schema, Valignano found the inhabitants of the coastline of the subcontinent under Portuguese dominion to be unequivocally inferior to Europeans:

> These people, who are almost black and go half naked, are universally contemptible and held to be base by the Portuguese and other Europeans; and the truth is that compared to them they are of little substance and lack refinement. They are, as Aristotle says, of a servile nature, because they are commonly poor, miserable and mean, and for any gain they will do the lowest things.[54]

Even caste, in which some Europeans saw a version of the cherished European principle of honour, was reduced in Valignano's view to superstition; a kernel of monotheistic truth had been occluded in

[52] Pyrard de Laval, *Voyage*, 767.

[53] Üçerler, 'Alessandro Valignano'.

[54] Valignano, *Historia*, 24–5.

India by monstrous error.[55] Whereas Xavier's contempt had been aimed at the brahmins, rather than the low-caste Parava converts, Valignano made no such distinction.[56]

Valignano articulated an evangelical vision in which the 'quality' of the converts was central. He represented a broader intellectual shift within the order, as hierarchical comparative ethnology became the primary means to understand the vast non-Christian world in which the Society evangelized. One need only compare Valignano to José Acosta, writing in Peru only a decade later, to see the reach of this model.[57] In Asia, in accordance with an ethnographic hierarchy reflecting Xavier's own judgement, Valignano tried to pivot the centre of the province away from Portuguese India to the missions in Japan and China.[58] Moreover, for the conversion of such 'superior' peoples, he advocated accommodatio.[59] By contrast, India commanded no such respect: to Valignano, it was no surprise that Salcete, 'full of many brahmins' and thus 'always given in the greatest manner to the abominable cult of idolatry and gentile superstitions', should be the setting for a massacre such as that at Cuncolim.[60] For a missionary like Stephens, whose sympathy for the people of Goa had only grown from his first, generous impressions, Valignano's indictment was troubling indeed.[61]

The visitor's attitude did not ingratiate those missionaries, most of whom were Portuguese themselves, who laboured along the Indian coastline under Portugal's dominion. The turning point in this conflict came around 1593, when Valignano petitioned Rome to institute

[55] Valignano, *Historia*, 25–32.

[56] On the general discourse of missionaries on the nature of the gentiles within the Portuguese world, see Ricardo Ventura's excellent dissertation, 'Conversão e Conversabilidade'. I am grateful to the author for sharing his work.

[57] Pagden, *The Fall of Natural Man*, 146–96.

[58] Aranha, 'Gerarchie razziali'.

[59] Naturally, not all Italian missionaries deemed brahminical culture as essentially inferior. Roberto Nobili's mission in Madurai, discussed later in the sixth chapter, is the obvious counter-example.

[60] Valignano to Claudio Aquaviva, Goa, 8 December 1583, *Documenta Indica* XII, 916–33.

[61] Stephens to his father, 10 November 1579, in Hakluyt, *The Principal Navigations*, vol. IV, 239–40.

a college in Macao to rival that of Goa. The Portuguese provincial, Francisco Cabral, could hardly have been more different in temperament and orientation to Valignano. Nuno Rodrigues, the procurator, noted that Cabral, in sharp contrast to Valignano, showed little application in promoting humanistic learning in the colleges.[62] Cabral fought the effort, arguing that the Visitor had siphoned away the most talented Jesuits arriving from Europe to Japan, while sending ill and unsuitable brothers to the struggling missions of India. Valignano, he charged, had also reduced Japan's contribution to the common expenses of the province by half, even though that vice-province made a considerable income from investments in silk, gold, and real estate. In light of these pressures, Cabral suggested that not only should the Indian and Japanese missions be separated into more manageable provinces, but that the troubled parishes in Salcete should be handed over to the care of the episcopacy.[63]

The Trials of Salcete

As always, the doubts about the mission in Salcete were expressed privately: in the public annual letter Cabral had sent a month before, he described the 11 churches and 27,123 Christians of Salcete in proud detail. He celebrated the great devotion of the converts, exemplified in several edifying tales, including one involving the foiling of an attempt by a few Christians to escape to the land of the infidels and 'take caste' again.[64]

The reality, as Cabral's private desire to be rid of the mission indicates, was quite different. In the fraught atmosphere of the wider eastern province, Stephens confronted his first serious personal challenge while serving as rector at the College in Margão. Stephens, at the age of forty-five, was described in an internal assessment as being of great intelligence, judgement and prudence, of sanguine

[62] Nuno Rodrigues to Claudio Aquaviva, Goa, 13 December 1595, *Documenta Indica* XVII, 453–4.

[63] Francisco Cabral to Claudia Aquaviva, Cochin, 15 December 1593, *Documenta Indica* XVI, 510–25.

[64] Francisco Cabral, Annual Letter of Province of India, Goa, 15 November 1593, *Documenta Indica* XVI, 319–26.

temperament and an excellent talent for conversion, despite a somewhat mediocre knowledge of cases—understandable in light of his interrupted theological study. Though he confirmed this assessment of Stephens's personal qualities, Nuno Rodrigues averred that he had little talent for administration, using Stephens as a case in point in arguing for limited terms of office for mission superiors.[65] Stephens had served as superior of the mission, after taking his final vows as coadjutor in 1589. In this capacity, Stephens had been responsible, among other things, for the management of the income of the mission. While the Portuguese monarchy guaranteed support to the mission from the income derived from the erstwhile temple lands, its administration was still open to debate. Moreover, the rapid acquisition of land by the Jesuit missions during the tenure of Stephens's predecessor, which continued under Stephens's leadership, became a source of controversy.[66]

The charges against Stephens were laid out most clearly by João da Cunha. By his own admission, Stephens was displeased with him and Cunha clearly wished to leave the mission in Salcete. Eventually, Cunha was dismissed from the order in 1596.[67] Still, his complaints in this instance do not seem baseless, even if coloured by personal animosity. Cunha had criticized Stephens for appropriating the income from a *palmar* (coconut palm grove) left by Antonio de Gois to the church of Colvá for the expenses of the college, of which Stephens was the rector. For pointing out this violation of the donor's wishes, Stephens and his supporters removed him from his parish. These events, Cunha claimed, led to scandal, not only in Salcete but in Goa too: those who had known Gois claimed that the Jesuits 'were neither God nor did they have His privileges to do as they wished, appropriating the income of Christians in ways neither licit nor honest'.

[65] See Catalogues of the Province of India, Goa, 15 December 1594, *Documenta Indica* XVI, 959.

[66] The documents of the College of Rachol and the tax registers of Salcete reveal that under Miguel Leitão's and Stephens's rectorships, the mission acquired significant amounts of land donations. See collections, GSHA, 824, Provisões do Colegio de Rachol; 3071, Foral de Salcete.

[67] João da Cunha to Claudio Aquaviva, Goa, 15 November 1593, *Documenta Indica* XVI, 272–87.

Cunha charged that there were murmurs within and beyond the order that the fathers of Salcete and their rector, Stephens, during his four years as superior, had convinced the new Christians to leave their land to the churches under Jesuit control. The converts were further influenced to ensure these donations would revert to the Company, should the administration of the churches be handed to non-Jesuits.[68] These practices led to rumours that the fathers wished to take these lands by any means. Moreover, these lands were ordinarily under the title of many claimants, who had rights through inheritance, royal donation, sale, or marriage. Thus, donations were often made as acts of vengeance to spite other claimants, or even as a means to assert exclusive title over disputed land. To compound these ills, the lands and their income were disposed of at the whim of Stephens and his vicars: Stephens had prohibited the appointment of independent stewards (*mordomo*) in the churches, who could be a source of opposition to the way the church income was used. Furthermore, Stephens attracted donations by promising the donors that the income would be used to build churches near their villages, thus freeing converts from the burden of a long and difficult journey to distant churches. These churches were never completed, even though the matter had reached the ears of the archbishop. Meanwhile, Stephens continued to appropriate the income for use in the college, while the churches remained without ornament or fell into disrepair.

Cunha was clearly in Francisco Cabral's orbit of influence, praising his compatriot unreservedly. As the above charges reveal, he also seemed to have been allied ideologically with Cabral in privileging the pastoral work of the churches over the humanistic enterprise of the colleges. Still, Cunha's claims regarding the disproportionate influence of the college and its rector in the structure and functioning of the mission was borne out in a far more neutral description of the mission penned by the German Gaspar Schuren.[69] While a systematic study of the land records of the mission during Stephens's tenure

[68] According to Cunha, the fathers involved with Stephens in this scheme were Paio Rodrigues, Gonçalo Carvalho, and Antonio Viegas.

[69] Gaspar Schuren to Province of Toledo, Salsete, 20 November 1593, *Documenta Indica* XVI, 383. Schuren's description is slightly erroneous in its particulars as there were in fact ten churches, of which six had residences.

as superior is beyond the scope of this study, there is certainly anecdotal evidence to bear out Cunha's claims regarding the disputes that occurred as a result of these transactions. Certainly, Stephens found himself adjudicating land titles, often with the seemingly free exercise of his own judgement in these matters and in ways that benefitted the Jesuits in land disputes.[70] There is certainly evidence, as Cunha claimed, that disputed land was given to the Jesuits as a strategy in the internal politics of Salcete; moreover, Jesuits often took sides in these disputes within and outside the village communities.[71]

The rumours of the wealth of the Salcete mission, as well as its dubious management, must have found sympathetic ears. Two years later, the thorny issue of the rents from the temple lands arose again. Salcete's income had been appropriated by the previous provincial, Pedro Martins, for the use of the house of catechumens in Goa. Valignano and Cabral confirmed the decision and Cabral even increased the burden on Salcete. Stephens's predecessor, Miguel Leitão, as well as Stephens himself, strongly protested. The decision, Stephens lamented, reflected the fact that 'the matters of Salcete are not well-favored, especially in comparison with some of those of Goa,

[70] See, for example, the notarial document attesting to the current ownership (not to mention the complicated history of donation and sale) of the palmar identified as 'bhattanchy Namassy' in the village of Margão penned by Stephens in GSHA, 3071, Foral de Salcete, vol. II, fl. 520. See also the document in which Stephens confirmed the possession of certain lands in Vargua granted by the Viceroy Francisco Mascarenhas to Bernal de Rodrigues, who was not identified as a new Christian, on the grounds that they had not been proven to be temple lands, although previous documentation seemed to imply that they were (GSHA, 3071, Foral de Salcete, vol. II, fl. 544). See also how Stephens confirmed the payment of a fine of 150 xerafins by Francisco Barreto, a indigenous Christian, for selling and trespassing on a land given in Vargua by the Viceroy Francisco Mascarenhas to Miguel Leitão, the former rector of Salsete in GSHA, 3071, Foral de Salcete, vol. II, fl. 546–546v.

[71] This can be seen in the case of the island of Juo (Rachol) by the gāunkārs of the village of Raya, who successfully had their 'traditional' rights to this land recognized in a dispute with the local judge, Francisco Dias, and then leased the land to the Jesuits. Amongst the ganvcars was one 'Thomas Estevão, son of Vitu Paï', suggesting that the English Jesuit had sponsored his baptism (GSHA, 824, Provisões do Colegio de Rachol, 14–26ff). See also ANTT, Cartorio dos Jesuítas, 87, Doc. 18.

such that the ends of the Company and those of Salcete are called different'.[72]

Stephens sought to exploit the factional divisions within the order: he averred that Valignano, had he remained longer to evaluate the needs of Salcete, would have seen the injustice effected by this appropriation of Salcete's income.[73] He could not believe that Valignano, if he had been well-informed, would not have fallen in with the opinion of experienced Jesuits and even theologians in Goa who agreed with Stephens and Leitão that the income should first be used to meet the needs of Salcete, with only the remainder being disbursed to the house of the catechumens.

Stephens enclosed a detailed account of the income of the mission, showing that temple rents were already smaller than the expenditures of Salcete. Increasing the burden would be intolerable, not least because priests would be ridden with debt, given the prohibition on alms-taking in Salcete. Moreover, the reassignment of the temple funds had already led to the closure of the house of catechumens and the hospital in Salcete, and the building and renovation of churches had stalled. The addition of a regulation prohibiting excessive rents was thus absurd, especially given the financial burdens placed on Salcete for the house of catechumens in Goa.[74] Stephens did acknowledge indirectly the rumours of malfeasance, when he claimed that the brahmins would give the Jesuits one set of accounts and present another to the viceroy. By doing so, Stephens claimed, they made it seem that the Jesuits, who conscientiously sent their accounts whenever any doubt was raised, presented false information to the Portuguese authorities.

Stephens's letter was a response to the growing dissatisfaction within the Jesuit hierarchy regarding the Salcete mission. Nonetheless, Cabral's

[72] Stephens, Rector, to Claudia Aquaviva, Margão, 25 November 1595, *Documenta Indica* XVII, 296.

[73] From references to Stephens in Valignano's personal letters when giving news of Italian missionaries in India, it appears that Valignano took some interest in Stephens and may even have considered him, however peripherally, as part of his circle of Roman-educated missionaries in the province. Still, given Valignano's unhelpfulness towards the Indian mission in general, Stephens often found himself on the side of the Portuguese faction.

[74] Stephens, 'Ynformación del Padre Rector de Salsete sobre el rendimiento de las rentas de los pagodes', Margão, 25 November 1595, *Documenta Indica* XVII, 298–311.

call to cede it to the episcopacy was not a universally popular opinion, with even Valignano considering it hasty. To hand over the reins was to ignore, as Nuno Rodrigues argued, the symbolic importance of the mission in Salcete, where large numbers of gentiles were still being baptized daily and which had required such apostolic zeal from the Jesuits.[75]

Though this particular controversy eventually blew over, the mission continued to be a troubled one. Writing a few years later, Stephens wrote sorrowfully of the situation in Salcete as he asked for more Jesuits to be sent to his beloved mission. So acute was the shortage that they were forced to allow churches to be administered 'by vicars who were not worthy of the office', or even to accept indigenous clerics. While Stephens was willing to acknowledge the future potential of indigenous clergy 'as they have some culture', he insisted that the mission needed more Jesuits to counteract the twin evils that were vitiating it.[76] The first was general ignorance among converts, who knew as little of Christianity as the gentiles.[77] The second, borne out by his experience administering the temple incomes and in his dealings over land in Salcete, was the general air of malice that permeated the parishes, full of litigations, quarrels, and false witnesses.

In these troubled times, Stephens found some reasons for hope in Salcete. The first was that 'this population of Margão is entirely made up of Christian brahmins', whose 'very intelligent and well-disposed children' attended the local school. Their education included a catechism, composed 'in the language of the country': Stephens reported that 'one discovers in the confessions that the knowledge of [this catechism], however little, is beneficial'. The final source of hope was that the Provincial Nuno Rodrigues had ordered some small chapels to be built in remote villages 'for the children to assemble for catechism'.[78]

[75] Nuno Rodrigues to Claudio Aquaviva, Goa, 13 December 1595, *Documenta Indica* XVII, 461–2.

[76] Stephens to Aquaviva, Margão, 6 December 1601, ARSI, Goa 15, 50–1ff.

[77] Stephens to Aquaviva, Margão, 6 December 1601, ARSI, Goa 15, 50–1ff. This assessment was also borne out by Francisco da Cunha, who claimed that the emphasis on baptism in the mission had led to a relative neglect of catechetical instruction. See Francisco da Cunha to Claudio Aquaviva, Margão, 23 November 1599, ARSI, Goa 14, 402f.

[78] Stephens to Claudio Aquaviva, Salsete, 5 December 1608, ARSI, Goa 16, 180f.

This letter thus indicated a new focus in Stephens's career: having left behind the fraught and worldly negotiations involved in the administration of the mission, Stephens increasingly devoted himself to brahmin converts, particularly children, and the development of a system of instruction for them. Again, the turn towards children, as in the case of Xavier, Nóbrega, and Anchieta, was an index of both frustration with present social conditions and the hope of founding an entirely new, and therefore pure, Christian community.

Stephens's work in the college of Margão was dealt yet another blow when the visitor Nicolau Pimenta decided in 1606 to shift the college to Rachol, as part of the ongoing contraction of the Jesuit mission. The close relationship the Jesuits had developed with the local Christians was evident. In a moving petition, the Christians of the village implored the Father General not to tear them from the heart and eyes of their priests. They acknowledged that the Jesuits would be safer in the fortress in Rachol, away from the periodic raids of gentiles that they faced in Margão. Though they understood that the Jesuits were primarily there to convert gentiles, they claimed that their need for ongoing instruction should not be ignored. Among the many signatories to this letter is Stephens, attesting to his own desire not to abandon the college for whose upkeep and development he had faced so many difficulties.[79]

It is difficult to reconstruct Stephens's later activities. What is clear is that the corrupt and fraught nature of Salcete as a mission space did not abate. In 1606, for example, when it is likely that Stephens was serving as socius to Nicolau Pimenta in Loutulim, the visitor uncovered a scandal that threatened to undermine the very foundations of the mission. In a secret coded letter to the Jesuit headquarters in Rome, Pimenta relayed that a woman had been procuring young new Christian girls in Salcete as prostitutes for some thirteen vicars.[80] Stephens's judgement that the vicars of Salcete were not worthy of their office had been amply borne out.

[79] The Christians of Margão, Salcete to Aquaviva, 6 December 1607, ARSI, Goa 16, 126–7ff. References to these raids can be found in many letters, such as Thomas Stephens, Rector, to Claudia Aquaviva, Margão, 25 November 1595, *Documenta Indica* XVII, 296.

[80] Nicolau Pimenta to Claudio Aquaviva, Goa, 6 December 1606, ARSI, Goa 9, 16–17ff. Identified among them are Mazarelli and Antonio Viegas.

In external matters, too, the turn of events was grim, as the increasing activity of Dutch pirates in India disrupted shipping and posed a serious threat to Portuguese dominion. These events had repercussions for the mission: thus in 1608, Stephens wrote to the Father General, stating that the new college had begun well, but the infestation of Dutch pirates, which had ended the sea traffic, made its progress precarious. This was at least in part because the financial outlay required for the project could not be met.[81] In the face of these difficulties and in his old age, Stephens increasingly retired to the literary work that would be his principal legacy.

Christ in the *Brahmapuri*

In 1608, Stephens wrote to Father General Aquaviva, 'It has been many years that I have greatly desired to see in this Province some books printed in the language and alphabet of the land, as there are in Malabar with great benefit for that Christianity.' Stephens claimed that the overworked provincial had ignored the request. Further, it had 'seemed impossible to cast so many matrices [printing moulds] totalling six hundred, since the characters are syllables and not alphabets like our twenty-four in Europe'.[82] The misunderstanding of the Nāgrī alphabet was one of the few defects in Stephens's knowledge of the languages of Salcete.[83] Despite his error, which made the prospect of printing books in local scripts seem prohibitively difficult, Stephens made every effort to make available Christian knowledge in locally accessible scripts and tongues.

The problem of translating sacred Christian knowledge into gentile tongues, particularly in the Americas, occupied missionaries from the dawn of the age of 'discoveries'.[84] Given the humanist turn of the sixteenth

[81] Stephens to Claudio Aquaviva, Salsete, 5 December 1608, ARSI, Goa 16, 180f.

[82] Stephens to Claudio Aquaviva, Salsete, 5 December 1608, ARSI, Goa 16, 180f.

[83] The same mistake is present in his discussion of the alphabet in his Kōṅkaṇī grammar, the 1640 expanded edition of which is reprinted in Cunha Rivara, *Grammatica da Lingua Concani*.

[84] The case of Quechua is exemplary here. See Sabine MacCormack's succinct discussion of the issues at stake in her classic essay, '"The Heart Has Its Reasons"'.

century, the key to adjudicating if a language was worthy of carrying the Christian word was its amenability to grammatical reduction in the Latin mould.[85] In India, the first such language to come under grammatical and missiological scrutiny was Tamil. In 1586 the Jesuit Henrique Henriques published the *Flos Sanctorum*, inaugurating a long tradition of Jesuit writing in Tamil.[86] For Stephens, this literary tradition was the inspiration for the creation of a parallel literary corpus in Salcete.

The culmination of Stephens's various vernacular efforts was precisely the work he hoped to print in local script: *Discurso sobre a vinda de Jesu Christo* (Discourse on the coming of Jesus Christ) (see Figure 5.1).[87] Unlike the workaday Kōṅkaṇī catechism and grammar he also authored as pastoral aids, this discourse was written in the high poetic language of the region, Marāṭhī, in the *ovī* metre.[88]

The composition of the work, which came to be popularly known as the *Kristapurāṇa*, was completed by 1614. Thereafter, it was dispatched, alongside a version in Portuguese, for inspection by the Inquisition to various authorities, including the first Jesuit in Salcete, Pedro Mascarenhas. He claimed to have verified that the version in the 'bramana marastta' language corresponded, 'as far as the language permits' with the version in Portuguese, suggesting that the use of

[85] The notion of linguistic reduction, as a corollary to Spanish colonial efforts to 'reduce' indigenous settlements in America, is borrowed from William F. Hanks's work, *Converting Words.*

[86] On the history of Tamil translations of Christian knowledge, see Županov, *Missionary Tropics*, 232–58.

[87] I have consulted Roman-script manuscripts of the text at the Pilar Seminary (the earliest extant manuscript, dating to 1609); two copies of the manuscript at the Thomas Stephens Konknni Kendr; and the printed edition (purportedly the third edition, printed in 1654) held at the Central Library, Panjim. Copies of the first two are now available digitally through the British Library, Endangered Archives Program, EAP636: Creating a digital archive of Indian Christian manuscripts. I have also consulted the earliest known nāgrī-script manuscript held in the Marsden Collection, SOAS, MS 12104. References will be cited from Stephens, *The Christian Puránna.*

[88] The catechism was printed in 1622, under the title *Doutrina Christam em Lingua Bramana Canarim.* A facsimile of the text, with an excellent critical introduction, has been published as Stephens, *Doutrina cristã.*

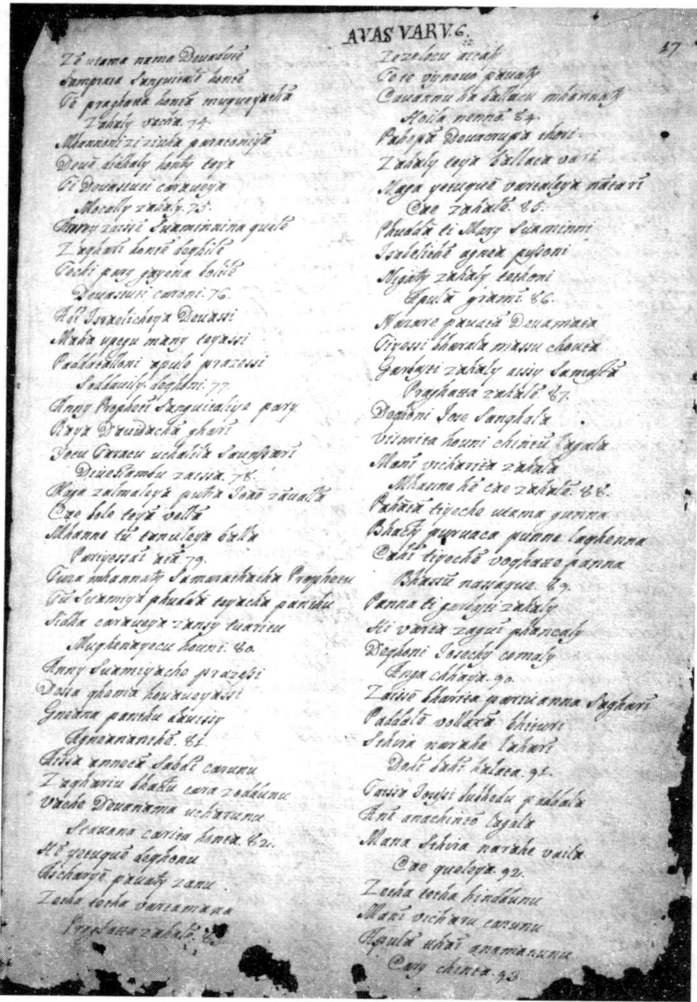

Figure 5.1 Page from the Earliest Known Manuscript of *Discurso sobre a vinda de Jesu Christo*. The manuscript is purported to date to 1609. It was found in a cowshed next to the old building of the Pilar Seminary in Goa in 1959.
Source: Courtesy of the British Library, the author, and Leonard Fernandes (British Library, EAP636/1/35pt1: Kristapurana [Part 1], available at http://eap.bl.uk/database/overview_item.a4d?catId=317818;r=17035, accessed on 17 September 2016).

the Marāṭhī language was associated with brahmins.[89] Provincial Francisco Vieira attested in 1615 that the work had been approved by various 'learned and serious' Jesuits.[90] The work was finally printed in Roman script in 1616. Stephens dedicated it to the archbishop primate of Goa, to whom he offered 'this poor present, which is a work composed in the mode of the land, and in a style that the indigenous most like, which contains an instruction and is like a catechism ... that which I with my weak talent in these wilds (*mattos*) of Salcette could make'.

Stephens's insistence on the location of the composition of the work 'in these wilds of Salcette' is suggestive of its insistently local orientation.[91] Within this circumscribed context, he desired as wide an audience as possible. As he wrote in the Marāṭhī preface:

> All this is written in the Marāṭhī language. Among the languages of this land, this language appeared fit for describing the things of God but as pure Marāṭhī is not understood by the middle (*madhima*) people, so that the fruit of this *purāṇa* may be enjoyed by many people, leaving aside the difficult expressions used by poets of the past, in the manner of contemporary poets I have made my poem easily intelligible by mixing in expressions of the simple language of the brahmins.[92]

The justification for the creation of the text given in the Portuguese dedication to the archbishop and to the reader in the Marāṭhī prose

[89] Saldanha, 'Introduction', in *The Christian Puránna*, lxxxvii. There is also internal evidence in the Kristapurana itself attesting to the completion of the composition in 1614. See Stephens, *Discurso*, 'Dussarem Purana', chapter 59, verses 119–20 in Stephens, *Doutrina cristã* 524.

[90] Francisco Vieira's licence, dated 22 June 1615, was also printed in the licences of the first edition of 1616 (Saldanha, 'Introduction', in *The Christian Puránna*, lxxxvii).

[91] My reading here is indebted to the apparatus laid out by Hanks regarding the need to attend to 'indexical centring in the deictic field' in analysing colonial discourses (Hanks, *Converting Words*, 103–11).

[92] Saldanha, 'Introduction', in *The Christian Puránna*, xvi. Malshe discusses how the language of the text is of the Gomantaki variety one may expect in the region but is unequivocally Marāṭhī (Malshe, 'Stīphansacyā Kristapurāṇācā Bhāśika āṇi Vāṅmayīna Abhyāsa'). A condensed version was published as Malshe, *Phā. Sṭiphansa āṇi tyācẽ Kristapurāṇa.*

preface was explicated at poetic length within the body of the text itself. In the first chapter, Stephens recounted how an anxious desire (*utcanttha*) arose in him to make known the ultimate śāstra. He decided to do so in the Marāṭhī language, which was among the languages of the continent like that of a lustrous gem amidst gravel, a blue diamond (*hira nilla*) amidst jewels, the jasmine among flowers and musk amongst fragrances, the peacock among birds, the wish-fulfilling tree (*calpataru*) amongst trees, the twelve signs of the zodiac amongst the stars, and the days of the sun and moon amongst all the days.[93] The allusive richness of these similes suggests the improbability of the sole authorship of the work by Stephens, which may better be read as a co-creation between Stephens and his brahmin converts.[94]

Yet, neither Stephens's personal desire nor the suitability of the Marāṭhī language for expressing Christian knowledge was sufficient justification for the writing of the life of Christ in this foreign tongue.[95] Such justification could arise only from the needs of the converts in his care. The following scene opened in a church in the land of Salcete, on a Sunday afternoon. Young Christian boys sat in catechism class before the padre, reciting the *Doutrina* (undoubtedly penned in Kōṅkaṇī by Stephens himself) with sweet voices, the echo of the pure law rising to the heavens. When catechism was completed, a brahmin engaged the padre in a debate. He began in a conciliatory tone, expressing his sincere belief that those who repeated the *Doutrina* would come to know the supreme God and, through its teachings,

[93] Stephens, *The Christian Purânna*, 6–7 ('Adi Puranna', chapter 1, verses 120–5).

[94] Malshe, in 'Stīphansacyā Kristapurāṇācā', shows a parallelism between the images employed here and those found in the Marāṭhī version of the *Yogavāsiṣṭha*, concluding that the Christian text displays deep knowledge of the Marāṭhī literary tradition but is nonetheless an original composition. Given Stephens's closeness with the brahmin convert community of Margão, perhaps his literary collaborators are listed among the signatories of The Christians of Margão, Salcete to Aquaviva, 6 December 1607, ARSI, Goa 16, 126–7ff.

[95] The anxiety of writing in the colonies in textual genres outside the purview of approved Jesuit writing conventions, evident in Nóbrega's writing of the *Diálogo*, can be deduced here too.

would be liberated. If the teachings of the *Doutrina* could be taught to them in a śāstra or a *purāṇa*, however, it would be better.[96]

The brahmin demanded, in other words, that Christian truth be expressed either as a technical treatise on the rules of the practice of a Christian life (śāstra) or as a narrative relating the history of the universe, the genealogies of God and of kings, and other cosmographical and philosophical matters from a Christian point of view (purāṇa). It was a demand for the translation of a foreign form of knowledge into a 'literate' indigenous genre: śāstra, as a technical treatise, would certainly be the provenance of the learned, while a purāṇa would stand in contrast to a more popular devotional poetry such as the *abhaṅg* in this period. The implication is that the catechism, as it was originally taught, was not understood to fall within the parameters of either indigenous genre.[97]

Although it is unspoken here, the request expressed the need for an indigenous literature appropriate to a convert population who could no longer read or recite non-Christian texts without violating the precepts of their new religion. For learned convert brahmins, the demand for Christian knowledge in elevated indigenous literary genres was a matter of recovering lost social capital. In the text, however, the need for such a translation was ascribed to the fallible nature of the convert. The brahmin argued that it was the nature of man, as the guru well knew, to contemplate new things again and again and to pass his time pleasantly, in idle repartee or in wandering the marketplace, forgetting the path of faith. In the land of the Franks, however, there were purāṇas to deliver them, books that allowed them to pass the time pleasantly but fruitfully. These, however, remained inaccessible to him and his compatriots since they had not learnt the language of the Franks. If in the land of the Franks one could find purāṇas written in the manner befitting that land, why was it that in the brahmin's land no such book was to be found? Speaking for his brethren, the brahmin concluded that if there were śāstras or purāṇas in Marāṭhī 'in our location (amā tthaī)', then the heart's desire of the

[96] Stephens, *The Christian Puránna*, 7 ('Adi Puranna', chapter 1, verses 126–34). The idiom here emphasizes the language of reasoned debate: 'Puranna charchecha vicharu/Mandilla tennẽ'.

[97] On the nature of oral literacy in India, with particular regard to the purāṇa, see Rao, 'Purāṇa as brahminic Ideology', 95.

people would be fulfilled.[98] Again, the insistence on the specific location of speech—in Salcete—is noteworthy.

The brahmin's reasoning was met with profound joy by the padre, who lauded him for his question but counselled patience, advising him that as the Franks say, Rome (Romanāgāri) was not built in a day. He assured him that god himself would fulfil the desire of the faithful listeners.[99] On the Sunday when the promised text was ready, the men of the brahmin village came together and entered the temple to find the Mother Church beautifully decorated.[100] In skilful brushstrokes, the text provides a piquant sketch of the village church: on both sides, the faithful saints rose in a wondrous parade, their gaze fixed upon the scene before them, and luxuriant green grass spread over the earth upon which the Christians walked joyfully. Seeing the decorated altar and the golden retable, their love for Christ could not be contained. In the temple, the fragrance of incense rose and scattered softly, as a zephyr played in the four directions. Then, in unison, everyone bent their knee and began to recite the praises of God. From his lofty seat, the padre gathered the Christians of the brahmin lineage, and many people sat to listen to the text. Making the sign of the holy cross, the padre began reciting, with his listeners asking questions. The souls of the listeners were stilled, their ears open, their five senses gathered. The padre thus decided to recount to them every Sunday 'the tales of the past'.[101]

This first chapter dramatized not only the conditions of the production of the text in the context of the exigencies of conversion in Salcete, but also of its oral performance. The regular recitation of and listening to the life of Christ in an appropriate language and genre took its place in a constellation of Christian activity, including the seven sacraments, that defined the life of the converts—in particular, those brahmin converts most receptive to such a literary retelling of Christian knowledge. The dialogical form of the text was indicative, as Stephens had suggested in the Portuguese dedication to the archbishop, of its function as a form of catechism.

[98] Stephens, *The Christian Puránna*, 7 ('Adi Puranna', chapter 1, verses 135–43).

[99] Stephens, *The Christian Puránna*, 8 ('Adi Puranna', chapter 1, verse 149).

[100] Stephens, *The Christian Puránna*, 9 ('Adi Puranna', chapter 1, verses 171–2).

[101] Stephens, *The Christian Puránna*, 9 ('Adi Puranna', chapter 1, verses 173–81).

This dialogical form was equally a generic marker appropriate to a purāṇa, as indicated by the reference to the common purāṇic trope of *phalaśruti*, or the fruit acquired through listening, which marks the relationship between narrator and listener in texts of this genre. In keeping with the catechetical and missiological precepts underlying the text, this trope is transformed somewhat: whereas Hindu purāṇas may list the material fruits of listening to the text and even attach conditions whereby the full fruits may not accrue to the listener without his complete devotion or appropriate payment to the reciter, the *Discurso* claims simply that the listener and the reciter would share equally in the fruits of happiness and virtuous deeds.[102]

This attentiveness to the generic markers of the purāṇa in the composition of the *Discurso* is profound. Consider the organization of the thirty-six chapters of the first book of the *Discurso*, the 'Adi Puranna', a version of the Old Testament teleologically oriented to the birth of Christ.[103] Stephens's organization of the biblical material is remarkable for its correspondence to the five distinguishing marks (*pañcalakṣaṇa*) of the purāṇa, namely cosmogony (*sarga*); destruction and recreation (*pratisarga*); the genealogy of God(s) and patriarchs (*vaṃśa*), the reigns of the Manus (*manvantarāṇi*); and the history of royal dynasties of the solar and lunar races (*vaṃśānucarita*). The early chapters on Christian cosmogony fit the rubric of sarga. The biblical flood—appropriately translated as *pralaya*, the eschatological term for the periodic dissolution of the universe—and its aftermath could be considered a form of pratisarga.[104] Even the biblical penchant for genealogies such as Genesis

[102] Stephens, *The Christian Puránna*, 8 ('Adi Puranna', chapter 1, verse 168). For a brief discussion of phalaśruti, see Brown, 'Purāṇa as Scripture', 74–5.

[103] Omissions from the Pentateuch include the Book of Leviticus and parts of the Book of Numbers and Deuteronomy. The history of Israel is told without reference to the books of Judges, Ruth, Judith, Tobias, Esther, and Maccabees. From the Book of Wisdom, Psalms, Proverbs, Ecclesiastes, the Book of Job, and Ecclesiasticus are omitted. Of the prophetic books, there is a heavy emphasis on Elias, Jeremiah, Ezekiel, and, in particular, Daniel. The most noteworthy addition to this material is the last chapter devoted to the Sibylline prophecies, which were gaining currency since Sixt Birck's edition of the text appeared in Basel in 1545.

[104] See, in particular, the seventh chapter about the flood entitled 'Pralaya Catha', and the first fifteen verses of the following chapter regarding God's covenant to Noah and man's resettlement of the world.

11, detailing the Abrahamic lineage, finds congenial generic ground in the Purāṇa.[105] Equally, the history of Israel was not out of place in a textual genre that has often served as the vehicle for historical narration in India. Given that even of the extant *Mahāpurāṇas*, these five topics account for less than 3 per cent of the textual corpus, the generic adaptation is all the more remarkable.[106]

When we consider Velcheru Narayana Rao's insight that these five distinguishing marks are to be understood not as a set of rigid conventions or empirically observed facts, but rather as an ideological frame that transforms whatever content is placed within it to correspond to a brahminic world view, the *Discurso* admirably fulfilled the brahmin's request for a local translation of Christian knowledge.[107] There is a profound emphasis on the brahminical nature of the audience: the village depicted in this chapter is repeatedly identified as a 'brahmapurī' or a village of brahmins.[108]

Stephens's marked brahminical bias in his efforts at literary accommodatio bore a formal similarity to Valignano's approach to conversion. Valignano's contempt for the indigenous peoples of India, and the brahmins in particular, should not distract us from noting that both their philosophies of conversion were based on a humanistic approach and an underlying emphasis on the 'quality' of converts. In other words, Stephens and Valignano appeared to share a hierarchical understanding of the conditions of accommodatio.[109]

The Poetics of Location

Stephens's adaptation of Christian knowledge to local circumstances was not confined to language and textual genre. The *Discurso* drew upon local realities to inform its exposition of biblical history. One can perceive this clearly in the eighth chapter from the first book, which describes the aftermath of the flood (covering roughly Genesis 9–13). The bulk of the chapter explains how it was that the recreated

[105] Stephens, *The Christian Puránna*, 47 ('Adi Puranna', chapter 8, verses 62–6).

[106] Rao, 'Purāṇa as brahminic Ideology', 86.

[107] Rao, 'Purāṇa as brahminic Ideology', 87–9.

[108] See, for example, Stephens, *The Christian Puránna*, 7–9 ('Adi Puranna', chapter 1, verses 135, 171, 178).

[109] See later.

world of men lost its linguistic unity and how idolatry entered the world.[110]

The text recounted how the great emperor (*chacravarty*) Nemrodu brought together innumerable workers to build a wondrous city. In the shadow of a huge fortress, various chiefs erected temples, vast markets, its lanes filled with songs and bustling confusion, and the clanging of temples. There was a royal temple, too, lofty and charming, with a golden cupola, and in the courtyard of the palace, a hall was erected upon stone pillars and decorated with flowers. Then the king built a tower of a new sort, of great height, its cupola reaching to the sky. Even though a pralaya was again foreseen, the people and the king ascended the tower. Suddenly, those workers who were constructing the tower began to speak different languages: when one asked for lime, the other brought him a stone brick and vice versa. Then the people began to wander, dispersing throughout the world; where there had been one language, there were now many in the various lands. Each set out in search of their own islands over the seas, and the lords of the world built cities and towns and shared the earth's riches across the various lands.[111]

In the linguistic world of Salcete, one could reasonably expect to find Kōṅkaṇī, Marāṭhī, and Portuguese, and quite possibly Kannaḍā, Sanskrit, and Persian; moreover, the area had been subject to three different polities of three different faiths in rapid succession. In such a location, this parable regarding the birth of linguistic diversity and a concomitant desire to find one's own land based on one's language must have seemed somewhat strange. Yet, as the *Discurso* insisted, the essential lesson of the parable was deeper: from that day on, vice entered the body of men. So crowded was the earth with sin that the worship of the lord was lost. Worse still, so crazed were the sinful that they forgot the creator and began to worship created things. The courtiers of a king, who could not bear the separation from his dead

[110] Stephens, *The Christian Puránna*, 45 ('Adi Puranna', chapter 8, verse 15).

[111] Stephens, *The Christian Puránna*, 45–6 ('Adi Puranna', chapter 8, verses 16–35). This identification of the emperor as Nimrod, which is not mentioned in Genesis, derives from the Jewish commentarial tradition, most likely Flavius Josephus's *Jewish Antiquities*. The *editio princeps* (first edition) of the Greek text had been published in Basel in 1544 but Latin translations of excerpts from the text had been in circulation for much of the medieval period. I am grateful to Arthur Dudney for confirming this hypothesis and for providing me with a synopsis of the Christian and humanist reception of the text.

son, made such an effort to console him that they built an effigy of the prince and installed it at the threshold, placing flowers at its feet and laying out victuals before the beautiful idol. After washing it, they worshipped, and thus idolatry began.[112]

This version of the origin of idolatry can be traced to the Book of Wisdom (Chapter 14:15–16), which, as Joan-Pau Rubiés has shown, was an important reference for Christian writers from at least the second-century apologetes.[113] More remarkable than this adaptation of the Christian theological tradition on idolatry in Marāṭhī verse is the distinctly local turn the discussion then takes in the text. Included among the examples of idolatry the text provides were those people who began to worship the 'devacharas, at whose appearance the sight darkens'.[114] Seeing them in dreams, they made idols of his image and took them from village to village worshipping it.[115] They gave honour to *bhūtas* (ghosts), worshipped all types of idols (*patma*), and forgot entirely the supreme Lord.[116]

The *Discurso* concluded that while the supreme Lord's strength makes heaven manifest, created things speak the sign of creation; thus men should worship only God.[117] This idea dated back to the Platonic and Stoic Christian reception of Jewish wisdom literature, which identified the central error of idolatry as the inability to differentiate between the Creator and his creation.[118] The consequences were unequivocal: those who worship *devchārs* will go to hell (*yema loca*) and will obtain all the suffering (*duqha*) of hell (*agnicondd*).[119]

The two translations of hell used here are revealing of a strategy that characterizes the whole *Discurso*. The first, 'yema loca', was a

[112] Stephens, *The Christian Puránna*, 46–7 ('Adi Puranna', chapter 8, verses 36–49).

[113] Pau-Rubiés, 'Theology', 576.

[114] Stephens, *The Christian Puránna*, 47 ('Adi Puranna', chapter 8, verses 50–3).

[115] Stephens, *The Christian Puránna*, 47 ('Adi Puranna', chapter 8, verse 54).

[116] Stephens, *The Christian Puránna*, 47 ('Adi Puranna', chapter 8, verse 55). The term 'patma' seems to be a local variation or corruption of the word *pratima*, also found in the text.

[117] Stephens, *The Christian Puránna*, 47 ('Adi Puranna', chapter 8, verses 46–7).

[118] On this tradition, see Pau-Rubiés, 'Theology', 576–8.

[119] Stephens, *The Christian Puránna*, 47 ('Adi Puranna', chapter 8, verse 58).

straightforward borrowing from the Hindu concept of the realm of the god of justice, Yama, who metes out appropriate punishments after death for accumulated sins. Although the notion of an *eternal* hell was alien, in such indigenous textual traditions as the medieval *Garuḍa Purāṇa*, in which lists of transgressions and their associated punishments are described in gruesome detail, the concept of suffering incurred in the afterlife was familiar. The second term, 'agni-condd', literally a confined space of fire, would evoke for a European listener the concept of a Dante-esque inferno; the connotations to a brahminical audience would be closer to that of the sacrificial fire (*agnī kund*). The association of the sufferings of hell with the most sacred symbol of Hindu ritual life is an audacious example of the deliberate reversal of values effected in the *Discurso*.

Still more intriguing is the reference to the devchār. D.D. Kosambi classifies this deity as a local figure that remained outside of brahminic ideological frameworks: 'In the first place, local pre-Brāhmaṇic priests of the *gāvḍos* still survive in places like Kholgor; their deities, where unabsorbed by Brāhmaṇic synthesis, have been converted to cacodemons, known generally as *devchār* but still worshipped by the lower castes as well as the *gāvḍos*.'[120] In this light, it appears that the brahmins supplied Stephens with the name of deities worshipped by religious rivals as a local translation for false gods. Manuel Magalhaes's ethnographic research in the Hindu village of Betki and other parts of Goa suggests that the significance of this deity is still more complicated.[121] In modern Goa, the term may be used pejoratively as a way to refer to the deities of a rival village or lineage. Devchārs are widely understood to be a deeply ambiguous class of deities, often associated with specific parts of a village such as a boundary, a tree, or certain sections of the fields. Thus, the *Discurso* sought to literally demonize these deities of place, strictly outside the brahminical pantheon of Vedic gods and tied to the land of Salcete.

Yet, conversion did not so easily displace these creatures, as the *Discurso* itself suggested. Hearing of Abraham's long indictment of the idolatry of the Chaldeans, a brahmin listener interrupted the priest's narrative. He conceded all that he had heard about the

[120] Kosambi, *Myth and Reality*, 166.

[121] Personal communication.

supreme Christian God and the prohibition of idolatry. Yet, he averred, devchārs and bhūtas were worshipped only out of self-interestedness: food offerings were made in the fields so that devchārs would not deceive them and gifts were given as bribes to evil spirits (*maruva*). This did not seem to be a sin, as he demonstrated with the help of several examples or similes (*upama*):[122]

> He said, Behold a king,
> Whom all the people honour,
> And whom all call their lord,
> Great and small.
>
> But at one time, the subjects
> To the king's governors (*nayaka*),
> Secretly gave bribes to the king's servants,
> For the profit of their soul (*atmahita*) ...
>
> And if the supreme lord
> Says in anger 'Torture him!' (*sattamara re*),
> Then he gives something to another messenger of the king
> In order that he should not suffer injury.
>
> The consequence of doing these things
> Is not to dishonour the supreme king.
> Similarly, to give a self-interested vow to an idol (*angauanna*)
> To appease the evil spirits
>
> Or some seen *devachara* is not to
> Denigrate or dishonour (*auacalla*) the Lord.[123]

In contrast to the padre's earlier usage, the brahmin imbued the term 'devachara' with striking specificity: the reference to offerings made in the field, for example, reflect present-day ritual practices associated with devchārs.[124] The analogy he employed established the worshipper's relationship to the supreme God and minor deities as equivalent to that of a subject to the king and his nāyakas. This was consonant not only with the memories of the structure of Vijayanagara rule, but

[122] Stephens, *The Christian Puránna*, 48 ('Adi Puranna', chapter 8, verse 83).

[123] Stephens, *The Christian Puránna*, 48 ('Adi Puranna', chapter 8, verses 84–9).

[124] Personal communication with Manuel Magalhães.

also of the Hindu conception of the central deity as a sovereign king.[125] In such a framework, minor tutelary deities and other entities could be conceived of as servants or nāyakas of the king within a supernatural hierarchy. This sanctioned the continued worship or ritual appeasement of these deities, without challenging the supremacy of the sovereign god. The brahmin thus argued that replacing belief of an earlier Hindu sovereign god with the Christian creator-God did not fundamentally change the convert's ritual relationship to these minor deities; they were still nāyakas of the supreme god with the ability to affect the lives of converts.

The brahmin's point required serious refutation since the Christian theological tradition on idolatry turned on a fundamental ambiguity, evident as far as back as Paul's epistles: idols were not only useless images, but also representatives of active, malevolent spirits.[126] It was, therefore, not possible to dismiss the view of the devchār as a living and powerful entity capable of intervening in human affairs, and thus requiring ritual bribery. The padre responded to the brahmin's upama, with fittingly syllogistic propositions:

> And if there were indeed many gods
> Then in your judgment
> Among them all
> Wouldn't one be the best?
>
> Then if out of all one was the greatest,
> Then you should call him the supreme lord,
> Who being powerful would not want another
> To be god.[127]

His argument was based not on the brahmin's conception of a sovereign god, capable of tolerating lesser deities as subordinates, but on a monotheistic God, who would brook no rival.[128] Yet, in collapsing the

125 Appadurai and Breckenridge, 'The South Indian Temple'.

126 Pau-Rubiés, 'Theology', 580. As Rubiés shows, Augustine, whose influence was pervasive in this period, carried forth Paul's view on idolatry.

127 Stephens, *The Christian Purânna*, 49 ('Adi Puranna', chapter 8, verses 96–7).

128 The basis for this image can be found in Exodus 20:5.

brahmin's theological possibility of worshipping both the supreme Christian God and lesser indigenous deities, the padre still had not dealt with the essential problem of theodicy the brahmin had raised: should one 'bribe' active and potentially malevolent spirits? The padre warned against such a temptation:

And if another belief comes to your mind,
Then you will say
Evil spirits (*margōt*) have afflicted people,
They bring stones and rocks and throw them at the temple.

Through sorcerers (*ghaddiya*) and astrologers
How many people are afflicted with pain;
They do evil by many means
To make someone better.

How many times good things happen,
The pain of how many goes away,
And to how many women
Sons are born.

'All this is by means of votive offerings,'
If they say that then to you
I will say as prescribed,
Pay attention.

The Evil Spirit (*maru*) afflicts man,
He throws stones upon the temple ...

At some time, mankind
Is afflicted by pain and trouble
But without the will of God,
Nothing can happen.

And if at some point
Man is freed from suffering
That is through the mercy of God ...

And if at some other time,
A woman gives birth to a son,
God is pleased with her
Is what it means.[129]

[129] Stephens, *The Christian Puránna*, 50 ('Adi Puranna', chapter 8, verses 117–25).

In a literary reversal of Portuguese temple-breaking campaigns, the padre compared the temptation of Hindu apostasy to that of evil spirits destroying the temple of Christ. The priest argued that the quotidian reasons for which the people of Salcete sought the intercessions of sorcerers and astrologers stemmed from a faulty assumption. They attributed the good fortune that followed to the efficacy of these rituals. Rather, everything that occurred, including these moments of good fortune, were the manifestation of the Christian God's will. By insisting upon the omnipotence of the Christian God, he undercut the brahmin's argument regarding the need to appease these deities and spirits in order to prevent misfortune. Still, the padre counselled staying alert to the deception of these local spirits, since they were the evil conception of the Deceiver, who found many ways to manage his kingdom of sin. Sensing man's misfortune, the devil enters his mind, telling him to go to the sorcerer and make a divination, and promising him relief from pain upon making the appropriate offerings. Similarly, if a barren woman was tempted by an evil spirit to make an offering, when through the grace of God she gives birth, an onlooker might say look, it is the fruit of the offering. 'Thus,' the padre thundered, 'does the evil spirit cheat greatly.'[130]

The transformation of the figure of the devchār into Satan was especially clear in the final example (upama) the padre gave to his listeners.[131] The story involved a man who went to the tax office of a king bearing a gift and encountered a lion at the bottom of the stairs of the royal palace. Falling at the lion's feet, he committed to its charge his gift and asked for mercy. Seeing this, the assembled court rang with laughter. Calling him a fool, they asked him for whom he had bought the gift. If he answered that he had bought it for the king, they would tell him he had been afflicted by idiocy, for the king was seated upon the throne above the shackled lion. Whereas the king honoured the gifts he received, the lion would simply consume them and eventually, its bearer. If the man instead answered that since the lion kills, he had brought it the gift, then the assembly would ask him

[130] Stephens, *The Christian Puránna*, 50–1 ('Adi Puranna', chapter 8, verses 123–37).

[131] Stephens, *The Christian Puránna*, 51 ('Adi Puranna', chapter 8, verse 138).

how could a shackled lion destroy him?[132] Employing this example, the padre explained how God, seated upon his lion-throne in heaven (*vaicunttha nagarī*), would bind the devchār in hell (*yemapurī*).[133] Whoever approached God with his gift, to him God would show mercy; whoever approached the devchār with his gift would lose not only the gift but would also be taken by the devchār.[134]

Countering the brahmin's original royal metaphor regarding the relations between god and devchārs, the padre's example subsumed the devchār into the Christian category of Satan. It is in this light that one can make sense of the padre's pronouncement to the Christians that the gods of the Hindus were devchārs, an identity which would have been meaningless under the divine hierarchy sketched out by the brahmin.[135] Moreover, in effecting this equivalence, the padre completed the exposition of the dual interpretation of gentile idolatry derived from the Augustinian tradition, as both the adherence to useless symbols and the worship of demonic entities.

The choice to cast a local deity such as the devchār as the primary translation of Satan throughout the *Discurso* is notable, particularly when we consider the availability of the Perso-Arabic term *shayṭān* in Marāṭhī, which is arguably closer semantically and theologically to the Christian word. (In the following decade, Etienne de la Croix would use precisely this term to refer to Satan throughout his vast opus on the life of St Peter in Marāṭhī, abandoning the usage pioneered by Stephens.[136]) This choice may in part be explained by the very ambiguity of the devchār as a potentially dangerous entity. The semantic field of the padre's discussion—involving sorcerers and witchdoctors

[132] Stephens, *The Christian Puránna*, 51 ('Adi Puranna', chapter 8, verses 139–48).

[133] Stephens, *The Christian Puránna*, 51 ('Adi Puranna', chapter 8, verse 141. Just as the realm of Yama was sublimated into the Christian concept of hell, Viṣṇu's abode is translated into the Christian heaven in the *Discurso*.

[134] Stephens, *The Christian Puránna*, 51 ('Adi Puranna', chapter 8, verses 141–2).

[135] Stephens, *The Christian Puránna*, 52 ('Adi Puranna', chapter 8, verse 173).

[136] Etienne de la Croix, *Discurso sobre a vida do Apostolo Sam Pedro* (Goa, 1634), BNP, microfilm, F. 198–9. In keeping with the brahminic register of Stephens's text, there is an almost remarkable avoidance of words of Perso-Arabic origin, suggesting an intentionality in this choice.

(ghaddiya), devchārs, margōts, bhūtas, and *prētas*—circumscribed a local level of (non-brahminical) religion.[137] Unlike the Sanskritic temple deities and their attendant ritual practitioners, these figures were decidedly ambivalent, associated with danger, power, and possibly pollution. For brahmin converts, therefore, the devchārs may have been more easily assimilated into the Christian figure of Satan.

Furthermore, the devchār, tied to specific parts of the village, stood in contrast to the major temple deities, who were often relocated to lands under Bijāpuri dominion after the temple-destruction campaigns in Salcete. With the flight of the temple gods, the parish priest was left to battle those entities in the village that were not dependent on vulnerable temples, but were instead tied to the land itself. Moreover, ritual practitioners such as witchdoctors and astrologers, whose activities were not bound by the temple complex, continued to influence the quotidian lives of the villagers after these campaigns. This accounts for the *Discurso*'s insistent focus on them, as opposed to temple priests, as idolatrous rivals.

Still, denuded of much of the structure of the Hindu temple complex, Salcete was not divested of the memories or influence of Hindu philosophical thought beyond popular, localized traditions of belief and practice. A Christian convert raised one final doubt: in their continent, he claimed, among certain Hindus, they believed that there was one sole God and that these same people proscribed the worship of bhūtas and the offering of gifts and foods to evil spirits. This being so, the Christian asked, should one cast aside such a good and proper path? Much as in Xavier's encounter with the brahmin scholar in south India, the troubling possibility of Hindu monotheism (or, more plausibly, monistic theism) reared its head. Stephens dealt with it decisively, if unsatisfactorily from a philosophical point of view: the Christian must cast aside this path since it was insufficient merely to admit the existence of one sole God. The true God *must* be identified as the Christian trinity of 'Pita Putru Spiritu Sanctu'.[138]

137 According to Manuel Magalhães, margōts in present day Ponda are the evil spirits of women killed in childbirth. The prēta is another pan-South Asian entity, commonly described as a hungry ghost.

138 Stephens, *The Christian Puránna*, 53 ('Adi Puranna', chapter 8, verses 180–4).

New Wine in Old Bottles

The expansive explanatory style of the *Discurso* and its attentiveness to its local context was used to make potentially unsavoury aspects of Christian ritual life palatable to the converts. This is most clearly exemplified in the twenty-second chapter of the second part of the second book, devoted to Jesus's first miracle as recounted in John 2.[139] In the land of Galilee, in the village of Cana, a wedding had been arranged, to which the head of the household in which the wedding was to take place (*vharaddy*) had summoned Jesus, his mother Mary, and his faithful disciples. Jesus's coming was not only the harbinger of the auspicious moment (*muhurta*), but he himself was described as the destroyer of obstacles (*vignanassu*), an epithet appropriately borrowed from Gaṇeśa, the indigenous deity commonly invoked to ensure propitious beginnings. While the guests were dining, the liquor ran out. Not seeing drink in the row of diners (*pancaty*) some guests began to complain, causing the bridegroom shame. Mary, the compassionate mother, was moved to pity and explained the situation to Jesus, urging her son to intervene. On Jesus's instructions, a server filled large, earthen storage vessels (*ranzanna*) with water. When the host of the wedding (*yajmanna*, literally the one who sponsors the sacrifice) tasted the water drawn from the vessels, he was amazed to find it had turned into wine. He told the bridegroom reproachfully that whereas most people served the best wine first, saving the inferior liquor for later, here they had hidden the best wine till the end. Seeing this miracle, the first public sign of his power, Jesus's disciples abandoned their remaining doubts about Jesus being the saviour.[140]

[139] The second book or 'Dussarem Purann'a consists of four parts: the first, comprising seventeen chapters, relates the story of Jesus's birth and childhood; the second is an account of his miracles and teachings, told in twenty-seven chapters; the third, in seven chapters, describes the Passion and crucifixion; while the last, consisting of eight chapters, deals with Christ's resurrection and entry into heaven. There are some additions to the scriptural material, particularly from Marian traditions. The focus on the life of Christ entailed omissions from the New Testament relating to the aftermath of his death, notably the Acts of the Apostles.

[140] Stephens, *The Christian Puránna*, 302–3 ('Dussarem Puranna, chapter 22, verses 4–25).

The miracle would have had resonance within the Marāṭhī literary universe: here, too, they were a sign of the religious figure's power, a means to inspire wonder within disciples and a mode of competition between saints, within and across sectarian bounds.[141] The miraculous revelation of God to a row of brahmin diners who insult in some way the saintly devotee, is a common trope in Marāṭhī bhakti poetry: by giving a visible sign of divinity, God reverses the humiliation and exalts the *sant* (saint).[142] Still, despite the allusive resonances, this particular miracle, which turned upon the changing of water into wine, was problematic in Salcete: as a listener pointed out to the padre, his people considered alcohol a pollutant (*vittallu*).[143]

The padre mounted a spirited defence of alcohol. In a passage resonant of his first letter of 1579 to his father, in which Stephens had marvelled at the diversity of nature in God's vast earth, the padre explained how there were many islands and continents on the earth, each granted by God to various people. Within this diversity, no land produced everything and each enjoyed its own fruits: the padre cited how from Hindustan came coconuts, pepper, the betel leaf and nut, mangoes, jackfruit, and clove, while from Ceylon came cinnamon.[144] In the land of the Franks, by the same token, grapes overflowed (*vossanddanna*), a choice of verb that connoted the notion of abundance common in interpretations of Jesus's first miracle. Since the people of Hindustan did not have grapes, the padre explained, they did not drink wine.

The padre offered a second pragmatic reason for the European consumption of alcohol. While in India because the sun travelled overhead there was no need for wine, in the land of the Franks, far removed from the sun, pure water was not always to be found. In a

[141] While magical competitions between Sufis and yogis are a common trope across north Indian literature, in the Marāṭhī tradition they could also occur within the same bhakti tradition (Green, 'Oral competition narratives'; Novetzke, *Religion and Public Memory*, 62–3).

[142] Mahīpatī relates such an episode about Nāmdev in the *Bhaktavijaya*. Similar examples exist in the hagiographic tradition of Eknāth: see Novetzke, 'The Brahmin Double', 242–3.

[143] Stephens, *The Christian Purānna*, 304 ('Dussarem Puranna', chapter 22, verse 28).

[144] Stephens, *The Christian Purānna*, 304 ('Dussarem Puranna', chapter 22, verses 29–34).

series of creative images, the padre explained to the inhabitants of sultry Salcete the hardships of a European winter. Upon the cold pervading the land, it would harden like stone, such that the water dried up. In that land, during the winter, water was struck with a hoe and carried in gunny bags upon the backs of asses. Where spittle struck the earth, it would dry up immediately and glitter like glass. If men lost their way in the mountains in the winter, they would lose their life, their body becoming as rigid as a stone doll. The drinking of wine was thus necessary in these wintry lands. Such was the grace of God that he had granted gifts to each society fitting to their homeland. Where the grape grew there was often no heat; thus it was mixed with water for use as wine. Where there was no grapevine and spring waters flowed, like in Salcete, wine was avoided and pure water was drunk instead. Thus, the padre admonished, one should not deem impure the various drinks God had granted to people, least of all the one which had been made pure by the son of God with his own blood.[145]

The padre then made a distinction between those who drank wine in a pure way, and those who drank to the point of intoxication and were thus polluted. Nobody, the padre acknowledged, could approve the liquor made in Hindustan from the juice of the palm or some other fruit tree (*calpavruqhea*) and then sold out of greed to the low (*adhama*) castes. Fools would take such liquor without mixing it with water. Those hapless folks fell about crippled with drink, causing distress to their sons and daughters and destroying the household. Coming home late at night and, upon finding that there was nothing to eat, these miserable men beat their wives, causing their children to create an uproar that roused the neighbours, who in turn would abuse the drunks. For drink, they would sell the land of their livelihoods, abandon agriculture, and lose all their wealth. Half-scorched by drink, their lifespan was destroyed little by little. If the Christians of Hindustan used this liquor, they would invite great ridicule and insults. Such liquor gave Satan (devachara) happiness, made God turn his face away, and caused the great saints suffering.[146]

[145] Stephens, *The Christian Purânna*, 304–5 ('Dussarem Puranna', chapter 22, verses 36–51).

[146] Stephens, *The Christian Purânna*, 305 ('Dussarem Puranna', chapter 22, verse 52–66).

In contrast to this vivid picture of the miseries of low-caste alcoholism in the villages of Salcete, the padre explained intoxication was *not* what the Christian ritual use of alcohol entailed: country liquor was *not* what Jesus had created from water. Among the seven sacraments, Jesus had created the two greatest: the first was baptism, which was of water, and the second that of the altar, involving the liquor made of grape juice. Thus, both water and wine were honoured. Still, among the two, water had no fragrance while wine had a good odour; water showed no hue whereas wine had colour; water had no taste while wine was flavourful, and where water was wintry cold, wine was warm and spicy (*tiqhu*). Just as Christ had made wine from water, in the same way, whoever with true mind took the baptismal water would leave the qualities of water and take on those of wine. The gentile soul, without fragrance or taste, without warmth and colour, which opened to Christianity would then take on qualities and colour (*gunnavarnu*); to this believer would come the taste of faith, the warmth born of God.[147]

The metaphor, beautiful in itself, was especially powerful as theological refutation in light of theistic Hindu philosophical strains centred on the *nirguna brāhman*. In either its monist or dualist varieties, these philosophies advanced the notion that the supreme reality (and hence, God) was without qualities, with the dualist version qualifying this formlessness as essentially material. In the padre's formulation, the soul of the gentile who drank only water was marked by its lack of qualities; the Christian, on the other hand, could taste, smell, and see the colours of God, his bhakti thus taking on the taste of the wine he drank during the Eucharist.

As this brilliant apologia for Christian ritual use of alcohol suggests, the *Discurso* followed a spirit of accommodation in the oldest theological sense, expressed in the rabbinical exegetical formula that 'the scriptures speak in the language of man'. Attentiveness to the local context of the production and enunciation of the text was not merely in service of a literary adaptation of Christian knowledge to a foreign language and genre; it was paramount to the effective explication of this knowledge to the converts who would listen to and eventually

[147] Stephens, *The Christian Puránna*, 305–6 ('Dussarem Puranna', chapter 22, verses 67–77).

recite this text. Nonetheless, there is no question here of religious tolerance or coexistence.[148]

The *Kriṣṭapurāṇa* proved deeply popular: as early as 1620, Jesuits were reporting the enthusiasm with which it was recited by converts, for whom it was a much needed replacement for the vernacular literature they had lost through conversion.[149] Precisely because of its popularity, it achieved a life within the convert community that exceeded the control of their Jesuit guardians.

An intriguing clue to the reception of the *Kriṣṭapurāṇa* within the convert community can be found in the Marsden manuscript, the earliest extant non-Roman version of the work, dating from the late seventeenth or early eighteenth century (see Figure 5.2). This manuscript, which shows two scribal hands, is largely the same as extant Roman-script versions, although it strikes a higher linguistic register, replacing many of the Portuguese loanwords with Sanskritic synonyms.[150] More importantly, it has one very significant omission.[151] The entire chapter dedicated to the wedding at Cana described above, of vital theological import since it describes Jesus's first miracle, seems to have been deliberately omitted from the text. It suggests that Stephens's beautiful attempt to explain the Christian use of alcohol was not entirely successful. At least certain circles of the convert community continued to maintain their own standards of ritual and theological propriety.

[148] Compare this elegant but firm refusal of the compatibility of gentile philosophies to Christian truths to Eknāth's famous and nearly contemporary *bhārūḍ* (drama poem), *Hindu-Turk Saṁvād*. The text performs the conflict between the Hindu and Muslim interlocutor with great gusto, before an amiable theological agreement is reached. The respective creeds, despite apparent differences, revealed the same essential truth, a position made possible by Eknāth's sublimation of advaita philosophy to the Sufi notion of *waḥdat al-wujūd* (literally the one-ness of being or unity of existence).

[149] Saldanha, 'Introduction', in Stephens, *The Christian Puránna*, xliii.

[150] Abbot, 'The Discovery of the Original Devanāgri Text'.

[151] The other change worth mentioning is the significantly redacted first chapter, which now retains only the briefest of dedications to the supreme God. It omitted the description of the village church, as well as the paean to the Marāṭhī language justifying its worthiness as a vehicle for Christian knowledge.

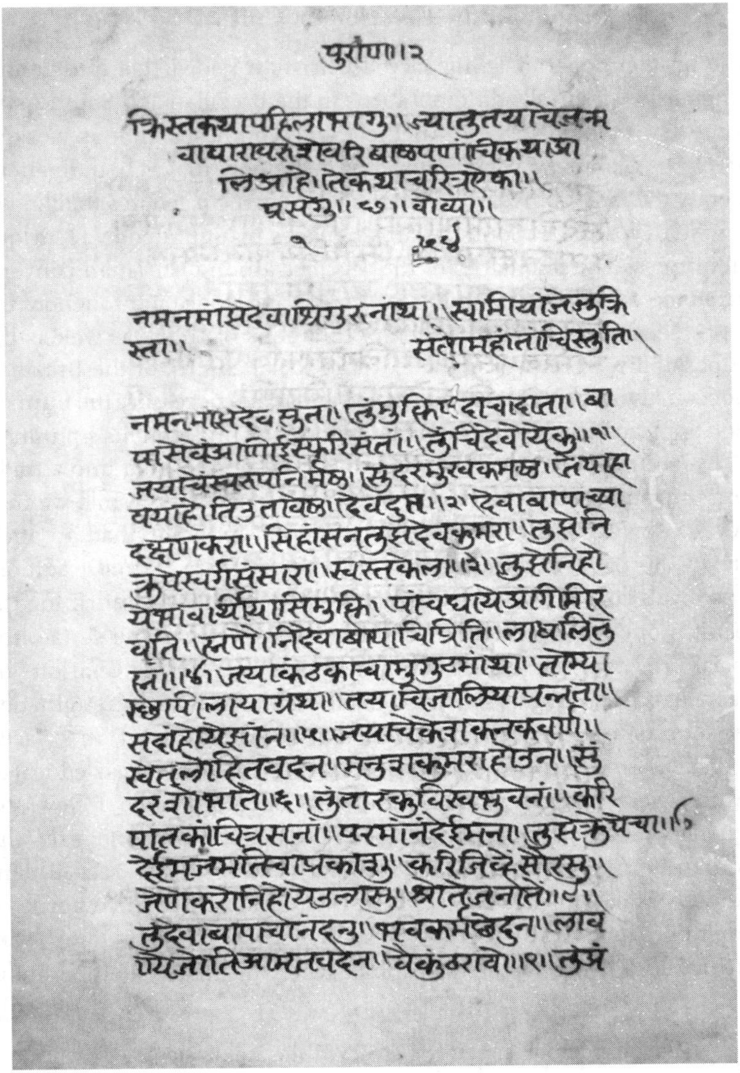

Figure 5.2 Marsden Manuscript of Stephens's *Kriṣṭapurāṇa*, page from Deva Puran; note that the scribal hand of the Adi Puran is different
Source: Courtesy of SOAS archives, with thanks to Wei Jiang for the photograph (MS 12104, SOAS, Marsden Collection).

Accommodatio and the Location of Culture

The problem of translating sacred Christian knowledge into gentile tongues took radically different turns in the Brazilian and South Asian contexts in which José de Anchieta and Thomas Stephens worked. Stephens's opus was not only founded upon the rich indigenous literary tradition of medieval Marāṭhī; it also participated in a tradition of Christian writing in South Asian languages inaugurated by Henrique Henriques. The popularity of the *Discurso* among Christian converts paved the way for Jesuit writing in Marāṭhī and Kōṅkaṇī throughout the seventeenth century.[152] The literary traditions of India, as well as the impossibility of imposing the extreme social control of the Brazilian aldeia in the subcontinent, nourished and made necessary the humanistic application of accommodatio epitomized by Stephens's purāṇa.

By contrast, Anchieta's poetic project did not flourish into a tradition of Jesuit literary writing in Brazilian vernaculars. While we may never know if Anchieta's reformulation of Tupí orality had an afterlife in the convert community's oral culture, as a *textual* tradition, Anchieta's corpus is unique. Given the laws of 1595–6 confirming the Jesuit monopoly over contact with the indigenous in the sertão, the social project of the aldeias continued unabated. Yet, as Charlotte de Castelnau L'Estoile has shown, even as Jesuits in Brazil strengthened the aldeias and cleaved ever more tightly to the Crown, they faced resistance from the Society's administration in Rome. Less-educated Jesuits were sent to Brazil, who were ill-equipped to follow the Ignatian dictat of learning the local language. Simultaneously, the Roman administration was increasingly averse to the recruitment of local men, who had linguistic and cultural competence borne of experience but were suspect precisely because of their long years in Brazil.[153] These factors, combined with the radical demographic

[152] Though none of these texts achieved the iconic status of Stephens's *Discurso*, the textual tradition inaugurated by that opus was rich. Etienne de la Croix's monumental *Discurso* was published a decade later. Following him as rector of the college was Antonio Saldanha, whose contribution to this literary tradition included, among other works, *Padva mhallalea xarantulea Sancto Antonichy Jivitua-catha*, a life of St Anthony of Padua. See Saldanha, *Santu Antonici jivitvakatha*.

[153] Castelnau L'Estoile, *Les Ouvriers d'une vigne stérile*.

reorientation of the mission and colony towards a largely African population, meant that Anchieta's literary project could not bequeath a tradition of Jesuit writing in indigenous languages.

One may also contend that Anchieta's project was no longer *possible* in the intellectual climes that came to prevail in the Jesuit order. Anchieta, much like Nóbrega, his predecessor and mentor, implicitly embraced a view of the Tupí that did not deem them to be at the bottom of a hierarchy of human civilization. Rather, as his poetry revealed, he saw them as a people possessed of a culture that demanded respect and attentive study.

This was a view increasingly out of step with the intellectual currents in the order. The clearest indicator, and perhaps harbinger, of this epistemic shift was the widespread circulation of José Acosta's *De Procuranda Indorum Salute* and the accompanying chapters from his moral history of the peoples of the New World.[154] Acosta's work was in many ways addressed to the same problem that had occupied Nóbrega—the definitive repudiation of the possibility that the Amerindian fell in some way outside the realm of humanity itself, thus rendering them incapable of Christian salvation. Yet, his solution differed considerably from Nóbrega's almost quietist resignation to the limited capacity of the missionary in bringing the Amerindian into the Christian fold.

Acosta's belief in the necessity of the ethnographic understanding of the gentiles to the evangelical process was axiomatic, 'for an understanding of their affairs will encourage them to believe in ours'. Moreover, such knowledge lent itself to an explicitly hierarchical comparative ethnology of three levels of barbarians. The first, which included the Chinese, and perhaps the Japanese and certain inhabitants of India, were the least removed from 'right reason' and 'what is

[154] Acosta's evangelical handbook was penned in 1577 in Lima, published in Seville in 1588 and republished in Salamanca in 1588 and Cologne in 1596. Subsequent editions were prefaced with the first two books of *De Natura Novi Orbis*. The handbook was widely circulated and came to be used as a textbook by the Jesui BNP, l of Natural Manachol, fl.rsden Collection, SOAS, MSam 4) held at the Central Library, Panjim. The handbook was widely circulated and came to be used as a textbook by the Jesuit order not only in the Americas, but also in Europe, North Africa, and in the Asian missions. See Pagden, *The Fall of Natural Man*, 198.

more important, [possessed] the use and the knowledge of letters, for wherever there are books and written monuments, people are more humane and more politic'. The second category consisted of immediately pre-literate societies, peoples like the Mexica and the Inca who possessed approximations to a writing system. They displayed a form of social organization proper to civilized men, forming empires and living in village settlements, and engaged in a barbaric but 'solemn religious cult'. The last and basest category, which in Acosta's estimation included all the peoples of Brazil, were characterized by complete illiteracy, and a concomitant lack of civilized social and religious life, marked by nomadism, animism, and cannibalism.[155]

As Adone Agnolin puts it, if in the beginning 'in the images between the Oriental and Occiental Indies ... the play of these images [of natives] produced ... the creation of a singular humanity', by the time Acosta was writing, this Augustinian anthropology was superseded by a hierarchical ethnology of humanity.[156] Moreover, the existence of such a typology of peoples required a similar typology of missionary practices appropriate to the conversion of each category of gentile. For the two highest categories, Acosta proscribed deculturation; rather, indigenous rites and customs could be translated, such that the gentile version would eventually be subsumed by Christian beliefs and practices. (Even so, apostolic preaching was only possible in the *Indias Orientales* [East Indies].[157]) In the lowest category, however, Acosta did not discern a culture—that is, a complex of rites, customs, and ceremonies—or social fabric that could be preserved during Christianization. In other words, civility could not exist in the realm of orality; thus accommodatio, as a form of cultural practice, was limited to the literate world.

In light of this schema, Anchieta's project was a striking violation of Acosta's precepts, while Stephens's accommodation to the literate culture of the brahmins of Salcete was entirely consonant. Thus, even as Jesuit interest in literizing and literarizing indigenous languages in Brazil sputtered, the following generation of Jesuits in India pursued ever more radical projects of accommodatio that transcended text to

155 Quoted in Pagden, *The Fall of Natural Man*, 158–64.
156 Agnolin, *Jesuítas e Selvagens*, 469.
157 Hosne, *The Jesuit Missions*, 168.

embrace mimetic praxis. Yet, the anomalous existence of Anchieta's corpus highlights precisely the naturalization of civilizational hierarchies that subtend so much of Europe's imperial thought—whether in the 'civilizing' logics of high and neo-colonialism, or in the Orientalist disciplines, which form the basis of modern religious studies.[158]

The devotion to the local that Anchieta and Stephens's practice of accommodatio entailed was entwined in a wider politics of the creation of imperialistic knowledge. Moreover, despite their attempts to set aside the distractions of the global currents of European imperial rivalries, neither could fully insulate himself and his missions. Soon, these global currents became impossible to ignore. It is in this context that an imperial imaginaire flowered among the following generation of Portuguese missionaries.

[158] On this latter issue, see Masuzawa, *The Invention of World Religion.*

III

RELIGION, *ACCOMMODATIO*, AND THE IMAGINATION OF EMPIRE

6

THEATRES OF EMPIRE

António Vieira and Baltasar Da Costa in Brazil and India

The increasingly fractious relationships between Portuguese and non-Portuguese missionaries that Thomas Stephens witnessed reflected anxieties caused by the growing fragility of the Portuguese empire. During the Spanish captivity, Portuguese holdings around the world became targets for the Dutch after the resumption of their hostilities against the Hapsburgs (see Figure 6.1). Simultaneously, an increasingly muscular papacy, after Urban VIII, expanded its own evangelical reach independent of the Iberian powers.

In this context, missionaries such as the great Jesuit António Vieira and his confrere and compatriot Baltasar da Costa had to negotiate the particularities of local missions within the vicissitudes of global politics. For Portuguese Jesuits, the Portuguese empire was more than a means to safeguard their local missions. Working in Brazil and India, they began to understand their own peripheral position in the politics of imperial rivalry, literally and figuratively. Their missions, which for them held deep religious significance, were rendered expendable or marginal in the global calculations of temporal power. To put it another way, local missions became theatres of global empire and missionaries such as Vieira and da Costa began to take on many complex roles to address their various audiences, local and global. Thus, they oscillated between a praxis based on local knowledge, in service of a missionary strategy of

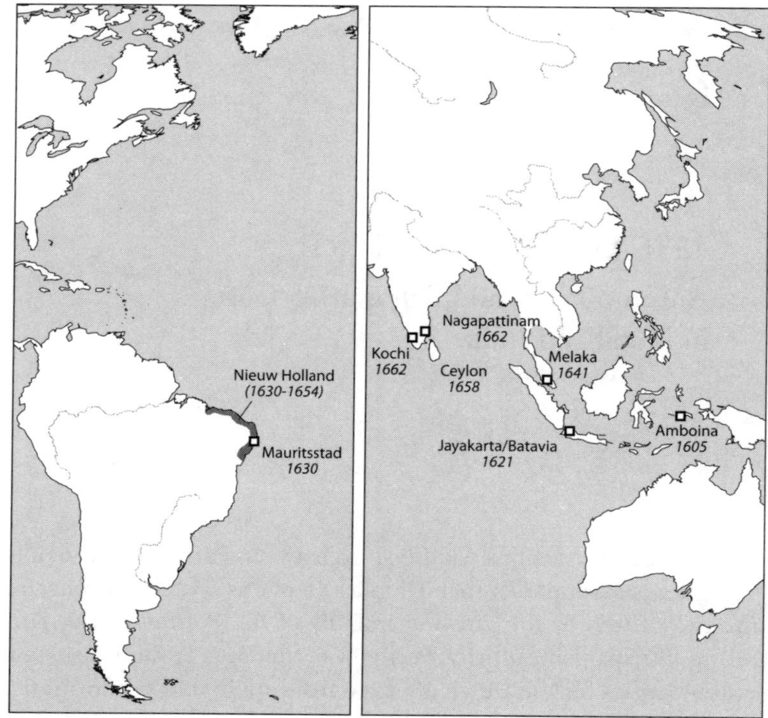

Figure 6.1 Dutch Assaults on the Portuguese Empire, Seventeenth Century
Source: The author (drawn by William Nelson).

accommodatio, and a performance of imperial vassalage in metropolitan spaces—without forgetting their commitment to their distant missions.

The first section of this chapter explores Vieira's career in Brazil, from its turbulent beginnings during the Dutch assaults in Bahia, to his post-Restoration efforts to renew the promise of mission and empire in the new frontiers of the Amazon. We then turn to the career of Baltasar da Costa in the south Indian mission of Madurai, tracing the shifting roles he inhabited in balancing his commitment to local accommodatio and the global Portuguese empire.

Colonial Signs, Imperial Visions

In 1621, the Jesuit brother Pedro de Basto, serving in the Malabar province, received this vision: 'God had shown him many figures, and first amongst them was Christ our Lord, with a stick in his hand full of shoots, and that he had seen alongside some writing, which when read said: *Punishment of Christendom in India*.'[1] Basto, born Pedro Machado, came to India in 1587 as a soldier. He joined the Jesuit order in Goa, and moved to south India in 1601, where he spent the rest of his life.[2] News of his visions spread quickly, such that there was 'no city in India, which was the site of a siege, war or battle, whether naval or terrestrial, that God did not manifest to [him].'[3] Religious and state officials, merchants and citizens sought his guidance in navigating, literally and metaphorically, the tricky waters of those turbulent times.[4]

Basto's visions began around 1594, the year of the successful Portuguese siege of Chaul, and one year before the Dutch rounded the Cape of Good Hope.[5] Thus began a series of costly engagements, which exposed the fragility of the Estado da Índia and wreaked havoc on its trade. By 1619, the Dutch established the centre of their eastern empire in Jakarta, under the Verenigde Oost-Indische Compagnie (VOC). Basto's visions confirmed that the systematic Dutch assault upon the Portuguese in the east was a measure of God's punishment.

[1] Queyros, *História da vida*, 255. Queyros's biography was based on a dossier of affidavits by those who had known Basto, as well as a spiritual autobiography Basto was directed to write by his superior, a resumé of which circulated throughout India, including among the lay clergy (Queyros, 'Aos que lerem', *História da vida*.)

[2] Soon after joining the order, Basto moved to the college in Cochin, where, over the next nine years, he began to establish his reputation for saintliness and prophetic ability. After a fight with a superior, Basto moved to Tuticorin, serving as spiritual coadjutor there for seventeen years, before returning to Cochin. He died in 1645. See Queyros, *História da vida*, 22, 33, 52–4, 59.

[3] Queyros, *História da vida*, 258. Queyros quotes here from Pedro de Basto's self-authored spiritual autobiography.

[4] A good proportion of the visions recorded in Queyros relate to shipwrecks or visions received in response to merchants who anxiously sought advice on whether certain voyages they were planning were propitious or not.

[5] Queyros, *História da vida*, 258.

It was not only the Portuguese east that experienced this divine wrath. The same year, the West-Indische Compagnie (WIC) was promulgated. In 1626, a young novice reported prophetic intimations of the Dutch invasion of Bahia to the Society of Jesus:

> A few days before the arrival of the enemies, two of our Fathers being in the choir, one of them saw Christ our Lord with a sword drawn against the city of Bahia, as one who threatened it. To the other, the same Lord appeared with three spears that appeared to shoot at the body of the church. Those who saw this well understood that it augured some great punishment.[6]

The writer António Vieira had been born in Lisbon to Cristóvão Vieira Ravasco and Maria de Azevedo (see Figure 6.2).[7] His father received an important clerkship in the newly created high court of Bahia and subsequently moved his family to Brazil.[8] António Vieira, who had come to the Jesuit college in Bahia at the age of fifteen, was serving as a novice on 8 May 1624 when the enemy's naval force was sighted.

The city was ill-prepared to ward off the attack. The governor, Diogo de Mendonça Furtado, gathered a force of some 3,000 men, while the bishop, Marcos Teixeira, set out, 'with a company of armed ecclesiasts, not only to animate the people, but, with sword in hand, to repel and attack the enemy, if necessary; and, running to all the stations, exhorted all, as a true prelate and pastor, to fight unto death for faith and king... '. Not unlike the karaíba, Jesuits and other clergy fanned through the streets, exhorting and confessing the soldiers, preparing 'with no less care their souls for death as their bodies for war'. Such was the religious fervour that 'it seemed to many opportune that God should give such a punishment'.[9]

The defences, both temporal and spiritual, proved pitiful: as the residents panicked, the bishop led an exodus out of the city.[10]

[6] Vieira, 'Carta anua de 1626', *Obras Escolhidas* I, 2.

[7] On Vieira's family background and his mixed race parentage, see Dutra, 'The Vieira Family'.

[8] Alden, 'Some Reflections on Antonio Vieira', 7. The article provides a useful introduction to Vieira's life and work.

[9] Vieira, 'Carta anua de 1626', *Obras Escolhidas* I, 3.

[10] Vieira, 'Carta anua de 1626', *Obras Escolhidas* I, 10. The allusion is Vieira's own.

Figure 6.2 António Vieira (1608–1697)
Source: John Carter Library, Brown University, Rhode Island, USA (Carolus Grandi, Celeberr.us P. Antonius Vieyra Soc. Jesu. Lusit. Vijssipon., 1742, John Carter Brown Archive of Early American Images, available at https://jcb.lunaimaging.com/luna/servlet/JCB~1~1, accessed on 6 September 2017).

After sacking the abandoned houses, the Dutch embarked upon an iconoclastic orgy, tearing the images of saints limb from limb, breaking crosses, profaning altars and sacred vestments, and using the chalices reserved for the Eucharist for the masses of Bacchus. Even in this dreadful scene Vieira perceived divine mercy, as God took upon himself the greater part of the punishment that the colony's sins had merited.[11] Nonetheless, the twin prophecies of the priests in the choir had come to pass: the city of Bahia had been pierced by the Dutch sword while its church was rent by the three spears of heresy, iconoclasm, and sacrilege.

Yet all was not lost: Bishop Teixeira organized an effective resistance in the countryside, aided greatly by loyal indigenous peoples, particularly those the Jesuits tended.[12] Again, a sign was given for this reversal of fortune:

> [The enemies] had struck a cross hoisted outside a chapel many times. A few days later, when our people, as usual, waited for them to jump ashore, the cross, which once stretched its arms from east to west, had half twisted upwards, leaving its base immobile, until its arms stood north to south, open to those who fought. It seemed to give signs to those who avenged its injuries. And while our people experienced this favor, the enemies felt it more ... fearing that the death, which had triumphed in our favor on land, would come [to them too at] sea.[13]

The sign was proved correct. Just as the resistance in the countryside checked Dutch ambition, eventually, on Easter morning of 1625, succour arrived from across the seas: an armada appeared, consisting of Portuguese, Spanish, and Neapolitan soldiers, who for once set aside the divisions of the Habsburg empire to expel the Dutch.[14] The reprieve, though a sign of divine favour, was also partial: Vieira's report ended on the ominous observation that while Salvador da Bahia was freed, the coast was infested with enemies.

Vieira's report, often haunting but not yet marked by the sharp political acumen of his later letters, did not reveal that the invasion of Bahia had been foretold by means other than divine omens. The complacent colony had ignored Spanish warnings of the coming attack, in part due to the truculence of the same Bishop Teixeira whom Vieira lionized.[15] The wider political backdrop of the invasion did not affect the contours

[11] Vieira, 'Carta anua de 1626', *Obras Escolhidas* I, 11.

[12] See especially Vieira, 'Carta anua de 1626', *Obras Escolhidas* I, 27, 35, 43.

[13] Vieira, 'Carta anua de 1626', *Obras Escolhidas* I, 21.

[14] Schwarz, 'The Voyage of the Vassals', 737.

[15] Edmundson, 'The Dutch Power in Brazil', 239–40.

of Vieira's account: for Vieira, writing as a missionary in the colony and far removed from the intricacies of Europe's endless wars, the invasion was experienced first and foremost as divine punishment, foretold in visions. The cause was apparent: as the mass confessions before the invasion revealed, 'ancient hatreds' and 'sins hidden by the silence of many years' had riddled the colony to such an extent that even its inhabitants recognized the merit of their punishment.[16]

The anxious note upon which the annual letter ended proved to be prescient. A successful year of buccaneering in the Atlantic Ocean in 1628 provided the WIC with both the funds and the ambition to launch another attempt upon Brazil. This time, however, Olivares showed none of the political will that had made possible the armada of 1625. Spain, forced to invest heavily in protecting its treasure fleets from Dutch assault, merely sent advance warning of Dutch plans and Matthias de Albuquerque to lead the defence in Brazil. A desultory war of attrition ensued, where both sides were victims as much to the enemy as to the hardships of the terrain. The only aid from Europe was a badly planned expedition funded entirely at Portuguese expense. By the time Duarte de Albuquerque, the proprietor of Pernambuco, approached the Dutch with an offer to pay an indemnity for its recovery, both he and the Dutch knew that little help could be expected from Spain. By 1635, when Vieira took his vows, Nieuw-Holland was firmly established.

If Brazil's position was precarious, Portuguese India was in undeniable crisis. In 1622, the Portuguese suffered the humiliating loss of Hormuz to a joint Anglo-Persian force. Belated attempts to seek non-military solutions to the crisis by mobilizing private mercantile interests saw the promulgation of the Companhia da Índia in 1628, which collapsed ignominiously five years later.[17] Two years later, the viceroy Conde de Linhares recognized the impossibility of repelling both Dutch and English incursions, especially in light of their alliances with hostile native polities. He thus signed a truce with the English in Surat.[18] The Dutch assault, however, continued

[16] Vieira, 'Carta anua de 1626', *Obras Escolhidas* I, 45.

[17] On the company, see Disney, *Twilight of the Pepper Empire* and de Silva, 'The Portuguese East India Company'.

[18] The viceroy had hoped the peace would pave the way for the undoing of the Dutch and leave the English and Portuguese as masters of all they surveyed. See Linhares, *Diário*, 267.

unabated: Goa was blockaded again in 1636 and Portuguese holdings in southern India, the seat of the Jesuit Malabar province, were in grave peril.

One of Basto's most celebrated visions bore remarkable resemblance to that reported by Vieira before the siege of Bahia. When Basto commended the beleaguered Estado da Índia to God, he saw 'God enraged against it, for the great sins that they had in all of India and saw on the banks of Goa an angel with a naked sword in hand, turned toward the city, as one who threatened'.[19] The vision, publicized by the Jesuits, reached the ears of the Archbishop Primate Dom Francisco dos Martyres. He ordered that the Blessed Sacrament be shown in the churches of the religious convents and parishes to implore divine mercy and favour. Prayers and rigorous penances were performed in Goa; other ports of Portuguese India followed suit. After three years of such petitions, prayers, and orations, Basto was rewarded with a vision of the same angel with its face and sword turned towards the sea and its back to Goa. Not long after, in 1639, the Dutch blockade of Goa ended, reinforcing Basto's reputation as a seer.[20] Eventually, news of his visions would reach the ears of António Vieira himself.

Foreign Nations Are the Rod of Divine Wrath

The religious establishment in Portuguese India and Brazil experienced the increasing encroachment of Dutch naval power similarly. Basto's many visions relating to the conflict with the Dutch in the east all turned on divine castigation.[21] The image of a rod was a recurring theme. Once, while praying for the deliverance of the Portuguese from the vexations of its enemies, God showed Basto a large stick, covered in knots. On another occasion, he saw a long rod and heard a clear, sonorous, funereal voice, saying *Punishment in the*

[19] Queyros, *História da vida*, 257. The vision was told to Francisco Brito de Almeyda, who recorded it in written form, which text Queyros quotes here.

[20] Queyros, *História da vida*, 258. Queyros mentions here how famous preachers like Diogo de Areda publicized this vision in sermons and other media.

[21] Goa was fertile ground for the theme of God's punishment and other preachers, including non-Portuguese ones such as António Ardizone Spinola, preached variations of it. See Winius, 'Millenarianism and Empire'.

Church of God.[22] The first cause of the empire's troubles was to be found not in European political rivalries; to focus on the immediate threat of the Dutch or its temporal causes would be to ignore its real significance.

The searing sermon that Vieira preached in 1640, when the Dutch had been ensconced in Pernambuco for a decade, also echoed this belief.[23] While acknowledging again the many sins of Brazil, now Vieira railed for mercy, focusing not on the cause of this punishment but on its consequences. Thinking undoubtedly of the freedom of religion offered in Nieuw-Holland, Vieira argued that in allowing the Portuguese to be so beaten by heretics, God was discrediting himself. Worse, it undermined the true faith in the eyes of the new Christian, the Tapuía barbarian, the inconstant Indian, and the African slave, all recently baptized and lacking catechetical instruction. If the cause of these events were to be found in Brazil, then consequences in Europe were immaterial. The Dutch conflict, in Vieira's reading, was first and foremost a threat to local Brazilian society. Defeat at their hands meant the erosion of the religious authority that underpinned Catholic civility.[24] Vieira predicted vividly what could be expected if God handed Brazil to the Dutch, echoing the descriptions of the wailing, abandoned townsmen of Salvador and of Dutch iconoclasm from his annual letter of 1626.

The need to drive home the consequences in Brazil was born from an increasing awareness of his colonial location, of its marginality, and even invisibility from the viewpoint of Europe. This is palpable in Vieira's sermon on St Anthony, given on the saint's day in his church in Bahia, after the Dutch barracks erected in front of it were uprooted in 1638. The sermon was a meditation on the promise God gave to Hezekiah through the prophet Isaiah to defend Judah from the Assyrian invasion: 'I will protect and save this city for my own

[22] Queyros, *História da vida*, 256.

[23] Vieira, 'Sermão pelo bom sucessos das armas de Portugal contra as da Holanda', *Obras Escolhidas* X, 72.

[24] Vieira, 'Sermão pelo bom sucessos das armas de Portugal contra as da Holanda', *Obras Escolhidas* X, 55. Vieira relies on the Book of Daniel here to draw a parallel with the situation of the humiliated Israelites, the veracity of whose God was questioned by the Egyptians upon seeing their miserable state.

sake and for the sake of my servant David.'[25] Vieira's sermon turned on the name of his beloved city, named for the Saviour and saved by him in a fulfilment of the promise given to Hezekiah, superimposing biblical prophecy onto colonial history. He invoked here the language of signs, crafting his sermon as an exercise in their interpretation. Yet, recent events and their significance, visible to all in the colony, which lacked a printing press, remained illegible in Europe:

> [Similar] victories, and others more minor than similar, are customarily printed in Europe in order to make public all over the world [while] we in America lack these trumpets of fame with which to have [our news] printed for the eyes of His Majesty and with which to gladden Portugal, Spain and all the Monarchy. In the words that I have proposed (which are from IV Kings, chapter 19) there seems to be a pattern so characteristic of our history.... What I will say or repeat, will be, if only pondered, what everyone saw.[26]

If this sermon revealed his frustration at the invisibility of Brazil in Europe, Vieira was even more explicit in articulating colonial resentment on the occasion of the visit of the viceroy in 1640. Preaching at the hospital of the Misericórdia in Bahia, Vieira began with a striking quotation from the prophet Malachi: 'The sun of justice shall come and it will bring health in its wings.' Using the prophecy, Vieira laid out the various complaints of Brazil to the viceroy, a long-delayed diagnosis of its colonial condition:

> The worst accident that Brazil had in its infirmity was in the hindrance to speech: many times, [Brazil] wished to complain, many times it wished to ask for a remedy for its ills, but the words always drowned in the throat, through either respect or violence; and if ever a groan came to the ears of those who must heal, there also came the voices of power which defeated the claims of reason. For this reason, today I'll be the interpreter of our illness ...[27]

[25] Vieira, 'Sermão de Santo António', *Obras Escolhidas* X, 1. The key phrase Vieira parses in this sermon is given as follows: *Protegam urbem hanc, et savabo eam propter me, et propter David, servum meum- IV, Kings, XIX.*

[26] Vieira, 'Sermão de Santo António', *Obras Escolhidas* X, 3–4. Vieira's point here is even more significant if we consider that the first printing press in Brazil did not arrive till the nineteenth century, when the Portuguese court itself was transplanted there while fleeing the Napoleonic wars.

[27] Vieira, 'Sermão da visitação de nossa senhora', *Obras Escolhidas* X, 88.

Keenly aware that 'what everybody saw' in Brazil was invisible in Europe, Vieira positioned himself as the voice for the silent and silenced Brazil, the interpreter of its signs and symptoms. Brazil's illness, its 'original sin', was an absence of justice, which had led to the loss of dominion in these lands:

> The reason why kingdoms and monarchies are not preserved under the same lord, the reason why they pass inconstantly from some nations to others, as we see is *propter injustitias*—through injustices. The injustices of Earth open the door to the justice of Heaven. And as foreign nations are the rod of divine wrath—*Assur virga furores mei*—with them we are deprived of country.[28]

The idea that the Dutch, as the Assyrians had been for Israelites, were the instrument of divine punishment was common to Basto as well.[29] Once, when Basto had prayed for divine retribution against the Dutch, he was rewarded instead with a vision of Christ who chastised him: 'With them, I want to punish India for I am not satisfied with her Christians and afterwards I will undo them like salt in water.'[30] Vieira's elaboration of the theme of punishment, however, went beyond the recognition of divine castigation. He did not apportion blame solely to the ills of colonial society, nor even ask for mercy; he instead alleged that it was the lack of colonial justice that allowed these ills to go unchecked and which had placed Brazil at such risk.

He was not speaking vaguely: his was a passionate indictment of a colonial system where brave soldiers received neither adequate support nor recognition for their efforts, while the undeserving reaped honours and wealth, making a mockery of attempts to restore Brazil.[31] He complained that colonial officials, 'the successors of Pilates in the world', hid the truth: one of the reasons that Brazil's true condition remained invisible in Europe was the dissimulation of colonial officials who painted an inaccurate picture for their metropolitan masters. Moreover, 'the people [were] undone in tributes and more

[28] Vieira, 'Sermão da visitação de nossa senhora', *Obras Escolhidas* X, 90.

[29] Funkenstein, *Perceptions of Jewish History*, 54. By the same token, Portugal, in its very powerlessness, like Israel, manifested its divine destiny and God's power.

[30] Queyros, *História da vida*, 399.

[31] Vieira, 'Sermão da visitação de nossa senhora', *Obras Escolhidas* X, 95.

tributes, in taxes and more taxes, in donations and more donations, in alms and more alms', without any profit or advantage. 'In its time,' Vieira noted bitterly, 'Pernambuco gave much; Bahia gave and gives much today and nothing is achieved, because what is taken from Brazil, is taken out of Brazil; what Brazil gives, Portugal takes.'[32] Still, despite the severity of his diagnosis, he had not lost hope: he ended the sermon with the 'happy prophecy' that Brazil would be restored.[33]

What Vieira's sermons and Basto's visions had in common was an attempt to make comprehensible in local terms the vicissitudes of global politics originating in Europe, and to imbue these events with meaning. This was a highly affective discourse, revealing the intensely felt despair of the beleaguered colonial Jesuits and their hopes for transcending these adversities, religious and political, through the correct interpretation of signs. In the imagination of these colonial Jesuits, these non-European locations were no less a privileged theatre in which divine will and Portuguese destiny were intertwined and enacted; instead, the colony was politically and religiously meaningful in itself and not merely a distant square on the chessboard of European politics.

A Kingdom Restored, an Empire in Peril

Many of Pedro de Basto's prophetic revelations related to the restoration of the Portuguese Crown.[34] News of Basto's visions travelled in garbled form to Lisbon, where it stimulated much debate, with some interpreters concluding that D. Sebastião was alive, while others disagreed.[35] When João IV acceded to the throne, it seemed Basto's revelations were confirmed. Following the accession, from 1 October 1641 to 27 June 1643, he experienced a series of visions, foretelling various victories, showing the king in glorious form, dressed in purple, accompanied by the sun.[36]

[32] Vieira, 'Sermão da visitação de nossa senhora', *Obras Escolhidas* X, 107.

[33] Vieira, 'Sermão da visitação de nossa senhora', *Obras Escolhidas* X, 110.

[34] Queyros, *História da vida*, 408.

[35] Queyros, *História da vida*, 418–21. The lively debate about the meaning of Basto's vision between the brothers at Lisbon and Coimbra may have been how Vieira first heard of Basto, when he came to João IV's court.

[36] Queyros, *História da vida*, 410–14.

Basto's visions were an index of the hope kindled by the restoration of the Portuguese Crown, in the kingdom and its empire. It was short-lived—although a truce with the Dutch was quickly reached, Portugal gained a new and powerful enemy in her former Spanish overlords. D. João IV, still putting down conspiracies for the restoration of Spanish rule in his own court, had neither the internal political strength nor external alliances to battle both powers.

Soon after the restoration, Vieira joined the court in Portugal, where he became a favoured advisor of D. João IV. In 1646, he was serving as ambassador to France when news reached him that colonists subject to the Dutch in Pernambuco hoped to launch a rebellion and restore Brazil to an autonomous Portugal. They were seeking Portugal's support in the endeavour. Vieira hastened to press upon the king 'the danger and difficulty of this enterprise,' believing the conspirators too optimistic of their ability to dislodge the Dutch. Vieira urged the king to reconsider the dangers of accepting the burden of war with Holland while Spain loomed hostile, because 'the Dutch are not only our neighbors in Brazil, but in India, China, Japan, Angola and in all parts of the earth and the sea, where their power is the greatest in the world'.[37]

Vieira's appraisal showed a distinctly new turn in his thought, proper to his metropolitan location and his new role in the Portuguese court. No longer was Brazil his sole concern. Nonetheless, as the Dutch planned to blockade Bahia, the matter had to be resolved. Vieira advocated that instead of open warfare, the Portuguese should buy back the lost province; the Dutch could be persuaded, provided a sufficiently large indemnity were paid and if certain members of the states-general were judiciously bribed.[38] Among his proposals for raising funds for the indemnity was a tribute to be exacted from the inhabitants of Brazil, which even Vieira acknowledged would be very large. He justified this new burden on the grounds that Pernambuco would be redeemed from the hands of their enemies and restored to the true faith. Further, it would ensure Brazil's financial security, as ports would be freed for the trade in sugar and slaves. Lastly, but

[37] Vieira, 'Ao Marquês de Nisa, Paris, a 11-III-1646', *Obras Escolhidas* I, 83.

[38] Vieira, 'Parecer sobre se restaurar Pernambuco', *Obras Escolhidas* III, 2. The opinion was written in Lisbon on 14 March 1647.

no less importantly, Portugal's other conquests would be safe from Dutch molestation.[39] Gone were his earlier concerns about the undue burden on colonial Brazil; gone too was his concern for Brazil's reception of such imperial demands.

When the Dutch proved unwilling to sell Pernambuco back to the Portuguese and the rebellion threatened the truce with Holland, Vieira proposed abandoning Pernambuco in order to avoid open war. Though he invoked his colonial experience to impress upon his audience the value of his proposal, the extent to which Vieira had abandoned his Brazil-centric understanding of the Dutch problem was apparent in this remarkable plea. The first objection Vieira foresaw to his proposal was to do with religion: to hand over Pernambuco would mean to leave it in the hands of heretics, thus abandoning the Catholics living there and preventing further propagation of the faith. Vieira's response was startling: first, under his plan, devout Catholics could leave Pernambuco with their movable property and live in Portuguese lands. Second, he denied that Pernambuco presented any further opportunities for the propagation of the faith, 'due to the lack of gentiles'. By handing over Pernambuco, where opportunities for conversion had been exhausted, the Crown would safeguard a vast domain, where huge numbers of Christians still lived. To support his claim, he tabulated the numbers of converts in every parish administered by the Jesuits in the Estado da Índia, from east Africa to Japan; they totalled over a million souls, a number that did not even include those tended by other orders and the episcopacy. Unlike Pernambuco, Vieira argued, in the east, opportunities for conversion still abounded, particularly in the four empires of China, Japan, Ethiopia, and Mughal India.[40] D. João IV's responsibilities as a Catholic monarch came down to a matter of numbers.

Vieira impressed upon him the continued cost to Bahia of the twenty-four year struggle in Pernambuco. He argued that the risk in which the king would place the eastern empire and the rest of Brazil for the sake of Pernambuco was unwarranted.[41] The rest of the

[39] Vieira, 'Parecer sobre se restaurar Pernambuco', *Obras Escolhidas* III, 13.

[40] Vieira, 'Papel a favor da entrega de Pernambuco aos Holandeses', *Obras Escolhidas* III, 30–4.

[41] Vieira, 'Papel a favor da entrega de Pernambuco aos Holandeses', *Obras Escolhidas* III, 35–6, 50–3, 60–1, 67.

paper analysed the military and diplomatic vulnerability of the far-flung empire in the event of war with the Dutch, concluding that in such an eventuality, Goa and Bahia would be taken with no effort.[42] Nevertheless, the bleak proposal did end on a hopeful note. In consolation of the small loss of Pernambuco, Vieira promised:

> We will [repossess] the fortress of Negumbo and the territories that belonged to it in Ceylon, when it was surrendered. We will open trade in the Rivers of Cuama, and the straits of Mecca; discover new drugs in Maranhão and Pará, we will take the Rio de Prata ... [Delay] what we now want to do for a more opportune time, in which not only will we come to take [back] what we now restore to [the Dutch], but [regain] all that they have so unjustly possessed in our Conquests ... [for] God has in store [for the Portuguese] the possession of the empire of the world.[43]

In this calculus of empire, possessions like Pernambuco, where the scope for conversion was exhausted, could be abandoned for new unexplored frontiers. These places held open the possibility for renewing Portugal's promise and destiny: that of bringing about the prophesied fifth empire in which mankind would be united under the Catholic Church and Portuguese Crown. Frontiers such as Maranhão and Mozambique promised not only new sources of commercial wealth, but also the possibility of bringing more gentiles into the Christian fold in preparation of the fifth empire.

To Dream of Empire in the Conquests

Vieira came to work in precisely these frontiers unexpectedly. Following a disastrous diplomatic mission in Italy, he was more or less compelled to give up his career as a statesman in Europe and return to his roots as a missionary in Brazil. He left with mixed emotions, but with a decided sense of divine ordination.[44] Once reconciled to his

[42] Vieira, 'Papel a favor da entrega de Pernambuco aos Holandeses', *Obras Escolhidas* III, 61–101.

[43] Vieira, 'Papel a favor da entrega de Pernambuco aos Holandeses', *Obras Escolhidas* III, 105–06.

[44] Vieira to Prince Teodósio, Cabo Verde, 25 December 1652, *Obras Escolhidas* I, 147.

departure from the exalted circles of European courts, he described his new life of apostolic simplicity with joy:

> I walk dressed here in the coarse cloth of the land, more brown than black; I work from morning to night; I spend part of it commending myself to God; I do not deal except with the least creature, do not go out but to remedy some soul, I cry for my sins and make others cry for theirs, and in the time that remains from these occupations, I read the books of mother Teresa and other similar readings.[45]

If Maranhão represented an opportunity for renewing his personal vocation, it was also a chance to revive the waning missionary enterprise in Brazil. Over the course of the seventeenth century, the missions in the old colonies had begun to crumble. In 1640, the long-standing conflict with colonists over the illegal enslavement of the indigenous led to the Society's complete expulsion from São Paulo, while in Rio de Janeiro and São Vicente similar conflicts had left the Jesuits in a precarious position. The missions in Maranhão and Pará offered a chance to start again: describing the state of Maranhão to the king, Vieira termed it deliberately 'the new world'.[46] It was indeed a new world: on canoes and rafts Vieira explored the Amazon, marvelling at the habits of turtles and the strange, cold-blooded land creatures known as *jabotis*, the crocodiles stirring under the shade of trees, and always those 'sad Indians' who fed and protected and guided their helpless Portuguese charges through this wondrous, dangerous landscape, 'without any payment but that they are called dogs and other, even more affronting names'.[47] The presence of these indigenous peoples was the greatest reason why Maranhão was a 'new world'. They presented an opportunity to re-enact the original colonization of Brazil and to rectify its 'original sin': the unjust captivity of the Amerindians, which, as Vieira reminded the king, was 'perhaps the main cause of all the punishments that are experienced in our Conquests'.[48] Yet, already

[45] Padre Francisco de Morais, Maranhão, 6 May 1653, *Obras Escolhidas* I, 151.

[46] Vieira to João IV, Maranhão, 20 May 1653, *Obras Escolhidas* I, 153.

[47] Vieira to Father Provincial of Brazil, Maranhão, 1654, *Obras Escolhidas* I, 163–71.

[48] Vieira to João IV, Maranhão, 20 May 1653, *Obras Escolhidas* I, 155.

'pure work and ill-treatment' by the colonists were killing off the indigenous inhabitants.[49]

Vieira was not the only one to imagine that Maranhão held the key to a new empire: it was a view shared by the Portuguese state too, albeit for largely financial reasons.[50] For all its promise, it was a lawless frontier: as Vieira put it, 'Maranhão and Pará are the La Rochelle of Portugal, a conquest to be conquered, and a land where His Majesty is named but not obeyed.'[51] This was partly why the Crown cleaved to the Jesuit mission in Maranhão as a means to extend and deepen its control over the territory.[52] Vieira left for Maranhão with renewed powers to ensure a Jesuit monopoly in that mission field; his arrival also coincided with that of a royal decree freeing all indigenous slaves in 1653.

Anxious not to alienate the colonists and aware of the realities of colonial economics, Vieira restrained himself from using the full range of powers granted to him by the king. Significantly, he compromised the Jesuit monopoly on the distribution of indigenous labour and refrained from enforcing the decree. The efforts were largely futile. The old refrain of Brazilian colonial history, of the struggle over the custody of indigenous peoples between Jesuits and colonists, rang out again.[53] The colonists alienated Amerindians from the Jesuits, 'partly with promises, partly with threats, partly by giving them too much to drink and driving them from their senses, partly by telling them that the fathers would take the many woman the chiefs were

[49] Vieira to Father Provincial of Brazil, Maranhão, 1654, *Obras Escolhidas* I, 171.

[50] See, for example, 'Representação da Concelho da Fazenda sobre as necessidades urgentes em que estava o Reyno, apontando os remedios', fl. 64, ANTT, Manuscritos da Livraria 1146, Microfilm 1337. The Conselho da Fazenda, which held sway over matters to do with the empire before the Duke of Cadaval usurped its authority to the Conselho de Ultramarino, declared that Maranhão 'promised a new empire'.

[51] Vieira to João IV, Maranhão, 4 April 1654, *Obras Escolhidas* I, 173.

[52] Vieira was well aware of the symbiotic basis of this relationship. See, for example, 'Parecer sobre a conversão e governo dos gentios e indios', in *Obras Ineditas*, 112.

[53] On the long-running conflict over the control of indigenous labour between the Jesuits and colonists, see Alden, 'Black Robes versus White Settlers'.

accustomed to from them'.[54] Moreover, for all the Crown's goodwill, Vieira could not trust its local representatives, as they would deliver indigenous people to the colonists instead of the missions. By 1654, Vieira was requesting an independent militia for the protection of the Jesuits in the sertão, under the jurisdiction of the missionaries save in case of outright war.[55] The entradas upon which the fate of Maranhão hinged, Vieira argued, required the complete independence of both missionaries and Amerindians from local authority for their continued success. Vieira emphasized that in the untrammelled world of the Amazonian backwaters—so different from the urban civilizations of India or Japan—the Portuguese interloper was entirely dependent upon Amerindians, who guided, protected, and even fed the missionaries. Further, 'if the Indians are diverted by the interests of the governors and do not rely solely on the religious, they will not go to the missions'. As 'the infamy and fear' of plantation labour and colonial oppression reached them, they retreated into the forests.[56] Only once they were convinced to leave the safety of the forests could they be subjected to the colony's myriad demands upon them, temporal and religious. The unfettered rapacity of the colonists and local state officials would thus make it harder to bring them into the ambit of colonial control.

Despite his warnings, the passage of a new law that allowed indigenous slavery in disguised form prompted Vieira to return to Lisbon in 1655 to fight for the autonomy of Amerindians and missionaries from both royal officials and colonists.[57] Vieira sought to bring home to Lisbon's political and ecclesiastical elites the needs of distant Maranhão, where capable missionaries would 'find the fruit that they go to procure from distant parts, like India and Japan, with fewer delays and more certainty'. He impressed upon them that the

[54] Vieira to João IV, Maranhão, 6 April, 1654, *Obras Escolhidas* I, 180.

[55] Vieira to João IV, Maranhão, 6 April, 1654, *Obras Escolhidas* I, 189.

[56] Vieira to João IV, Maranhão, 6 April, 1654, *Obras Escolhidas* I, 195.

[57] Vieira strongly recommended that indigenous chiefs remain in charge of their own villages, with no other Portuguese superior. See Vieira, 'Parecer sobre a conversão e governo dos Indios', *Obras Escolhidas* V, 4. He also warned that if each colonist claimed jurisdiction over the Indians who worked for him, the result would be a serious violation of the king's relationship to his own vassals. Vieira, 'Responde-se ao segundo papel que tem titulo de "Breve Notícia do Gentio do Brasil", *Obras Escolhidas* V, 21.

conservation of the colony depended on the well-being and goodwill of the Amerindians. Thus, defending their freedom in these lawless lands was crucial.[58] Otherwise, the Amazon would witness the re-enactment of Brazil's disorderly history, instead of fulfilling its promise as an ever-expanding frontier of the Church and the Portuguese empire:

> In most parts of our Brazil, disorder prevailed, as the sovereignty of Portugal entered to possess its lands and wrest the freedom of its natives until it extinguished them ... [T]his last portion of the Amazon river of Jesus Christ waited for a zealous and effective minister of His Majesty. ... Descend those gentiles that are convenient for the service of the colonists ... [T]hrough the lower rivers, one may see infinite Indians, already Catholic and domesticated, ready to serve the Portuguese in their cities and villages....[59]

For Vieira, there was no conflict of interest between the demands of the Portuguese empire and those of the missionary enterprise. All it required was a certain moderation upon the part of the colonists, and both Church and empire would stand master over an infinitude of indigenous peoples in the Amazon, who would provide for all their needs. This passage, perhaps more clearly than any other, obviates a romantic or anachronistic reading of Vieira's defence of the freedom of the Amerindians. One may argue that this was a rhetorical manoeuvre to make his demands more palatable to the Crown. Its consistency with the rest of his thought and his overwhelming concern for the Portuguese empire suggests that this vision indeed represented his utopia.

Upon his return to Brazil, Vieira continued his campaign to keep Maranhão in the hearts and minds of those in Portugal. After the Portuguese defeated Spain at Elvas, a victory widely considered to be miraculous, Vieira reminded them of the equally miraculous victories Portugal experienced in these distant lands:

> At the same time in which miraculous victories are written about from the Kingdom to the Conquests, we in the Conquests write to the kingdom of victories too, which, with as much or more reason, may be called miraculous. There, God triumphs with blood, with destructions, with tears and

[58] Vieira, 'Responde-se ao segundo papel que tem titulo de "Breve Notícia do Gentio do Brasil", *Obras Escolhidas* V, 24.

[59] Vieira, 'Responde-se ao segundo papel que tem titulo de "Breve Notícia do Gentio do Brasil", *Obras Escolhidas* V, 25–6.

> with the pain of Christianity; here He wins without blood, without destructions, without war and even without expenses ... As much as [the church] feels diminished and attenuated by the blood which flows in Europe, it is enlarged and grown with the people, nations and provinces which it wins and acquires in America.[60]

The victory of which Vieira wrote was a rapprochement with the 'Nheengaíbas', or those deemed from the Tupí point of view to speak a barbarous tongue, inhabitants of the island of Marajó. Members of this group had allied themselves with the Dutch and were considered extraordinarily ferocious and barbarous, much like the Tapuía of the early days of Brazil. Vieira sought to circumvent a planned war by the colonists against the group by offering the latter a peace treaty. The colonists had a vested interest in fomenting war, not only because it would allow them to enslave the enemy under the pretext of just war, but because, in promoting warfare between indigenous groups, they could exploit the right to capture *índios da corda*, prisoners of war of other indigenous peoples. Once enslaved, from the Jesuit perspective, they would be lost to the faith.

The treaty, in Vieira's eyes, bloodlessly secured Portuguese temporal and spiritual rule in the Amazon, as much as military victory had done at Elvas. Vieira reminded the king that Portugal was much more than the kingdom; its conquests were as integral to Portugal and to the universal Church as the slim land on the edge of Iberia where the king held his court. As he had done many years ago in Bahia, Vieira insisted that the conquest was no less a privileged theatre of the enactment of divine will as the kingdom. Moreover, the missives sent from the kingdom could not inscribe the complete history of the church; to read this, one must also read the missives sent from the conquests.

Vieira was well aware that the pronouncements from the kingdom carried a weight that missives from the colonies could not. In an infamous commentary on the mystical strophes attributed to Gonçalo Eanes Bandarra entitled *Esperanças de Portugal* [Hopes of Portugal], Vieira described to the bishop of Japan the circumstances in which he composed the work: in a canoe on the Amazon.[61] Written

[60] Vieira to Afonso VI, Maranhão, 28 November 1659, *Obras Escolhidas* I, 196–7.

[61] Vieira, 'Esperanças de Portugal', in *Obras Ineditas*, 83.

in 1659, the work ran against conventional Sebastianist interpretations of Bandarra and argued that the strophes prophesied the return of João IV, Vieira's late patron. It was he, and not the ill-fated Sebastião, who had been prophesied to restore the full glory of Portugal. Though the body of the text encompassed the world in its analysis, flitting from Constantinople to Rome, Sicily to Angola, Spain to the Levant, Vieira ended the epistle by reminding the reader again of the setting in which it was written:

> And I too will bid farewell of my prophet, who brings in such a pilgrim part of Maranhão to Lisbon ... its own truth. So he says in the prologue of his *sapataria*, which are all the verses with which I want to conclude:
>
> Always I walk occupied
> For my good vocation
> If I lived in Lisbon
> I would be more prized.[62]

In this poignant ventriloquism, one can sense Vieira's rueful understanding of his colonial location—of what it meant to dream and write of empire at its margins. By 1661, the Jesuits were expelled from Maranhão, due partly to the circulation of Vieira's querulous reports of the behaviour of the colonists and the imprisonment by the missionaries of an indigenous chief, Lopo de Sousa Guarapaúba, who was allied with the colonists. Vieira found himself again returning to Europe.[63] If 'the seed is the word of God', the harvest of this land of promise had proved bitter to its sowers.[64]

[62] Vieira, 'Esperanças de Portugal', in *Obras Ineditas*, 129.

[63] 'Representação de Jorge Sampayo e Carvalho contra os padres da Companhia de Jesus, expondo os motives que teve o povo para os expulsar do Maranhão', in Barão de Studart, *Documentos*, Doc. 267; Vieira to Afonso VI, Praias do Cumá, 21 May 1661, *Obras Escolhidas* I, 226–8.

[64] The reference to Luke 8:11 is from the famous 'Sermão de Sexagésima', which Vieira preached in Lisbon in 1655, in which he gave vent to the sense of injury shared by the missionaries of Maranhão. A major subtext of the sermon was the unflattering comparison of the preachers in Portugal with the Jesuit missionaries in Maranhão and elsewhere, which contributed to the hostility of the ecclesiastical establishment in Portugal to Vieira (Vieira, 'Sermão de Sexagésima', in *Sermões*, vol. 1, 31).

Opening Again the Forests of Heathenism

Regardless of the belief among missionaries of the religious significance of their colonial theatres of activity, missions in the Portuguese world had become vulnerable on all fronts. The Malabar province of Basto's day was not only beset politically, economically, and militarily by the Dutch, on the ecclesiastical front too it was riddled with controversy. The Jesuit order had received a great honour in the election of Francisco Ros as bishop to the St Thomas Christians of Malabar, who had been coerced into accepting the Roman rite at the Synod of Diamper in 1599. When the Syrian Christians objected to their subjection to the see of Goa and demanded direct submission only to the Pope, Ros became archbishop. In 1605, to the great resentment of his see, he moved the archbishopric to Kodungallur from the traditional seat of the metropolitan in Ankāmali, on the grounds that it was safer to base the see under the protection of the Portuguese fortress of Cranganore than to remain at the mercy of the Hindu ruler who claimed Ankāmali. The St Thomas Christians opposed Ros and his successors at every turn in an effort to maintain their traditions and autonomy.[65]

The existence of dual Episcopal authority, in the bishoprics based in Kochi and in Kodungallur, further complicated the mission field. During his time on the Fishery Coast, Basto witnessed a bitter jurisdictional dispute over control of the Paravas, when the bishop of Kochi, the Franciscan André de Santa Maria, attempted to pass authority over the mission in Thoothukudi (Tuticorin) from the Jesuits to his own vicars. The Jesuits retreated with their converts to an island, arguing that this was an unrelated move to protect the Parava from the exploitation of local kings. Their opponents, however, interpreted the move as a hostile act, intended to maintain jurisdiction over the Parava at all costs. Despite their protestations of the undying loyalty of their flock, Jesuits themselves acknowledged that at least one powerful Parava headman was aiding the bishop's cause. Nearly two

[65] Thomaz, 'A carta que mandaram os Padres da Índia da China e da Magna China'; Oliveira e Costa, 'Os Portugueses e a cristandade siro-malabar (1498–1530)'; Subrahmanyam, 'Dom Frei Aleixo de Meneses'; Županov, 'One Civility, but Multiple Religions'; Cunha Rivara, *Synodo Diocesano*.

decades later, the Jesuit viewpoint carried the day with the authorities in Goa and Lisbon, and they retained their historic mission.[66] Still, on both sides of the south Indian coast, the hegemony of the Jesuits was clearly eroding.

In this darkening political and religious landscape, there was one mission that flickered with hope: Madurai. When Alberto Laerzio hoped to breathe new life into the mission and 'open again the forests of that heathenism', he turned to Basto. He was visited with visions of the apostles St Peter and St Paul 'planting a green shoot in a field', which grew 'until it reached the size of a tree', with 'two branches, one towards the east, and the other towards the west'. The western branch, however, was foreshortened, while the eastern one remained fresh and bore fruit. The sign, taken to indicate the propitiousness of the Madurai mission, was conveyed to its missionaries.[67]

Basto's vision seemed to contradict the reality of a mission, languishing in the shadow of the burgeoning Nāyaka state, which had begun inauspiciously enough: from 1595 to 1606, the Jesuit Gonçalo Fernandes effected not a single conversion, tending instead to the Parava who had emigrated there from the Fishery Coast or who visited Madurai for trade. When Laerzio sent Roberto Nobili to Madurai, he found that Fernandes and his converts existed outside caste society, as members of the unclean *parangi kulam*, the caste of foreigners. Recognizing this barrier to conversion, Nobili experimented with new modes of self-presentation based first upon his noble lineage and eventually on the model of a brahmin ascetic (see Figure 6.3). Much like Stephens, Nobili adopted wholesale a brahminical view of caste society, and adapted his missionary strategy to it. He acquiesced to brahminical custom not only in his person, but also by making important concessions to his high-caste neophytes, allowing them

[66] Queyros devotes a large part of his biography of Basto to this episode, including transcriptions of original letters of complaint sent by the fathers to Rome as well as responses from Goa and Lisbon confirming their rights. See Queyros, *História da vida*, 60–120. For an anti-Jesuit view of the Fishery Coast missions, see 'Historia della costa de Pescaria, 1633', ASPF, Scritture Originali Riferite nelle Congregazioni Generali (SG), 40 (Orientali Relazioni), 506–16ff.

[67] Queyros, *História da vida*, 55.

Figure 6.3 Baltasar da Costa's Sketch of Roberto Nobili as a *Sannyāsi*
Source: Academia das Ciências de Lisboa, Portugal (Costa, *Catecismo em que se explicao todas as verdades Catholicas necessarias pera a salvacao com excellentissima ordem*, 1661, Academia das Ciencias, Vermelha, 698).

to maintain separation from lower-caste converts, retain the *pūnūl* (sacred thread), the *kuḍumi* (tuft of hair), and the practices of ablutions and wearing sandal paste.[68] Nobili would confess to Fernandes in secret at night, a practice later extended by the missionaries to lower caste converts so as not to jeopardize their standing among the higher castes.

Nobili's innovations deeply offended Gonçalo Fernandes. After the Italian Alberto Laerzio's departure and the succession of the Portuguese Pero Fernandes as provincial, Gonçalo Fernandes found the climate favourable to voice again his profound disagreement with the new method. He perceived Nobili's strategy as a dangerous descent

[68] Paolo Aranha has shown just how radical some of the accommodations effected by Nobili were, particularly in death rituals. Aranha, 'Missionary Constructions of Hinduism'.

into paganism and an affront to the Portuguese, who were closely identified with the parangi identity from which Nobili had worked so hard to distance himself. A debate ensued, within and beyond the Jesuit order, involving the highest echelons of church authority. Nearly two decades later, as Ines Županov's pioneering study has shown, Nobili's erudite arguments and political sophistication carried the day in 1623.[69] Still, even with all these concessions, the number of brahmin converts in 1622 was only twenty-nine.[70]

The issue of caste, despite Nobili's innovations, continued to blight the mission. In 1638, amidst a series of uplifting narratives of indigenous conversions, Manuel Martins included a case of a man of the merchant caste, 'honored among castes', who joined the low-caste Parava mission. As Martins explained, he would now be 'reputed to be of low caste, with whom the honored gentiles do not deal in political customs, because they cannot distinguish between political and religious customs'. (The gloss was necessary, given Nobili's insistence that the customs associated with brahminism were not religious in nature, but indicated social and political status—a reading contradicted by the loss of caste entailed in conversion here.) Martins explained that he had converted in order to marry a Christian fisherwoman, but was then 'despised by his relatives, among them an older sister'.

Many years later, when the marriage foundered, the merchant went inland 'to the land of the gentiles', in search of his sister. While there, 'he hid the insignia of the Christians ... [and] lived thus for some months'. Serendipitously, the merchant found that his sister in the meanwhile had heard the Christian law, as 'distinct from caste' and from 'political customs', and had been convinced of its truth. After seeing various sacred images and a crucifix, she declared to the priest that she already recognized the cross: it was frequently found outside the gates of churches and she had spent her childhood close to a Parava village. She revealed that she had not understood it as a sign of sacred mysteries, but merely as something that the lower castes adored. She may not have been entirely wrong: from the sixteenth century, trading networks facilitated the spread of

[69] Županov, *Disputed Mission*.

[70] Nobili had more success with other members of the upper castes, but brahmin converts proved rare.

independent shrines, and cults of Xavier and St James (Yāgappaṉ) had spread into the interior. Apart from the sign of the cross or occasionally an image of the Virgin Mary, these shrines and their associated worship did not resemble the cult of European saints.[71] Thus, the cross may not have been unequivocally associated with the new faith in the Tamil country.

When she received baptism and Martins gave her crucifixes of wood, she balked, asking for one of glass. Martins explained that since the Paravas commonly wore crucifixes of wood on their chests, great 'disgust' had affected her 'imagination' of these 'insignias of the low people'. Even though she revered the cross, she dared not accept one, unless it was made of a different material. Still, Martins claimed, both brother and sister lived, 'with no fear of disgrace', as Christians in their 'interior and exterior'.[72]

Martins's narrative bristled with tensions. By his own admission, the original impetus of the merchant's conversion and willingness to join the low-caste Parava was the desire to marry a Parava girl. In explaining the consequences of this conversion, though he adhered to Nobili's definition of caste as a social or political custom independent of religion, Martins was forced to concede that the members of caste society themselves were unaware of this distinction. His description of the sister's conversion revealed the popular perception of Christianity and the powerful disgust at its association with the lower castes that pervaded even the imagination of (high-caste) converts. Yet, he insisted that these converts were Christians inside and out. The internal contradictions and limitations of Nobili's position on caste and its consequences for the mission were apparent. Martins reported that in that year, 50 people of honoured castes in Tiruchirappalli and 70 in Madurai had joined 500 low-caste converts in accepting Christianity. Even after twenty years, Nobili's *sannyāsi* model was not reaping a rich harvest amongst the higher castes; the mission's demographic base remained lower caste.[73]

A further impetus to change came when, in Tiruchirappalli, a pious convert of the blacksmith caste convinced a Paraiyan *paṇṭāram*,

[71] Bayly, *Saints, Goddesses and Kings*, 379–419.

[72] Manuel Martins, Madurai, 20 October 1638, ARSI Goa 53, 112v–113v.

[73] Manuel Martins, Madurai, 20 October 1638, ARSI Goa 53, 112v–113v.

a non-brahmin Śaiva penitent, of the Christian truth. The untouchable penitent approached Antonio Vico for baptism and instruction.[74] Vico took the risk and converted the paṇṭāram, exhorting him in turn to convert his many followers. Some 300 Paraiyan converts then built their own church. Vico and Martins visited it stealthily, fearing the consequences should their high-caste converts learn of it. (Again, Basto proved decisive in encouraging Martins to baptize the Paraiyan.) When the high-caste converts realized the Jesuits were baptizing the Paraiyans in secret, they destroyed the Paraiyan church and arrested the paṇṭāram and chief catechumens. It was clear the Jesuit sannyāsis could not mix with the Paraiyan converts. Catechumens, acting as priests, tended the roughly 200 converts, until the Provincial Manuel de Azevedo sent someone to take charge of them.

It was in this reinvention of the mission that Baltasar da Costa would play a crucial role. Born in 1610 in Aldeia Nova, Costa entered the Society on 20 June 1627, in Lisbon. After studying Latin and philosophy in Coimbra, he sailed for Goa on 13 April 1635, on the same boat that carried the future martyr Marcello Mastrilli, as well as Basto's future biographer, Fernão de Queyros. Costa completed his studies and joined the mission to the Paravas on the Fishery Coast, entangled at the time in a jurisdictional tussle with the lay clergy.[75]

Costa received his call to the Madurai mission and on 4 July 1640, and in the garb of a paṇṭāram with bored ears, he left for Karur. His superiors believed that there, four days' journey outside Madurai, he would be able to cultivate the Paraiyans without offending the 'nobility' of the Madurai mission.[76] Even now, in his new garb, he continued to follow the precepts of Nobili, tending to the Paraiyan only under cover of night. He was, however, much impressed with their devotion and their unity, 'as if they were the children of the same father'.

[74] On the origins of the paṇṭāram mission, see the third section of Baltasar da Costa, 'Relação Annua da Missão de Maduré desde Outubro de 644 até o de 646 para Padre Francisco Barreto Procurador Geral a Roma pela Provincia do Sul', Madurai, 14 October 1646, Jesuit Madurai Mission Archives, Shembaganur, Tamil Nadu, India [hereinafter JMMA], No. 432.

[75] Manoel de Azevedo to Mutio Vitelleschi, Coulam, 1 January 1639, ARSI Goa 18, 155–6v.

[76] Baltasar da Costa, Madurai, August 1640, JMMA, 420.

Costa's trials started early—after receiving permission from the local Nāyaka revenue official to build a church, the brahmins and paṇṭārams of the local temples warned the *maniyakkārar* (local dominant non-brahmin caste) that they would leave if the church was built, since it was Costa's intention to destroy their gods.[77] Eventually, Costa received a plot on the other side of river to erect a church that the Christians could attend without drawing attention to themselves. The Paraiyans could hear mass without entering the main church, which had a special enclosure for them. The rudimentary church quickly attracted seventy new converts, when Costa's activities were interrupted by a fresh crisis.

Rumours were circulating of a coming persecution of the Christians in Tiruchirappalli and it took little provocation to turn rumour into reality. Sebastião Maya described the immediate cause of the persecution from prison.[78] A wealthy and powerful Paraiyan sought a Christian neophyte's daughter for marriage and was refused, since he had not converted. Enraged, he enlisted 'a great number of Pandaras, malignant people' and, bearing great gifts, they approached Vacantarayapillai. This was 'a man of low condition by blood' who had risen to great influence in the court, since his sister had been taken from a temple by the Nāyaka himself as his courtesan. The repression began in Tiruchirappalli, the seat of the Nāyaka court, and on Sunday 22 July 1640 soldiers burst into the church. They seized the brahmin who was helping at mass, imprisoning him upon royal orders for preaching, despite 'being a brahmin', a 'new law' to the Paraiyans. Father Martins offered himself as the most culpable and was summarily imprisoned and then exiled. The brahmin convert and thirty others remained in prison. Martins travelled towards Senji, but sent a neophyte to warn Baltasar da Costa in Karur and Maya and Nobili in Madurai. The warning arrived too late: by the time he reached Madurai, Maya and Nobili had already been imprisoned.

[77] On Nāyaka efforts to widen the religious bases of their support by spreading their donative activities outside the ambit of Hindu religious institutions, see Rao, Shulman, and Subrahmanyam, *Symbols of Substance*, 89–90.

[78] Sebastião de Maya to Provincial Manoel de Azevedo, 'Relação da persiguição da christandade de Maduré e prisão dos padres daquella missão', Madurai, 8 August 1640, ARSI Goa 53, 123–6ff.

Maya's report revealed a basic problem in the Madurai mission's adoption of accommodatio based on brahminical norms of purity: while such an ideology was operational in the region, the Nāyaka polities began to elaborate a radically different ideology of kingship and hierarchy in the region. As Rao, Shulman, and Subrahmanyam have shown, this ideology centred on their proud identity as śudra kings 'with strong links to trade ... [and] a marked heroic and martial orientation, in contrast with other trading groups'.[79] The Nāyakas did away with 'the formal identification of kingship with the ideology of dharmic norms, as well as ... the still vital distinction between the worlds of temple and palace'.[80] Here, the brahmin was unequivocally the servant of the king so that 'the Dumontian portrayal of a hierarchical order of ever more encompassing forms culminating in the brahmin (with an encompassed, even 'secularized' Kshatriya ruler beneath him) simply cannot describe Nāyaka society or the political order it produced.'[81] The Nāyaka court's 'stable dramatis personae' consisted of three elements: 'first, the self-made, individualized hero who wins himself a throne, in the complete absence of any proper royal pedigree; second, the merchant-lord who underwrites this assumption of power; third, the courtesans who confer—as only they are able to—symbolic recognition of the achieved status'.[82] These peculiarly Nāyaka scripts of power can be seen in Maya's description of the rich Paraiyan affronted by the refusal of a girl who would confer upon him the symbolic status due to him; of Vacantarayapillai and his origins and rise to power; and of the treatment of the brahmin seized in the church. This Nāyaka form of power not only exceeded and competed with the brahminical ideology of purity; it revealed the vulnerability of a missionary strategy that relied purely on this latter system in their lands.

Nobili eventually managed to send word to Costa, instructing him to go to Madurai to tend to the Christians there, but in his black cassock since a foreign priest was preferable to a low-caste paṇṭāram.[83]

[79] Rao, Shulman, and Subrahmanyam, *Symbols of Substance*, 73–4

[80] Rao, Shulman, and Subrahmanyam, *Symbols of Substance*, 67.

[81] Rao, Shulman, and Subrahmanyam, *Symbols of Substance*, 79.

[82] Rao, Shulman, and Subrahmanyam, *Symbols of Substance*, 20.

[83] Baltasar da Costa, Madurai, August 1640, JMMA, 420.

This episode marked the beginning of the play of identities necessary to navigate the Nāyaka context that would define Costa's career.

Ethnography, *Accommodatio*, and *Imitatio* in Costa's *Paṇṭāram* Mission

Though Costa's reverence for Nobili was beyond doubt, given his ethnographic understanding of Madurai, he was highly sceptical of the sannyāsi missionary model. In a letter Costa penned in 1646, he displayed a remarkable understanding of the nature of the Nāyaka kingdom.[84] In his description of Tirumala Nāyaka's kingdom, he demonstrated the extent to which Nāyaka political culture centred on wealth and conspicuous consumption. He described the courtesans, the sumptuous processions, and the king's ritualized public appearances. He also noted the nature of the nominal overlordship of Vijayanagara, which continued to be an important means of legitimation for the kingdom, although Costa misrecognized this relationship and characterized the Nāyaka's actions as disloyal. He also noted the financial burden on agriculture caused by this political system, describing the rapacious modes of taxation and the poverty of the people, and recounted common jokes about the acquisitiveness of the Nāyaka king.

In the same letter, Costa analysed the castes of the land. He described the traditional four-part division: brahmins, the first caste that sprang forth from the breast of Brahma; the komatis or cettis of the third caste, who emerged from his thighs, and the śudras, emerging from his feet. In this division, Costa noted, no mention is made of the low castes (that is, the untouchables), who constituted the majority of the Christians. He championed these castes as the best, employing Christian metaphors of the greatness of the humble. Discarding the traditional schema, Costa offered a tripartite division of high, middle, and low castes, corresponding to brahmins; kings and merchant castes such as komatis, and śudras; and the Paraiyans.

Costa's description of the brahmins was savagely critical. He noted their divine pretentions, their dress and physical insignia, their separation from other castes, and other constrictions related to purity.

[84] Baltasar da Costa, 'Relação Annua'.

Costa found them highly superstitious and also interested solely in their own bellies, a trope reminiscent of Xavier's description of the brahmins. Costa also implied that their practices of marriage, particularly the giving of a bride price, left women as virtual slaves. He acknowledged their intelligence and excellent memory, their facility for mathematics and accuracy in predicting eclipses, their study of philosophy, medicine, music, and dancing, and their system of disputation, which he judged to be different from that in Europe. He also described their ascetics, the sannyāsis.

Costa then moved on to his second group, in which the kings occupied the first place. He noted the heroic ideal they embodied, observing that they were born soldiers who died bravely. Next, he dealt with the trading castes, followed by brief descriptions of marriage customs, kinship relations, and certain peculiarities of a subset of the Veḷḷāḷa caste.[85] It was a very astute understanding of the nature of Nāyaka kingship, which combined the warrior-like qualities of the kingly castes, without denying their śudra origins, and in which wealth, earned through trade and commerce, was a means to political power. He thus correctly classified the kings alongside these left-hand castes, the political elites of Nāyaka society.

Costa was most sympathetic to the Paraiyans, who, as he explicitly noted, in many ways mirrored the brahmins. The Paraiyan yogīs, for example, were blessed with prodigious memories but whereas the brahmins specialized in superstition, they learned the moral sayings of a saint whom Costa suspected was contemporaneous with, if not a disciple of, St Thomas the apostle. The saint was Tiruvaḷḷuvar, the author of the *Tirukkuṟaḷ*, one of the most important texts in the Tamil canon, dating between the Caṅkam age and the beginnings of bhakti in Tamil Nadu (ca. 450–550 AD).[86] The Paraiyan claimed the author was the issue of a brahmin and a Paraiyan woman, since the vaḷḷuvan is a Paraiyan caste of royal drummers who served as ritual practitioners for the Paraiyans. By the late sixteenth century, the Portuguese were aware of his standing in the Tamil religious landscape and had

[85] Costa's report has a similar sensitivity to the minutia of local custom displayed in Gonçalo Fernandes's treatise of 1616. See Fernandes, *Tratado do Padre Gonçalo*.

[86] Zvelebil, *The Smile of Murugan*, 155–71.

begun to cast him as a disciple of St Thomas.[87] Costa, continuing this tradition, spoke highly of the ethical principles of the poet, who he claimed had declared that God should become man and suffer.[88] The high standing of this poet among the Paraiyan contributed to Costa's belief that they were naturally pious and amenable to the Christian faith.

By contrast, Costa's biggest complaint about the brahmins was that despite their intelligence, they remained implacably obstinate, with two in three brahmin converts apostasizing. It was this obduracy that destroyed Nobili's project, which rested on the faulty assumption that the conversion of the kingdom rested upon converting brahmins, since they were so revered.

Still, Costa was adamant that this was no reason to abandon the underlying *method* Nobili had elaborated. First, since brahmins could not accept religion from those of an inferior caste, the method kept the door open for them. The mere fact that there were brahmin Christians justified the preservation of the sannyāsi mission as other castes could reassuredly follow in their footsteps.[89] Unlike Gonçalo Fernandes, Costa agreed with the crucial distinction Nobili had drawn between caste and faith. He supported the effort to debunk the idea that conversion would entail the loss of caste, an error that Nobili had attributed to linguistically incompetent early missionaries, who had asked the indigenous to become Christians and enter the caste of the Portuguese.

The most important reason, however, for defending Nobili's mission was because of the example it set of missionary endeavour: 'Just consider,' Costa wrote, 'the great honor and credit that follows our company ... [for] doing such extreme things, that, not content with depriving [missionaries] for all their life of their own country, but also the customs with which they grew up, exchanging them for others as

[87] Subrahmanyam, *Penumbral Visions* 37–8; Blackburn, 'Corruption and Redemption'.

[88] This may have been an interpretation of *Tirukkuṟal*, 318: 'Whose soul has felt the bitter smart of wrong, how can/He wrongs inflict on ever-living soul of man?'

[89] Martins makes a similar argument for the value of the sannyāsi model even as brahmin converts declined. See Manuel Martins, Satyamangalam, 31 October 1651, ARSI, Goa 53, 219–22ff.

barbarous as they are difficult, acting with brahmins, as brahmins, with Pâreas, as Pâreas.'[90] Costa's words here are an ironic echo of Nobili's own, on the special aptitude of Italian missionaries for radical accommodatio in comparison to the Portuguese: Italian missionaries, Nobili averred, could cast off their national customs with ease, becoming 'all to all', which the Portuguese could not do without great difficulty.[91] Costa, in his person and praxis, belied Nobili's judgement of the capacity for accommodatio of Portuguese missionaries.

This difficulty was no reason to abandon Nobili's method: 'Nor should those be heard who say that such a mode cannot be conserved due to its difficulty, for they do an evident injury to the spirit of the Company, for its sons, [even] with news of the slow fires of Japan, still do not step back from that mission.'[92] In his reference to Japan, Costa may well have been thinking of the martyrdom of Mastrilli, his erstwhile companion on the long voyage to the Indies. It was not an idle comparison: he reported that Basto had once seen a vision of 'rivers of the blood of martyrs running' while praying for Madurai. He had told Costa to 'be greatly consoled that in Madurai there is another Japan'.[93] The Madurai mission, as Costa impressed upon his confreres in Portugal, was comparable in worthiness to Japan.[94] He exhorted his brothers in Portugal to devote themselves to it, not by downplaying its hardships but by emphasizing them. In this light, Nobili's method was invaluable not because of its limited success in converting brahmins but because of its value as an exemplum of the devoted life of a missionary. To use Costa's own metaphor, Nobili's method was picked out against the dark background of his relative failure among the brahmins, like stars that shine brighter against the obscurity of the night.

Costa's critique of Nobili's ethnography and his simultaneous defence of his method rested on a subtle distinction between the principles of accommodatio and imitatio, another concept with deep

90 Baltasar da Costa, 'Relação Annua'.

91 Roberto Nobili, Madurai, 21 October 1610, ARSI, Goa 51, 165f.

92 Baltasar da Costa, 'Relação Annua'.

93 Baltasar da Costa, 'Relação Annua', 14.

94 Although Costa would not witness the fulfilment of this prophecy, he was instrumental in recruiting João de Brito to the Madurai mission, in which he was later martyred.

theological and rhetorical roots. 'Imitatio christi' was not only the orienting principle for the Christian life, but the foundation of a praxis centred on exemplary lives, most obviously but not exclusively evident in the cult of saints. As Augustine revealed in his *Confessions*, itself intended as an exemplary conversion narrative, imitation, though not a substitute for divine grace, is an instrument of it. This was one reason why, in Augustine's account, pagans who lacked the 'pattern of divine humility' were unable to return to God.[95]

Costa's defence of Nobili's method thus rested on its exemplary value in the tradition of Christian imitatio to other missionaries, more than for its success as accommodatio to Madurai society. This idea is most explicitly expressed in Costa's epitaph to Nobili.[96] Nobili, the sun that rose in the West to set in the East, illuminated many others, most notably the missionaries who followed him to Madurai, the 'stars' who would illumine the firmament of Madurai, 'borrowing the light' of that original sun, 'as mirrors reflecting the Sun's rays produce as many Suns as there are mirrors'. In exhorting his confreres to come to Madurai, Costa explained that through his method, Nobili lived on: 'Madura has as many Nobilis as there are laborers.' Thus, Costa was claiming that though he dressed in the garb of a paṇṭāram he was actually mimicking Nobili, not in a simple sense of reproducing his likeness, but rather in a procedural sense, like a mirror borrowing the light of a sun to become another sun.

Nobili's *method* was thus of indisputable value for Christian imitatio; the sannyāsi model, however, was flawed as a template for accommodatio in Madurai since it was based on a faulty ethnography of Madurai society that gave inordinate importance to brahmins. Costa's ethnographic schema, which gave prime importance to the new Nāyaka elites, instead suggested a different object for Jesuit mimetic practice in Madurai, one aimed precisely at accommodating these elites rather than intractable brahmins.

Costa was not suggesting that accommodatio and imitatio were opposed, in and of themselves. The dovetailing of these concepts in

[95] Herdt, *Putting on Virtue*, 66–71.

[96] The epitaph is included at the end of Costa' translation of Nobili's Tamil catechism. See Baltasar da Costa, *Catecismo em que se explicão todas as verdades Catholicas necessárias pera a salvação com excellentissima ordem*, 1661, AC, Vermelha, 698.

the idea of providing a pattern of Christian virtue, accommodated stylistically to a particular audience, nourished much early modern thought, not least Jesuit pedagogical theatre.[97] Nonetheless, if this period witnessed a flowering in the religious and rhetorical theory and practice of imitatio, it saw a concomitant preoccupation with hypocrisy and dissimulation, one manifestation of which was precisely anti-theatricality.[98]

For a Jesuit to style himself as paṇṭāram was thus a fraught affair, since it placed him uncomfortably close to the morally ambiguous figure of the actor, not to mention the object of his mimesis, a pagan priest. This discomfort is obvious in Costa's description of the paṇṭārams, the model for his mimetic practice. Their 'incredible' activities Costa compared to the character Don Pablos de Buscón from Francisco de Quevedo's picaresque novel, a swindler who failed in his two goals of learning virtue and becoming a gentleman. The allusion suggested not only the upstart social ambition of these religious penitents, who served members of the second category of castes of Nāyaka elites in Costa's schema; it was also a pointed comment on their inability to orient themselves to spiritual, rather than social, values. The critique was coupled with an attempt to distance himself from those who served as his model in Madurai: Costa claimed he had adopted the dress of the most respectable among them, enclosing a sketch for reference, since the others wore attire that was either comical or went nearly naked in demonic fashion.

In this report and others, the paṇṭārams are Costa's antagonists *as well as* his distorted mirror image.[99] Both struggled for the hearts of

[97] Baltasar da Costa, *Catecismo em que se explicão todas as verdades Catholicas necessárias pera a salvação com excellentissima ordem*, 1661, AC, Vermelha, 128–70. The rhetorical idea of style, which allowed that excellence could be achieved by a variety of incomparable means provided a general framework to bring together accommodatio and imitatio in Jesuit pedagogical theatre, particularly outside Europe in such works as José de Anchieta's Tupí plays (Ginzburg, *Wooden Eyes*, 110–12).

[98] The classic works on these subjects, which have since generated much scholarship, are: Zagorin, *Ways of Lying*; Barish, *The Anti-theatrical Prejudice*.

[99] The term is taken from René Girard's discussion of the violence towards the rival born of mimetic desire. See Girard, *Violence and the Sacred*, 152–8, 174–8.

the lower castes. Yet, Costa's critique of the sannyāsi mission's focus on brahmins and his sympathy for lower castes suggested that along with markers of paṇṭāram identity upon his body, he had adopted the social viewpoint of the paṇṭāram. This was based not on brahminical ritual purity, but on Nāyaka notions of power and hierarchy that had led to the dramatic rise of the very castes the paṇṭārams served.

Costa's seemingly paradoxical relationship to the paṇṭāram is best considered in light of the rich variety of mimetic practices entailed by imitatio in humanist thought, which allowed both the obscuring of a model, whether through a digestive or dissimulative process, as well its explicit acknowledgement through *aemulatio*, whether as tribute or as competitive critique.[100] Thus, Costa's mimetic practice could be strictly dissimulative, for the purposes of camouflage while travelling through bandit country.[101] It could also be eristic, invoking the model precisely to highlight difference from it.

One can discern this in Costa's skilful negotiations of the Nāyaka courts. Given that Nāyaka kings claimed equal dominion over both temple and court, dissolving their traditional separation, Costa often insisted on staging his religious disputations with the paṇṭārams before the Nāyaka rulers and not in temples.[102] One such royal audience occurred before the Nāyaka in Sathyamangalam. Costa was seeking the Nāyaka's intervention against some laws promulgated under the aegis of the local paṇṭārams. These laws would force all inhabitants to contribute to the sacrifice during a feast, undoing the conversions Costa and his catechists had effected in the region. Costa reported his exchange with the king:

> [The Nāyaka asked] 'this law that you preach, is it one of the four of these parts?' 'The good merchant' I replied, 'if he wants to make good fortune, when he goes to foreign kingdoms, does not carry to it the merchandise which they have in abundance and just so the merchant of salvation of

[100] Pigman, 'Versions of Imitation'.

[101] Baltasar da Costa, 'Relazione del successo nella Missione de Maduré delli 8 di Iuglio 1643 insino a 29 d'outobre de 1644', JMMA, 430, 24.

[102] Županov has compared Nobili's career to a Telegu chieftain. Regardless of the aptness of that particular characterization, it should be clear here that Costa was not attempting to become a 'chieftain' himself (*Disputed Mission*, 182).

souls does not do well to bring in this kingdom laws which are taught in it. The law which I preach is as different from yours, as the truth from falsehood.'[103]

Costa's paṇṭāram identity and behaviour was a means to make palatable without denying the novelty he was bringing into the Tamil country, a newness that was both coin and danger in this religious marketplace. In the same way that he brought foreign gifts like organs and prisms for Nāyaka kings, he brought a new law to their courts.

The mercantile metaphor was singularly apt for the Nāyaka audience, whose courtly literature celebrated wealth and commerce in new ways. Costa's comparison of himself to a merchant was befitting both as a paṇṭāram, priest to the merchant castes, and as a Jesuit missionary. The use of commerce, discursively and literally, for the missionary enterprise was sanctioned by the example of Xavier himself, who relied on a private trader to carry him from India to new vistas.[104] The comparison also allowed Costa to invoke the benevolent view that local people could take of European merchants.[105]

As the multivalence of this metaphor suggests, Costa's mimetic self-fashioning drew upon the familiar figures of the paṇṭāram and the European merchants in the Tamil country, as much as his Jesuit predecessors. Moreover, his mimetic practice affirmed difference as vociferously as it claimed likeness, drawing attention to or obscuring the various European and Tamil models on which his persona was based. As a Christian missionary to the non-brahmin castes of Madurai, the success of his enterprise depended on seeming like a paṇṭāram but differentiating himself from the Hindu priests who bore that name. In the lands of the Nāyaka kings, who so valued commerce and wealth and wondrous new things, Costa wished to appear as a foreign merchant who brought spiritual not material wares. To maintain the legitimacy of his missionary practice and of the Madurai

[103] Costa, 'Relazione'.

[104] Županov, *Missionary Tropics*, 50–65.

[105] This view was expressed by the contemporary Tamil poet Venkatadhvarin thus: '[The Hunas] would not unjustly extort the property of others and [they] never speak false; they invent wondrous articles and inflict punishment on convicts by the law: observe this virtue of the mischievous Hunas' (Veṅkaṭādhvarin, *Viswagunadarsana*, 78).

mission in the larger Jesuit order, Costa both embraced his role as a committed disciple of Nobili, while subtly setting himself apart from his mentor.

The Limits of *Accommadatio*

Costa's paṇṭāram mission witnessed a rapid increase in the number of converts, and shortly after his death, it replaced the sannyāsi model entirely.[106] On the surface, this alone seems a testament to the success of Costa's mimetic model. Yet, the extent to which this 'success' was a result of Costa's own agency is doubtful. As Costa himself acknowledged, without the energy and activity of indigenous converts, the mission would have foundered. In 1646, there were only two sannyāsi fathers, Nobili and Martins, who interacted solely with the highest castes, and two paṇṭāram Jesuits—Costa himself and Manuel Alvarez. With so few missionaries, they relied heavily on indigenous catechists, some of whom Costa described in detail.

First among them was the catechist Savery Rayan, or Peter Xavier, whose zeal for conversion Costa considered a credit to his eponymous patron saint. Peter Xavier proved particularly useful because of his knowledge of 'all the sects of this land', so that even scholars feared debating him. He had come to Christianity through a curious act of will and reason: discontented with the tenets of various indigenous creeds and learning that the Portuguese worshipped 'one god', he had set out towards São Tomé and serendipitously met Christians in Tiruchirappalli. After his catechism and baptism, abandoning his military career, he dedicated himself to conversion and lived a life of commendable austerity. Constantine, the second catechist, had been a yogī before his conversion. He faced ostracism from his relatives with equanimity and his former life again proved useful in providing ammunition against disputants. Costa mentioned in particular his training in music, which allowed him to gather crowds wherever they went, thus providing alms for their travels and drawing in potential

[106] Županov, *Disputed Mission*, 235. The sannyāsi mission ended in 1673. Even the paṇṭāram model was not sustainable in the long run due to the lack of missionaries and the willingness of converted clans to turn to other ritual practitioners.

converts. The next, Glorioso, the man secretly inducted by Vico at the behest of the convert from the blacksmith caste, was a Paraiyan, the first of his caste to become a Christian. Glorioso had brought several hundred of his disciples into the fold, who in turn continued to provide alms for his sustenance.[107]

As these brief biographies reveal, conversion in the Madurai mission was often directed largely by indigenous people. Costa's report of the conversions in Sathyamangalam is instructive, not least because, as he joyfully reported, the conversion of the 200 high-caste Veḷḷāḷa catechumens occurred through the proselytization of a lowly Paraiyan. Much like the blacksmith convert who had taken the Paraiyan yogī to Vico, the Paraiyan convert came with a deputation of the Veḷḷāḷa leaders to request instruction and baptism. Costa went to Madurai to consult with Nobili before undertaking the journey, but sent Peter Xavier along with them. By the time Costa arrived, the catechumens were ready for baptism. The entire process occurred without a single action taken by the European Jesuits themselves.[108]

Through conversion, indigenous catechists found new avenues for religious and political leadership in Madurai, regardless of caste. Moreover, these catechists were significantly more effective in evangelizing to their brethren than the Jesuits themselves. While Costa's successful adoption of Nāyaka symbolic expressions of power allowed his followers to claim a legitimate form of authorization for their activities in Nāyaka society, the artifice of mimicry was never quite erased.[109] Thus, Jesuit paṇṭārams remained in a precarious position in Nāyaka society: one need consider only the periodic persecutions, culminating in the later martyrdom of Jõao de Brito, to see the limited efficacy of Jesuit accommodatio as Nāyaka political praxis.

[107] Costa mentioned three others in addition: Xavier of the Veḷḷāḷa caste, a friend of Peter Xavier, a fact which had played a role in his interest in the new religion and eventual conversion; Yesupattan, a high-caste convert; and Yesuvadien, one of the first converts of Tiruchirappalli.

[108] Costa, 'Relazione'.

[109] On the way in which mimicry, in taking on 'the insignia of authority', can lay bare the symbolic expression of power in a subversive way, see Bhabha, *The Location of Culture*, 172. Note that his discussion is explicitly intended for the case of mimicry in a colonial context, which Costa was not strictly operating within.

To some extent, this careful difference maintained by Costa was incumbent upon him as a Catholic missionary. In imitating gentile penitents, he could not abandon the ontological ground upon which his faith and vocation was founded. Moreover, he had to differentiate himself from his 'pagan' mirrors and foils in the eyes of potential converts.[110] Still, the efficacy of the indigenous catechists did raise the question of why they could not be made full clergy or even Jesuits in their own right, making moot the need for mimesis as a missionary strategy: Unlike Xavier, who never rid himself of his suspicions of the *kanakkappiḷḷai*, Costa was effusive in his praise of the indigenous catechists.[111] It would appear that the alterity maintained through mimesis of Tamil religious figures by Jesuits was less threatening than the erasure of difference implied by the full acceptance of Tamil converts into the Society.

The paradox of maintaining radical accommodatio with a strict policy against recruiting indigenous Jesuits was made sharper by the shifting attitude of Rome. In much the same way that the Dutch continued to erode Portuguese temporal authority, the papacy was increasingly infringing upon its religious jurisdiction, ceded in the Padroado. The beginnings of this encroachment could be traced to the bull *Apostolicae sedis* of 1608, in which the Jesuit monopoly of Japan secured under the Padroado was revoked, in part because of the inability of the Portuguese to defend their rights under the Philippine union.[112] This process quickened with the establishment of the Congregation of the Propaganda Fide, a product of Rome's ambitions after the Council of Trent to reconcile the schismatics, heretics, and gentiles to itself. It reflected an increasing papal desire for autonomy, regardless of the jurisdictional claims of the Catholic monarchies, in pursuing its goals.[113]

[110] On the dialectical relationship between alterity and mimesis, see Taussig, *Mimesis and Alterity*, 129.

[111] See, for example, Costa, 'Annua da missam de Madurê', 9 September 1653, JMMA 446, 5f.

[112] Boxer, *The Christian Century in Japan*, 239–41; Paiva, 'A Igreja e o poder', 135–85.

[113] On the transformation of the papacy in this period in a manner resembling an early modern monarchy, see Prodi, *Il Sovrano Pontifice*.

The basic orientation of the Propaganda Fide's attitude towards India had its origins in a series of letters written on 8 June 1630, sent by the collector in Lisbon. He provided a clear assessment of the state of Christendom in the Portuguese empire to the Congregation. His first point was an insistence on the superiority of Italian missionaries for India, due to their talents and temperament. He then asserted that it was not enough for European missionaries to speak the native language: in his opinion, the church would remain always a 'child without force if its doors were not opened to the natives', who were better equipped to convert their brethren because of their 'natural affection and heredity' than Europeans.[114] Moreover, given the political uncertainty, a native clergy would ensure stability: speaking particularly of Ceylon, although the collector's point was valid for much of Malabar, he noted that because of the political turbulence and uncertainty in the seas, there was the constant 'risk of losing everything in a moment'.[115] In India, brahmins, as 'noble' people of ability, were capable of becoming an indigenous clergy. The collector reflected the European adoption of brahminical views of caste society: the fifth provincial Council of Goa of 1606, for example, prohibited conferring sacred orders to members of the lower castes, and specified that only brahmins or other castes of 'noble' reputation should be admitted as ministers of the church.

The collector's views were an echo of a long-forgotten dream: Xavier, upon first arriving in Goa, had expressed a similar sentiment in his enthusiastic hopes for the new College of Goa, which had originally intended to train students of different languages, countries, and races to spread Christianity in their lands. Xavier's optimism regarding an indigenous clergy disappeared during his apprenticeship in southern India. Despite Ignatius's objections, he ushered in what became a lasting policy of not recruiting indigenous peoples into the Society. The collector was well aware that such prejudices had hampered the project to create an indigenous clergy, as the 'men of the kingdom' had a 'very low concept of the Indians' and their capacities for such

[114] Letter of the collector dated 8 June 1630, ASPF, SG, 98 (Lettere Spagna, Portogallo Indie Svizzera Colonia 1630), 85f.

[115] Letter of the collector dated 8 June 1630, ASPF, SG, 98 (Lettere Spagna, Portogallo Indie Svizzera Colonia 1630), 77–8f.

office. The collector pointed out that the teachings of St Thomas had been preserved in the hearts of Indians for all these centuries. Moreover, brahmins and other nobles were of great eminence in both letters and virtue, practicing chastity and abstinence from food over and above that known from ancient philosophers. Despite this, not only were they barred from the clergy, but were even treated poorly after baptism.[116]

The claim was somewhat exaggerated: though converts were barred from the religious orders, indigenous catechists and lay clergy had been crucial to the church in India. In Goa especially, the number and influence of the indigenous clergy in the seventeenth century can be gauged from the fact that they eventually instituted their own religious order, the remarkable Congregação do Oratório de Goa, which pursued its own missionary project.[117] The collector's admiring references to Italian missionaries and the virtues of brahmins was suggestive of his sympathy for the notorious Madurai mission of Roberto Nobili. Nonetheless, he was clear that this was a lesser strategy than instituting an indigenous clergy. He insisted that the European missionary's knowledge of local language and custom was insufficient for successful evangelization; ultimately, those best suited to convert a particular society were their own brethren, due to their 'natural affection and heredity.'

The collector's views carried Rome: the Congregation was clearly worried about the Portuguese state limiting access of non-Portuguese missionaries to its lands.[118] The resentment at the influence of non-Portuguese missionaries in the Estado was genuine and a matter of long-standing political concern.[119] Not long before the collector wrote,

[116] Letter of the collector dated 8 June 1630, ASPF, SG, 98 (Lettere Spagna, Portogallo Indie Svizzera Colonia 1630), 85f.

[117] Županov, 'Goan Brahmans in the Land of Promise'; Tavares, *Jesuítas e Inquisidores em Goa*, 234–42. For a general discussion of the issue of native clergy, see Mercês de Melo S.J., *The Recruitment and Formation of the Native Clergy of India*.

[118] See 'Considerationi intorno alli punti contenuti nelle lettere del Colletor de Portogallo sotto la data delli 8 de Giugno 1630', ASPF, SG, 98 (Lettere Spagna, Portogallo Indie Svizzera Colonia 1630), 96f.

[119] See, for example, the appended prohibitions of unlicensed missionaries from Rome or any other part of Europe coming to India dating from 1627

for example, the Crown advised the General of the Society of Jesus to appoint only Portuguese superiors, because this most suited 'governance, quietude and the cultivation of souls' in that state.[120] In this light, Rome enthusiastically adopted the collector's recommendations for creating an indigenous clergy, a policy which led to the controversial appointment of the Goan brahmin Mateus de Castro as vicar apostolic of Bijāpur in 1637.[121] Although he spent much of his career fighting for the recognition due to him as a consecrated bishop from ecclesiastical and Portuguese state officials, it was an important turning point in the history of the church in India. Indigenous Christians found a new avenue of support, particularly in struggles against the Jesuits: the indigenous archdeacon of the St Thomas Christians, for example, skilfully leveraged Rome's increasing resentment of the Jesuit monopoly of the Malabar missions in his struggles against the archbishop.[122]

Rome's intervention in India cast doubts upon the assumptions underlying Nobili's method: what need was there for Europeans to

---

to 1631 in Doc. 30, 29 January 1666, AHU, India 49. The Congregation was much more successfully kept out of Brazil, since access to the New World still depended on the favour of the Iberian monarchies. See, for example, ASPF, Fondo Scritture Riferite nei Congressi, America Meridionale, vol. 1 (1649–1713), 52–3f, in which foreign missionaries seek advice regarding the requirement that missionaries swear fidelity to the king of Portugal before embarking for Brazil.

[120] Letter of king to Conde de Linhares, Lisbon, 31 January 1629, ARSI, Goa 18, 125f. The order was a keenly felt blow to the Italian members of the company. See Letter of Gaspar Fernandes to Vitelleschi, Cochin, 2 December 1630, ARSI Goa 18, 124v.

[121] On Mateus de Castro and his position between the padraodo and the papacy, see Sorge, *Matteo de Castro*.

[122] The archdeacon reported in 1629 'that for 40 years now that [we] are governed by the Jesuits, they have not made the fruit of martyrs, as in Japan, even less have they converted the idolaters, because these fathers do not wish any other Religious to come into these parts'. This portion of the text was highlighted in the manuscript preserved in the archives of the Propaganda Fide. Furthermore, the collector's reports of 8 June 1630 had been immediately preceded by a sympathetic report of the Archdeacon's claims to the Congregation. See ASPF, SG, 98 (Lettere Spagna, Portogallo Indie Svizzera Colonia 1630), 81f.

contort themselves, to forego their own culture, if converts could ably spread the gospel themselves? The changing views of the papacy underlined the fundamental inconsistency and paternalism in Jesuit attitudes towards indigenous peoples. If Jesuit missionaries were willing to undergo the rigours of accommodatio (at least for those cultures deemed worthy), they were unwilling to consider indigenous converts equal partners in the business of evangelism.

In the Courts of Kings

The ambitions of the Propaganda Fide in India grew in lockstep with Dutch designs on the Estado. The brief hope of respite from Dutch aggression occasioned by the decade-long armistice signed in June 1641 was quickly dashed. The Dutch continued to strengthen their position in Ceylon and by 1652 they were again attacking Portuguese forts there. The viceroyalty could hardly provide adequate support, not least because Bijāpur marched against Goa in 1654. Colombo fell on 12 May 1656. Less than a year later, the Dutch admiral Rijklof van Goens made the fallen fortress the base for an alarming attack on the Coromandel coast, with a blockaded Goa unable to provide support. The trail of destruction continued till Malabar, before orders arrived in Kannur from Batavia to halt further operations. In 1660, Batavia sent another fleet to Malabar and continued the blockade of Goa, preventing the passage of reinforcements to Ceylon or word to Europe. With the aid of the Samūtiri of Kozhikode, by early 1663, the Dutch captured both Kodungallur and Kochi, the two key Portuguese fortresses on the Malabar coast. With their loss and the concomitant destruction of the Jesuit colleges, the Society lost much of the institutional infrastructure of the province.

Spurred by the fact that southern India was slipping quickly out of Catholic temporal jurisdiction, the papacy began to step up its efforts. By 1658, the year when Ceylon was definitively lost to the Dutch, it launched its own missionary efforts, with the establishment of the Societé des Missions Etrangéres in Paris.[123] The reaction from the

[123] The principles set out by the Congregation for the new missionary society were astoundingly similar to those first detailed by and in response to the collector's letters of 1630 (Bernard, *Les instructions de la S.C. 'de Propaganda'*).

Estado da Índia was expectedly hostile, not least because of the influx of foreign missionaries to the region.[124] These missionaries were viewed, not entirely without reason, as little more than the advance guard of foreign imperial ambitions, who would stir local sentiment against the Portuguese.[125] The impoverished Estado da Índia could barely acquit the demands of the Padroado.[126] The traditional Jesuit strategy of asserting loyalty to the Estado da Índia and the Padroado to garner Portuguese support in their various disputes, particularly against the episcopacy, was increasingly ineffective.[127]

In Madurai, Costa felt these winds of change. After the fall of Kochi, the financial strain on the mission became even more acute.[128] Costa's concern, however, was not solely directed to the Madurai mission. Portuguese attrition in both temporal and spiritual domains had begun to awaken in him the calls of his own 'natural affection and heredity', which he had so proudly set aside in conforming himself to the demands of Nobili's method. Though imitatio was intimately connected to personal transformation in Christian thought, Costa's

[124] See, for example, the viceroy's concerns that the new bishop of the Serra, a French Carmelite, would bring in more foreign missionaries (Doc. 23, 12 September 1661, AHU India 44).

[125] See, for example, the complaints about the French bishop of the Serra and also against Mateus de Castro for stirring indigenous subjects of the Estado da Índia, the Mughals, and the Dutch against the Portuguese (Doc. 57, 12 January, 1662, AHU India 44). The fact that the French Crown did attempt to set up a company under the aegis of the Societé des Missions Etrangéres, to the disapprobation of the Catholic monarchies and Rome, did not inspire confidence in the purity of purpose of the new enterprise.

[126] On the inability to support the Padroado financially, see, for example, Doc. 116, 29 August, 1662, AHU, India, 45.

[127] See, for example, Doc. 123, '*Petição do Collegio de Cochim*', ANTT, Cartório Jesuítico, 90; Doc. 26, 16 September 1661, AHU India, 44. For a chronology of the fractious relationship between the Jesuits and papal representatives in the east, see Doc. 19, 19, Breve ragguaglio di ciò, che è accaduto nelle Indie Orientali fra i Vicari Apostolici, et i Missionari d.a Comp.a di Gièsù dall anno 1662 fino al 1684," BNI, Fondo gesuitico, 1255.

[128] See, for example, Doc. 66, 'Palmar de Bety para a missão de Maduré', ANTT, Cartório Jesuítico, 90; Doc. 34, 'Copia de hum papel que a Provincia de Cochin mandou ao nosso Reverendo Padre Geral Vincencio Carrafa o anno de 648', BNI, Fondo gesuitico, 1384.

mimetic practice did not result in a complete 'casting-off' of his Portuguese heritage. Despite Costa's determination to disprove Nobili's doubts regarding the mimetic ability of the Portuguese to become 'all to all', Costa never overcame his particular concern for Portugal and its empire. While he was undoubtedly committed to his missionary vocation, unlike the agents of the Propaganda Fide, he was also concerned for the Portuguese empire for its own sake and not solely as an expedient for universal conversion. Yet, much like Vieira, Costa's concern for the preservation of the Portuguese empire was inseparable from his vocation as a missionary and his particular commitment to his local mission of Madurai.

This unity of purpose can be glimpsed in Costa's prefatory notes to his translation of Nobili's short catechism from Tamil into Portuguese, composed in 1661.[129] To the reader, Costa addressed a vigorous defence of Nobili's method, arguing that he had not hidden the Passion from his converts in Madurai, but that instead the catechism allowed a gradual but solid process of spiritual learning for the converts.[130] Using a series of mercantile metaphors, he explained the purpose of translating a work meant exclusively for gentiles speaking a specific language in a remote mission. Knowing the difficulty that missionaries had in learning the language, such that many were struck mute like 'merchants who leave the shore to search for necessities each day with too large a coin', Costa explained that in the east the language barrier loomed like the Tower of Babel as the single greatest hurdle to evangelizing. Further, to trust in *topazes* or interpreters, who were essentially 'mercenaries', was unwise. The work would thus allow missionaries to be 'merchants who not only had the large coin of wisdom, but also the little one of words with which they could communicate'.[131] The exhortation was reminiscent of his performance as a foreign merchant of spiritual wares at the Sathyamangalam court. The transactional metaphor continued in his

[129] Costa, *Catecismo*. The fact that the work can be found in the old Franciscan library in Lisbon indicates that its reception extended beyond the Jesuit order, and beyond the viceroyalty of Goa.

[130] Costa, *Catecismo*, 3–6. The charge of hiding the Passion was a common one levelled at Jesuit missionaries in the east, particularly in Japan.

[131] Costa, *Catecismo*, 6v–7v.

final exhortation embedded in Nobili's epitaph, appended at the end of the translation: describing how Nobili had drawn gold from the viscera of this infertile land, Costa exhorted the 'traders' 'who conduct the Society's transaction' to buy the 'Madurean field in which such treasure is hidden', to repay with interest the debts owed to the Lord.

His note attested to his ardent commitment to the Tamil language and to the Madurai mission.[132] The work, however, as a translation into Portuguese, also brought Madurai into conversation with Portugal, which could claim no dominion over it. The text was thus not merely for the benefit of fellow missionaries who may find themselves in the Tamil country. As Costa put it, to dedicate his translation of Nobili's Tamil catechism to the Portuguese king 'was no free action but due obligation'. It was a reflection of the original obligation placed by Christ upon D. Alfonso Henriques, 'primogenitor of twelve lords of Portugal' when he appeared to him 'in that mysterious vision ... on the field of Ourique'. Christ chose D. Alfonso Henriques as king of Portugal but also 'as defender and preacher of His holy Law, by means of his vassals ... when He told him these memorable words, which extend to his descendants: *I chose them for my reapers in distant lands*'. Costa reminded the present king of Portugal that he had inherited both 'the scepter and the good distribution of the divine law, which is contained in the book I offer your Majesty'.[133]

Beginning with the divine acclamation of the founder-king Afonso Henriques, Costa constructed a continuous tradition of Portuguese kingship—sidestepping neatly both the Philipine interruption and the transition from the House of Avis to that of Braganza. If the Portuguese king was bound to spread the faith 'by means of his vassals', Costa, as a vassal, was bound to the king in turn to help him fulfil his obligation to Christ. The writing, translation, and dedication of a Tamil catechism thus served as the enactment, but also the reminder, of a series of mutually constitutive obligations, subtended

132 Among his works was a grammar of the Tamil language (Costa, 'Arte Tamulica', CL, MS M34).

133 Costa, *Catecismo*, 1–3. The dedication is dated Madurai, 12 February 1661. The battle of Ourique, where Afonso Henrique defeated a Muslim army following this vision, was a touchstone of Lusitanian millenarian thought, particularly in this period.

by the original obligation of the Portuguese king to Christ. By casting himself as both missionary and vassal, Costa presented his work as an act of feudal and divine obligation. In turn, he reminded the king of his twin obligations to defend his vassals and spread the divine law in distant lands. In doing so, Costa effected a subtle slippage in his own location from Madurai, the realm of gentile kings, to the Estado da Índia, the dominion of the Portuguese king. In this slippage lay perhaps more than a wistful desire that Madurai should be brought into the Portuguese as well as the Catholic fold.

This desire may be read in Costa's notion that to fulfil his obligations, God had given to the Portuguese king two armies with two sorts of weapons: the first of well-tempered and fine metal, the second of prayers, sacrifices, and the most strong sword of the word of God, which St Paul judged to be the stronger of the two. These weapons were united and joined, like two blades on the same divine sword. Costa reminded the king that in the Estado da Índia, the Dutch were operating 'the mystery of evil'. To face this enemy, the king did not lack valorous soldiers and captains; nor did he lack zealous preachers and apostolic missionaries, especially in the complex ecclesiastical field of Malabar. What was lacking, however, was the unity of the two blades of this sword; this alone prevented victory. Some ministers said that the money spent from the royal incomes on the evangelical ministers was misused; some captains claimed that while they shed their blood and had no barracks, the preachers ate in safety. These voices, Costa warned, were raised in their own interest and not that of the common good.

Both the soldiers, who wielded the material weapons, and the preachers, who wielded spiritual ones, lacked favour, not through any fault of the king but due to bad ministers, more concerned with self-interest than pursuing the goals that God had given the king. It was an echo of Vieira's diagnosis of Brazil's colonial condition. In offering his work of translation to the king, Costa claimed he had completed an act of justice, giving the king his due: in notifying the king of the cause of his many losses, Costa was fulfilling his obligations as a loyal vassal. In doing so, Costa asserted his own right to be recognized as a vassal of the king, even if he were in distant lands, even if he laboured not as a state official or a soldier in the king's army, but as a missionary in the realm of gentile kings. Through the act of translation, Costa transported and submitted himself to another royal court, this time in Lisbon, in which he claimed his position as a vassal and not as a foreign missionary. His supplication may even have borne fruit: Costa's name was one among the three possible candidates from the Jesuit order that the king was considering for the bishopric of Kodungallur in 1663.[134]

* * *

In these movements, back and forth between the Tamil country and Portugal, mediated by shifting roles and languages, Costa resembled Vieira's movements between Brazil and Portugal, between his commitments as a missionary of the Society of Jesus in Madurai and his obligations as a Portuguese subject. Costa adopted many masks in the course of his missionary career—the black cassock of the Society; the bored ears and robes of the paṇṭāram; the loyal disciple of Nobili, who sought like a mirror reflecting sunlight to disseminate his master's method not only in Madurai, but in Goa and Lisbon; the foreign merchant of spiritual wares in the Nāyaka courts; and the loyal vassal of the Portuguese king. Yet, underlying this diversity of roles was an attempt to find a unity of purpose, to intertwine, despite their contradictions, the demands of his particular location in Madurai; his commitment to the spread of the universal Church; and, last but not least, the call of his 'natural affection and heredity' as a vassal of the Portuguese empire. It was a struggle Vieira, shuttling between the backwaters of Maranhão and the glittering courts of Lisbon and Rome, knew well.

Unlike Vieira, Costa faced the added burden of bringing his missionary realm, ruled in fact by foreign gentile kings, under the conceptual umbrella of the Portuguese domain. His desire to defend Portuguese dominion in India was undiminished by a lifetime of mimetic practice in the Tamil country. Similarly, Vieira's sense of alienation in the forgotten colonies did not diminish his commitment to the empire. It is to the unripened fruit of their shared commitment to Portuguese temporal and spiritual dominion that we now turn.

134 Doc. 49, 'De episcopis quos Rex Lusitaniae vult constituere in Indiis ex Societate 1663', BNI, Fondo gesuitico, 1255.

7

THE EMPIRE OF APOSTLES

> I do not wish to believe in prophecy ... but I cannot deny what I have seen and will see.[1]

This chapter explores an imaginaire of empire, in an era when the Portuguese were militarily beset on all fronts and were unable to enforce the terms of the Padroado. This imaginaire was a response to the interruption and reinstatement of an independent Crown and to these conditions. It developed over the course of the seventeenth century among Portuguese Jesuits such as António Vieira, Baltasar da Costa, and others who laboured in the 'conquests', for whom the changing circumstances of the world had exposed the fissures and contradictions in their three primary commitments: the first, to a notion of the meaningfulness and specificity of their local missionary space; the second, to the universalist enterprise of Catholic evangelism; and the third, to the global ambitions of Portuguese temporal domain.

Portuguese notions of empire have not received as much scholarly attention as its Spanish counterpart, although recently this imbalance is beginning to be redressed. Antonio Vasconcelos Saldanha's erudite work, for example, considers the problem from the standpoint of legal history, exploring how the far eastern empire was conceived through treaties. Giuseppe Marcocci, on the other hand, uses an approach

[1] Vieira to Duarte Ribeiro de Macedo, Rome, 26 September 1670, *Obras Escolhidas* II, 23–4.

akin to Anthony Pagden's work on sixteenth-century Spanish debates on its New World empire, focusing heavily on debates about the Portuguese expansion in canon law and amidst theologians.[2] While these and other works fill a woefully neglected historiographical gap, this chapter is less concerned with providing a global overview of a notion of Portuguese empire than with exploring the specificities of one such imaginaire among several. Even in the sixteenth century, the extreme factionalism of the Portuguese court that spurred the first wave of expansion made it difficult for a coherent ideology of empire to emerge in Portugal.[3] Certainly in the seventeenth century, as the debates sketched later in the chapter demonstrate, it is difficult to find *a* single coherent notion of empire around which political action and state policy, let alone religious activity, coalesced. Perhaps the strongest unifying thread was a certain millenarianism that emerged as a response to the death of D. Sebastião and the Spanish captivity. Still, even Sebastianists and those inspired by the mystical poet Gonçalo Eanes Bandarra were not a uniform breed. As we shall see, Portugal's prophetic traditions and foundational myths were deployed to support precisely opposite notions of Portugal and its empire.

This chapter begins by considering the ways in which this imaginaire was articulated and disseminated, with all its recurring discursive patterns through visions and the genre of historical prophecy among Portuguese Jesuits. It will then explore how this imaginaire informed the failed attempt to institute a company to save the Estado da Índia, a project whose failure marked the end of this phase of imperial thinking.

Between History and Prophecy: Awaiting the Fifth Empire

> Midnight ... as I was preparing to go to Choir, I was led to see a celestial globe, and a rod of an incomprehensible majesty, which, with the greatest speed, was laying the [longitudinal lines], which the Arabs call *azimudes*. Then with all brevity, it laid the other lines that run from east to west, which we call parallels and the Arabs *almucantarath*. All these lines were of a golden color ... Then it delineated all the 48 constellations, the five zones and finally all the lines and figures that mathematicians consider.

2 Saldanha, *Iustum Imperium*; Marcocci, *L'Invenzione di un impero*.

3 On this issue, see Thomaz, *De Ceuta a Timor*.

> Completing this work, which to all showed in itself a beautiful pilgrimage, it said to me: This is to be understood spiritually.[4]

For Pedro de Basto, this particular call from God, who called for 'all the Globe to recognize for whom it is saved', added even greater urgency to his prayers for universal conversion. That very day Basto was granted still more visions during mass that revealed what exactly would constitute a truly global Christianity:

> In the first there appeared a very large coat of arms or shield, covered with innumerable people, dressed for a feast and most joyful, and it had the color of the sun. In the other mass, I saw a ball or globe of the world, covered in people dressed in red, who appeared most happy, and above, a royal crown of notable grandeur.[5]

The vision was repeated thrice, and each time Basto heard a voice, explaining God's will that 'his empire will join the three different peoples, of three crowns, and will unite them beneath one alone'. Basto's was a double vision, spiritual and temporal. On the one hand, the globe encircled and picked out in glowing lines, marked the beautiful 'pilgrimage' of the spread of Catholicism. On the other, the globe and its three principle peoples were united in God's empire under one Crown. To Basto's biographer, Fernão de Queyros, the identity of these three peoples was obvious: gentiles, Moors, and Jews. It was equally obvious that only Portugal's kings could lay legitimate claim to that one Crown that would unite them in God's empire.

This vision bore more than a little resemblance to that of the Fifth Empire elaborated by António Vieira in the 'História do Futuro' (History of the Future). This famous unfinished work was written during his incarceration of 1663–7, after *Esperanças de Portugal* came to the attention of the Inquisition.[6] Vieira lived, as he noted, in an age of empires: in Asia, the vast empire of China and of the Tartars, of Persia

[4] Queyros, *História da vida*, 417–18. He quotes here from Basto's spiritual autobiography.

[5] Queyros, *História da vida*, 417–18.

[6] Other similar works written in this period included the prolegomenon to the *História*, and two representations to the Inquisition in his own defence. On Vieira's millenarian writings, see Cohen, 'Millenarian Themes in the Writings of António Vieira'; Besselaar, *António Vieira*; Jordán, 'The Empire of the Future'.

and of the Mughals; in Africa, that of Ethiopia; in Europe, Germany, which had the name of empire if not its grandeur, and Spain, which had the grandeur but not the name.[7] Yet, these were but feeble facsimiles of those polities worthy of the designation of empire, of which there had been four since the creation of the world: the Assyrians or Babylonians; the Persians; the Greeks, which began and ended with Alexander; and the Romans, which had disintegrated into the ten kingdoms of Portugal, Castile, France, England, Sweden, Denmark, Muscovy, Poland, the empire of Turkey, and the Holy Roman Empire, comprising Italy and Germany.[8]

Analysing the prophecies of Daniel and the visions of Zachariah, Vieira argued that these four empires constituted one age of the world, each empire a part of a single statue of time, which was undone by Christ. There was to be, however, one last great empire—that of Christ himself. Based on Daniel's prophecy that the empire would grow and exact obeisance from kings, Vieira deduced that it would be mundane rather than other-worldly.[9]

As the empire of Christ, it was necessarily a spiritual empire. Vieira insisted, however, that it was also a temporal empire, although this did not imply that it would be subject to the same vicissitudes of time, nor focus on the external majesty and pomp of other worldly empires.[10] Christ united the divine and the human in his person, and thus, as man, universal dominion over all other kings pertained to him.[11] He was not merely the rightful king of the Jewish people amidst whom he was born; even amidst the gentiles, his coming had been foreshadowed by divine signs and prophecy. This explained why the three Oriental kings, from the three parts of the known world of that time, came to offer tribute to the newborn Christ. Simultaneously, the Sybilline oracles revealed that gentiles in the west too foresaw the coming of Christ with even greater clarity than the elliptical biblical prophets.[12]

[7] Vieira, 'História de Futuro', in *Obras Escolhidas* IX, 1.

[8] Vieira, 'História de Futuro', in *Obras Escolhidas* IX, 2–5, 14.

[9] Vieira, 'História de Futuro', in *Obras Escolhidas* IX, 39–43, 48–9, 51.

[10] Vieira, 'História de Futuro', in *Obras Escolhidas* IX, 54–7, 64.

[11] Vieira, 'História de Futuro', in *Obras Escolhidas* IX, 78.

[12] Vieira, 'História de Futuro', in *Obras Escolhidas* IX, 86, 137–8. Vieira noted that some blamed the obscurantism of the Jewish prophets for the blindness of the Jews in not recognizing in Christ their messiah.

Vieira insisted on the role the Jews had played in spreading news of the coming of the messiah. Jerusalem, the most cosmopolitan city of the ancient world and the seat of its greatest empire, had attracted men of all languages, colours, and nations.[13] Sacred history was replete with stories of embassies, confederations, wars, treaties of peace, of correspondence, and intercourse of all kinds between the Hebrew people and the gentile nations. Furthermore, Jews travelling on political business spread word of the messiah throughout the gentile world.[14] The most important vehicle, however, was the commercial instincts of the Jews, their 'natural greed ... and the genius, industry and particular inclination this nation always had for commerce and merchandise'. This inclination 'served divine Providence, leading them gently to the most remote lands and regions'. When the merchants left Judea, 'in the bales of merchandise that they carried, the Savior of the world placed his too'.[15]

Throughout this prophetic exegesis, Vieira brought subtly into view the past and present condition of the Portuguese empire. In keeping with the concerns of the age of companies, Vieira was acutely aware of the role of commerce in the business of religion, which Vieira imbued with a biblical pedigree. Vieira also drew on Portuguese imperial history and the precedent set by Francis Xavier to demonstrate that 'it is not a new thing in God ... to put faith on the back of interest':

> The first king of Portugal to title himself *King of commerce of Ethiopia, Arabia, Persia and India* was he who introduced the faith in India, in Persia, in Arabia and in Ethiopia ... St Thomas, who carried the Gospel from Brazil to India when there was no commerce, had to walk (as is tradition) on the waves, for he did not have someone to carry him; and the second Apostle of the Orient, wishing to preach in China, outlined that the preacher should enter as a merchant, so that Faith had a place as merchandise.[16]

In particular, Vieira reached an important conclusion about the role of the Jews in the biblical past, future, and present: the Jews were destined to carry the faith to the gentiles.[17] In this function, their commercial instinct, indeed their greed, had and would play a great part.

[13] Vieira, 'História de Futuro', in *Obras Escolhidas* IX, 92, 94.
[14] Vieira, 'História de Futuro', in *Obras Escolhidas* IX, 97–8.
[15] Vieira, 'História de Futuro', in *Obras Escolhidas* IX, 101–2.
[16] Vieira, 'História de Futuro', in *Obras Escolhidas* IX, 103.
[17] Vieira, 'História de Futuro', in *Obras Escolhidas* IX, 111–13.

From the plan of the rest of the incomplete work, we know Vieira intended to argue that the prophesied empire would be brought about by the universal conversion of all men, including gentiles and Jews, who would thus be united. Gentiles would convert first: the hallowed kingdom would begin with the end of the empire of the Turks and their conversion. The supreme pontiff and evangelical preachers, who would bring about universal conversion, would be supported by the authority, power, and arms of a temporal prince, who would be emperor and universal monarch of the world. This prince would thus serve as the vicar of Christ in the temporal realm, just as the Pope claimed that name in the spiritual domain. The temporal seat of this empire would be Portugal.[18]

Vieira, unlike Basto, did not claim outright the divine inspiration of prophecy in asserting authority for his vision of the fifth empire.[19] Still, his work shared a common function with prophecy—the uncovering of time:

> Time, like the World, has two hemispheres: one above and visible, which is the past, the other below and invisible, which is the future ... From this point [in the present] begins our history, by which we will discover the new regions and the new inhabitants of this second hemisphere of time, which are the antipodes of the past.[20]

Just as Costa had drawn upon the founding mythology of Afonso Henrique and the reigns of Manuel and João III in crafting his dedication of Nobili's catechism, Vieira invoked a grander time in Portugal's history. He too drew upon the age of discoveries, in which the Portuguese had set forth in search of the Indies, discovering

[18] Vieira, 'História de Futuro', in *Obras Escolhidas* IX, 161–70.

[19] Vieira remained equivocal about labelling his work prophecy, unsurprisingly perhaps, given the Inquisition's grim view. For example, to his great friend Rodrigo de Meneses, referring to his belief that the Marquis of Marialva would defeat the Turks and prepare the way for the fifth empire, Vieira wrote: 'The hopes, which I do not wish to call prophecies, will be arranged through his numbered footsteps.' See Vieira to Rodrigo de Meneses, Rome, 15 February 1670, *Obras Escolhidas* II, 15.

[20] Vieira, 'Livro Anteprimeiro da História do Futuro', in *História do Futuro*, vol. I, 31.

Brazil in the antipodes of the world. The reader of his *História do Futuro* would similarly undertake a voyage of discovery towards the horizon of time, in which the future of Portugal would be uncovered in the antipodes of the past. This uncovering would occur through Vieira's particular mode of prophetical exegesis, resulting not in the obscurities of prophecy but in the specificities of a history of the future. If Moses, who revealed the history of creation, was a prophet of the past, Vieira positioned himself as a historian of the future:

> The prophets did not call their prophecies history, for they did not conserve in them either the style or the laws of history. They did not distinguish the ages, did not signal the places. They did not individuate people, did not follow the order of cases and events, and all that they saw and all they said is enveloped in metaphors, wrapped in figures, obscured in enigmas, and told or sung in phrases proper to the prophetic spirit and style, more accommodating of the majesty and admiration of mysteries than of their news and intelligence.[21]

By contrast, Vieira's method was 'to observe religiously and punctiliously all the laws of history', so that the reader could 'perceive the order and succession of things'. Since Vieira would 'distinguish between ages and years, signal provinces and cities, name nations and even people', he could call his work a history of the future.[22] In other words, for Vieira, historical events pertain to qualitatively different ages and thus must be 'accompanied by their circumstances', that is, contextualized. Furthermore, Vieira contended that this historical method, its precision, could be applied to the future, forming the basis of his mode of prophetic exegesis.

The roots of this historical approach may be traced back to the remarkable work by the great Portuguese humanist Fernão de Oliveira, *História de Portugal*. Written in 1580, the year the Portuguese Crown lost its autonomy, it was an attempt to place Portuguese history within the matrix of biblical chronology, drawing heavily on the twin foundational myths of Afonso Henrique and of the patriarch

[21] Vieira, 'Livro Anteprimeiro da História do Futuro', in *História do Futuro*, vol. I, 31–2.

[22] Vieira, 'Livro Anteprimeiro da História do Futuro', in *História do Futuro*, vol. I, 31–2.

Tubal, who mediated the foundation of the kingdom in theological law during the post-diluvian repopulation of the earth.[23]

Vieira was part of an age that Amos Funkenstein has marked as a watershed in the development from its theological origins of historicism, both as methodology and as an interpretive orientation.[24] Vieira, for example, was a contemporary and acquaintance of Menasseh Ben Israel, who wrote *Esperança de Israel* (Hope of Israel)] in 1650, a result of his reading of the enormous body of materials on the natives of America, from José Acosta to Garcilaso de la Vega and Pedro Cieza y Leon. He averred that Amerindians were one of the lost tribes of Israel; their discovery was the first step in the recovery of the promised land and they would be the first to go to Israel. When his pamphlet was translated into English in 1652 as *The Hope of Israel*, it even precipitated Cromwell's readmission of the Jews to England.[25] Parallels with Vieira abound, from the echo of the title of Vieira's *Esperanças de Portugal*, to the privileged position of the indigenous peoples of the New World in both their schema. Vieira may even have hoped that his own *Esperanças de Portugal* and subsequent writings would facilitate the readmission of the New Christians, as his Jewish counterpart's work had done in England. More importantly, the two works share a methodological orientation of prophetical exegesis, which turns precisely on the principle of divine accommodation, that is, the notion that God allows that 'scripture speaks a human language'. For these thinkers, scripture must be interpreted contextually, with attention to both the time and place of its articulation, thus making allowance for the temporally bound and contingent nature of humanity.[26]

Vieira's contemporary and confrere, Fernão de Queyros, also displayed this marriage of historical method and the elucidation of the future in his exposition of Basto's visions. Queyros, born in 1617 in Canavezes, Portugal, and having joined the order in Coimbra

[23] The text, with an excellent critical introduction, is reproduced in Franco, *O Mito de Portugal*.

[24] Funkenstein, *Theology and the Scientific Imagination*.

[25] Wolf, *Menasseh Ben Israel's Mission*, which includes a reprint of *The Hope of Israel*; Schorsch, 'From Messianism to Realpolitik'; Cogley, 'Some Other Kinde of Being and Condition'.

[26] Funkenstein, *Theology and the Scientific Imagination*, 222–70.

in 1631, sailed to India in 1635 on the same boat as Baltasar da Costa. Like Costa, he met Basto when he landed in Cochin and was duly impressed by the visionary. Serving in India during the Dutch assaults in south India, Queyros felt the loss of Portuguese dominion as keenly as Vieira and Costa, a fact evident in both his history of Ceylon (which was essentially a means to make sense of its loss to the Dutch), as well as in his biography of Basto.[27]

In the introduction, Queyros described in detail the sources upon which he based his *History* of Basto's life—chiefly the spiritual autobiography of Basto and the dossier of affidavits of those who had known him personally and attested to the various visions Basto had communicated to them.[28] Queyros claimed that he had deposited all his sources in the archive of the province of Malabar in the Jesuit house in Goa so that the veracity of his work could be checked for all time. He was also fully aware that witnesses who were still alive could easily discredit his whole work, should he deviate from the documents. Further, he explained that although he had not begun the work with the intention of relating the political events of the east, it was not possible to demonstrate what God had revealed to Basto without giving notice of these events, hampered as he had been by the lack of documents. Unlike the writers of the lives of saints, who embellished their work with 'one or another erudition, from the Sacred or the profane', Queyros 'without reproving other opinions', followed whenever possible 'the rigor of history'. Still, Queyros included an exegesis of Daniel's prophecies in the work: unlike Vieira, he argued that it was the Romans, not the Greeks, who constituted the third, while the fourth empire was that of the Muslim Caliphs. Naturally, he agreed with Vieira that the fifth empire would be Portuguese.

[27] On Queyros's other writings, particularly his history of Ceylon, which has a similar orientation to historical method and prophecy, see Strathern, 'Re-reading Queiros'; Abeyasinghe, 'History as Polemics and Propaganda'. Queyros also maintained a strong interest in Ethiopia. For a brief summary of his life and writings see, Schurhammer, 'Unpublished Manuscripts of Fr. Fernão de Queiroz, S.J.'.

[28] Queyros, 'Aos que lerem', *História da vida*. Queyros was also careful to mention that he himself had met Basto only once, in 1635, the same year Costa came to India and right in the beginning of Queyros's career as a Jesuit and his time in India. The brief encounter left a lasting impression upon him.

Despite slight variations, the unity and coherence of the imaginaire of the Portuguese empire here is clear. Whether in the mode of history or prophecy, whether expressed in the metaphors, symbols, and images of visions or in the orderly, contextual language of history or exegesis, Basto, Vieira, Queyros, Costa and others struggled against the vagaries of time of Portugal's present misfortunes.

Moreover, this imperial imaginaire had many adherents other than these figures, both within and beyond the Jesuit order, in other locations than those considered here. Paulo da Trindade, the outstanding figure of the Franciscan mission in India, is an obvious case in point. His magnum opus, *Conquista Espiritual do Oriente* (The Spiritual Conquest of the Orient), written in the 1630s, married history and prophesy in much the same way as Vieira and Fernão Queyros; indeed, Queyros relied heavily on Trindade's work in writing his history of Ceylon, another work concerned with the idea of the Portuguese fifth empire. The strictly literalist Sebastianist Frei Sebastião de Paiva is another worthy point of comparison; despite his metropolitan career, Paiva cited the biography of Anchieta penned by Rodrigues as well as Camões's epic in constructing his theory of the fifth empire. The use of such evocatively 'colonial' figures is in itself revealing of the scope of his vision.[29]

These thinkers struggled to defend a shared vision of a globe: one that was encircled spiritually and temporally, by Catholicism and by the Portuguese empire. Moreover, unlike the present condition of the Portuguese, so buffeted by the storms of Europe's imperial rivalries, the fifth empire would be immune to time's vagaries. It would be brought about by universal conversion, including of the infidels and the gentiles, in which missionaries would play a crucial role: an empire ruled not by apostles but that could only be wrought by apostolic labour.

Slaying Idolatry with the Sword of Judaism

For all the erudition and originality of the 'História do Futuro', many of its ideas were germinating in rather different form during Vieira's

[29] Trindade, *Conquista Espiritual do Oriente*; Paiva, *Tratado da Quinta Monarquia*.

service in the court of João IV. In 1643, Vieira penned a proposal to the king, in which he outlined the miserable state of the country and the need to entice Jewish merchants to restore its financial standing.[30] Vieira began by noting that 'all human things are subject to the inconstancy of the ages, and none more than monarchies, those principally which, having powerful and neighboring enemies ... have not yet put out firm roots'.[31] It was an awareness of the tyranny of time on the fortunes of Portugal that haunted all his works, especially the 'História do Futuro', in which a vision of a Portugal freed from 'the inconstancy of the ages' emerged clearly.

Vieira enumerated the dangers facing Portugal, both 'the forces interior to the kingdom', who were still loyal to Castile, as well as those 'external in the Conquests'. The latter included the Dutch, who were disinclined to honour the truce of 1641, and the French, flexing their imperial muscles.[32] Neither the kingdom nor the conquests were financially capable of averting these dangers. Diplomatically, too, Portugal was weak: even the Pope had not received the Portuguese ambassador and not a single foreign ambassador graced the Portuguese court.[33] These conditions did not inspire confidence amongst businessmen, 'whose judgment, founded upon their own interest, was always the most certain'.[34]

Yet, Portugal had one untapped resource in its new Christian community: 'Through all the kingdoms and provinces of Europe are spread a great number of Portuguese merchants, men of enormous capital, who carry in their hands the majority of the commerce and riches of the world.' There was some truth to this enduring trope—the majority of Lisbon's merchants at any given time in the seventeenth century were new Christians.[35] The new Christian and Jewish

[30] Vieira, 'Proposta feita a el-rei D. João IV', *Obras Escolhidas* IV, 1–26.

[31] Vieira, 'Proposta feita a el-rei D. João IV', *Obras Escolhidas* IV, 1.

[32] Vieira, 'Proposta feita a el-rei D. João IV', *Obras Escolhidas* IV, 2–8.

[33] Vieira, 'Proposta feita a el-rei D. João IV', *Obras Escolhidas* IV, 9.

[34] Vieira, 'Proposta feita a el-rei D. João IV', *Obras Escolhidas* IV.

[35] Smith, 'The Mercantile Class of Portugal and Brazil'. Their influence was not exclusive of course: not only did old Christian merchants have long-established ties to this community, they played a vital part in the Portuguese restoration and the Brazil commerce (Smith, 'Old Christian Merchants').

diaspora, particularly of Portuguese extraction, were crucial to the functioning of early modern trade—even when, for the sake of their Jewish faith, they were forced to reside in exile outside Portugal.[36] In this light, there emerged a group of thinkers who advocated greater liberties for the new Christian communities to stimulate Portuguese commerce.[37] Notable examples included the new Christian merchant Duarte Gomez Solis, who advocated that Portuguese Jews should be allowed to profess and practice their faith openly in Goa or Kochi.[38] Unlike Solis and other mercantilist thinkers of the era, however, for Vieira, commerce was a means to a religious end, not the goal in itself.

Still, Vieira's faith in the love of homeland among the new Christian community ran deep: 'All of them,' he argued, 'for the love they have for Portugal, as their country, and for His Majesty, as their natural king, are desirous of returning to the kingdom and serving His Majesty with their incomes, as they do for foreign kings.'[39] There was no canonical objection to welcoming back these merchants of Jewish extraction; the Pope himself not only allowed new Christians, but even Jews to live and worship in his realms.[40] The presence of foreign merchants from Protestant nations in Portugal highlighted how self-defeating the exclusion of Portuguese merchants of Jewish extraction was for a nation founded on commerce. When one considered the contagious nature of the Lutheran heresy compared to the non-evangelical nature of Judaism, the policy was more absurd still.[41] Was it not, Vieira asked, to the greater service of God to use the money of the new Christians to propagate the Catholic faith, instead of allowing it to support the armies of heretical powers?[42]

[36] Israel, *Diasporas within a Diaspora*; Trivellato, *The Familiarity of Strangers*; Studnicki-Gizbert, *A Nation upon the Ocean Sea*; Almeida Mendes, 'Les réseaux de la traite ibérique'.

[37] Hanson, *Economy and Society*, 113–18.

[38] Wachtel, 'The "Marrano" Mercantilist Theory of Duarte Gomes Solis'.

[39] Vieira, 'Proposta feita a el-rei D. João IV', *Obras Escolhidas* IV, 11.

[40] Vieira, 'Proposta feita a el-rei D. João IV', *Obras Escolhidas* IV, 15–19.

[41] Vieira, 'Proposta feita a el-rei D. João IV', *Obras Escolhidas* IV, 20–2. Vieira explicitly referred to the Protestant infection of Pernambuco.

[42] Vieira, 'Proposta feita a el-rei D. João IV', *Obras Escolhidas* IV, 22. Portuguese Jews had actually contributed less than a percent of the capital

Vieira thus urged João IV to fight, 'slaying idolatry with the sword of Judaism'. His confidence came both from biblical history and prophesy: just as God had conquered Israel with the treasures of Egypt, 'the sons of Jacob will come to the aid of the hidden king, and by means of this support, they will come to the knowledge of the truth of Christ'.[43] Here in germinal form was the notion elaborated at such length in the 'História do Futuro' that the gentiles would be converted through the aid of the Jews in preparation of a 'miraculous' empire. The mode of reasoning Vieira employed here to support his claim would reach fruition in the 'História do Futuro'; here too, the biblical past, interpreted correctly, laid bare the future.

Vieira also invoked royal precedent: D. Manuel admitted the new Christians to the realm, promising them that they would not be treated differently from the old Christians; D. João III honoured this commitment.[44] Furthermore, these two kings, under whom Portugal's empire reached its zenith, were the happiest of Portugal. Their reigns were the most prosperous, as much spiritually as temporally, as they spread the Faith and enriched the kingdom.[45] D. Sebastião, on the other hand, had revoked this promise of his ancestor; 'the events of Portugal in the time of his reign' and the following seventy years 'of tears' of the Spanish captivity were 'good testimonies' of the result.[46] Vieira stopped just shy of proclaiming that the presence of the new Christians was intimately tied to the fortunes of Portugal.

In Vieira's long-standing project of financing companies of the sort that had propelled the Dutch to such prosperity using new Christian

---

of the Dutch West India Company. See Israel, *The Dutch Republic and the Hispanic World*, 127.

[43] Vieira, 'Proposta feita a el-rei D. João IV', *Obras Escolhidas* IV, 22–4.

[44] On this original promise to the new Christians, see 'Privilegios, que o Senhor Rey D. Manoel concedeo aos Christãos Novos ... por cartas de 1 e 3 de Março de 1507', ANTT, Armário Jesuítico, 29, Doc. 1.

[45] On this original promise to the new Christians, see 'Privilegios, que o Senhor Rey D. Manoel concedeo aos Christãos Novos ... por cartas de 1 e 3 de Março de 1507', ANTT, Armário Jesuítico, 29, Doc. 1, 25.

[46] On this original promise to the new Christians, see 'Privilegios, que o Senhor Rey D. Manoel concedeo aos Christãos Novos ... por cartas de 1 e 3 de Março de 1507', ANTT, Armário Jesuítico, 29, Doc. 1, 25.

capital he saw one great obstacle: the Portuguese Inquisition, that 'fortress of Rossio'.[47] The Inquisition had considerably intensified its activities in the 1620s, with the majority of crimes related to Judaizing.[48] This reflected the increasing preoccupation with *limpeza de sangue*[49] from the sixteenth century onwards. It also reflected an emerging jurisdictional division of labour in which the episcopacy focused on the old Christians, while the Inquisition concerned itself with the new Christian community.[50]

As early as 1646, Vieira wrote a proposal on the need to change the rules or *estilos* of the Holy Office in Portugal. He focused in particular on the confiscation of goods of those accused by the Inquisition, a rule that strongly deterred the investment of new Christian capital in Portugal.[51] When the entire Brazil trade was under terminal threat by the Dutch, the moment for launching the Companhia Geral do Comércio do Brasil finally came. The Company charter of 10 March 1649 granted it monopoly rights over wine, cod, oil, and flour, the four most important goods sent from Portugal to Brazil, as well as the right to collect a tribute tax, the *avarias*. In return, the Company would supply an armed escort to Portuguese shipping. In addition, an ordinance of 6 February 1649, guaranteed that *all* stockholders of the Company, including new Christians and foreigners, were exempt from the confiscation of goods and capital. The latter ordinance drew the ire of the Inquisition, as expected. On the other hand, the

[47] Israël-Savator Révah's seminal article characterized the relationship of the Jesuits to the Inquisition as one of hostility based on the new Christian question: 'Les Jésuites Portugais contre l'Inquisition'. For a more nuanced, recent treatment, see Franco and Tavares, *Jesuitas e Inquisição.*

[48] Magalhaes, 'Em busca dos "tempos" da inquisição (1573–1615)'. For a recent historiographical survey, see Marcocci, 'Towards a History of the Portuguese Inquisition'.

[49] *Limpeza de sangue* denotes purity of blood, free from new Christian heritage.

[50] Carneiro, *Preconceito Racial em Portugal e Brasil Colônia*; Paiva, 'Inquisição e visitas pastorais'. For an opposite view to Paiva on the relative harmony between the episcopacy and the Inquisition, see Marcocci, *I custodi dell'ortodossia.*

[51] Vieira, 'Proposta que fez ao Serenissimo Rei D. João IV a favor da gente de nação', *Obras Escolhidas* IV, 27–62.

Crown compelled all new Christians to invest in the company in 1650, under threat of inquisitorial persecution. Despite this provision, the Inquisition continued to criticize the project, enlisting the aid of the three estates in doing so. There was precedent for the vociferous opposition of the Inquisition—it had reacted similarly to the founding of the first Company of India.[52]

Despite this opposition, the company was established as Vieira wished. The traditional historiography of the Companhia, since the pioneering work of J. Lucio de Azevedo and Charles Boxer, granted Vieira the interpretation he himself placed on the event—Vieira brokered the financing for the company, principally through his friend, the Bahian merchant Duarte de Silva, in the teeth of Inquisitorial opposition.[53] Over time, the focus on Vieira's role and the attribution of the company almost exclusively to new Christian interests has received a critical reappraisal: beginning with David Grant Smith's pioneering work, a new view is emerging of the role of both old and new Christians with links to interested foreign merchants who sought to preserve the Brazil trade.[54] Regardless, when the Company finally secured Pernambuco in 1654, capturing too part of the Dutch navy, Vieira's personal sense of vindication and accomplishment was intense, lasting till his death.[55] Moreover, it provided the impetus for his single-minded effort to create a company dedicated to the Estado da Índia, founded and maintained like the Brazil company through new Christian capital.

[52] See, for example, 'Representações do estado eclesiastico, da Nobreza e do Povo a S.M. sobre dever-se abolir a Companhia do Brazil, anno 1654', ANTT, Manuscritos da Livraria, microfilm 1337. On the Inquisition's reaction to the eastern company, see Disney, *Twilight of the Pepper Empire*, 90–3.

[53] Azevedo, *História de António Vieira*; Boxer, 'Padre António Vieira S.J.'

[54] See, for example, Freire Costa, *O Transporte no Atlântico*. Evaldo Cabral Mello has also revised his views, emphasizing the need to reconsider Vieira's role and focus on other actors in *O Negócio do Brasil*.

[55] Vieira to Conde de Ericeira, Bahia, 23 May 1688, *Obras Escolhidas* I, 53–75. Parrying the somewhat critical appraisal of his activities after the Restoration in the first part of the Conde's *História de Portugal Restaurado*, published in 1679, Vieira offered the foundation of the Brazil company as his greatest defence.

Yet, these plans were continually vulnerable to the waves of anti-Semitic prejudice that simmered just beneath the surface of Portuguese society. On 10 May 1670, the church of Odivelas, near Lisbon, was robbed of some sacred objects and its edifice was damaged. The news rippled through the country, stirring a wave of virulent anti-Semitism across cities in the Portugal kingdom, from Lisbon to Bahia. Amidst outpourings of Catholic piety, in masses and processions and public agitations, the blame was laid squarely at the door of the new Christians. (As it happened, the boy responsible, Antônio Ferreira, was of that community; his arrest and execution served only to fan the flames of anti-Semitism.) Within six weeks of the attack, the regent D. Pedro began to promulgate a series of laws against new Christians, culminating in the expulsion of all those who had abjured to serious transgressions since 1604, a not inconsiderable number.[56] Over the next eighteen months, the Holy Office and the Crown stripped new Christians of the right to mount horses, travel in litters or coaches, wear silk, gold or jewels or hold public office, and, for those accused of Judaism, hold royal contracts or honorific posts.

Vieira received word of these events in Rome. The events precipitating his departure to Rome were, as usual, highly contingent on the politics of the Portuguese court. After his condemnation by the Inquisition in 1667, which prohibited him from preaching, teaching, or writing, Vieira was briefly reinstated when D. Afonso VI was deposed on 1 January 1668 and D. Pedro, friend to the Jesuits, assumed effective power. The Inquisition's order was largely overturned but very soon after, Vieira again fell out of favour with the court. Vieira's bitterness at D. Pedro's change of heart was clear in the letter he wrote to Queen Catarina of England, complaining that 'the company of the commerce of Brazil, which restored Pernambuco and Angola and gave capital to the kingdom to defend itself, for being my invention and will has brought me to this fortune'.[57]

[56] See 'Decreto do Princepe D. Pedro ... A 25 de Agosto de 1671', ANTT, Armário Jesuítico, 29, Doc. 13.

[57] Vieira to D. Catarina of England, Rome, 21 December 1669, *Obras Escolhidas* II, 11. He also subtly evaded D. Pedro's attempts to bring him back into his control. See Vieira to D. Pedro, Rome, 7 September 1671, *Obras Escolhidas* II, 37.

He withdrew to Rome, ostensibly to campaign for the canonization of the forty Jesuits who were martyred by Calvinist corsairs off the coast of the Canaries in 1570, but in fact to press his own case in Rome against the Portuguese Inquisition. His talents brought him recognition in Rome, yet Vieira remained dissatisfied: once, after preaching his first sermon in Italian, he noted ruefully, 'I know the language of Maranhão, and Portuguese, and it is a great misfortune that, being able to serve with either of these my country and my prince, I have at this age to study a foreign tongue to serve, and without fruit, foreign tastes too.'[58]

Despite these personal preoccupations, Vieira followed Portugal's fortunes with mounting frustration, both at its continually weak and unimpressive position in the European theatre of power, and its blindness to the imminent danger of losing its eastern possessions to rival imperial powers:

> I do not have patience to read the gazettes of the world, and to see spoken in them of all the princes and kingdoms and only of ours a perpetual silence, as if Portugal were a corner of *terra incognita*. France battles England and Holland over India, and we, having peace and soldiers, abandoned that which cost so much [Portuguese] blood and devotion to the kings.[59]

The successful end of the War of Devolution left France free to pursue its imperial ambitions, though Portugal at least secured recognition of its independence from Spain under the terms of the final peace. Thus, when news of the fresh persecutions of the new Christians reached Vieira, he feared the consequences for Portuguese commerce and for the country's imperial possessions, which depended upon this wealth. While acknowledging the injured sensibilities of the old Christians, Vieira argued that the treatment of the new Christians, after Odivelas, was ultimately self-defeating. He listed five problems stemming from the new Christians: (*a*) 'the contagion of blood through mixing with the new Christians'; (*b*) continued Judaizing; (*c*) the infamy brought to Catholic Portugal through the *nação* (Portuguese Jewish diaspora);

[58] Vieira to Rodrigo de Meneses, Rome, 22 October 1672, *Obras Escolhidas* II, 92–3.

[59] Vieira to Rodrigo de Meneses, Rome, 23 February 1671, *Obras Escolhidas* II 28–9.

(*d*) 'the loss of the Conquests, with the extension of heresy and impediment to the propagation of the faith' caused by the community's investment in foreign powers; and (*e*) 'the diversion and extinction of commerce', as the new Christians carried their capital to safer harbours across Europe 'for fear of confiscation'.[60]

It was the latter two problems that most alarmed Vieira. Moreover, the Inquisition, Vieira argued, was unable to remedy any of these ills and other solutions were needed:

> Shit, says St Augustine, out of its place dirties the house, and put in its place fertilizes the field; and, applying this doctrine and analogy to our case, with the greatest of doctors I say, Sir, the Jews should be removed from where they dirty the house and placed where they fertilize the field. So acts the Pope, and the Roman Church ... Remove from Portugal the Jews, the sacrileges, the offences to God and keep in Portugal the merchants, the commerce, the opulence....[61]

In other words, Vieira advocated not for the return of crypto-Jews, but for good Christians of Jewish extraction. These new Christians, vulnerable to the caprices of the Inquisition, were unnecessarily barred from putting their commercial instincts and capital to the service of the empire and its religious mission.

In Rome, Vieira wrote wryly, he wished for a measure of the zeal of the Portugal, and in Portugal for a measure of the insight of Rome. The problem was the inordinate myopia of the Portuguese, who 'neither remembered the past, nor looked to the future, nor even disposed of the present'. Portugal remained woefully inattentive to the dangers of Castile, England, Holland, and France, and lacked not only capital, 'which was the fundament of power, of respect and of the preservation of monarchies', but also the means to raise it, as Genoans, French,

60 Vieira to Rodrigo de Meneses, Rome, 24 October 1671, *Obras Escolhidas* II, 40–2.

61 Vieira to Rodrigo de Meneses, Rome, 24 October 1671, *Obras Escolhidas* II, 40–2. Vieira told his friend that the contents of this letter were meant for his eyes only, wary no doubt of advertising such a contrary opinion in this time of heightened anti-Semitism. The unusually harsh language towards the new Christians may also have been a rhetorical compromise, rather than a true measure of his attitude, as Hernani Cidade and António Sérgio suggest.

English, and Dutch and all the other nations in India, not to mention those in Africa, robbed what little they had.[62]

Vieira claimed that popular opinion in Rome was one of disbelief at the short-sightedness of the Portuguese: 'Oh! If you heard laughing the most saintly and most learned men of the World at the implications of what we call the zeal for faith, losing thousands of leagues ... when we want to preserve inches!'[63] Vieira also found welcome support for his views in the Jesuit house in Rome from some newly arrived missionaries from the East, including Baltasar da Costa:

> Father Juzarte [the procurator of Japan], who loves His Majesty and has many particular obligations because of this, has arrived here, and another father [Costa], equally zealous and loving of the kingdom ... Both lamented that which I have cried for so long. They say that all the gentiles of India have a mortal hatred for the Dutch and sigh for us and say: 'Portuguese, why do you sleep, why do you not come to rescue us from this tyranny?'[64]

The conversations with these missionaries from the east were highly edifying, particularly with regard to what was necessary for the preservation of the eastern empire. Vieira passed on its gist to the Portuguese ambassador in Paris, Duarte Ribeiro de Macedo. Both Costa and the procurator from Japan, Pedro Zuzarte, 'very well-versed in all the conquests', agreed that 'it would be easy to restore what is lost, if Portugal had the money to pay the soldiers promptly'. Mercenaries, who had drifted to the service of the Dutch, would return to the Portuguese fold, and gentile kings were eager to aid the Portuguese. Without money, however, 'all other diligence is useless', and all those sent from Portugal to India 'will die for pure

[62] Vieira to Rodrigo de Meneses, Rome, 21 November 1671, *Obras Escolhidas* II, 48.

[63] Vieira to Rodrigo de Meneses, Rome, 21 November 1671, *Obras Escolhidas* II, 49.

[64] Vieira to Rodrigo de Meneses, Rome, 21 November 1671, *Obras Escolhidas* II. Though the clamouring for the Portuguese amidst the gentile nations was undoubtedly a fond fantasy, it was true that 'gentile nations', wary of the Dutch, did buttress the Portuguese as a counter-weight. See, for example, Golconda's attempts to foil Dutch ambition as described in Galletti et al., *The Dutch in Malabar*, 11.

abandonment'. Vieira, however, was pessimistic: 'I do not expect us to do one thing for profit.'[65]

From the innumerable references to the problem of paying soldiers in the letters from the viceroys of Goa to the Conselho de Ultramarino, Zuzarte and Costa's opinions clearly had some currency, even if it grossly over-simplified the problems facing the Estado. Still, the need for wealth to preserve the eastern empire was acute. From his conversation with the Genoese, who had long experience of India, Vieira learned that Portuguese commerce there was finished: Goa imported everything, and all of this trade was in the hands of foreigners. Ships left empty, as merchants were reluctant to travel there for fear that their capital would be lost for lack of spices in which to trade. Given the military needs of the Estado, this dire financial condition was especially worrying.[66]

Vieira was also aware of the increasing encroachment of the papacy upon the rights of the Padroado and wary of the French imperial designs that underlay the activities of the Propaganda Fide missionaries. He wrote, for example, that he had read a book translated from French in which the author declared that under the pretext of faith and evangelization, the French king wished to move into India.[67] On another occasion, Vieira expounded upon this plot at greater length:

> Today I read a manifesto of a French bishop, of those sent to India, that in Paris they had a seminary for the conversion of the East, raised through royal expenses, to continue the propagation of the Faith through an eastern company or companies of the same nation, and that the same seminary was erected with the apostolic authority of Alexandre VII and assisted all the mission with great favors and indulgences from the Congregation of the Propaganda, as if there were no Portugal in world, nor were our privileges valid.[68]

[65] Vieira to Duarte Ribeiro de Macedo, Rome, 5 January 1672, *Obras Escolhidas* II, 56–7.

[66] Vieira to Duarte Ribeiro de Macedo, Rome, 11 March 1672, *Obras Escolhidas* II, 66–9.

[67] Vieira to Duarte Ribeiro de Macedo, Rome, 22 November 1672, *Obras Escolhidas* II, 96–7.

[68] Vieira to Duarte Ribeiro de Macedo, Rome, 26 July 1672, *Obras Escolhidas* II, 78–9.

The spiritual attrition of the Portuguese empire was no less worrying than its temporal one.

Despite his misgivings, Vieira still held out hope for preserving the Estado da Índia, relying again on his understanding of the sacral destiny of Portugal and the prophecies that spoke of it. He spoke of his confidence to the ambassador: 'Of our provisions and instruments, I expect little, but I have great confidence in He who gave us Pernambuco and Angola, which by some miracle is still reserved for this state, for whose faith we have sacrificed so much blood [*sic*].' Vieira remembered that 'a saintly brother that we had in India, called Basto, whose prophecies are approved with continuing experiences, said that God showed him three cities with the arms of Portugal and mitres above'. Since Basto did not recognize the cities, Vieira reported, his superiors commanded him to draw them. From the images, they 'knew clearly that they were Ormuz, Malaca and Sacatrá'. Vieira said that if this prophecy came to pass, 'we will be encouraged to believe the other things that he also predicted, of the greatest expectation and glory of Portugal and the Church'.[69] Still, even with these intimations of divine favour in Basto's visions, a practical solution had to be sought. To Vieira, the answer was obvious: a Company of India, the counterpart to that which had saved Brazil.

The Company of India

On 14 July 1672, after arriving in Lisbon from Rome, Baltasar da Costa sent a memorial on the Dutch violation of the peace with Portugal.[70] He was in Lisbon in his capacity as procurator for the Malabar province. The brief memorandum was largely related to the persecution by the Dutch of the Jesuit missionaries in the Malabar province. He also reported the continuing intrigues of the Dutch with indigenous kings to dispossess both the Portuguese and the Jesuits: Costa mentioned the Nāyaka rulers repeatedly, reflecting his special preoccupation with the Madurai mission.

[69] Vieira to Duarte Ribeiro de Macedo, Rome, 12 January 1672, *Obras Escolhidas* II, 59.

[70] 'Do que os Olandeses tem feito na India ... por Baltasar da Costa', 14 July 1672, fl. 365, BA, 50-V-37.

The memorandum expressed Costa's commitment to both Portuguese rule and Catholic evangelism as well as his commitment to the local missions of the Malabar province. Still, it did not garner the notoriety of his letter of 7 September 1672 to the confessor of D. Pedro, the Jesuit Manuel Fernandes. The proposal contained some measures that had occurred to him for recuperating India, which he urged Fernandes to recommend to the prince.[71] India, Costa reminded Fernandes, was conquered through power in the sea; now, however, Portuguese possessions were lost wherever they touched the sea. The great need, therefore, was for naval power. Costa claimed that ships could be cheaply manufactured in India, which had wood and workers and expertise for this enterprise. Still, capital was necessary and with India exhausted, there was one other resource to fund this enterprise without emptying the royal treasury. This strategy contravened 'no law, neither divine nor human'. If the prince granted a general pardon to the 'people of the nation', an act with considerable precedence in Portugal, and ameliorated the rigours of the Holy Office, they would remain in Portugal without fear, as they do in Rome. They would then create a company for India, which would solve all of its problems. The company would secure the growth of commerce and the royal treasury, as well as allowing the prince to make war upon his enemies. To restrict the Holy Office in this way could not be wrong since it would conform to the very standards that the Pope himself, the vicar of Christ on earth and the head of the Church, had in his dealings with people of Jewish origin.

The hand may have been Costa's but the imprint of Vieira's thought, gleaned no doubt from their conversations in the Roman house, is clear throughout the letter. Just three days after the date of this letter, Vieira wrote to Rodrigo de Meneses from Rome: 'When our alliance with England and France over India is discussed, I lose patience, remembering how many times I spoke of the Oriental Company, with which we could have recovered our own very easily.'[72] A few days later, he wrote to Duarte Ribeiro de Macedo that he had

[71] 'Carta original do Jesuita Balthazar da Costa, para o Confessor do Princepe ... Em 7 de Setembro de 1672', ANTT, Armário Jesuítico, 29, Doc. 14.

[72] Vieira to Rodrigo de Meneses, Rome, 10 September 1672, 85–6.

received news of Costa's proposal for the Oriental company. He noted approvingly that this measure would circumvent the need to rely on uncertain allies, who were also imperial rivals. As he put it, 'I always desired a company and not companions.'[73] Naturally, given his lack of favour in Pedro's court and his long history of conflict with the Inquisition, Vieira could not have proposed such a solution himself. Costa and Fernandes, on the other hand, who between them could claim the authority of experience of the east and the ear of D. Pedro, were far better placed to make such a suggestion.

Costa's role in the matter ended when he died during a voyage back to India in 1673 with a new mission for Madurai that included the future martyr João de Brito. In Lisbon, however, his letter precipitated a remarkable controversy, which dragged on for nearly a decade.[74] The new Christians, aided by Manuel Fernandes and underwritten by a group of extremely wealthy merchants, chief among them Manuel da Gama de Padua, made good on the opening Costa had provided.[75] They presented a proposal to the prince regent seeking a general pardon, leave to take recourse to the Pope, and the right to be judged in conformity with the standards of the Roman Inquisition. They offered in exchange to bear the costs of creating a company for India and the one-time cost of sending and maintaining 5,000 men to India. In addition, beginning in 1674, they

[73] Vieira to Duarte Ribeiro de Macedo, Rome, 22 November 1672, *Obras Escolhidas* II, 96–7.

[74] Relevant documents are to be found in ANTT, Armário Jesuítico, maços 29–30. In his classic work on mercantilism in baroque Portugal, Carl Hanson treats this episode as demonstrative of the conflict between a landed aristocracy and a mercantile class, in which the former was allied with the Holy Office and the petty bourgeoisie. See Hanson, *Economy and Society*, 89–123. By contrast, José Eduardo Franco analyses it from the point of view of the long history of the relationship between the Jesuits and the Inquisition. See Franco, 'A Companhia de Jesus e a Inquisição'. My concern here is rather the competing imaginaires of Portugal, and the relative weight given to the colonies in these visions, that emerge in this debate.

[75] 'Conferencia original da letra do confessor Manoel Fernandes com os Christaos Novos ...', ANTT, Armário Jesuítico, 29, Doc. 16. 'Reflexões originaes da letra de Manoel da Gama de Padua ...', ANTT, Armário Jesuítico, 29, Doc. 17.

undertook to send 1,200 men each year to India, providing 20,000 *cruzados* for the maintenance of soldiers. They would also bear the costs of the voyage of all missionaries to India and the costs of the bishops of India, giving 20,000 *reais* to the ambassador or resident of Rome.[76]

In the final proposal, the influence of their Jesuit advisors and facilitators is apparent: the new Christians averred that their pledges were made for the increase of the faith and not as a bribe for a general pardon, a discursive move that was strengthened by the inclusion of their commitment to pay for the costs of the Padroado bishops as well as missionaries to the east. (The offer to pay the Portuguese resident in Rome echoes exactly Vieira's concern that the resident Gaspar de Abreu had not been paid in Rome.[77]) Moreover, the use of new Christian resources for the support of the conversion of the gentiles conformed precisely to Vieira's notion of the particular role of the Jews in bringing about the Fifth Empire.

The proposal was accepted, but the direct challenge to the Portuguese Inquisition did not go unanswered. In the first consultation on their part, dated April 1673, the Inquisition attacked the notion that Portugal's Holy Office should conform to Roman standards. If the Crown had reason and justice for denying all that the apostolic see desired, justifiably declining bishops imposed by Rome or resisting those sent by the Congregation of Propaganda Fide, then it was clear that not everything done in Rome could be justly practiced in Portugal. To conform to Rome's inquisitorial standards, as proposed by the new Christians, would be equivalent to ceding royal prerogative.[78] They urged the Crown not to make the kingdom, in which Christ himself told their first king that he wished to build his

[76] For the full development of this proposal, see 'Primeiro projecto que os Christãos Novos prezentarão ... Em 1672', ANTT, Armário Jesuítico, 29, Doc. 15; 'Proposta dos Christãos Novos da Letra do Padre Manoel Fernandes ... Em Março de 1673', ANTT, Armário Jesuítico, 29, Doc. 18; 'Segundo projecto, que offererecerão os Christãos Novos ao Princepe ... Em o anno de 1673', ANTT, Armário Jesuítico, 29, Doc. 20.

[77] Vieira to Duarte Ribeiro de Macedo, Rome, 5 January 1672, *Obras Escolhidas* II, 57.

[78] 'Primeira consulta feita pela Inquizição ao Principe ... Em Abril de 1673', 13vf., ANTT, Armário Jesuítico, 29, Doc. 21.

empire, an asylum for heresy and a new promised land for the Jews.[79] To allow Judaism to take root in Portugal for the highly uncertain enterprise of converting the gentiles of India was hardly a worthwhile proposition. They reminded the prince of the perfidy and greed of the new Christians, who would undoubtedly hide their true wealth from the Crown and renege on their commitments once the Holy Office had been irretrievably weakened.[80] Drawing upon the same sense of the sacred destiny of Portugal, the same foundational myth of Afonso Henrique's vision of Christ at Ourique, the Inquisition presented a vision of Portugal in direct opposition to the imaginaire of the Jesuit missionaries. Here, Portuguese dominion in the gentile lands and the missionary enterprise were not vital; instead, the discursive emphasis was on the direct relationship that the Portuguese king had with Christ, thus affording him relative independence from the Pope in determining the destiny and religious policies of his realm.

The new Christian faction, ably aided by their Jesuit supporters, rebutted each point of the Inquisition's consultation.[81] To bolster their

[79] 'Primeira consulta feita pela Inquizição ao Principe ... Em Abril de 1673', 8f., ANTT, Armário Jesuítico, 29, Doc. 21

[80] 'Primeira consulta feita pela Inquizição ao Principe ... Em Abril de 1673', 8f., ANTT, Armário Jesuítico, 29, Doc. 21.

[81] For the full evolution of Father Manuel Dias's response, see ANTT, Armário Jesuítico, 29, Doc. 22, 'Papel da letra do Padre Manoel Dias ... impugnando a primeira consulta do Santo Officio. Em Abril de 1673'; Doc. 23, 'Variação da letra do Padre Manoel Diaz ...'; Doc. 28, 'Papel da letra do Padre Manuel Diaz....'; Doc. 91 is almost identical to Doc. 23. Manuel Fernandes provided his own, no doubt highly influential, opinion, to D. Pedro in his capacity as his confessor: Doc. 29, 'Parecer da letra do Padre Manoel Fernandes...'. See also Doc. 27, 'Primeira e segunda copia de hum discurso que por parte dos Christãos novos se deu a alguns ministros de SA...'. An anonymous opinion, which was almost undoubtedly that of Vieira, argued vociferously that the new Christians, as members of the Catholic Church, could not be impeded from appealing to the head of that Church. See Doc. 36, 'Parecer que se entende ser do Padre Antonio Vieyra....' Vieira's private letters echoed this opinion. See Vieira to Duarte Ribeiro de Macedo, Rome, 31 January 1673, *Obras Escolhidas* II, 117. There was already royal precedent for this: Joao IV had given the new Christians permission to seek recourse to the Pope regarding the practices of the Inquisition in an authorization dated 10 December 1649.

argument they compiled (highly selective) lists and descriptions of new Christians, who had been forced by fear of the Inquisition to flee Portugal, including clergymen and members of religious orders, who were living as good Catholics in other countries.[82] The new Christian merchants reiterated their financial commitment to the project.[83] Meanwhile, learned doctors were found who would aver that the Crown could not impede the new Christians from taking recourse to the Pope. Not surprisingly, the predominant figures in these lists were missionaries from various orders with experience in the 'conquests', including Pedro Zuzarte, with whom Vieira had conversed so fruitfully in Rome; the bishops and bishop-elects of Angola, Kochi, Malacca, and Meliapor; and scholars from the Jesuit colleges, including Baltasar Telles, author of an important history of Ethiopia.[84]

In this dossier of opinions, the fact that the new Christian proposal would conserve the missionary enterprise in the colonies was heavily emphasized.[85] Francisco Abreu Godinho argued, for example, that if Charles V could allow the Jews to remain in their faith in his realm because of the aid they provided in fighting the Turk, then why could Portugal not admit those Jews who had left their errors behind to fight the 'Ādil Shāh of Bijāpur? The conquest of Africa was hindered when the Moriscos went there; the progress of Holland began when the Jews went there—from these examples, he concluded, like Vieira, that when such groups remain in the lands of infidels, they impoverish the Catholic kingdoms. Since they could not conquer the Moors, the Portuguese should at least ensure that they themselves were not conquered by heretics. Thus, they should encourage the new Christians to go to the lands of the infidels. In Brazil, Portugal could claim only those lands that the sea wets, lacking the people to populate

[82] 'Lista de varios Christãos Novos ... ', ANTT, Armório Jesuítico, 29, Doc. 25.

[83] 'Obrigação original de Manoel da Gama de Padua ... Feita em 12 de Junho de 1673 ...', ANTT, Armório Jesuítico, 29, Doc. 31.

[84] 'Primeira e segunda lista dos doutores ...', ANTT, Armório Jesuítico, 29, Doc. 35. Most importantly for the new Christian proposal, the list included the Archbishop of Lisbon. Interestingly, the list also included the confessor of the late João IV, who had long struggled for control against the Inquisition.

[85] 'Pareceres de Francisco de Almada, Francisco de Abreu Godinho e de outros doutores, lentes e ministros ...', ANTT, Armório Jesuítico, 29, Doc. 38.

the interior. If strangers were permitted to populate these lands, Brazil would be lost, since it was only natural that these foreigners would wish to be under the dominion of their own king. By contrast, populating the land with Jews bore no such danger, because it was proven in the tribunal of God Himself that this nation cannot have a king. Furthermore, he asked, who would believe that the Portuguese crossed the seas to make the gentile a catechumen, if they impeded the baptized from remaining faithful?[86]

The fault lines of the dispute thus followed the relative importance placed on the 'conquests' versus the kingdom in interpretations of the foundational myth of Portugal, and of its sacral destiny and responsibility. Thus, the inquisitorial position was not automatically opposed by all Jesuits: Nuno da Cunha wrote from the São Roque house, advising D. Pedro against accepting the new Christian proposal, even as Manuel Fernandes lobbied for it. Perhaps, the fact that Nuno da Cunha was not a missionary in the colonies has more to do with his orientation in this debate than his identity as a member of the Jesuit order.[87] Furthermore, the Holy Office was not devoid of support from prominent ecclesiastical figures either.[88] Nonetheless, the new Christian proposal carried the day and D. Pedro sent their requests to the Pope for examination.[89]

[86] '"Pareceres de Francisco de Almada, Francisco de Abreu Godinho e de outros doutores, lentes e ministros ...'," ANTT, Armório Jesuítico, 29, Doc. 38, 15v–16. Francisco de Abreu Godinho was careful to note that he was an old Christian right at the outset of the opinion he penned. It is interesting to note that he had penned a tract on the original scandal of Odivelas, 'Declaração ao Príncipe no sacrilego de sacato de Odivellas anno de 1671'. See Machado, *Summario da Bibliotheca luzitana*, 40.

[87] Nuno da Cunha, 5 January 1674, ANTT, Armório Jesuítico, 29, Doc. 64; 'Carta em Latim do Padre Manoel Fernandes Confessor do Princepe para o Cardeal Secretario de Estado ... Sem data', ANTT, Armório Jesuítico, 29, Doc. 59.

[88] 'Carta Original do secretario Francisco Correa de Lacerda para o padre confessor ... Em 3 de Agosto de 1673', ANTT, Armório Jesuítico, 29, Doc. 41; 'Carta do Bispo de Leiria Pedro Vieyra da Sylva ao Princpe ... Em 6 de Agosto de 1673', ANTT, Armório Jesuítico, 29, Doc. 42.

[89] 'Primeira carta que o Princepe D. Pedro escreveo ao Pontificie ...', ANTT, Armório Jesuítico, 29, Doc. 45.

The Inquisition quickly put forth a second consultation condemning the move, in which India was not mentioned even once and the entire new Christian proposal was cast as the machinations of António Vieira.[90] The Holy Office also prepared to send its own representative to Rome to counteract the procurators of the new Christians, who was courting papal favour.[91] Again, a series of disputes ensued, with opinions proffered by theologians on both sides of the debate, culminating in yet another consultation of the Holy Office.[92]

The Inquisition, however, had a distinct advantage in its metropolitan location and orientation—unlike the distant viceroys and colonial officials of India, natural allies to the new Christian proposal, the Inquisition could count on the immediate presence of many old Christians in Portugal. For many of them, the conquests were relatively unimportant and their anti-Semitic prejudices were likely to trump their concern for the faraway empire. A groundswell of popular support buoyed the argument of the Holy Office, as satirical pamphlets and anti-Semitic rumours swirled through the streets of Lisbon.[93] When the palace conspiracy of 1673 underscored D. Pedro's vulnerability as a usurper, the Lisbon Cortes forced the Crown to retract the founding of the company.

Even the project of conforming the *estilos* (conventions) of the Portuguese Inquisition to that of Rome was eventually defeated. Vieira's support in this regard was of limited efficacy. Only years after the original papal order demanding that the Portuguese Inquisition send its cases for review to Rome, were two exemplary cases sent. In 1680, Manuel da Gama da Pádua passed away, and Manuel Fernandes

[90] 'Segunda consulta do concelho geral do santo officio ... Em 11 de Agosto de 1673', ANTT, Armório Jesuítico, 29, Doc. 47.

[91] 'Carta do Tribunal da Inquizição ao Princepe ... Em 25 de Agosto de 1673', ANTT, Armório Jesuítico, 29, Doc. 49; 'Francisco de Azevedo aos Procuradores dos christãos novos ... Em 2 de Dez. de 1673', ANTT, Armório Jesuítico, 29, Doc. 57.

[92] 'Parecer de vinte e tres teologos que opinarão contra o Recurso dos Christãos novos. Em 28 de Agosto de 1673', ANTT, Armório Jesuítico, 29, Doc. 50; 'A testação do Reytor da universidade da Evora ... Em 29 de Agosto de 1673', ANTT, Armório Jesuítico, 29, Doc. 51A; 'Terceira consulta de Santo Officio ... 12 September 1673', ANTT, Armório Jesuítico, 29, Doc. 53.

[93] Franco, 'A Companhia de Jesus e a Inquisição', 20–1.

excused himself from the post of royal confessor under orders from the Jesuit Father General. By August 1681, the Pope re-established the full functionality of the Portuguese Inquisition. D. Pedro himself presided over the first auto-da-fé conducted in Lisbon, amid general festivities, in 1682.[94]

It was perhaps not entirely surprising that the stand-off between the papacy and D. Pedro would end in such a way: even as these negotiations took place, the Pope approached the Portuguese court for assistance in fighting the Ottomans.[95] The vicissitudes of Europe's politics had again trumped the needs of the 'conquests', which remained invisible to the metropole. Like Costa before him, Vieira returned to his colonial home, in Maranhão, abandoning his imperial projects for the rigours of the mission, where he would finally end his life in 1697.

The Limits of an Imperial *Imaginaire*

The imaginaire of Portugal and its empire articulated by the Jesuit protagonists of this chapter clearly found resonance amidst those sections of Portuguese society which considered Portugal's imperial possessions *and* its obligation to spread Catholicism throughout these possessions as integral to Portugal's identity and destiny. This imaginaire was by no means hegemonic; nor even were all other competing visions of Portugal current in this period insensible to the place of the conquests.[96] Nonetheless, to highlight the very specificities of this imaginaire, it may be useful to consider its limits.

[94] Hanson, *Economy and Society*, 89–123.

[95] 'Breve do Papa Innocencio XI a SA o principe D. Pedro ... 28 November 1677', ANTT, Documentos da Biblioteca Nacional de Paris, Caixa 2, Doc. 109. On Vieira's continuing involvement see, for example, letters 70, 74–6, 78–80 in *Obras Escolhidas* II.

[96] Marcocci contends that the Holy Office had its own particular view of global empire (Marcocci, 'A Fé de um Império', 100). His notion of an independent inquisitorial colonialism, does veer a little close to the suggestion that a project of global empire requires only a disciplinary structure of transnational proportions. Nonetheless, this is a promising line of enquiry that deserves further research.

One such limit can be discerned in a project articulated by Vieira's frequent correspondent and friend, Duarte Ribeiro de Macedo. His time as ambassador for Portugal in France introduced him to the economic thought of Colbert, which he applied to the particular case of Portugal in his best-known work, *Discurso sobre a introdução das artes no Reino*, in 1675.[97] He focused first on the need to improve Portugal's balance of trade by reducing its recent reliance on foreign luxury goods. This reliance was due to the Dutch disruption of Portugal's near monopoly on Oriental products and of its monopoly on sugar. He contended that the erosion of Portugal's bullion could be remedied only through manufacturing, using Castile's decline as a negative example. The second part of the work proposed complementing the natural resources of the conquests with manufacturing in Portugal to revive Portugal's commercial fortunes. This would prevent Portugal's European rivals from gaining effective control of the colonial markets and thus of the colonies themselves.

The work that concerns us here, however, was a treatise on the transplantation of the things of India to Brazil, dated 10 May 1675.[98] Ribeiro de Macedo began by recounting a conversation with the British ambassador to Paris. They were speaking vaguely about the British colonies in Virginia and the Portuguese ones in Brazil, when Montague revealed that the British king had once proclaimed to the court that he knew that his brother-in-law, the Portuguese king, had the means to destroy the Dutch. Upon reflection, Ribeiro de Macedo came to believe that the cryptic remark of the English king had referred to the possibility of simply transplanting valuable spices from the beleaguered east to secure Brazil. This would circumvent the deleterious effects on Portuguese commerce of the loss of dominion in the east to the Dutch.

He relied on the principles of natural philosophy, which showed that the conditions found in the latitudes in the northern hemisphere of the world were the same as those found in the corresponding latitude in the southern half, to prove the plan was workable. The second chapter detailed previous Portuguese experiences with

[97] On his brand of Colbertism, see Hanson, *Economy and Society*, 126–40.

[98] Duarte Ribeiro de Macedo, *Discurso Político sobre a introdução das artes*, 1801, 18-25vff., AC, Vermelha, 281.

transplantation, in particular that of orange trees from China, which were now ubiquitous in Portugal. He supported his claims in the third chapter through books emerging from the Royal Society in London, which also dealt with transplantation. In the fourth, he showed the particular suitability of the Portuguese realm for this project. The fifth outlined a plan to put his ideas into action, involving, above all, the transplantation of cloves and cinnamon from the eastern empire to the lush lands of Maranhão.

This plan was not a little influenced by his long-standing correspondence with Vieira: the ambassador repeatedly sought from Vieira, as well as from his fellow missionaries, specialized local knowledge of the conquests. Thus, in 1672, he had approached Vieira to ask Zuzarte if there was any possibility of selling an eastern port belonging to the Portuguese to a Catholic nation, as compensation for the aid necessary to recuperate Sri Lanka and Malacca.[99] Zuzarte's apparently responded that it would be best not to give any port, but if absolutely necessary, Chaul may be suitable. Vieira seconded the reluctance to give up any port; he recommended again the creation of an oriental company through judicious enticements to new Christians. The Jesuits were thus united in their reluctance to consider the loss of colonial territory unless absolutely necessary, a reluctance that Ribeiro de Macedo seemed to have overcome with more ease.

Similarly, with regard to his plan to transplant Indian spices to Maranhão, the ambassador sought Vieira's advice; Vieira acquiesced to its feasibility in a letter the ambassador quoted in his treatise. Vieira noted that D. Manuel had actually ordered that all Indian plants be transplanted in Brazil to save the eastern commerce, but this early experiment was abandoned, although ginger continued to grow in Brazil.[100]

In both situations, Ribeiro de Macedo viewed the conquests as interchangeable possessions at the disposal of the Crown for its own economic interest; there was no attempt to imbue these colonial locations themselves with any meaning or consider its local specificity. The question of what would happen to the missions in the east if the

[99] Vieira to Duarte Ribeiro de Macedo, Rome, 29 February 1672, *Obras Escolhidas* II, 66–7.

[100] Quoted in Ribeiro de Macedo, *Discurso Político*, 23f.

oriental possessions became financially redundant to the Portuguese was simply irrelevant; one colonial location was much like another, as long as they were on corresponding latitudes.

The contrast could not have been clearer with Vieira's infamous *Papel forte*, in which he had advocated accepting the loss of Pernambuco to secure the rest of the Portuguese conquests. Vieira had begun *first* by considering the religious implications of such a move. Even though Vieira claimed that the project of transplanting the spices of the east in Brazil was the second of the two charges given to him by João IV, it had been at best a practical, but by no means preferable, alternative if his original and much cherished plan to save the east through an oriental company were to fail.[101] Transplantation, like everything else in Vieira's thought, held deep religious significance. As he explained in a sermon given in Rome:

> You cannot plant the Faith without transplanting those who sow. Not in vain did Christ say *Pater meus est Agricola* [John 15:1, My father is the gardener]. God was with the Portuguese like the gardener of lights. The gardener sows in little land thereafter to have in plenty. Portugal was a little land, but there God made a seminary of light for the transplanting of the world.[102]

Thus, first God created and saved Portugal, 'that chosen seminary of faith and light', so that eventually 'some lights would illuminate Africa, others Asia, others America, some to Brazil, others India, others to the Mogor and others to Japan and China'.[103]

The image seemed to echo the one that Costa employed to describe Nobili, as a sun whose light other mirrors would continue to reflect in Madurai. Missionaries would carry the shoots of the light of faith to sow in all corners of the world. Transplanted from Portugal, 'faith planted itself in the three parts of the world', eventually 'subjecting all three to His empire, as Lord'.[104] Moreover, as Vieira and Costa's commitments to Maranhão and Madurai demonstrate, to the Jesuit

[101] Vieira to Conde da Ericeira, Bahia, 23 May 1688, *Obras Escolhidas* II, 58. The letter discusses Ribeiro de Macedo's project, mentioning the anecdote of the English king with which Ribeiro began his work.

[102] Vieira, *Sermões de Roma*, 199–200.

[103] Vieira, *Sermões de Roma*, 199–200.

[104] Vieira, *Sermões de Roma*, 199–200.

missionaries, one mission space, as long as it held open the possibility of new conversions, was not simply interchangeable with another.

If Ribeiro de Macedo's strictly economic vision of the conquests represented one extreme, the remarkable paper sent to the Propaganda Fide by a Spanish friar in 1674 was another.[105] Demonstrating a commendable knowledge of India, the author argued that in order to promote Christianity, the Congregation should conform to the particularities of the ruler in each region of the east. Thus, in the Portuguese lands, it was foolish to promote the ecclesiastical superiority of indigenous Christians in the face of the natural resentment of the Portuguese. By contrast, such a policy would be ideal in the lands ruled by gentile kings, especially in the Mughal empire. Conforming to the particularities of the ruler would thus guarantee access to the missionaries. As evidence of his claim, he mentioned his own friendship with the Dutch captain in Kochi and included a copy of the passport granted to him by the Dutch. It served as a concrete reminder of the access a missionary could gain from such a willingness to accept the political status quo.

Again, the contrast with the imperial imaginaire of the Portuguese Jesuits is clear. For this papal agent, the primary goal was spreading Catholicism, regardless of who held temporal dominion. For Portuguese Jesuits like Vieira and Costa, it was not enough to maintain a deeply local understanding of their mission space and their commitment to evangelizing within it; they were simultaneously impelled to harmonize this with a larger vision not only of universal Catholicism, but of global Portuguese dominion.

While the specificities of this imaginaire emerged most clearly during the 1670s, it was also then that the imaginaire, so productive of thought and action, finally began to crumble under the weight of historical contingency. One can see this perhaps most clearly in the way in which Vieira remembered his failed project of the company of India at the end of his career and life. Defending himself from the critical stance of the Conde da Ericeira's *Historia de Portugal*, Vieira

[105] 'Informatione Generale dello stato miserabile dell'India Orientale', 302–23f., ASPF, Scritture Riferite nei Congressi Indie Orientali, 40 (Relazioni). The author is most likely the Spanish Carmelite José Carmona, who eventually made his way to Mexico via the Philippines.

staked his reputation on his role in the creation of the Company of Brazil. The utility of the Company, Vieira asserted, could be gauged from the fact that it preserved Brazil, which in turn sustained the war with Castile, saved the kingdom *and* restored Pernambuco. Furthermore, Vieira claimed, if he had been able to found an eastern Company, India would not have reached the state it was in.[106]

In this defiant sentence, the embers of his 'hopes for Portugal' undoubtedly still smouldered. The switch in temporal register, indicating that the possibilities for preserving India were now consigned solely to a lost moment in the past, was telling. Vieira had long maintained his imaginaire of empire in the face of present circumstances, by asserting that the very fact that the prophecies foretelling the Fifth Empire had not yet come true validated them in terms of genre as prophecy.[107] When Vieira articulated this imaginaire in the mode of prophetical exegesis, in the mode of a history of the future, it was a powerful basis of action. The move to the past tense revealed finally that the imaginaire, at least in the variant Vieira promoted, was no longer a viable basis for action and had been effectively defeated by historical contingency.

Neither the Portuguese empire nor the various imperial imaginaires it engendered collapsed with the end of Vieira's career. Still, even as other frontiers, especially Mozambique, began to emerge in the Portuguese imagination as new sites to re-found the promise of the empire, Vieira's disillusionment marked the end of this particular imaginaire of an empire of apostles.[108] The radical disjuncture between

106 Vieira to Conde da Ericeira, Bahia, 23 May 1688, *Obras Escolhidas* II, 57–8.

107 See Cohen, 'Millenarian Themes'. Queyros uses a similar strategy to defend Basto's legitimacy as a prophet.

108 D. Pedro's later reign saw an attempt to colonize Mozambique through military means and to found a settler colony there. It is interesting to note that at much the same time as the India company was being debated, another proposal for company to aid in the colonization of Mozambique had also arrived at Pedro's court, ostensibly supported by a group of Muslim subjects resident in Goa, or more likely Daman and Diu. See 'Tratado das noticias para a companhia', 474f., BA, 50-V-37, Doc. 165; 'Papel feito pellos Mouros Portugueses que estão em França e dezeias vir ao Reyno', 320–2ff., BA, 51-IX-33; 'Tratado das noticias para a companhia do Estado da India', 333–9ff., BA, 51-IX-33.

the self-aggrandizing narrative of empire and its harsh realities had become too sharp to ignore. By the following century, as Portugal responded to the changing currents of the Enlightenment, the Society of Jesus would come to be expelled from its domain. These pioneering missionaries, and the role they played in the actual and discursive production of empire, would thus be consigned to the past—but not before leaving a lasting legacy that has fuelled imperial thinking and nostalgia well into the present.

EPILOGUE

Modern Millenarians and the Empire of Liberty

On 22 August 2007, President George W. Bush addressed the national convention of Veterans of Foreign Wars in Kansas City, Missouri, at the height of the Iraq War.[1] Surrounded by survivors of America's past wars, he sought to read the current conflict in light of history, in which the war in Iraq was but another moment in the inexorable expansion of the American 'empire of liberty'.[2] The new enemy empire of 'the radical caliphate envisioned by Osama bin Laden', President Bush declared, was merely a contemporary incarnation of an older enemy: imperial Japan, which too had surprised Americans with an attack on its own soil. Left unsaid was the intermediary stage in the evolution of American enemies: the Soviet state, which President Reagan had tellingly dubbed the 'evil empire' before the National Association of Evangelicals in 1983.[3] Much like his predecessor, President Bush

[1] 'Transcript of President Bush's Speech at the Veterans of Foreign Wars Convention', *The New York Times*, 22 August 2007, available at http://www.nytimes.com/2007/08/22/washington/w23policytext.html, accessed on 10 October 2016.

[2] On the historical roots of the Bush doctrine, stretching back to Thomas Jefferson, see Immerman, *Empire for Liberty*.

[3] 'Evil Empire Speech', *Voices of Democracy. The U.S. Oratory Project*, 8 March 1983, available at http://voicesofdemocracy.umd.edu/reagan-evil-empire-speech-text/, accessed on 13 October 2016.

harkened to religion: in his exhortation to stay the course in the war, he reminded his listeners that 'the greatest arsenal of democracy is the desire for liberty written into the human heart by our Creator'.

Nonetheless, in his recourse to history, President Bush focused not on the well-known triumphs of the American military, but rather on a war that had become emblematic of its folly: Vietnam. The lesson of Vietnam, according to the president, was not a lesson regarding the arrogance of imperial ambition but a fable regarding the cost of defeatism. Bush argued that 'the price to our withdrawal from Vietnam' was new enemies emboldened by Osama bin Laden's declaration that 'the American people had risen against their government's war in Vietnam. And they must do the same today.' Attrition in Iraq would thus constitute a repetition of the real mistake of Vietnam.

Subtly, the defeat in Vietnam was transformed into victory halted. The speech was in line with a revisionist view of the Vietnam War that was crystallizing in national discourse. On Veteran's Day in 2004, while American troops occupied Iraq, the National Museum of American History inaugurated an exhibition entitled 'The Price of Freedom: Americans at War'. It highlighted 'the history and contributions of the American people (but focusing primarily on the military's role) in preserving and protecting freedom and democracy'. The section on the Vietnam War leads seamlessly to a replica of a chunk of the Berlin Wall, completing the arc of American victory. While the inclusion of the Iraq War in the exhibition elicited some concern, the Vietnam War was now part of the arc of American triumphalism.[4]

President Bush's reference to Vietnam was not accidental. In March 2007, the grim pictures that emerged from the darkness of Abu Ghraib had shown that those who defended 'civilization' had themselves descended into barbarism. As criticism of the war effort mounted, a military surge, launched in February 2007, failed to bring stability. In May 2007, American casualties in the war reached its peak, with a toll of 126 soldiers, while the horrific count of Iraqi death increased by a further 1,700 that month.[5] When the violence abated by year end, many observers attributed it not to American military might, but to other factors such as the Sunni Awakening and the

[4] Bob Thompson, 'A Tug of War', *Washington Post*, 7 November 2004.

[5] Biddle et al., 'Testing the Surge'.

completion of ethnic cleansing along sectarian lines.[6] The realities of empire were messy—and bloody.

In the face of the manifest failures of the 'empire of liberty', President Bush appealed to both history and religion in urging his listeners to resist the temptation to doubt American imperial destiny. The defence of triumphalism was more than just of rhetorical significance: one study has shown that Iraqi insurgent attacks against American military targets spiked in periods following public criticism of the war in the USA, resulting in more American casualties even while there were fewer deaths overall.[7] The grandiose arc of imperial discourse did not merely belie the contingent, contested, and constrained nature of imperial power; it functioned, long-term, to shore up that power.

In pushing for continued support of the war, President Bush pointed to the distance between the imperial metropolis and its colonial agents, suggesting that the former was not sufficiently apprised of the progress made by the latter. A war started on imperfect information continued in the same vein. The information gap between the metropolis and its imperial outposts allowed President Bush to maintain a triumphalist vision of empire, despite its failures, and thus to continue to feed the imperial machinery in search of predestined victory.

The Church Says 'NO'

On the afternoon of 9 July 2015, Pope Francis addressed the World Meeting of Popular Movements in Santa Cruz, Bolivia. In an analysis that appeared to update his countryman Raúl Prebisch's theories of *dependencia* for the age of neoliberal globalization, the Pope mounted a scathing critique of contemporary colonialism. As rapacious corporations raid the environment and pauperize indigenous peoples, and developing countries struggle to maintain their autonomy in the face of 'ideological colonialism', the Pope exhorted: 'Let us say NO to forms of colonialism old and new. Let us say YES to the encounter between peoples and cultures.' In a sharp departure from his predecessor, the Pope emeritus Benedict XVI, Pope Francis acknowledged the

6 Biddle et al., 'Testing the Surge'; John Agnew et al., 'Baghdad Nights'.

7 Iyengar and Monten, 'Is There an "Emboldment" Effect?'

implication of the Church in the long history of colonialism, 'humbly [asking] for forgiveness, not only for the offences of the Church herself, but also for crimes committed against the native peoples during the so-called conquest of America'.[8]

The speech was in keeping with a vision for the universal church that the Pope, when he was still known as Jorge Bergoglio, had sketched out during the pre-conclave General Congregation meetings of the Cardinals, of a 'Church [that] is called to come out of herself and to go to the peripheries'.[9] The speech, widely credited for his election to the papacy, was hailed as a sign of the coming revival of a moribund Church, plagued with scandals and whose demographic centre had pivoted away from Europe, even as its leadership remained ensconced in Rome. His words, as much as his person as the first Latin American and Jesuit to serve as pontiff for the Catholic church, seemed a harbinger for a new era for the Church.

Observing this historical election whilst living in Italy, I was not immune to this sense of newness entering the world. The excitement was infectious, particularly among the elated communities of Latin American migrants. Yet, reading Pope Francis's words, it was not the newness of his vision of the apostolic church of the twenty-first century that impressed me. Rather, I was struck by the resonance of his words with the sentiments expressed by so many of his forbears, who had devoted their lives as missionaries of the Society of Jesus in the geographical peripheries of the Church. In the image of the Church that goes out of herself to these peripheries, Pope Francis could draw upon a long and illustrious genealogy of his confreres who had done

[8] 'Pope Francis: Speech at World Meeting of Popular Movements', *Vatican Radio*, 10 July 2015, available at http://en.radiovaticana.va/news/2015/07/10/pope_francis_speech_at_world_meeting_of_popular_movements/1157291, accessed on 20 October 2016.

[9] 'Bergoglio's Intervention: A Diagnosis of the Problems of the Church', *Vatican Radio*, 27 March 2013, available at. http://en.radiovaticana.va/news/2013/03/27/bergoglios_intervention:_a_diagnosis_of_the_problems_in_the_church/en1-677269, accessed on 10 June 2013. The original italicized phrase reads: 'Dei Verbum religiose audience et fidente proclamans', a reference to the opening words of the 1965 Dogmatic Constitution on Divine Revelation.

precisely that. His namesake, the first Jesuit missionary to India, St Francis Xavier, had first exhorted his brethren in Europe to come out of themselves. Urging them to stop the pursuit of letters or ecclesiastical benefices in the comfort of a familiar home, Xavier railed that if they truly studied the account God would take of them and of their given talents, they would say, 'Send me where you will, and if you desire, even to the Indies.'[10]

Pope Francis's words not only evoked this particular strand of the history of the Church coming out of herself; as his speech in Bolivia suggested, he hoped to address too the intimate involvement of the evangelical Church with European conquest and imperialism. In his own way, therefore, Pope Francis is attempting to decolonize the Church. Little wonder that so many of the saints canonized under his pontificate, including José de Anchieta, had laboured in the non-European world. Unlike Benedict XVI, Pope Francis wished not to defend a Eurocentric understanding of the Church but rather to promote a universal Church that had become 'a part of the identity' of the peoples of the former colonies of Europe. For Pope Francis, a figure like the apostle of Sri Lanka, José Vaz (1651–1711), the Goan brahmin oratorian missionary who had never travelled to Europe, was an exemplary missionary in the multi-religious context of an indigenous kingdom. If the vehicle of Portuguese imperialism had brought the Church to his ancestral lands, the saint had carried that zeal to other shores of the Indian Ocean on the steam of his own zeal. For his homily, the Pope thus chose the biblical quotation: 'All the ends of the earth will see the salvation of our God' (Is 52:10).[11]

[10] Xavier to the Society in Rome, Cochin, 15 January 1544, *Epistolae* I: 167. The quotation, *Mitte me quo vis: et si expedit, etiam ad Indos*, is a play on what St Thomas was supposed to have said, according to the thirteenth-century hagiologist, Jacopo da Voragine, in his famous *Legenda Aurea*: 'Domine, mitte me quo vis, praeter ad Indos' [Lord, send me where you will, except the Indies].

[11] 'Full text: Pope Francis' address for Canonization of St Joseph Vaz', *Catholic Herald*, 14 January 2015, available at http://www.catholicherald.co.uk/news/2015/01/14/full-text-pope-francis-address-for-canonisation-of-st-joseph-vaz/, accessed on 29 October 2016.

This attempt at decolonizing the Church is naturally grounded in the fundament of Catholic theology. The Pope has repeatedly invoked this notion, for example, to critique attempts to make development aid conditional upon the promotion of Western progressive ideas of gender, sexuality, and marriage in developing countries that run counter to the Church's teachings.[12] Many secular critics of the colonial structure of development aid may agree with the thrust of his analysis that conditional aid limits the autonomy of decolonized nations. These same secular critics are just as likely to balk at championing oppressive sexual and gender regimes in the name of preserving 'tradition'. Unlike them, Pope Francis *cannot* view Catholic doctrine itself as merely an ideology, which may be complicit in colonizing enterprises.

The Work of History

The key puzzle that this book wrestles with is this: how European accommodation to the local, the experience of give-and-take in the non-European world, and the many attendant experiences of failure led to an enduring vision of cultural and political dominion. It is a refrain that continues to ring through the discordant trumpet call of Euro-American imperialist discourse—even today, after decades of failed wars and 'interventions'. Amnesia and ignorance, particularly of the fraught, contingent, and violent nature of imperial power, are the smouldering embers that constantly threaten to engulf the world in new conflagrations of imperial violence. Yet, this is part of the design of empire. The imperfect flow of information between the metropolis and its imperial outposts is not merely incidental: it is necessary to the maintenance of the triumphant self-definition of empire, in the face of its vagaries.

The conventions of Jesuit epistolary production mandated that the messy and unpleasant realities of the missions of the Indies be

[12] See, for example, 'In-flight Press Conference of His Holiness Pope Francis from the Philippines to Rome', 19 January 2015, available at https://w2.vatican.va/content/francesco/en/speeches/2015/january/documents/papa-francesco_20150119_srilanka-filippine-conferenza-stampa.html, accessed on 17 October 2016.

relegated to private correspondence, while publicly circulated letters celebrated its successes. The result was the widespread circulation, through the vehicle of Jesuit writing, of an image of the Indies as a land of evangelical and imperial opportunity throughout the sixteenth century. When Portuguese temporal and spiritual dominion was in crisis in the following century, the intertwining of religion and history in the genre of historical prophecy allowed for a discursive construction of a religious vision of empire that belied this crisis and mobilized resources in defence of empire. The imperial wars that beset our so-called secular age continue to depend on such self-aggrandizing and self-fulfilling prophetic visions of empire. Further, though the Church under Pope Francis is confronting its own imperial past, the muscular resurgence of Euro-Christian cultural supremacists looms over the domestic landscape in both Europe and the US.

I offer these contemporary moments as a coda to this book to make two points regarding the historian's task in addressing the entangled history of religion and empire. First, regardless of the deep roots of Catholicism in the non-European world and the Church's own attempts to confront its colonial past, the historian, as a secular figure, remains crucial to the task of decolonizing our understanding of the Church. This requires keeping in view both the ways in which the Church has served as a handmaiden to empire and the ways in which the dictates of evangelism have run counter to the demands of imperial power.

Second, in studying empire, we must not be seduced by its own narratives of invincibility and inevitability: indeed, this is one of the most insidious modes through which empires survive. To reify these narratives, if only to critique them, may unwittingly serve to strengthen empire. The historicization and demystification of empire is crucial to the work of anti-imperialism. It is in that spirit that this book was written.

GLOSSARY OF KEY TERMS

accommodatio	(Latin) literally, accommodation. Integral to Jesuit praxis in adapting a spiritual message to the capacities and tastes of their audience, as long as it conformed to Catholic orthodoxy
aldeia	(Portuguese) Jesuit-controlled villages of indigenous converts in Brazil
auto-da-fé	(Portuguese) Ritual of public penance to which apostates and heretics were condemned by the Inquisition
carta de doação	(Portuguese) medieval instrument in which the Crown ceded a concession of a captaincy to a donatary captaincy, which established the boundaries of the captaincy, granted possession in perpetuity and heredity, and ceded civil and criminal jurisdiction over the area of the captaincy. Complemented by the *foral*, which outlined the rights and responsibilities of colonists with respect to both the donatary captain and the Crown, in establishing new settlements
cartaz	(Portuguese) sea-pass or licence
casado	(Portuguese) literally, householder. Socio-juridical category of Portuguese private citizens settled in colonies

christão novo	(Portuguese) new Christian, referring most often to indigenous or Jewish converts
entrada	(Portuguese) expeditions into the interior of Brazil to 'descend' indigenous peoples to the coast, either as slaves destined for the *fazendas* or to the *aldeias*
Estado da Índia	(Portuguese) State of India, referring to the eastern holdings of the Portuguese empire, administered from Goa
feitoria	(Portuguese) fortified trading post
fazenda	(Portuguese) large estate or farm or, increasingly after the rise of sugar in Brazil after 1580, plantation
foral	(Portuguese) legal basis for the foundation of a Portuguese settlement, a charter setting out the rights of settlers and the Crown's prerogatives
gāunkār	(Kōṅkaṇī) male patrilineal descendant of those considered the original inhabitants of a village in Goa; effective landholder and patron of the village
gentio	(Portuguese) gentile
hijuela	(Spanish) instituted by Ignatius in 1541, these were private letters which dealt with internal matters and were meant for a specific or limited audience. These were appended on a separate sheet from edifying letters, which missionaries had to write to report their activities and were meant for public circulation
imaginaire	(French) a cosmological term referring to a specific imagined world or the ensemble of what is imagined
Imitatio Christi	(Latin) the imitation of Christ
Índias	(Spanish/Portuguese) the Indies, which primarily referred to the extra-European spaces encountered by the Europeans in the 'age of discoveries'. In missionary usage,

could refer to imperfectly Christianized areas of Europe (*Índias por acá*) as much as the Indies beyond Europe's shores (*Índias por allá*)

índio — (Spanish/Portuguese) literally, Indian. The indigenous peoples of the Indies, including those in the Americas as well as the Indian subcontinent. When modified with the qualifier *ladino*, it indicated an indigenous person with European cultural and linguistic fluency

kanakkappiḷḷai — (Tamil) indigenous catechists. Jesuit missionaries relied upon these figures as part of a growing infrastructure, which included secular figures such as interpreters (*topazes*), Portuguese and indigenous civil authorities such as bailiffs (*meirinhos*) and *paṭṭaṅkaṭṭi* (indigenous village headmen) to convert and minister to the indigenous population of Tamil Nadu

karaíba — (Tupí) wandering stranger-prophet

limpeza de sangue — (Portuguese) literally, purity or cleanliness of blood. Socio-legal concept indicating pure old Christian lineage

língua geral da costa — the indigenous lingua franca of the Brazilian coast

meirinho — (Portuguese) bailiff

nāyaka — military governors of the Vijayanagara empire, who emerged as leaders of independent kingdoms in southern India after the fall of the empire

Padroado — (Portuguese) literally, patronage. The arrangement between the papacy and the Portuguese Crown that ceded to the latter the right to administer various aspects of the church in its domain

pagode — (Portuguese) ambiguous term referring to both idols and temples in the east

pajé	(Tupí) indigenous shaman
paṭṭaṅkaṭṭi	(Tamil) village overseers or headmen, referring here specifically to the Parava of the Fishery Coast
purāṇa	(Sanskrit) genre of texts consisting of historical and cosmological narratives, including accounts of the creation of the universe to its destruction, genealogies of kings, heroes and gods, and philosophical and religious speculation
śāstra	(Sanskrit) a treatise or manual of technical or specialized knowledge
sertão	(Portuguese) backlands of the interior, away from coastal settlements
Tapuía	Tupí term indicating peoples who did not speak Tupí, usually referring to inimical Gê-speaking peoples
vila	(Portuguese) a Portuguese village or small town

BIBLIOGRAPHY

Archives and Libraries

AC Academia das Ciências, Lisbon, Portugal
AHU Arquivo Histórico de Ultramarino, Lisbon, Portugal
ANTT Arquivo Nacional de Torro do Tombo, Lisbon, Portugal
ARSI Archivum Historicum Societatis Iesu, Rome, Italy
ASPF Archivo Storico della Sacra Congregazione per l'Evangelizzazione dei Popoli de Propaganda Fide, Italy
BA Biblioteca da Ajuda, Lisbon, Portugal
BNI Biblioteca Nazionale, Rome, Italy
BNP Biblioteca Nacional, Lisbon, Portugal
BNRJ Biblioteca Nacional, Rio de Janeiro, Brazil
CL Central Library, Panjim, Goa, India
GSHA Goa State Historical Archives, Panjim, Goa, India
JMMA Jesuit Madurai Mission Archives, Shembaganur, Tamil Nadu, India
SC Stonyhurst College Collections Archives, Clitheroe, Lancashire, UK
SOAS Archives and Special Collections, SOAS Library, SOAS University of London, UK

Published Primary Sources

Anchieta, José de. *Arte de grammatica da lingoa mais usada na costa do Brasil feita pelo P. Joseph de Anchieta*, edited by Julio Platzmann. Leipzig: B.G. Teubner, 1876.

———. *De gestis Mendi de Saa*. São Paulo, Armando Cardoso, 1970.

———. *Obras Completas*, vol. 6, *Cartas: Correspondência ativa e passiva* [*OC* 6], edited by Hélio Abranches Viotti. São Paulo: Edições Loyola, 1984.

———. *Poesia*, edited by Maria de Lourdes de Paula Martins. Belo Horizonte: Editora Itataia, 1989.

———. *Teatro de Anchieta*, edited by Armando Cardoso. São Paulo: Edições Loyola, 1977.

Aquinas, Thomas. *The Summa Theologica*, translated by the fathers of the English Dominican province. Westminster, MD: Christian Classics, 1981. First published in 1912–36.

'Assento do Conselho da Fazenda declarando o Estado senhorio directo das terras aldeanas e prohibindo doação dellas, July 5, 1649'. In *Bosquejo Historico*, edited by Nery Xavier, pp. 236–7.

Augustine of Hippo. *The City of God against the Pagans*, translated by R.W. Dyson. New York: Columbia University, 1998.

———. *De Doctrina Christiana*, translated and edited by R.P.H. Green. Oxford: Oxford University, 1995.

———. *Exposition of the Psalms 1–32*, translated by Marie Boulding. New York: Augustinian Heritage Institute, 2000.

———. *Saint Augustine: Confessions*, translated by Henry Chadwick. Oxford: Oxford University, 1991.

———. *The Trinity*, translated by Stephen McKenna. Washington, D.C.: Catholic University of America Press, 1963.

Barão de Studart, ed. *Documentos para a história do Brasil e especialmente a do Ceará*, vol. 4. Fortaleza: Coleção Studart, 1921.

Barbosa Machado, Diogo. *Summario da Bibliotheca luzitana, Tomo II*. Lisboa, 1786.

Barros, João de. *Décadas da Asia, Década Primeira, Parte Segunda*. Lisbon: Regia Officina Typografica, 1777 [1552].

Bernard, Jacqueline, ed. *Les instructions de la S.C. 'de Propaganda' aux Vicaires Apostoliques des royaumes du Tonkin et de Cochinchine (1659)*. Paris: Siry, 1971.

Bobadilla, Nicolaus. 1913. *Gesta et scripta*. Madrid: Typis Gabrielis Lopez del Horno, 1970.

Bouchon, Geneviève and Luís Filipe Thomaz. *Voyage dans les deltas du Gange et de l'Irraouaddy. Relation portugaise anonyme (1521)*. Paris: Fondation Calouste Gulbenkian, Centre Culturel Portugais, 1988.

Bulhão Pato, Raimundo de, ed. *Cartas de Affonso de Albuquerque, seguidas de Documentos que as elucidam*, vols I–III. Lisbon: Typographia da Academia Real das Sciencias, 1884–1935.

Cabral, Amílcar Lopes da Costa. 'National Liberation and Culture'. *Transition*, vol. 45 (1974): 12–17.

Caminha, Pero Vaz de. 'A Carta do Pero Vaz de Caminha'. Brazil: Ministério da Cultura, Fundação Biblioteca Nacional, Departamento Nacional de Livro, u.d. Available at http://objdigital.bn.br/Acervo_Digital/Livros_eletronicos/carta.pdf, accessed on 27 July 2016.

da Cunha Rivara, J.H., ed. *Archivo Portuguez Oriental*. Nova Goa: Imprensa Nacional, 1865.

———. *Grammatica da Lingua Concani composta pelo Padre Thomaz Estevão e acrescentada pello Padre Diogo Ribeiro da mesma Cõpanhia*. Nova Goa: Imprensa Nacional, 1857.

———, ed. *Synodo Diocesano da Igreja e Bispado de Angamale dos antigos Christãos de S. Thome das Serras do Malavar das partes da India Oriental, Archivo Portuguez Oriental*. Nova Goa, 1992 [1862].

d'Évreux, Yves. *Voyages dans le nord du Brésil fait durant les années 1613 et 1614*. Paris: Librairie A. Franck, 1864.

Fernandes, Gonçalo. *Tratado do Padre Gonçalo Fernandes Trancoso sobre o Hinduísmo*, edited by Josef Wicki, S.J. Lisboa: Centro de Estudos Históricos Ultramarinos, 1973.

Foley, H. *Records of the English Province of the Society of Jesus*, vol. 3. London, 1878.

Ford, J.D.M., ed. *Letters of John III*. Cambridge: Harvard University, 1931.

Galletti, A., A.J. van der Burg and P. Groot, eds. *Selections from the Records of the Madras Government: The Dutch in Malabar*. Madras: Government Press, 1911.

Ganss, George E., trans. and ed. *The Constitutions of the Society of Jesus*. St Louis: Institute of Jesuit Sources, 1970.

Greenlee, William, trans. *The Voyage of Pedro Álvares Cabral to Brazil and India from Contemporary Documents and Narratives*. London: Hakluyt Society, 1938.

Gundert, Hermann. *Keralolpatti*, translated by T. Madhava Menon. Thiruvananthapuram: International School of Dravidian Linguistics, 2003.

Hakluyt, Richard, ed. *The Principal Navigations, Voyages, Traffiques and Discoveries of the English Nation*, vol. IV. London: J.M. Dent & Co., 1907.

———, ed. *The Principal Navigations, Voyages, Traffiques, and Discoveries of the English Nation*, vol. V. Glasgow: James MacLehose and Sons, 1904.

Ignatius of Loyola. *Epistolae et Instructiones Sancti ignatii de Loyola*, vols I–XII. Rome: Monumenta Historica Societatis Iesu, 1964–8.

———. *Los Ejercicios Espirituales de San Ignacio de Loyola*, edited by M.R.P. Juan Roothaan, S.J. and R.P. Teodoro Toni, S.J. Zaragoza: Editorial Hechos y Dichos, 1959 (3rd ed.).

———. *Monumenta Ignatiana ex autographis vel ex antiquioribus exemplis collecta*, vol. I. Rome: Monumenta Historica Societatis Iesu, 1964.

Jonge, K.J. de. *De Opkomst van het Nederlandsch gezag in Oost-Indië (1595–1610)*, vol. 3. Amsterdam: Frederik Muller, 1865.

Leite, Serafim. *Cartas dos primeiros Jesuítas do Brasil*. Coimbra: Tipografia de Atlántida. 1956–8.

———. *Monumenta Brasiliae*, vols I–IV. Rome: Monumenta Historica Societatis Iesus, 1956–60.

———. *Novas cartas jesuíticas*. São Paulo: Companhia Editora Nacional, 1940.

Léry, Jean de. *Histoire d'un voyage faict en la terre du Brésil*, vol. II, edited by Paul Gaffarel. Paris: Alphonse Lemerre, 1880.

Linhares, Miguel de Noronha. *Diário do Terceiro Conde de Linhares, Vice-rei da India*. Lisbon: Biblioteca Nacional, 1937.

Linschoten, Jan van Huyghen. *The Voyage of John Huyghen van Linschoten to the East Indies*, vol. II, edited by Pieter Anton Tiele. London: Whiting and Co., 1885.

Luther, Martin. *A Prelude to the Babylonian Captivity of the* Church (1520). Available at http://www.projectwittenberg.org/etext/luther/babylonian/babylonian.htm, accessed on 4 January 2018.

Ma'abari I, Zainuddin. *Ahlil Iman Ala Jihadi Abdati Sulban*, translated by. K.M. Mohamed. Calicut: Other Books, 2013.

Ma'abari II, Zainuddin. *Tuhfat al-Mujāhidīn: A Historical Epic of the Sixteenth Century*, translated by S. Muhammad Husayn Nainar. Kuala Lumpur/Calicut: Islamic Book Trust, 2006.

Magalhães Gândavo, Pero de. 1573. *Tratado da Terra do Brasil*. Belo Horizonte: Itatiaia, 1980.

Nóbrega, Manuel da. *Cartas do Brasil e mais escritos*, edited by Serafim Leite. Coimbra: Universidade de Coimbra. 1955.

Olivelle, Patrick, trans. and ed. *The Law Code of Manu*. New York: Oxford University Press, 2004.

Paiva, Sebastião de. *Tratado da Quinta Monarquia*, edited by José Eduardo Franco and Arnaldo do Espírito Santo. Lisbon: Colleção Pensamento Português, Imprensa Nacional- Casa de Moeda, 2006.

Pliny the Elder. *The Natural History*, translated by John Bostock and H.T. Riley. London: George Bell & Sons, 1890.

Pope, G.U. *The Sacred Kurral of Tiruvalluva Nayanar*. New Delhi: Asian Educational Service, 2000 [1886].

Pyrard de Laval, François. *Voyage de Pyrard de Laval aux Indes orientales (1601–1611), Tome II: Goa, l'empire maritime portugais et le séjour au Brésil*, edited by Xavier de Castro. Paris: Éditions Chandeigne-Libraire Portugais, 1998.

Queyros, Fernão de. *História da vida do veneravel Irmão Pedro de Basto*. Lisbon: Officina de Miguel Deslandes, 1689. Available at http://purl.pt/22283, accessed on 4 January 2018.

Rodrigues, Pero. *Vida do Padre José de Anchieta da Companhia de Jesus*. São Paulo: Edições Loyola, 1981 [1617].

Rumeu de Armas, Antonio. 'Una carta inédita del Apostolo del Brasil, Beato José de Anchieta al Rey Felipe II: La expedición de Diego Flores de Valdes al Magallanes'. *Hispania*, vol. 45, no. 159 (1985): 5–32.

Ryley, J. Horton. *Ralph Fitch, England's Pioneer to India and Burma, His Companions and Contemporaries, with His Remarkable Narrative Told in His Own Words*. London: T. F. Unwin, 1899.

Sá, Artur Basílio de. *Documentação para a história das missões do Padroado português do Oriente, Insulindia*, vols I–II. Lisboa: Agência Geral das Colónias/ Agência Geral do Ultramar, 1954–5.

Saldanha, Antonio de. *Santo Antonichi Acharya*, edited by A.K. Priolkar. Bombay: Marathi Samshodhan Mandal, 1963 [1655].

———. *Santu Antonici jivitvakatha*, edited by A.K. Priolkar. Mumbai: Marathi Sansodhanamandala, 1956 [1655].

Salvador, Vicente do. *História do Brasil*. Rio de Janeiro: Biblioteca Nacional, 1889 [1627].

Silva Rego, António da. *Documentação para a história das missões do Padroado português do Oriente, Indía*, vols I–XI. Lisboa: Agência Geral das Colónias/ Agência Geral do Ultramar, 1947–55.

Sousa, Pero Lopes de. *Diario de Navegação da armada que á terra do Brasil em 1520 sob a capitania-mor de Martim Affonso de Souza escripto por seu irmão* Lisbon: Typographia da Sociedade Propagadora dos Conhecimentos Uteís, 1839 [reprint].

Stephens, Thomas. *Doutrina cristã, em língua concani, por Tómas Estevão, S.J., impressa em Rachol (Goa) em 1622*, edited by Mariano Saldanha. Lisbon: Divisão de Publicações e Biblioteca, Agência Geral das Colónias, 1945.

———. *The Christian Puránna of Father Thomas Stephens of the Society of Jesus*, edited by Joseph L. Saldanha. Mangalore: Simon Alvares, 1907.

Telles, Balthezar. 1645. *Chronica da Companhia de Iesu, da Provincia de Portugal*, vol. 2. Lisbon: Paulo Graesbeeck, 1647.

Trindade, Paulo da. *Conquista Espiritual do Oriente*, edited by Felix Lopes. Lisbon, 1960–7.

Valignano, Alessandro. *Historia del principio y progreso de la Compañia de Jesús en las Indias Orientales 1542–64*, edited by Josef Wicki. Rome: Institutum Historicum Societatis Iesu, 1944.

Veṅkaṭādhvarin. *Viswagunadarsana; or Mirror of Mundane Qualities*, translated by Caveli Venkata Ramaswami. Calcutta, 1825.

Venkatesananda, Swami and Christopher Chapple, eds. *The Concise Yoga Vāsiṣṭha*. Albany: State University of New York Press, 1984.

Vieira, António. *História do Futuro*, vol. 1, edited by António Sérgio and Hernani Cidade. Lisboa: Sá da Costa, 2008.

———. *Obras Escolhidas (Cartas I)*, edited by António Sérgio and Hernani Cidade. Lisboa: Livraria Sá da Costa, 1951.

———. *Obras Escolhidas*, vol. III, *Obras Várias I*, edited by António Sérgio and Hernani Cidade. Lisboa: Livraria Sá da Costa, 1997 (2nd edition).

———. *Obras Escolhidas*, vol. IV, *Obras Várias II*, edited by António Sérgio and Hernani Cidade. Lisboa: Sá da Costa, 1951.

———. *Obras Escolhidas*, vol. V, *Obras Várias III*, edited by António Sérgio and Hernani Cidade. Lisboa: Livraria Sá da Costa, 1951.

———. *Obras Escolhidas*, vol. IX, *História do futuro II*, edited by António Sérgio and Hernani Cidade. Lisboa: Livraria Sá da Costa, 1953.

———. *Obras Escolhidas*, vol. X, *Sermões I* edited by António Sérgio and Hernani Cidade. Lisboa: Livraria Sá da Costa, 1996 (2nd edition).

———. *Obras Ineditas do Padre Antonio Vieira*, vol. III. Lisboa: J.M.C. Seabra & T. Q. Antunes, 1857.

———. *Sermões*, vol. 1 edited by Alcir Pécora. São Paulo: Hedra, 2001.

———. *Sermões de Roma e outros textos*, edited by Manuel Correia Fernandes. Estarreja: Mel Editores, 2009.

Wicki, Joseph, ed. *Documenta Indica*, vols XVII–XVIII. Rome: Institutum Historicum Societatis Iesu, 1988.

———, ed. *Documenta Indica*, vols I–XIV. Rome: Institutum Historicum Societatis Iesu, 1940–79.

Wicki, Joseph and John Gomes, eds. *Documenta Indica*, vols XV–XVI. Rome: Institutum Societatis Iesu 1981, 1984.

Xavier, Filipe Nery, ed. *Bosquejo Historico das Communidades das Aldeas dos Concelhos das Ildas, Salsete e Bardez*, vol. 1. Bastora, Goa: Typographia Rangel, 1903.

Xavier, Francisco. *Epistolae S. Francesci Xaverii*, vols I–II edited by Georg Schurhammer and Josef Wicki. Rome: Monumenta Historica Soc. Iesu, 1944.

———. *Monumenta Xaveriana*, vol. I. Madrid: Augustino Avrial, 1899–1900.

Secondary Sources

Abbot, Justin E. 'The Discovery of the Original Devanāgri Text of the Christian Purāna of Thomas Stevens'. *Bulletin of the School of Oriental Studies*, vol. 2, no. 4, 1923: 679–83.

Abeyasinghe, T. 'History as Polemics and Propaganda: An Examination of Fernão de Queiros' History of Ceylon'. *Journal of the Royal Asiatic Society*, Sri Lanka Branch, vol. 25 (1981): 28–69.

Abranches Viotti, Hélio, S.J. *Anchieta o apóstolo do Brasil*. São Paulo: Edições Loyola, 1991.

Adorno, Rolena. *Guaman Poma: Writing and Resistance in Colonial Peru*. Austin: University of Texas Press, 1986.

Agnew, John, Thomas W. Gillespie, Jorge Gonzalez, and Brian Min. 'Baghdad Nights: Evaluating the US Military "Surge" Using Nighttime Light Signatures'. *Environment and Planning A*, vol. 40, no. 10 (2008): 2285–95.

Agnolin, Adone. *Jesuítas e Selvagens. A Negociação da Fé no encontro catequético-ritual Americano-tupi (séc. XVI–XVII)*. São Paulo: Ed. Humanitas, 2007.

Agnolin, Adone, Carlos Alberto de Moura Ribeiro Zeron, Maria Cristina Cortez Wissenbach, and Marina de Mello e Souza, eds. *Contextos Missionários. Religião e Poder no Império Português*. São Paulo: Hucitec Editora, 2011.

D'Agostino, Peter R. 'Orthodoxy or Decorum? Missionary Discourse, Religious Representations, and Historical Knowledge'. *Church History*, vol. 72, no. 4 (2003): 703–35.

Alam, Muzaffar and Sanjay Subrahmanyam. 'Frank Disputations: Catholics and Muslims in the Court of Jahangir, (1608–11)'. *Indian Economic and Social History Review*, vol. 46, no. 4 (2009): 457–511.

———. *Writing the Mughal World*. New York: Columbia University Press, 2011.

Albuquerque, Luís de and José Pereira da Costa. 'Cartas de "servicos" da Índia (1500–1550)'. *Mare Liberum*, vol. 1 (1990): 309–96.

Alden, Dauril. 'Black Robes versus White Settlers: The Struggle for "Freedom of the Indians" in Colonial Brazil'. In *Attitudes of Colonial Power toward the American Indian*, edited by Howard Peckham and Charles Gibson. Salt Lake City: University of Utah Press, 1969.

———. 'Changing Jesuit Perceptions of the Brasis during the Sixteenth Century'. *Journal of World History*, vol. 3 (1992): 205–18.

———. *The Making of an Enterprise: The Society of Jesus in Portugal, Its Empire, and Beyond, 1540–1750*. Stanford: Stanford University Press, 1996.

———. 'Some Reflections on António Vieira: Seventeenth Century Troubleshooter and Troublemaker'. *Luso-Brazilian Review*, vol. 40, no. 1 (António Vieira and the Luso-Brazilian Baroque) (2003): 7–16.

Almeida Mendes, Antonio de. 'Les réseaux de la traite ibérique dans l'Atlantique nord (1440–1640)'. *Annales HSC* (2008): 739–68.

Appadurai, Arjun and Carol Breckenridge. 'The South Indian Temple: Authority, Honor and Redistribution'. *Contributions to Indian Sociology*, vol. 10, no. 2 (1976): 187–211.

Aranha, Paolo. 'Gerarchie razziali e adattamento culturale: la "ipotesi Valignano"'. In *Alessandro Valignano S.I.: Uomo del Rinascimento: Ponte tra Oriente e Occidente*, edited by Adolfo Tamburello, M. Antoni J. Üçerler, S.J., and Marisa Di Russo. Roma: Institutum Historicum Societatis Iesu, 2008: 77–98.

———. 'Missionary Constructions of Hinduism and Caste in the Controversy on the Malabar Rites (17th–18th Centuries)'. Paper presented at the conference 'Rethinking Religion in India'. New Delhi: Indira Gandhi National Center for the Arts, 21–4 January 2008.

———. 'Roberto Nobili e il dialogo interreligioso?' In *Roberto Nobili (1577–1656): Missionario gesuita poliziano: Atti del convegno Montepulciano 20 ottobre 2007*, edited by Matteo Sanfilippo and Carlo Prezzolini (Perugia: Guerra Edizioni, 2008).

Axelrod, Paul and Michelle A. Fuerch. 'Flight of the Deities: Hindu Resistance in Portuguese Goa'. *Modern Asian Studies*, vol. 30, no. 2 (1996): 387–21.

Azevedo, João Lúcio de. *História de António Vieira*. Lisboa: Clássica Editora, 1992 (reprint).

Baer, Helmut David. 'The Fruit of Charity: Using the Neighbor in *De Doctrina Christiana'*. *The Journal of Religious Ethics*, vol. 24, no. 1 (1996): 47–64.

Bailey, Gauvin Alexander. *Art on the Jesuit Missions in Asia and Latin America, 1542–1773*. Toronto: University of Toronto, 1999.

Balandier, Georges. 'La situation coloniale: approche théorique'. *Cahiers internationaux de Sociologie*, vol. 11 (1951): 44–79.

Barish, Jonas. *The Anti-theatrical Prejudice*. Berkeley: University of California, 1980.

Barreto Xavier, Angela. *A Invenção de Goa*. Lisboa: Instituto de Ciências Sociais da Universidade de Lisboa, 2008.

Barros, Maria Cândida D.M. 'The Office of Lingua: A Portrait of the Religious Tupi Interpreter in Brazil in the Sixteenth Century'. *Itinerario*, vol. 25, no. 2 (2001): 110–40.

Bayly, Susan. *Saints, Goddesses and Kings: Muslims and Christians in South Indian Society*. Cambridge: Cambridge University Press, 1989.

Benassar, Bartolomé. 'Frontières religieuses entre Islam et chrètiente: l'expèrience vècue par les "renègats"'. In *Les frontières religieuses en Europe du xv au xvii siècle*, edited by Robert Sauzet, 71–8. Paris: Librairie Philosophiqie J. Vrin, 1992.

———. *The Spanish Character: Attitudes and Mentalities from the Sixteenth to the Nineteenth Century*, translated by Benjamin Keen. Berkeley: University of California Press, 1979.

Bernardes de Carvalho, Rita. 'A "Snapshot" of a Portuguese Community in Southeast Asia: The Bandel of Siam, 1684–86'. In *Portuguese and*

Luso-Asian Legacies in Southeast Asia, 1511–2011, edited by Laura Jarnagin, 44–66. Singapore: Institute for Southeast Asian Studies, 2012.

Besselaar, Jose van den. *António Vieira: Profecia e polêmica*. Rio de Janeiro: Editora da Universidade do Rio de Janeiro, 2002.

Béteille, André. *Caste, Class and Power*. Berkeley: University of California Press, 1971.

Bhabha, Homi. *The Location of Culture*. New York: Routledge, 2006 [1994].

Biddle, Stephen, Jeffrey Friedman, and Jacob Shapiro. 'Testing the Surge. Why Did Violence Decline in Iraq in 2007?' *International Security*, vol. 37, no. 1 (2012): 7–40.

Blackburn, Stuart. 'Corruption and Redemption: the Legend of Valluvar and Tamil Literary History'. *Modern Asian Studies*, vol. 34, no. 2 (May 2000): 449–82.

Bouwsma, William. 'The Two Faces of Humanism. Stoicism and Augustinianism in Renaissance Thought'. In *Itinerarium Italicum: The Profile of the Italian Renaissance in the Mirror of Its European Transformations*, edited by Paul Oskar Kristeller, Thomas A. Brady, and Heiko Augustinus Oberman, 3–60. Leiden: Brill, 1975.

Boxer, Charles. *The Christian Century in Japan, 1549–1650*. Lisbon: Carcanet, 1993.

———. *The Dutch Seaborne Empire*. London: Hutchinson, 1965.

———. 'Padre António Vieira S.J. and the Institution of the Brazil Company in 1649'. *Hispanic American Historical Review*, vol. 29, no. 4 (1949): 474–97.

Brown, C. Mackenzie. 'Purāṇa as Scripture: From Sound to Image of the Holy Word in the Hindu Tradition'. *History of Religions*, vol. 26, no. 1 (1986): 68–86.

Buarque de Holanda, Sérgio. *Visão de paraíso: os motivos edênicos no descobrimento e colonização do Brasil*. Rio de Janeiro: José Olympio, 1959.

Buber, Martin. *Good and Evil*. New York: Scribner, 1953.

Cabral, Evaldo Mello de. *O Negócio do Brasil. Portugal, os Países Baixos e o Nordeste (1641–1669)*. Lisboa: CNCDP, 2001 (2nd edition).

Cannell, Fenella. 'The Christianity of Anthropology'. *Journal of the Royal Anthropological Institute*, vol. 11, no. 2 (2005): 335–56.

Carneiro da Cunha, Manuela, ed. *História dos índios no Brasil*. São Paulo: Companhia das Letras, 1992.

———. 'Os Imagens de índios do Brasil: o século XVI'. In *América Latina: Palavra, literatura e cultura*, edited by Ana Pizarro, 151–72. Campinas: Editora da Unicamp, 1993.

———. *Os mortos e os outros: uma análise do sistema funerário e da noção de pessoa entre os índios Krahó*. São Paulo: Hucitec, 1978.

Carneiro da Cunha, Manuela and Eduardo Viveiros de Castro. 'Vingança e temporalidade: Os Tupinamba'. *Journal de la Societé des Américanistes* 171 (1985): 191–208.

Casale, Giancarlo. 'The Ottoman Administration of the Spice Trade in the Sixteenth-Century Red Sea and Persian Gulf'. *Journal of the Economic and Social history of the Orient*, vol. 49, no. 2 (2006): 170–98.

Castelnau L'Estoile, Charlotte de. *Les Ouvriers d'une vigne stérile: Les Jésuites et la conversion des Indiens au Brésil 1580–1620.* Paris: Centre Culturel Calouste Gulbenkian, 2000.

Castelnau-L'Estoile, Charlotte de and Carlos Alberto de Moura Ribeiro Zeron. '"Une mission glorieuse et profitable": réforme missionaire et économie sucrière dans la province Jésuite du Brésil au début du XVIIe siècle'. *Revue de synthèse*, vol. 4, nos 2–3 (1999): 335–58.

Castelnau-L'Estoile, Charlotte de, Marie-Lucie Copete, Aliocha Maldavsky, and Ines G. Županov, eds. *Missions d'Évangélisation et circulation des savoirs. XVI–XVIII siècle.* Madrid: Collection de la Casa de Velázquez, 2011.

Chakravarti, Ananya. 'In the Language of the Land: Indigenous Conversion in Jesuit Public Letters from Brazil and India'. *Journal of Early Modern History* 17 (2013): 505–24.

———. 'Invisible Cities: Natural and Social Space in Colonial Brazil'. In *Cities and the Circulation of Culture in the Atlantic World: From the Early Modern to Modernism*, edited by Leonard von Morzé. Palgrave, 2017.

Chatterjee, Partha. *The Nation and Its Fragments.* Princeton: Princeton University Press, 1993.

Clastres, Hélène. *The Land without Evil: Tupí-Guaraní Prophetism*, translated by Jacqueline Grenez Brovender. Urbana: University of Illinois, 1995.

Clendinnen, Inga. *Ambivalent Conquests: Maya and Spaniard in Yucatan, 1517–1570.* Cambridge: Cambridge University Press, 1989.

———. '"Fierce and Unnatural Cruelty": Cortés and the Conquest of Mexico'. *Representations*, vol. 33 (1991): 65–100

Clossey, Luke. *Salvation and Globaliztion in the Early Jesuit Missions.* Cambridge: Cambridge University Press, 2011.

Coates, Timothy. 'The Early Modern Portuguese Empire: A Commentary on Recent Studies'. *Sixteenth Century Journal*, vol. 37, no. 1 (2006): 83–90.

Cogley, Richard W. '"Some Other Kinde of Being and Condition": The Controversy in Mid-Seventeenth Century England over the Peopling of America'. *Journal of the History of Ideas*, vol. 68, no. 1 (2007): 35–56.

Cohen, Thomas. *The Fire of Tongues: António Vieira and the Missionary Church in Brazil and Portugal.* Stanford: Stanford University Press, 1998.

———. 'Millenarian Themes in the Writings of António Vieira'. *Luso-Brazilian Review*, vol. 28, no. 1 (Messianism and Millenarianism in the Luso-Brazilian World) (Summer 1991): 23–46.

Cohn, Bernard. *Colonialism and Its Forms of Knowledge*. Princeton: Princeton University Press, 1996.

Colley, Linda. 'Going Native, Telling Tales: Captivity, Collaboration and Empire'. *Past and Present*, vol. 168, no. 1 (2000): 170–93.

Collins, Steven. *Nirvana and Other Buddhist Felicities: Utopias of the Pali Imaginaire*. Cambridge: Cambridge University Press, 1998.

Costa, Leonor Freire. *O Transporte no Atlântico e a Companhia Geral do Comércio do Brasil (1580–1663)*. Lisboa: CNCDP, 2002.

Daher, Andrea. *A Oralidade Perdida. Ensaios de histôria das práticas letradas.* Rio de Janeiro: Editora Civilização Brasileira, 2012.

Davis, Richard H. *Lives of Indian Images*. New Delhi: Motilal Banarsidass, 1999.

Derrett, John Duncan Martin. *Essays in Classical and Modern Hindu Law*, vol. II. Leiden: Brill, 1977.

Dirks, Nicholas. *The Hollow Crown*. Cambridge: Cambridge University Press, 1987.

Disney, Anthony R. *Twilight of the Pepper Empire: Portuguese Trade in Southwest India in the Early Seventeenth Century*. Cambridge, MA: Harvard University Press, 1978.

Dominian, Helen G. *Apostle of Brazil: The Biography of Padre José de Anchieta, S.J., (1534–1597)*. New York: Exposition Press, 1958.

Doniger, Wendy. *Dreams, Illusions and Other Realities*. Chicago: University of Chicago Press, 1984.

———. 'The Origins of Heresy in Hindu Mythology'. *History of Religions*, vol. 10, no. 4 (1971): 271–333.

Dutra, Francis. 'The Vieira Family and the Order of Christ'. *Luso-Brazilian Review*, vol. 40, no. 1 (Special issue: António Vieira and the Luso-Brazilian Baroque) (2003): 17–31.

Eaton, Richard. *A Social History of the Deccan 1300–1761*. New Delhi: Cambridge University Press, 2005.

Eaton, Richard. *Sufis of Bijapur, 1300–1700*. Princeton: Princeton University Press, 1978.

Edmundson, George. 'The Dutch Power in Brazil, 1624–54: Part I—The Struggle for Bahia (1624–1627)'. *English Historical Review*, vol. 11, no. 42 (1896): 231–59.

Elliot, J.H. *The Old World and the New, 1492–1650*. Cambridge: Cambridge University Press, 1971.

Falcao, Nelson M. *Kristapurana: A Christian–Hindu Encounter*. Gujarat: Gujarat Sahitya Prakash, 2003.

Fausto, Carlos. 'Feasting on People: Eating Animals and Humans in Amazonia'. *Current Anthropology*, vol. 48, no. 4 (2007): 497–530.

———. 'Fragmentos de história e cultura Tupinambá'. In Carneiro da Cunha, *História dos Índios no Brasil*.

Fernandes, Florestan. *A função social da Guerra na sociedade Tupinambá*. São Paulo: Editôra da Universidade de São Paulo, 1970.

Fernández-Armesto, Felipe. *The Canary Islands after the Conquest: The Making of a Colonial Society in the Early Sixteenth Century*. Oxford: Oxford University Press, 1982.

Flores, Jorge Manuel. *Os Portugueses e o Mar de Ceilão: Trato, Diplomaci e Guerra (1498–1543)*. Lisbon: Edições Cosmos, 1998.

Franco, José Eduardo. 'A Companhia de Jesus e a Inquisição: afectos e desafectos entre duas instituições influentes (Séculos XVI–XVII)'. In *Actas do Congresso Internacional Atlântico de Antigo Regime (Espaço Atlântico de Antigo Regime: poderes e sociedades)*. Lisboa, 2005.

———. *O Mito de Portugal*. Lisboa: Editora Roma, 2000.

Franco, José Eduardo and Célia Cristina da Silva Tavares. *Jesuitas e Inquisição: Cumplicidades e Confrontações*. Rio de Janeiro: Editora da Universidade do Estado do Rio de Janeiro, 2007.

Freire, José Bessa Ribamar and Maria Carlota Rosa, eds. *Línguas gerais: Política linguística e catequese na América do Sul no período colonial*. Rio de Janeiro: Eduerj, 2003.

Freire Costa, Leonor. *O Transporte no Atlântico e a Companhia Geral do Comércio do Brasil (1580–1663)*. Lisboa: CNCDP, 2002.

Friedrich, Markus. 'Government and Information-Management in Early Modern Europe. The Case of the Society of Jesus (1540–1773)'. *Journal of Early Modern History*, vol. 12, no. 6 (2008): 539–63.

Funkenstein, Amos. *Perceptions of Jewish History*. Berkeley: University of California Press, 1993.

———. *Theology and the Scientific Imagination from the Middle Ages to the Seventeenth Century*. Princeton: Princeton University Press, 1986.

García-Arenal, Mercedes. 'Moriscos and Indians: A Comparative Approach'. In *The Middle East and Europe: Encounters and Exchanges*, edited by Geert Jan Van Gelder and Ed de Moor, 39–55. Amsterdam: Rodopi B. V. Editions, 1992.

Ginzburg, Carlo. *Wooden Eyes: Nine Reflections on Distance*, translated by Martin Ryle and Kate Soper. New York: Columbia University, 2001.

Girard, René. *Violence and the Sacred*, translated by Patrick Gregory. London: Continuum, 2005.

Grafton, Anthony. *New Worlds, Ancient Texts: The Power of Tradition and the Shock of Discovery*. Cambridge: Harvard University, 1992.

Graus, František. 'The Church and Its Critics'. In *Anticlericalism in Late Medieval and Early Modern Europe*, edited by Peter A. Dykema and Heiko A. Oberman, 65–81. Leiden: Brill, 1993.

Green, Nile. 'Oral Competition Narratives of Muslim and Hindu Saints in the Deccan'. *Asian Folklore Studies*, vol. 63 (2004): 221–42.

Hanks, William F. *Converting Words: Maya in the Age of the Cross*. Berkeley: University of California Press, 2010.

Hanson, Carl. *Economy and Society in Baroque Portugal*. Minneapolis: University of Minnesota Press, 1981.

Heras, Henry. *The Aravidu Dynasty of Vijayanagara*. Bombay: Indian Historical Research Institute, St. Xavier's College, 1927.

———. 'Decay of the Portuguese Power in India'. *Journal of the Historical Society of Bombay*, vol. 1 (March 1928): 26.

Herdt, Jennifer A. *Putting on Virtue: The Legacy of the Splendid Vices*. Chicago: University of Chicago Press, 2008.

Hess, Andrew C. *The Forgotten Frontier: A History of the Sixteenth Century Ibero-African Frontier*. Chicago: University of Chicago Press, 1978.

Eng Seng Ho, 'Empire through Diasporic Eyes: A View from the Other Boat'. *Comparative Studies of Society and History*, vol. 46, no. 2: 210–46.

Hopkins, A.G. 'Back to the Future: From National History to Imperial History'. *Past and Present*, no. 164 (August 1999): 198–243.

Hosne, Ana Carolina. *The Jesuit Missions to China and Peru, 1570–1610: Expectations and Appraisals of Expansionism*. London and New York: Routledge, 2001.

Hugh-Jones, Stephen. 'Yesterday's Luxuries, Tomorrow's Necessities: Business and Barter in Northwest Amazon'. In *Barter, Exchange and Value*, edited by C. Humphreys and S. Hugh-Jones, 42–74. Cambridge: Cambridge University Press, 1992.

Imbruglia, Girolamo. 'Ideali di civilizzazione: la Compagnia di Gesù e le missioni (1550–1600)'. In *Il Nuovo Mondo nella Coscienza Italiana e Tedesca*, edited by Adriano Prosperi and Wolfgang Reinhard. Bologna: Società editrice il Mulino, 1992.

Immerman, Richard H. *Empire for Liberty: A History of American Imperialism from Benjamin Franklin to Paul Wolfowitz*. Princeton, N.J.: Princeton University Press, 2009.

Israel, Jonathan I. *Diasporas within a Diaspora: Jews, Crypto-Jews and the World Maritime Empires, 1540–1740*. Leiden: Brill, 2002.

———. *The Dutch Republic and the Hispanic World*. Oxford: University of Oxford Press, 1982.

Iyengar, Radha and Jonathan Monten. 'Is There an "Emboldment" Effect? Evidence from the Insurgency in Iraq'. *National Bureau of Economic Research Working Paper Series*, Working Paper No. 13839, 2008.

Jordán, Maria. 'The Empire of the Future and the Chosen People: Father António Vieira and the Prophetic Tradition in the Hispanic World'. *Luso-Brazilian Review*, vol. 40, no. 1 (special issue: António Vieira and the Luso-Brazilian Baroque) (Summer 2003): 45–57.

Joseph, Gilbert. 'On the Trail of Latin American Bandits: A Reexamination of Peasant Resistance', *Latin American Research Review*, vol. 25 (1990): 7–53.

Karashima, Noboru. *A Concordance of Nayakas: The Vijayanagara Inscriptions in South India*. New Delhi: Oxford University Press, 2002.

Klor de Alva, J. Jorge. 'Colonialism and Postcolonialism as (Latin) American Mirages'. *Colonial Latin American Review*, vol. 1, no. 1–2 (1992): 3–23.

Kosambi, Damodar Dharmanand. *An Introduction to the Study of Indian History*. Bombay: Popular Book Depot, 1952.

———. *Myth and Reality*. Mumbai: Popular Prakashan, 2005 [1962]

Lafaye, Jacques. *Quetzalcoatl and Guadalupe: The Formation of Mexican National Consciousness, 1531–1813*, translated by Benjamin Keen. Chicago: University of Chicago, 1976.

Langfur, Hal. 'Recovering Brazil's Indigenous Pasts'. In *Native Brazil: Beyond the Convert and the Cannibal, 1500–1900*, edited by Hal Langfur. Albuquerque: University of New Mexico Press, 2014.

Lee, Kittiya. 'Conversing in Colony: The Brasílica and the Vulgar in Portuguese America, 1500–1579'. PhD thesis, Johns Hopkins University, 2005.

Leite, Serafim. *Breve itinerário para uma biografia do P. Manuel da Nóbrega, fundador da Província do Brasil e da cidade de São Paulo, 1517–1570*. Lisboa: Edições Brotéria, 1955.

———. *História da Companhia de Jesus no Brasil*. Rio de Janeiro: Civilização Brasileira, 1938–50.

———. *Nóbrega e a fundação de São Paulo*. Lisboa: Instituto de Intercâmbio Luso Brasileiro, 1953.

Lestringant, Frank. *Mapping the Renaissance World, The Geographical Imagination in the Age of Discovery*, translated by David Fausett. Berkeley: University of California, 1994.

Claude Lévi-Strauss. *The Story of Lynx*, translated by Catherine Tihanyi. Chicago: University of Chicago Press, 1995.

Lyons, John. *Exemplum: The Rhetoric of Example in Early Modern France and Italy*. Princeton: Princeton University Press, 1989.

MacCormack, Sabine. '"The Heart Has Its Reasons": Predicaments of Missionary Christianity in Early Colonial Peru'. *Hispanic American Historical Review*, vol. 65, no. 3 (1985): 447–51.

Madeira-Santos, Catarina. *Goa é a Chave de toda a India: Perfil politico da capital do Estado da India, 1505–1570*. Lisbon: CNCDP, 1999.

Magalhaes, Joaquim Romero. 'Em busca dos "tempos" da inquisição (1573–1615)'. *Revista da história das ideias*, vol. 9 (1987): 1–228.

Mallon, Florencia. 'The Promise and Dilemma of Subaltern Studies: Perspectives from Latin American History', *American Historical Review*, vol. 99, no. 5 (1994): 1491–515.

Malshe, S.G. Phā. *Sṭiphansa āṇi tyācẽ Kristapurāṇa*. Mumbai: Marāṭhī Sanshodan Mandal, 1965.

———. '*Stīphansacyā Kristapurāṇācā Bhāśika āṇi Vāṅmayīna Abhyāsa*'. PhD thesis no. 2689, Jawaharlal Nehru Memorial Library, Kalina Campus, University of Bombay, 1961.

Mamdani, Mahmood. *When Does a Settler Become a Native? Reflections on the Colonial Roots of Citizenship in Equatorial and South Africa*. Cape Town: University of Cape Town, 1998.

Marchant, Alexander. *From Barter to Slavery*. Baltimore, MD: Johns Hopkins University, 1942.

Marcocci, Giuseppe. 'La coscienza di un impero: Politica, teologia e diritto nel Portogallo del Cinquecento'. PhD thesis, Scuola Normale Superiore, Pisa, 2007–8.

———. *I custodi dell'ortodossia. Inquisizione e Chiesa nel Portogallo del Cinquecento*. Roma: Edizioni di Storia e Letteratura, 2004.

———. 'A Fé de um Império: a Inquisição no mundo português de quinhentos'. *Revista de História*, São Paulo, no. 164 (January/June 2011): 65–100.

———. *L'Invenzione di un impero: Politica e cultura nel mondo portoghese, 1450–1600*. Roma: Carocci, 2011.

———. 'Towards a History of the Portuguese Inquisition Trends in Modern Historiography (1974–2009)'. *Revue de l'histoire des religions*, vol. 227, no. 3 (2010): 355–93.

Margadent, Jo Burr. 'Introduction: Constructing Selves in Historical Perspective'. In *The New Biography: Performing Femininity in Nineteenth Century France*, edited by Jo Burr Margadant. Berkeley: University of California Press, 2000.

Masuzawa, Tomoko. *The Invention of World Religion: Or, How European Universalism Was Preserved in the Language of Pluralism*. Chicago: University of Chicago Press, 2005.

McGinness, Anne. 'Transforming Indigenous Vice to Virtue on the Stages of Colonial Brazil: An Analysis of Jesuit Theater and the Plays of José de Anchieta'. *Lusitania Sacra*, vol. 23 (2011): 41–57.

Mello e Souza, Laura de. *Inferno Atlântico*. São Paulo: Companhia das Letras, 1993.

Mercês de Melo, Carlos, S.J. *The Recruitment and Formation of the Native Clergy of India (16th–19th Century). An Historico-Canonical Study*. Lisboa: Agência Geral do Ultramar, Divisão de Publicações e Biblioteca, 1955.

Mesquita, Roque. *Madhva's Unknown Literary Sources: Some Observations*. New Delhi: Aditi Prakashan, 2000.

Metcalf, Alida C. *Go-betweens and the Colonization of Brazil, 1500–1600.* Austin: University of Texas Press, 2005.

———. 'The Entradas of Bahia of the Sixteenth Century'. *The Americas,* vol. 61, no. 3 (2005): 373–400.

Métraux, Alfred. 1928. *A religião dos Tupinambás e suas relações com a das demais tribus Tupi-Guaranis,* translated by E. Pinto. São Paulo: Companhia Editôra Nacional, 1979.

Momigliano, Arnaldo. *The Classical Foundations of Modern Historiography.* Berkeley: University of California Press, 1990.

———. 'The Place of Herodotus in the History of Historiography'. *History,* vol. 43 (1958): 1–13.

Monteiro, John Manuel. 'The Crises and Transformations of Invaded Societies: Coastal Brazil in the Sixteenth Century'. In *The Cambridge History of the Native Peoples of the Americas,* vol. III, *South America,* Part I, edited by Stuart Schwarz and Frank Solomon. Cambridge: Cambridge University, 1999: 973–1024.

———. *Negros da terra: Índios e bandeirantes nas origens de São Paulo.* São Paulo: Companhia das Letras, 1994.

Moog, Clodomir Vianna. *Bandeirantes e pioneiros.* Porto Alegre: Globo, 1973 (10th edition).

Richard Morse. *The Bandeirantes: The Historical Role of the Brazilian Pathfinders.* New York: Alfred A. Knopf, 1965.

Moya, José C. 'A Continent of Immigrants: Postcolonial Shifts in the Western Hemisphere'. *Hispanic American Historical Review,* vol. 86, no. 1 (2006): 1–28.

Nasaw, David. 'Introduction'. *American Historical Review* (Roundtable: Historians and Biography), vol. 114, no. 3 (2009): 573–8.

De Nicólas, Antonio T. *Powers of Imagining: Ignatius de Loyola: A Philosophical Hermeneutic of Imagining through the Collected Works of Ignatius de Loyola.* Albany: State University of New York Press, 1986.

Novetzke, Christian. 'The Brahmin Double: The Brahminical Construction of Anti-Brahminism and Anti-Caste Sentiment in the Religious Cultures of Precolonial Maharashtra'. *South Asian History and Culture,* vol. 2, no. 2 (2011): 242–3.

Novetzke, Christian. *Religion and Public Memory: A Cultural History of Saint Namdev in India.* New York: Columbia University, 2008.

O'Malley, John. *The First Jesuits.* Cambridge, MA: Harvard University Press, 1993.

Oakdale, Suzanne. 'The Commensality of "Contact", "Pacification" and Inter-Ethnic Relations in the Amazon: Kayabi Autobiographical Perspectives'. *Journal of the Royal Anthropological Institute,* vol. 14, no. 4 (2008): 791–807.

Obeyesekere, Gananath. *The Apotheosis of Captain Cook: European Mythmaking in the Pacific*. Princeton: Princeton University Press, 1992.

Oliveira e Costa, João Paulo. 'Os Portugueses e a cristandade siro-malabar (1498–1530)'. *Studia*, no. 52 (1994): 121–78.

Pagden, Anthony. *European Encounters with the New World*. New Haven: Yale University Press, 1994.

———. *The Fall of Natural Man: The American Indian and the Origins of Comparative Ethnology*. Cambridge: Cambridge University Press, 1982.

———. *Lords of All the World: Ideologies of Empire in Spain, Britain and France, c. 1500–1800*. New Haven: Yale University Press, 1995.

Paiva, José Pedro. 'A Igreja e o poder'. In *História religiosa de Portugal*, vol. 2, edited by Carlos Moreira Azevedo, 135–85. Lisboa: Círculo dos Leitores, 2000.

———. 'Inquisição e visitas pastorais. Dois mecanismo complementares de controle social?' *Revista de História das Ideias*, vol. 10 (1989): 85–102.

Pau-Rubíes, Joan. 'Theology, Ethnography and the Historicization of Idolatry'. *Journal of the History of Ideas*, vol. 67, no. 4 (2006): 571–96.

———. *Travel and Ethnology in the Renaissance: South India through European Eyes, 1250–1625*. Cambridge: Cambridge University Press, 2002.

Pearson, M.N. *Merchants and Rulers in Gujarat*. Berkeley: University of California Press, 1974.

Pigman, G.W. 'Versions of Imitation in the Renaissance'. *Renaissance Quarterly*, vol. 33, no. 1 (1980): 1–32.

Pompa, Cristina. *Religião como tradução: missionários, Tupi e Tapuia no Brasil colonial*. Bauru: EDUSC, 2003.

Pratt, Mary Louise. *Imperial Eyes: Travel Writing and Transculturation*. London: Routledge, 1992.

———. 'Arts of the Contact Zone'. *Profession* (1991): 33–40.

Prodi, Paolo. *Il Sovrano Pontifice: un corpo e due anime: la monarchia papale nella prima età moderna*. Bologna: Il Mulino, 1982.

Prosperi, Adriano. '*Otras Indias*: Missionari della Contra-Riforma tra contadini e selvaggi'. In *Scienze, credenze, occulte, livelli di cultura, Atti del Convegno Internazionale di Studi, Florence, 1980*, 205–34. Florence: Olschki, 1982.

Quijano, Aníbal. 'Colonialidad y Modernidad/Racionalidad'. *Perú Indígena*, vol. 13, no. 29 (1992): 11–20.

Ramos, Manuel João. *Essays in Christian Mythology: The Metamorphosis of Prester John*. Lanham, MD: University Press of America, 2006.

Randles, W.G.L. 'Peuples sauvages' et 'états despotiques': la pertinence, au XVIe siècle, de la grille aristotélicienne pour classes les nouvelles societies révélées par les Découvertes au Brésil, en Afrique et an Asie'. *Mare Liberum*, vol. 3 (1991): 299–307.

Rao, Velcheru Narayana. 'Purāṇa as Brahminic Ideology'. In *Purāṇa Perrenis: Reciprocity and Transformation in Hindu and Jaina Texts*, edited by Wendy Doniger. Albany: SUNY Press, 1993.

Rao, Velcheru Narayana, David Shulman, and Sanjay Subrahmanyam. *Symbols of Substance*. New Delhi: Oxford University Press, 1992.

Ratzinger, Joseph. 'The Spiritual Roots of Europe: Yesterday, Today and Tomorrow'. In *Without Roots: The West, Relativism, Christianity, Islam*, edited by Joesph Ratzinger and Marcello Pera (New York, NY: Basic Books, 2007): 51–80.

Révah, Israël-Savator. 'Jean Cointa, sieur des Boulez, execute par l'Inquisition de Goa en 1572'. *Annali Sezione Romana II* (2 July 1961): 71–5.

———. 'Les Jésuites Portugais contre l'Inquisition: la campagne pour la fondation de la Compagnie Génerale du Commerce du Brésil'. *Études Portugaises* (1975): 155–83.

Revel, Jacques, ed. *Jeux d'échelles. La micro-analyse à l'expérience*. Paris: Gallimard, 1998.

Robinson, Rowena. 'Cuncolim: Weaving a Tale of Resistance'. *Economic and Political Weekly*, vol. 32, no. 7 (1997): 334–40.

Roche, Patrick. *Fishermen of the Coromandel*. New Delhi: Manohar, 1984.

Roosevelt, Anna C. 'The Rise and Fall of the Amazon Chiefdoms'. *L'Homme*, nos 126/128 (1993): 255–83.

Sahlins, Marshall. *How 'Natives' Think: About Captain Cook, For Example*. Chicago: University of Chicago Press, 1995.

Said, Edward. *Orientalism*. New York: Pantheon, 1978.

Saldanha, Antonio Vasconcelos. *Iustum Imperium dos tratados como Fundamento do Império dos Portugueses no Oriente*. Lisboa: Fundação Oriente, 1997.

Saldanha, M.J. Gabriel de. *História de Goa: Política*. New Delhi: Asian Educational Services, 1979.

Sanderson, Alexis. 'Purity and Power among the Brāhmans of Kashmir'. In *The Category of the Person*, edited by Steven Collins and Michael Carrithers. Cambridge: Cambridge University Press, 1985.

Santos-Granero, Fernando. 'Of Fear and Friendship: Amazonian Sociality beyond Kinship and Affinity'. *Journal of the Royal Anthropological Institute*, vol. 13, no. 1 (2007): 1–18.

Schorsch, Ismael. 'From Messianism to Realpolitik: Menasseh Ben Israel and the Readmission of the Jews to England'. *Proceedings of the American Academy for Jewish Research*, vol. 45 (1978): 187–208.

Schurhammer, Georg, S.J. *Francis Xavier: His Life, His Times*, translated by M. Joseph Costelloe, S.J. Rome: Jesuit Historical Institute, 1976–82.

Schurhammer, Georg. *Gesamelte Studien*, vol. II, *Orientalia*. Rome: Institutum Historicum SI, 1963.

———. 'Thomas Stephens'. *Orientalia*, Lisboa: Centro de Estudos Históricos Ultramarinos, 1963.

———. 'Unpublished Manuscripts of Fr. Fernão de Queiroz, S.J.'. *Bulletin of the School of Oriental Studies*, vol. 5, no. 2 (1929): 209–27.

Schwartz, Stuart, ed. *Implicit Understandings: Observing, Reporting, and Reflecting on the Encounters between Europeans and Other Peoples in the Early Modern Era*. Cambridge: Cambridge University Press, 1994.

———. 'Indian Labor and New World Plantations: European Demands and Indian Responses in Northeastern Brazil'. *American Historical Review*, vol. 83, no. 1 (February 1978): 43–79.

———. 'The Voyage of the Vassals: Royal Power, Noble Obligations, and Merchant Capital before the Portuguese Restoration of Independence, 1624–1640'. *American Historical Review*, vol. 96, no. 3 (June 1991): 735–62.

Seijas, Tatiana. *Asian Slaves in Colonial Mexico: From Chinos to Indios*. New York: Cambridge University Press, 2014.

Siauve, Suzanne. *Le Doctrine de Madhva*. Pondicherry: Institut français d'indologie, 1968.

de Silva, Chandra Richard. 'The Portuguese East India Company, 1628–1633'. *Luso-Brazilian Review*, vol. 11, no. 2 (1974): 152–205.

Sivaraman, K. *Śaivism in Philosophical Perspective: A Study of the Formative Concepts, Problems and Methods of Śaiva Siddhānta*. Delhi: Motilal Banarsidass, 2001 (reprint).

Skyhawk, Hugh van. '"... In This Bushy Land of Salsette ...": Father Thomas Stephens and the Kristapurāṇa'. In *Studies in Early Modern Indo-Aryan Languages, Literature, and Culture*, edited by Alan W. Entwistle, Carol Salomon, Heidi Pauwels, and Michael C. Shapiro, 363–78. New Delhi: Manohar, 1999.

Smith, David Grant. 'The Mercantile Class of Portugal and Brazil in the Seventeenth Century: A Socio-Economic Study of the Merchants of Lisbon and Bahia, 1620–1690'. PhD thesis, University of Texas, 1975.

———. 'Old Christian Merchants and the Foundation of the Brazil Company', *Hispanic American Historical Review*, vol. 2 (1974): 233–59.

Snyder, Jon R. *Dissimulation and the Culture of Secrecy in Early Modern Europe*. Berkeley: University of California, 2009.

Somerville, Charles. *The Secularization of Early Modern England: From Religious Culture to Religious Faith*. New York: Oxford University Press, 1992.

Sorge, Giuseppe. *Matteo de Castro (1594–1677) profilo di una figura emblematica del conflitto giurisdizionale tra Goa e Roma nel secolo 17*. Bologna: CLUEB, 1986.

Sousa Pinto, Paulo Jorge. 'Purse and Sword: D. Henrique *Bendahara* and Portuguese Melaka in the Late 16th Century'. In *Sinners and Saints: The*

Successors of Vasco da Gama, edited by Sanjay Subrahmanyam, 75–93. New Delhi: Oxford University Press, 1995.

Stein, Burton. *Vijayanagara*. Cambridge: Cambridge University Press, 1989.

Stern, Steve J. 'Paradigms of Conquest: History, Historiography, and Politics'. *Journal of Latin American Studies* 24 [quincentenary supplement] (1992): 1–34.

Stoker, Valerie. 'Conceiving the Canon in Dvaita Vedānta: Madhva's Doctrine of "All Sacred Lore"'. *Numen*, vol. 51, no. 1 (2004): 47–77.

Strathern, Alan. 'Re-Reading Queiros: Some Neglected Aspects of the Conquista'. *Sri Lanka Journal of the Humanities*, vol. 26 (2000): 1–28.

Studnicki-Gizbert, Daviken. *A Nation upon the Ocean Sea: Portugal's Atlanta: Diaspora and the Crues of the Spanish Empire, 1492–1640*. Oxford: Oxford University Press, 2007.

Sturm, Fred Gillette. '"Estes Têm Alma como Nós?": Manuel da Nóbrega's View of the Brazilian Indios'. In *Empire in Transition: The Portuguese World in the Time of Camões*, edited by Alfred Hower and Richard A. Preto-Rodas, 72–82. Gainesville: University of Florida, 1985.

Subrahmanyam, Sanjay. 'Dom Frei Aleixo de Meneses (1559–1517) et l'échec des tentative d'indigénisation du christianisme en Inde'. *Archives des sciences socials des religions*, vol. 103, no. 103 (1998): 21–42.

———. *Explorations in Connected History*. New Delhi: Oxford University Press, 2005.

———. 'Holding the World in Balance: The Connected Histories of the Iberian Overseas Empires, 1500–1640'. *American Historical Review*, vol. 112, no. 5 (2007): 1370–2.

———. 'Making India Gama: The Project of Dom Aires da Gama (1519) and Its Meaning'. *Mare Liberum*, vol. 16 (1998): 33–55.

———. 'Noble Harvest from the Sea: Managing the Pearl Fishery of Mannar, 1500–1925'. In *Institutions and Economic Change in South Asia*, edited by Burton Stein and Sanjay Subrahmanyam, 134–72. New Delhi: Oxford University Press, 1996.

———. *Penumbral Visions: Making Polities in Early Modern South India*. Ann Arbor: University of Michigan Press, 2001.

———. *The Political Economy of Commerce: Southern India, 1500–1650*. Cambridge: Cambridge University, 2002.

———. *The Portuguese Empire in Asia, 1500–1700: A Political and Economic History*. New York: Longman, 1993.

———. 'Profiles in Transition: Of Adventurers and Administrators in South India, 1750–1810'. In *Land, Politics and Trade in South Asia*, edited by Sanjay Subrahmanyam. New Delhi: Oxford University Press, 2004.

———. 'The Tail Wags the Dog or Some Aspects of the External Relations of the Estado da India, 1570–1600'. *Moyen Orient et Ocean Indien* 5 (1988): 131–60.

———. 'On World Historians in the Sixteenth Century'. *Representations,* vol. 91, no. 1 (2005): 26–57.

Taussig, Michael. *Mimesis and Alterity*. New York: Routledge, 1993.

Tavares, Célia Cristina. *Jesuítas e Inquisidores em Goa: a cristandade insular (1540–1682)*. Lisboa: Roma Editora, 2004.

Tavárez, David. 'Naming the Trinity: From Ideologies of Translation to Dialectics of Reception in Colonial Nahua Texts, 1547–1771'. *Colonial Latin American Review*, vol. 9, no. 1, (2000): 21–47.

Taylor, Barbara. 'Separations of Soul: Solitude, Biography, History'. *American Historical Review* (Roundtable: Historians and Biography), vol. 114, no. 3 (2009): 640–51.

Taylor, Charles. *A Secular Age*. Cambridge, MA: Harvard University Press, 2007.

Thomaz, Luís Filipe. 'A carta que mandaram os Padres da Índia da China e da Magna China-um relato siriaco da chegada dos Portugueses ao Malabar'. *Revista da Universidade de Coimbra*, vol. 36 (1991): 119–81.

———. *De Ceuta a Timor.* Linda a Velha, Portugal: DIFEL, 1994.

———. 'Portuguese Control on the Arabian Sea and the Bay of Bengal—A Comparative Study'. In *Commerce and Culture in the Bay of Bengal*, edited by Om Prakash and Denys Lombard, 138–43. New Delhi, 1999.

Todorov, Tzvetan. *The Conquest of America*. New York: Harper Collins, 1982.

Trivellato, Francesca. *The Familiarity of Strangers: The Sephardic Diaspora, Livorno and Cross-Cultural Trade in the Early Modern Period*. New Haven: Yale University Press, 2009.

Tucci Carneiro, Maria Luiza. *Preconceito Racial em Portugal e Brasil Colônia. Os Cristãos-Novos e o Mito da Pureza do Sangue*. São Paulo: Perspectiva, 1983.

Üçerler, Antoni J, S.J. 'Alessandro Valignano: Man, Missionary, and Writer'. *Renaissance Studies*, vol. 17, no. 3 (2003): 337–66.

Vainfas, Ronaldo. *A Heresia dos Índios: catolicismo e rebeldia no Brasil colonial.* São Paulo: Companhia das Letras, 1995.

———. *Traição. Um jesuíta a serviço do Brasil holandês processado pela Inquisição*. São Paulo: Companhia das Letras, 2008.

Veluthat, Kesavan. *The Early Medieval in South India*. New Delhi: Oxford University Press, 2001.

Ventura, Ricardo. 'Conversão e Conversabilidade. Discursos da missão e do gentio na documentação do Padroado Português do Oriente (séculos XVI e XVII)'. PhD thesis, Faculdade de Letras da Universidade da Lisboa, July 2011.

Viegas, Susana. 'Ethnography and Public Categories: The Making of Compatible Agendas in Contemporary Anthropological Practices'. *Etnográfica*, vol. 14, no. 1 (2010): 135–58.

Vilaça, Aparecida. 'Chronically Unstable Bodies: Reflections on Amazonian Corporalities'. *Journal of the Royal Anthropological Institute*, vol. 11 (2005): 445–64.

———. 'Conversão, predação e perspectiva'. *Mana*, vol. 14, no. 1 (2008): 173–204.

———. 'Cristãos sem fé: alguns aspectos da conversão dos Wari'. *Mana*, vol. 2, no. 1 (1996): 109–37.

Viveiros de Castro, Eduardo. *Araweté: os deuses canibais*. Jorge Zahar Editor, 1986.

———. *From the Enemy's Point of View: Humanity and Divinity in an Amazonian Society*, translated by Catherine Howard. Chicago: University of Chicago, 1992.

———. 'Exchanging Perspectives: The Transformation of Objects in Subjects in Amerindian Ontologies'. *Common Knowledge*, vol. 10, no. 3 (2004): 463–484.

———. *A inconstância da alma selvagem e outros ensaios de antropologia*. São Paulo: Cosac & Naify, 2002.

Wachtel, Nathan. 'The "Marrano" Mercantilist Theory of Duarte Gomes Solis'. *Jewish Quarterly Review*, vol. 101, no. 2 (2011): 164–88.

Wilde, Guillermo. *Religión y poder en las misiones de Guaraníes*. Buenos Aires: Editorial SB, 2009.

Winius, G.D. 'Millenarianism and Empire: Portugese Asian Decline and the "Crise de Conscience" of the Missionaries'. *Itinerario*, vol. 11, no. 2 (1987): 37–51.

Wolf, Lucien. *Menasseh Ben Israel's Mission to Oliver Cromwell*. London: Macmillan and Company, 1901.

Wolfe, Patrick. *Settler Colonialism and the Transformation of Anthropology: The Politics and Poetics of an Ethnographic Event*. London: Cassell, 1999.

Young, Richard F. 'Francis Xavier in the Perspective of the Shaivite Brahmins of Tirucendur Temple'. In *Hindu–Christian Dialogue: Perspectives and Encounters*, edited by Harold G. Coward. Maryknoll: Orbis Books, 1990.

Zagorin, Perez. *Ways of Lying: Dissimulation, Persecution and Conformity in Early Modern Europe*. Cambridge: Harvard University Press, 1990.

Županov, Ines G. *Disputed Mission: Jesuit Experiments and Brahmanical Knowledge in Seventeenth-Century India*. New Delhi: Oxford University Press, 1999.

———. 'Goan Brahmans in the Land of Promise: Missionaries, Spies and Gentiles in Seventeenth- and Eighteenth-Century Sri Lanka'. In

Re-exploring the Links: History and Constructed Histories between Portugal and Sri Lanka, edited by Jorge Manuel Flores, 171–210. Wiesbaden: Otto Harrassowitz, 2007.

———. *Missionary Tropics: The Catholic Frontier in India (16th–17th Centuries)*. Ann Arbor: University of Michigan Press, 2005.

———. '"One Civility, but Multiple Religions": Jesuit Mission among St. Thomas Christians in India (16th–17th Centuries)'. *Journal of Early Modern History*, vol. 9, nos 3–4, (2005): 284–325.

———. 'Prosélytisme et pluralisme religieux: Deux expériences missionnaires en Inde aux XVIe et XVIIe siècles'. *Archives de sciences sociales des religions*, 39e Année, no. 87 (1994): 35–56.

Zvelebil, Kamil. *The Smile of Murugan on Tamil Literature of South India*. Leiden: Brill, 1975.

INDEX

accommodatio, practice of 7, 9–13, 17, 23, 177, 179, 208, 226–7, 259–60, 263–4; experiments in 89; in missionary praxis 131
Acosta, José 192, 225, 287
African slaves 50, 88, 158, 239; importation of 50
Aimbiré (chief) 155–7, 171–5
Aimoré 75–6
Akbar, Mughal emperor 51, 187
Albuquerque, Afonso de 44–5
aldeias 23, 92–3, 129–30, 159–62, 164–6, 168, 171–2, 175–7, 224
Alvarez, Gonçalo 119–21, 124–7, 130–1, 268
Amazonia 36, 50
Amerindians 2, 23, 109–10, 119–31, 159–60, 225, 248–9, 287; disposition of 136; occupation of 39; perspectivalism of 109, 112
Añanga 137, 164, 165, 172
Anchieta, José de 6, 23–4, 139–59, 164–5, 167–71, 173–7, 179, 199, 224–5, 227, 319; career in Brazil 158; poems of 175; works of 176
Angola 243, 251, 295, 300, 305
Añhangaçu 162–4, 166
Aquaviva, Rudolfo Fr. Gen. 186, 200
Aranha, Francisco Br. 122, 151, 186
ascetic(s) 76, 253, 261. See also *sannyāsi*
Augustine, Saint 9, 82, 118, 122–7, 129, 264; anthropology of 96, 123–4, 126, 128, 226
Azevedo, Inácio de 169, 234
Azpilcueta Navarro, Martín de 74–5, 87

Bandarra, Gonçalo Eanes 250–1, 281
baptism 42, 63–4, 73, 108, 116, 120, 148, 221, 256–7, 268–9, 272
Bardez 182n16, 183, 185
Barros, João de 43, 104
Barzaeus, Gaspar 117–18, 130
Basto, Pedro de 233, 238, 241–3, 252–3, 257, 263, 282, 285, 287–9, 300
Benedict XVI 1–5, 317, 319
Bergoglio, Jorge. *See* Francis, Pope
Bernard (brahmin convert) 187–9
Berno, Petro 182, 186, 188
Bijāpur 183–4, 273–4
Book of Wisdom 207n104, 210

brahmins 85, 95–106, 113–15, 129, 186, 202–6, 208, 211–14, 216–17, 258–64, 271–2; kinds of 100; and path to salvation 97; as priest 13; Xavier on 261
Brazil 15, 21, 39, 42, 72, 83; accident in 240; Church in 52; indigenous inhabitants of 35
Bush, George W. 315–17

Cabral, Francisco 43, 193, 195
Cabral, Pedro Álvares 33, 34–5, 42–3, 59
Cabral, Francisco 193, 195–6, 198
Caetano, Cardinal 87, 88n128
Caminha, Pero Vaz de 34–9, 42, 120
cannibalism 89, 92, 113, 128, 130, 137–8, 163–4, 176–7, 226; and Bishop Sardinha 92, 128–9, 176; Cururupeba and 174; Tupí ritual 137–8, 177
Cape of Good Hope 26, 190, 233
Caramuru, Diogo Álvares 73
Carijós 75–7, 84, 88, 148
Castilians 125, 148, 167
catechism 73, 79, 105, 142, 145, 155, 198–9, 203–6, 268, 285; in Kōṅkaṇī 201, 201n88; in Tamil 104, 264n98, 276, 277; in TupÍ 81
catechumens 110, 143–7, 196–7, 257, 269, 306
Catholic: church 8; education 180–5; evangelism 6, 52, 280; faith 89, 130, 182, 291; Rome as empire 5
Catholicism 4, 25, 92, 140, 282, 289, 312, 321; as identity of Portugal 308

Christianity 2–5, 17, 59, 72, 116, 144–5, 166, 198, 200, 221, 256; civility in 91, 135, 142, 156, 168, 176; conversion in 60, 64, 95, 106, 125; creator-God in 213; devil in 137, 159, 165, 172; faith in 43, 89, 95, 113, 121, 162, 185, 262; God in 9, 82, 100, 107, 110–11, 142, 163, 215; indigenous adoption of 4; knowledge in 98, 112, 200–1, 204–6, 208, 221, 224; spread of 3; virtue in 265
Christians 30, 75–9, 89, 115–16, 150–3, 193–4, 206, 255–6, 258–60, 292–3, 295–6, 307
church: and empire 4–5, 249; and European identity 5; institutional infrastructure of 52; land for 195, 258; built by Nāyaka officials 258
Coimbra 57, 90, 141, 149, 176, 257, 287
colonization 43, 49, 246
Columbus, Christopher 55
Congregation of the Propaganda Fide 270–1, 274, 276, 299, 303, 312
confessions 87, 107, 127, 199, 234, 264
conversion(s) 56–9, 93, 95–8, 102–4, 112–14, 116, 118–20, 127–31, 184–5, 187–8, 268–9; of Brazil 139; ostracism over 268; in Sathyamangalam 269
Correia, Pero 84, 148, 170
corsair 48, 169, 170, 296
cosmology 9, 21, 38, 41–2, 98, 108–9, 112–13, 116, 165
Costa, Baltasar da 6, 22, 24–5, 231–2, 257–8, 280, 288, 298, 300–2; in Madurai mission 232. See also *paṇṭāram*
crusaders 145, 148, 151
Cunha, Nuno da 183, 306

d'Évreux, Yves 135–6
deities 45, 62, 81, 211, 213–15, 217

demon(s) 75–6, 100, 105, 111, 115, 137, 159–60, 162–5, 171–3
Devchārs 211–13, 215–17
Devil 105, 113, 137, 159–60, 162, 163, 164, 165–7, 172, 215; Xavier's on 113; worship of 105
Discurso sobre a vinda de Jesu Christo (Discourse on the Coming of Jesus Christ) 180, 202–23; *Adi Puranna* as part of 205–7
Diu 44, 60
Dutch 5, 24, 190–1, 236–9, 241, 243–5, 274, 292–3, 298, 300, 309; assaults of 237, 239, 274, 288
dvaita-vādin (dualist) 103–44

Eanes, Cosme 59, 85
Eknāth 201, 219, 222
El Dorado 34, 48
Esperanças de Portugal 250, 282, 287
Estado da Índia 25, 44–5, 48, 50, 52, 179, 190, 233, 274–5, 278, 299–300
Evangelical Church 5, 7, 319
evangelization 4–7, 9, 23, 33, 58, 62, 91, 121, 152, 183, 269; in Goa 47

Fernandes, Gonçalo 253–4, 261–2, 301–2
Fernandes, Manuel 301–2, 306–7
Francis, Pope 317–21

Gama, Vasco da 26, 28, 34, 43, 55, 59
gentiles 34–5, 43, 58–9, 63, 69–70, 77–80, 85, 95–6, 127, 198–9, 282–5
Goa 43–5, 47–8, 59–60, 85–6, 178–80, 182–3, 186–90, 192–4, 196–7, 238, 271–2; coastal region of 45; religious monopoly in 47
Guaixará 171–3
Guaraní 75, 148, 170

Henriques, D. Alfonso 277, 285–6, 304
Hindu-Turk Samvād 222n149
História do Futuro 282, 289–90, 292
Holy Trinity 127, 104–5
humanism 96, 118–19, 177

Iberia 1, 58–9, 71, 250
idolatry 9, 37, 42, 63, 104–6, 110, 113, 183, 191–2, 208, 210–13
Ignatius, Fr 11–12, 56–7, 59–60, 70–2, 79, 87, 118, 141, 143–5, 178
imperialism 2, 5, 319
Indian Ocean 26, 30, 33–4, 43–4, 47–8, 190, 319
Indies 8–9, 55–60, 69–73, 77–8, 81, 95–6, 105–7, 117, 129, 178–9, 319–21
indigenous: Christians 273; conversions 23, 255; deity 218; enslavement of 50, 150, 157; as natives 19, 43, 226, 249, 271, 287; population 3–4, 8, 18–19, 34, 36, 49–50, 52, 73, 92–3, 246–7, 249–50; societies 17, 21, 42, 71, 112; warriors 151, 162
Iperuí 153, 157, 171
Islam 1–2, 29–30, 32, 58–9, 71–2, 95, 106, 130
Italian missionaries 263, 271–2

Japan: Costa and 263, 298; Jesuit missions in 192, 193, 270, 273n124, 276n132; Vieira and 244, 248, 250; Xavier in 56, 70–1, 114–16, 118
Japanese 191, 225
Jesuits: 7–8, 10–12, 23, 88–9, 92, 107–8, 118–19, 124, 138–9, 143–8, 153–7, 196–9, 246–8, 251–3; *accommodatio* by 11, 139, 269; in

Brazil 83–93, 224; as missionaries 8–10, 58, 71, 73, 131, 138, 185, 267, 274, 300, 304; missionary space of 6, 22, 56, 92, 94, 280; missions of 23, 73, 91, 94, 176, 181, 183, 194, 199; Portuguese as 24, 231, 280–1, 312
Jesus Christ 3, 6–7, 52, 55, 60, 79, 93, 105, 108, 122–5, 168–71, 175, 215, 218–19, 221–2, 233–4, 277, 283, 303–4; in *Brahmapuri* 200–8
Jews 30, 58, 63, 70, 123–4, 127, 282, 284–5, 291–2, 297, 303–6; as converts 58–9; customs of 9. *See also* Judaism
João III, D. 49, 80, 183, 285, 292
João IV 242–4, 251, 290, 292, 311
John, Prester 55, 67, 72, 95
Judaism 71, 95, 289, 291–2, 295, 304
justice 65, 67, 90, 211, 240–1, 278, 303

Kannur (Cannanore) 30–1, 274
karaíba (travelling shaman-prophets) 38, 41, 91, 107, 137–8, 153–4, 234
Kochi 27, 31–2, 43–5, 252, 274–5, 291, 305
Kodungallur 30, 252, 274, 279
Kollam 30–1, 65–8
Kozhikode/Calicut 27–8, 32–3, 42
Kriṣṭapurāṇa 202, 202n90, 222–3

la Croix, Etienne de 191, 216, 224
Laerzio, Alberto 253–4
Latin America 3–4, 18–20
Linschoten, Jan van Huyghen 189–90

Ma'abari I, Sheikh Zainuddīn 28, 44
Ma'abari II, Sheikh Zainuddīn 26, 28–9, 33
Macedo, Duarte Ribeiro de 280, 298, 300–1, 309–10, 312
Madhva 101–2, 103n25
Madurai 24, 65, 232, 253, 256–60, 263–5, 267, 269, 275–9, 302, 311
Madurai mission 253, 257, 259, 263–4, 267, 269, 275, 277, 300
Malabar 26, 28–34, 39, 43, 200, 233, 238, 252, 271, 273–4, 278, 288, 300–1
Malacca 60, 114, 305, 310
Mamelucos 15, 50, 148, 150
Mansilhas, Francisco 64, 67
Manuel, D. 6, 21, 34–5, 37, 42–3, 52, 55, 57, 135, 292, 310
Maranhão 135–6, 245–9, 251, 279, 296, 308, 310–11 Marathi bhakti poetry 219
Martins, Manuel 255–8, 268
martyrdom 169–71, 173; of Edmund Campion 180; of Jõao de Brito 269; of Mastrilli 263
martyrs 144, 148, 151, 167, 169–70, 175, 188, 263; saints as 173, 175–6
Mascarenhas, Pedro 183, 202
mass confessions 64, 237
Mastrilli, Marcello 257, 263
merchants 15, 28, 32, 180, 189, 233, 255, 266–7, 276, 284, 290–1; Christians 291; Jewish 290; of Lisbon 290
missionaries 6–12, 71–3, 117–19, 138–9, 148–9, 248, 251–4, 262–4, 271–9, 303–6, 310–12; non-Portuguese 24, 231, 272
missionary enterprise 5, 8, 12, 94, 101, 141, 182, 249, 267, 304–5; in Brazil 85, 119, 149, 246; Portuguese commitment to 69

Moors 43, 58, 70, 84, 106, 113, 184, 282, 305; Xavier and 106, 113
Moroupiaroêra 162–4
Mozambique 245, 313

Na Vila de Vitória 165–8, 175
Navarro, Doctor 73, 83, 107–8
Nāyaka, Tirumala 260; courts of 258–9, 266, 279
Nāyakas 213, 259, 261, 264–5, 269
Nicodemism 101, 103, 106
Nieuw-Holland 237, 239
Nobili, Roberto 253–5, 257–60, 262–4, 268–9, 272, 277, 279, 311; innovations 254–5, 263–4, 273, 275–6; mission of 262
Nóbrega, Manuel da 6, 21, 37, 52, 55, 57, 72–84, 86–96, 106–13, 119–24, 128–31, 135–9, 148–9, 153–4, 157, 225; and Brazil 57; innovative mission of 78; to Simão Rodrigues 139
Nogueira, Matheus Br. 92, 119–28, 131
Nunes, Leonardo Fr. 72, 84, 119

Ottomans 44, 59, 308

Pacheco, Afonso 184, 186
padres 137, 204–6, 212–16, 219–21
Padroado 24, 52, 60, 90, 94, 179, 191, 270, 275, 280, 299
Padua, Manuel da Gama de 302, 307
pagans 9, 104, 106, 113, 117, 126, 129, 142, 174, 264; beliefs of 106; warrior 144
Paiva, Frei Sebastião de 289
Paṇṭāram mission 266–8
Paṇṭārams 257–8, 264–7, 279
Papacy 8, 270, 274, 299, 308, 318
Paraiyans 257–62, 269; converts 257; church of 257
Parava mission 106, 255
Paravas 62–7, 96–8, 102–3, 252–3, 256–7
peace 65, 148, 152–8, 168, 173, 176–7, 284, 296, 300; treaty of 155, 250
Pedro, D. 295, 301–2, 306–8
penance 58, 107
Pereira, Rui 92–3
Pernambuco 49, 87, 237, 239, 242–5, 300, 311
persecution 58, 115, 171, 178–9, 258, 294, 300
Perumāl, Pāndya Vettum 65–7
Philip II 166, 174, 184
Pimenta, Nicolau 199–200
Pindobuçu 155, 157; as sorcerers 154
Pirataráka 163–5
Piratininga 49, 91, 140, 142, 144, 149–53, 158
Pires, AntóniobFr. 72–3
Pounde, Thomas 180–2, 189

Queyros, Fernão de 257, 282, 287–9

Rodrigues, Diogo 73, 78, 184, 289
Rodrigues, Nuno 193–4, 198
Rodrigues, Simão 57, 59, 77, 85, 88, 178
Rodrigues, Vicente Br. 72–3

Sá, Estácio de 158, 176
Sá, Mem de 23, 92–3, 128, 130, 151, 159, 174, 176–7; campaign of 1560 150, 177
Śaiva Siddhāntins 99, 104
Salcete 23, 179–80, 182–6, 188, 192–202, 204–6, 209, 211, 215,

9–21; Englishmen in
; mission to 186, 196, 198
Antonio Vasconcelos 224,
280
Salvador da Bahía 93, 234, 236, 238–40, 242, 244–5, 250
salvation 12, 97, 117–18, 122–3, 125, 127, 266, 319
Samaritans 123–4
Samutiri of Kozhikode 29, 31–3, 43–4, 62, 274; as Zamorim of Calicut 29
sannyāsi(s): mission of 257, 261–2; Costa on 266; model of 264, 268
Santo, Espírito 119, 158, 160, 162
São Vicente 49, 91, 143, 149, 157–9, 246
Saravaia 171–3
Sardinha, Pero Fernandes 85, 87, 89; Bishop 92, 128, 130, 176; and Brazilian mission 86; pacification campaign of 23, 93, 130, 176
Satan 165–6, 174, 215–17, 220
Schuren, Gaspar 191, 195
Sebastião 242, 281, 292
sertão 50, 79, 91, 112, 119, 128, 140, 147–8, 159–60, 172, 224
Shāh, Ādil 29, 44–5, 183, 305
shaman (*pajé*) 13, 37–8, 41, 79, 108–10, 112–13, 138, 144–7, 153, 155–6, 158; Amerindians as 13
Society of Jesus 6–7, 52, 55, 79, 93, 180, 182, 234, 273, 279, 314. See also *karaíba*
sorcerers 107–8, 144, 154–5, 214–16; Nóbrega on 107
Sousa, Martim Afonso de 48–50, 58, 151–2, 175
Sousa, Tomé de 72, 78, 90
sovereignty 32–3, 41–2, 49, 67, 92, 119, 167, 249
Spice Islands 113–14
spice trade 32, 48; in pepper 26, 28, 82, 190, 219
St Lawrence 171–3, 175
St Paul 78, 126, 253, 278
St Sebastian 81, 172
St Thomas 55, 80–2, 252, 261–2, 272–3, 284
St Thomas Christians 252, 273
Stephens, Thomas 6, 23–4, 178–83, 185–9, 191–201, 203–4, 206, 208, 216–17, 219, 222; friendship with Pounde 181; *purāna* of 224
Subrahmanyam, Sanjay 44, 50–1, 56, 252, 259
Syrian Christians 34, 252

Tamoios of Rio de Janeiro 125, 150–5, 157–8; captive among 158
Tatapytéra 162–3
Teixeira, Marcos 234, 236
Temininós 163, 172
Tibiriçá 143–4, 151–2
Tirucendur 62, 99, 103, 110; Murugan temple in 97, *see also under* Xavier, Francis (St.)
Tupana 106, 111
Tupí(s) 39, 75–83, 87, 111–13, 128–31, 137–40, 142–3, 153–5, 157–64, 168–9, 171–7; Anchieta's reformulation of 224; culture of 23, 137–8, 140; incarnation of Christian devil in 165; shamans of 156; society of 39, 42, 42n4, 78, 146; songs of 138–9, 141–2; warfare of 137, 150, 163, 165, 177; warriors of 136, 145, 150, 152, 174–5
Tupínambás 76, 163, 172
Tupiniquin 141, 149–52, 155, 157–8

universal church 5, 7–8, 10, 17, 24, 250, 279, 318–19

Valerian 173–4; persecutions of 171
Valignano, Alessandro 179, 191–3, 196–8, 208
Varman, Unni Keralā Tiruvadi 66, 68
Vaz, Miguel 59, 183
Venadu 65, 68
Vereenigde Oost-Indische Compagnie (VOC) 190, 233
Vieira, António 6, 24–5, 203, 231–2, 234–51, 280, 282–303, 305–7; sermons of 239–40, 242
Vijayanagara 51, 68, 183, 260
violence 4, 28, 33, 63, 140, 144, 146–7, 151–2, 163, 169–73, 188
Viveiros de Castro, Eduardo 81, 112, 138, 155

warriors 41–2, 136–7, 139, 145–6, 148, 150, 152, 162–4, 169–70, 173, 175
West-Indische Compagnie (WIC) 234, 237

Xavier, Francis (St) 6, 8, 21, 23, 52, 56–60, 63–72, 83, 85, 87, 93–107, 112–19, 130–1, 145, 270–1, 284, 319; to China 70; and conversion 58–60; death of 72; and humanism 119; on Indian mission field 70; and indigenous clergy 271; meeting Ignatius of Loyola 56; at Tirucendur 99, 103

Zomé 80–1
Zuzarte, Pedro 298–9, 305, 310

ABOUT THE AUTHOR

Ananya Chakravarti is assistant professor of South Asian and Indian Ocean history at Georgetown University, Washington D.C., USA. Previously, she was the Abdelhadi H. Taher Professor of comparative religion at The American University in Cairo, Egypt. Her work focuses on the intersection of religion and empire, and global and local historical methods. Her interests lie in early modern South Asia, the Portuguese empire, colonial Brazil, history of religions, history of emotions, and spatial history.